THE
COLLEGE
PRESS
NIV
COMMENTARY

ACTS

THE COLLEGE PRESS NIV COMMENTARY

ACTS

DENNIS GAERTNER, Ph.D.

New Testament Series Co-Editors:

Jack Cottrell, Ph.D.
Cincinnati Bible Seminary

Tony Ash, Ph.D.
Abilene Christian University

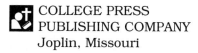
COLLEGE PRESS
PUBLISHING COMPANY
Joplin, Missouri

Library of Congress Cataloging-in-Publication Data

Gaertner, Dennis.
    Acts / Dennis Gaertner. — Rev. ed.
      p.   cm. — (The College Press NIV commentary)
    Includes bibliographic references (p. 37).
    ISBN 0-89900-626-4 (hard cover)
    1. Bible. N.T. Acts—Commentaries. I. Bible. N.T. Acts. English.
New International. 1995. II. Title. III. Series.
BS2625.3.G34 1995
226.6'077—dc20   95-3735
                                                         CIP

FOREWORD

The Book of Acts is pivotal not only in our understanding of the events which established the church of Jesus Christ, but also for providing a connecting link between the four Gospels and the Epistles of the New Testament. Without this record our knowledge of how the message of Jesus Christ came to be a missionary plea to the whole world would be severely weakened.

Beyond this use of Acts, the accounts of faithful servants of the Lord who risked so much of themselves in carrying the gospel into strange and often unfriendly territories will always be a challenge to me personally. I find in Acts a powerful indictment of any tendency I have to be timid about my faith. The men and women whom God called (whether recorded in Acts or not) will be justified on judgment day if they look suspiciously at our inability to reach out to our world effectively with the gospel of Jesus Christ.

I hope that this work will serve to challenge students of the Word. I have attempted to bring together as much information as possible from a number of perspectives, including textual data, historical facts, archaeological discoveries, theological interpretations, and practical insights, as well as concerns which are consistent with the churches of the Restoration Movement. In so doing, my prayer is that those whose desire is to be nourished by the Word and led by the Spirit will find here a study worth their effort.

For the help I have received on this project I am sincerely grateful. I could not have attempted such a work without those who have contributed to my educational training at Great Lakes Bible College, Cincinnati Christian Seminary, and Southern Baptist Theological Seminary. Also my colleagues at Johnson Bible College have been very helpful. Most of all my thanks goes to my wife, Joy, and my children, Rachel and Ben, who have been patient through the very long process of producing this study.

As the reader begins this study my prayer is that the truth of Acts will bear much fruit. May God "open a door" for his Word so that it may be proclaimed faithfully by his servants no matter what the opposition (Col 4:3).

A WORD
FROM THE PUBLISHER

Years ago a movement was begun with the dream of uniting all Christians on the basis of a common purpose (world evangelism) under a common authority (the Word of God). The College Press NIV Commentary Series is a serious effort to join the scholarship of two branches of this unity movement so as to speak with one voice concerning the Word of God. Our desire is to provide a resource for your study of the New Testament that will benefit you whether you are preparing a Bible School lesson, a sermon, a college course, or your own personal devotions. Today as we survey the wreckage of a broken world, we must turn again to the Lord and his Word, unite under his banner and communicate the life-giving message to those who are in desperate need. This is our purpose.

ABBREVIATIONS

AUSS . . . Andrews University Seminary Studies
BA . . . Biblical Archaeology
BAR . . . Biblical Archaeology Review
BiblThecSac . . . Bibliotheca Sacra
BJRL . . . Bulletin of the John Rylands Library
BTr . . . Bible Translator
ChrSt . . . Christian Standard
ed. . . . edited by
EQ . . . Evangelical Quarterly
ExpT . . . Expository Times
HTR . . . Harvard Theological Review
JBL . . . Journal of Biblical Literature
JSNT . . . Journal of Studies in the New Testament
JETS . . . Journal of the Evangelical Theological Society
JTS . . . Journal of Theological Studies
n. . . . note
NovT . . . Novum Testamentum
RevEx . . . Review and Expositor
TB . . . Tyndale Bulletin
TDNT . . . Theological Dictionary of the New Testament
TS . . . Theological Studies
trans . . . translated by
WThJ . . . Westminster Theological Journal

INTRODUCTION

As early as the second century the title "The Acts of the Apostles" was given to this document.[1] Before that time the work probably circulated with its companion volume, "The Gospel of Luke." When the other three Gospels were collected and the New Testament was formed, The Gospel of Luke and The Acts of the Apostles were separated. Both were included in the New Testament as books of history.

AUTHORSHIP

Like the Third Gospel, the Book of Acts does not identify its author. Evidence must be gathered, therefore, from both within the document itself and from references to the document in early church history.

The strongest evidence within the Book of Acts is its Prologue (1:1-3). When the Prologue of Acts is compared with the Prologue of the Third Gospel (1:1-4), the similarities are striking.[2] Both books mention the name Theophilus as the recipient. Acts refers to "the former book," implying that the Third Gospel is that book. Acts also intends to begin the story at the point that the Third Gospel ends it—the ascension of Christ. The style of Greek used in both cases is polished and formal. The implication that both works were written by the same author is unavoidable.[3]

---

[1]This title is found in both Vaticanus and Beza. For a summary of the range of issues facing students of Acts, see W.C. van Unnik, "Luke-Acts, A Storm Center in Contemporary Scholarship," in *Studies in Luke-Acts*, ed. Leander Keck and J.L. Martyn (Philadelphia: Fortress, 1980), pp. 15-32.

[2]See Charles Talbert, *Literary Patterns, Theological Themes and the Genre of Luke-Acts* (Missoula: Scholars Press, 1974), pp. 58-61.

[3]General agreement exists among New Testament scholars on the point that both the Third Gospel and Acts are products of the same author.

In addition, the passages in Acts which use the pronoun "we" imply an eyewitness account.[4] Appearing toward the end of Acts, these passages give the impression that whoever was writing the book was also present when some of the recorded events took place. It seems that the author makes himself a companion of Paul at these points in the narrative (Acts 16:10-17; 20:5-21:18; 27:1-28:16). At other points in the record the author was content to use "they" in describing events.

Inevitably, then, the question of authorship focuses on Paul's traveling companions. Because some of the "we" sections overlap with Paul's years in prison at both Caesarea and Rome, the companions who were with him at that time become prime candidates. When Paul wrote the letters to Philemon and to the Colossians from prison, Luke was one of the companions Paul mentioned (Phlm 23-24; Col 4:10-17).

Another line of reasoning was proposed by W.K. Hobart in 1882. He analyzed the vocabulary of Acts and concluded that the language indicated that the author of Acts was a physician.[5] This proposal did not survive the scrutiny of scholarship for long. By

---

[4]This is the traditional view and can be traced back as far as Irenaeus in the second century. Others argue that the "we-passages" come from a separate source which was used by Luke in the composition of Acts. The Tübingen school took this position and argued that Acts was written in the second century. Martin Dibelius took the position that the "we-passages" came from a diary written by one of the traveling companions of Paul. See his "The Acts of the Apostles in the Setting of the History of Early Christian Literature," *Studies in the Acts of the Apostles*, trans. M. Ling (London: SCM, 1956), pp. 192-205. The difficulty with these latter two views is that the Lukan style is present throughout all of them, as pointed out by Adolf Harnack in *Luke the Physician*, trans. J.R. Wilkinson (New York: Putnam's, 1907), pp. 26-120. Others have contended that the "we-passages" are a literary device. Vernon Robbins thinks that they are included in the accounts of sea voyages in imitation of a common literary device used in the ancient world. See his "By Land and by Sea: The We-Passages and Ancient Sea Voyages," *Perspectives on Luke in Luke-Acts*, ed. Charles Talbert (Edinburgh: T & T Clark, 1978), pp. 215-242. But the "we-passages" are not consistently confined to the sea voyages in Acts, and not all the sea voyages use the first person. See comments on 16:10.

[5]See his *The Medical Language of St. Luke* (London: Longmans Green, 1882).

1920 H.J. Cadbury offered a study which showed that much of the language which Hobart considered "technical" medical terminology was in use by such nonmedical writers as Josephus, Plutarch, and Lucian.[6] The most that can be said for this evidence today is that the terminology of Acts is compatible with authorship by a person with a medical background.

These pieces of evidence are consistent with the external evidence. Though references to The Acts of the Apostles do not appear as early in the church fathers as do references to other books of the New Testament, they do appear nonetheless. Diognetus (A.D. 130) and *The Didache* (A.D. 140) allude to the work, as does *The Epistle of the Churches of Vienne and Lyons* (A.D. 177), according to Eusebius. The latter source quotes the words of Stephen's prayer in which he asks that his accusers not have their sin charged against them (*Ecclesiastical History* V.2). Similarly, Irenaeus (A.D. 180), Clement of Alexandria (A.D. 190), Tertullian (A.D. 200), and Eusebius (A.D. 325) quote from Acts without naming their source.[7]

In addition to this evidence, many early church writers refer to the Third Gospel as written by Luke.[8] This is important since the internal evidence makes the author of the Third Gospel the same as the author of Acts. Such testimony comes from the Muratorian Canon (A.D. 170). Irenaeus, Clement of Alexandria, Tertullian, and Jerome, on the other hand, speak directly of Acts as written by Luke.

Much attention has also been given to the sources used by Luke in writing Acts. Harnack was the primary scholar who promoted the position that underlying Acts are several sources. He argued that one could detect first an "Antioch" source, then a second source describing Paul's conversion, and finally a third source which contained the "Jerusalem Caesarean" tradition. This third source,

---

[6]See his *Style and Literary Method of Luke* Part 1 (Cambridge: Harvard University Press, 1920). See also his later article entitled "Lexical Notes on Luke-Acts: V. Luke and the Horse-Doctors," *JBL* 52 (1933): 55-65.

[7]For a summary of this evidence see Gareth Reese, *New Testament History: A Critical and Exegetical Commentary on the Book of Acts* (Joplin, MO: College Press, 1991), pp. xxiv-xxv.

[8]Donald Guthrie, *New Testament Introduction* (Downers Grove, IL: InterVarsity, 1970), pp. 98-100,110.

he said, was actually two sources blended together, one more reliable than the other.[9]

Harnack's proposals ran into trouble on a couple of counts. His approach seemed dominated by a rationalism which excised the miraculous from the text. In addition his theories about the parallels between the two "Jerusalem Caesarean" sources did not hold up under the scrutiny of Joachim Jeremias and others.[10]

Another proposal regarding written sources for Acts came from C.C. Torrey. He argued that an Aramaic source was used in the composition of Acts 1-15, but absent from Acts 16-28.[11] This argument was made on the basis of Semitisms which he found in these earlier chapters. Later scholars argued that these terms and phrases are best explained as coming from the Septuagint or the synagogue.[12]

Also among the possible sources for Acts are oral traditions. C.J. Hemer lists dozens of passages which he thinks are best explained as deriving from reports passed along verbally to Luke.[13]

In recent years scholars have been far more interested in Luke as a writer and theologian than as a compiler of sources. In some cases studies have concentrated on comparing Luke's style with other ancient writers.[14]

With the work of Hans Conzelmann in 1953 the emphasis on Luke's theology as reflected in Acts became pronounced.[15] This

---

[9]See Adolf Harnack, *The Acts of the Apostles*, trans. J.R. Wilkinson (London: Williams & Norgate, 1909), 162-202. See also the summary of Harnack's views presented by Jacques Dupont, T*he Sources of Acts: The Present Position*, trans. Kathleen Pond (London: Darton, Longman & Todd, 1964), pp. 35-41.

[10]See Dupont, *Sources*, pp. 42-46.

[11]C.C. Torrey, *The Composition and Date of Acts* (Cambridge: Harvard University Press, 1916). See the summary of his argument in Ward Gasque, *A History of the Criticism of the Acts of the Apostles* (Tübingen: Mohr, 1975), pp. 165-167.

[12]See Fred Horton, Jr., "Reflections on the Semitisms of Luke-Acts," *Perspectives on Luke-Acts*, ed. Charles Talbert (Edinburgh: T & T Clark, 1978), pp. 1-23.

[13]C.J. Hemer, *The Book of Acts in the Setting of Hellenistic History*, ed. Conrad Gempf (Winona Lake, IN: Eisenbrauns, 1990), pp. 335-364.

[14]See Cadbury, *The Making of Luke-Acts* (New York: MacMillan, 1927).

[15]The English translation of Conzelmann's *Die Mitte der Zeit* came out

perspective continues to dominate scholarly discussions today. One problem with this perspective is that it frequently ignores or denies the value of Acts as a historical record of events in the early church.[16]

DATE OF WRITING

Acts 1:1 indicates that Luke wanted Acts to serve as the second volume of a two-volume work. For this reason Acts must be dated at the same time or later than the Gospel of Luke. The earliest dates that scholars assign to Luke are in the late 50s. Festus had already ascended to power when Acts was written, an event which is dated in A.D. 60. These boundaries fix the earliest date for Acts.

The real question is how late can Acts be dated. Some radical Bible critics have dated Acts as late as A.D. 115-130.[17] This date reduces the chances that Luke was the author. Many scholars fix the date between A.D. 70-80.[18] The reasons often given for this date have to do with the subject matter of Luke's Gospel, especially Luke 21:5-38. In these verses Jesus speaks of the destruction of Jerusalem. His description is so vivid that many scholars believe Luke must have recorded it after the event had occurred in A.D. 70.

---

seven years later as *The Theology of St. Luke*, trans. G. Buswell (New York: Harper & Row, 1960).

[16]See I.H. Marshall, *Luke: Historian and Theologian* (Grand Rapids: Zondervan, 1970). See also E.M. Blaiklock, "The Acts of the Apostles as a Document of First Century History," in *Apostolic History and the Gospel*, ed. W.W. Gasque, Ralph Martin (Grand Rapids: Eerdmans, 1970), pp. 41-54.

[17]Gasque, *History of Criticism*, pp. 21ff. The influence of F.C. Baur forced scholars first to examine the purpose of Acts within the framework of the conflict between Pauline and Petrine circles. This "tendency criticism" initiated by Baur and the Tübingen school continued to find expression in the followers of Baur, who pushed the Book of Acts to a much later date in their reconstruction of New Testament developments. C.J. Hemer gives a list with the names of scholars and the dates they assign to Acts, which ranges from the earliest at A.D. 57 to the latest at A.D. 135. See his *Book of Acts*, pp. 365-410. A factor in dating Acts is the issue of whether Luke knew and used the letters of Paul—a topic which continues to draw the attention of scholars. See, for example, William Walker, "Acts and the Pauline Corpus Reconsidered," *JSNT* 24 (1985): 3-23.

[18]Guthrie, pp. 345-346.

One question which must arise in discussing the date of Acts has to do with the last verses of the Book. Acts closes with a description of the Apostle Paul under house-arrest in Rome. He was taken there to stand trial before Caesar. The account ends by noting that he remained there "two whole years," preaching the gospel as he waited for his accusers to arrive. Tradition indicates that he was martyred in Rome during the reign of Nero (A.D. 54-68). The question to be answered is whether Paul was martyred during this Roman imprisonment. If so, why didn't Luke record Paul's death in Acts? Is the absence of any word on Paul's death significant? Was Luke avoiding the issue in order to preserve his focus on the victorious progress of the church? If so, maybe Acts was meant to end at this point in the story. This would allow for Acts to be written later than the year of Paul's death. The date of writing could then be fixed somewhere between A.D. 70-80.[19]

On the other hand, it may be that Luke does not record Paul's death because it had not occurred when he wrote Acts, meaning that the dating of Acts would be earlier. If Luke finished Acts before Paul's death occurred, the work must be dated somewhere in the early or mid 60s. Church tradition (especially Jerome and Eusebius) dates Paul's martyrdom in Rome around A.D. 67-68. Many scholars believe, however, that Paul was released from his house-arrest described in Acts 28. They argue that he resumed his missionary travels until the day he was once again arrested and taken to Rome. They also contend that the Pastoral letters (1, 2 Timothy and Titus) were written before this second imprisonment.[20] If this is true, then Acts may have been written at the end of Paul's first imprisonment, or about A.D. 63.

---

[19]Even a conservative scholar like Bruce has no difficulty with a date this late. He says that the composition came after "sufficient time has elapsed for the author to look back in tranquility over the course of events and present them in a more balanced perspective than would have been possible for one writing *in mediis rebus*." This date, he says, could have been "a decade or two later than the last events which he records." See his "Chronological Questions in the Acts of the Apostles," *BJRL* 68 (1986): 273-295.

[20]Ibid., pp. 596-599.

THEME OF ACTS

Acts opens with a statement from Jesus which seems to set the tone for the entire work. Jesus promises the Apostles that they will receive power in the form of the Holy Spirit (see 1:8). He then tells them that they will be his "witnesses in Jerusalem, and in all Judea and Samaria, and to the ends of the earth" (NIV). This theme of being a witness for the gospel is carried throughout the Book of Acts.[21] Consider the following verses in Acts:

1:22 — the replacement for Judas had to be a witness of Christ's resurrection

2:32 — Peter's sermon on Pentecost emphasized that the apostles were witnesses of the resurrection

3:15 — after healing the beggar Peter proclaimed the resurrected Christ and that the apostles were witnesses

4:20 — the apostles told the Jewish authorities they could not help proclaiming what they had seen and heard

5:32 — when the apostles were again persecuted they said they must obey God because they were witnesses along with the Holy Spirit

8:25 — Peter and John went to Samaria where they "testified and proclaimed the word of the Lord"

10:39 — Peter proclaimed to Cornelius that he was a witness to the ministry of Jesus

13:31 — Paul told the crowd in Pisidian Antioch that Jesus' followers had witnessed Christ's resurrection

22:15 — Ananias went to Paul with the message that Paul would be a witness to all men of what he had seen and heard

23:11 — God appeared to Paul encouraging him that he would testify in Rome concerning the Lord

---

[21]Many scholars during the history of studies in Acts have argued for a two-part division in the material of Acts—the first consisting of chapters 1-12, and the second chapters 13-28. See Gasque, *History*, pp. 25, 33, 36, 79, 88, 111, 133. J.W. Shepard arranges the material in a similar way in *The Life and Letters of the Apostle Paul: An Exegetical Study* (Grand Rapids: Eerdmans, 1956), p. 26.

These references do not include the numerous passages in which individuals are found witnessing falsely (e.g., 6:13; 7:58; 24:1; 25:7).

As the witnesses for Christ carried the gospel toward the far reaches of the world, the church advanced everywhere. This theme is also important in Acts.[22] The expansion of the church is presented in a historical context. Luke even dates some of the events in his record by using key Roman names and events as reference points (see 12:1,19; 18:12; 23:24; 24:24; 25:1, 23).

As Acts 1:8 indicates, Luke shows how the gospel prevailed wherever it was proclaimed. In Jerusalem, huge numbers were baptized on the Day of Pentecost. Later, thousands were added (4:4), even though the believers were being persecuted by the Jewish authorities. Such incidents as the striking down of Ananias and Sapphira and the dissension over the ministry to Hellenistic widows did not slow down the rapid increase of converts to the gospel (5:14; 6:1,7).

Beyond the walls of Jerusalem, the gospel also found fertile ground for growth. After the conversion of Saul of Tarsus, the church in Judea, Galilee, and Samaria experienced peace and saw its numbers increasing (9:31). Peter's work in Lydda bore rich fruit (9:35) and his raising of Tabitha in Joppa brought many to believe in the Lord (9:42).

The ever-widening influence of the gospel was felt beyond Judea and Samaria as well. Antioch saw increasing numbers of believers, especially among the Gentile populations (11:21,24). The cities of southern Galatia felt the gospel's impact as Paul and Barnabas evangelized in places like Lystra, Iconium, and Derbe (see 14:1,21). Later, Paul and Silas revisited these cities and more growth came (see 16:5). On this same missionary journey Paul and Silas even crossed into Macedonia where the results were the same (see 17:12). The gospel continued to conquer hearts and minds for Christ with each passing day.

Through all of Luke's record, the role of the Holy Spirit is highlighted. From the Day of Pentecost when he was poured out (see 2:14ff), the Spirit was essential to God's purposes for the proclamation of the gospel. When the men were chosen to administer the

---

[22]Charles Cosgrove sees an emphasis on divine providence expressed throughout Acts especially in terms of the "divine *dei*." See his "The Divine *dei* in Luke-Acts," *NovT* 26 (1984): 168-190.

benevolence to widows, Stephen was appointed because he was a man full of "faith and of the Holy Spirit" (see 6:5). In Samaria the new converts received a visit from the apostles who placed their hands on them, granting them the power of the Holy Spirit (see 8:17). This was a power which Simon the Sorcerer wanted to buy (see 8:18). Philip heard from the Spirit that he was to go to the chariot of the Ethiopian (see 8:29). While Peter was preaching to Cornelius, the Holy Spirit came on the listeners, interrupting Peter's address (see 10:44). Barnabas and Saul were first selected as missionaries at Antioch when the Spirit spoke to the church (see 13:2). Their travels were guided by the Holy Spirit (see 16:7) and in Ephesus Paul rebaptized believers who had not received the Spirit (see 19:1-7).[23] When Paul addressed the Ephesian elders, he reminded them that they had become leaders because of the Spirit's ministry (see 21:28).

While Acts emphasizes that the apostles received the power of the Spirit (1:8), it also emphasizes how they used this power. They faithfully bore witness for Christ. Acts underscores the work of the apostles, or at least some of the apostles. Roughly speaking, Acts 1-12 focuses on the work of the Apostle Peter. His role in the choosing of a successor for Judas (see 1:15ff) and the preaching on the Day of Pentecost (see 2:14ff) open the book. Almost every chapter which follows contains some report on the work of Peter. He and John heal the lame man (see 3:1-10), and then stand before the Sanhedrin (see 4:1-22). He confronts Ananias and Sapphira (see 5:1-11) and Simon the Sorcerer (see 8:9-25). He experiences the vision which results in the preaching to Cornelius and the conversion of his family (see 10:9-48). He then defends his actions before the church leaders in Jerusalem (see 11:1-18). Finally, he miraculously escapes imprisonment by Herod (see 12:1-19).

With Acts 13 the spotlight shifts to the Apostle Paul.[24] Paul and Barnabas are sent from Antioch as missionaries (see 13:2). Their

---

[23]The development of this theme is the major emphasis of Frank Stagg's *The Book of Acts: The Early Struggle for an Unhindered Gospel* (Nashville: Broadman Press, 1955). See also William L. Blevins, "The Early Church: Acts 1-5," *RevEx* 71 (1974): 463-474.

[24]The striking parallels Luke draws between the ministries of Peter and Paul are the subject of Talbert's attention. *Literary Patterns*, pp. 23-25. Reese discusses a number of the attacks which have been brought against the

report at the Jerusalem conference is crucial (see 15:12), and though they cannot agree about John Mark, a second missionary journey is undertaken by Paul and Silas (see 15:40). The second journey is followed immediately by a third (see 18:23), and then comes the account of Paul's tragic visit to Jerusalem and his arrest in the temple (see 21:30). The rest of the book describes the series of hearings Paul endures and his transport to Caesarea and on to Rome. Paul's ministry as a Roman prisoner is the focus of the final comment in Acts. For two whole years Paul stayed there in his own rented house and welcomed all who came to see him. Boldly and without hindrance he preached the kingdom of God and taught about the Lord Jesus Christ (28:30-31).

THE PURPOSE OF ACTS

For years scholars have puzzled over why Luke produced Acts.[25] Comparing the opening of Acts with that of Luke's Gospel shows that a particular disciple named Theophilus was central to Luke's motives. Was he a new convert? Was he a wealthy patron? Was he an influential Christian? These questions have no obvious answer.

Luke implies in the opening of the gospel that he had carefully researched his material (see Luke 1:1-4). He was concerned to provide a proper sequence of events. He shows awareness of other accounts which have been written concerning Jesus.

One purpose often noted is a historical one. Luke wanted to provide a historical record of the events of Jesus' life and the progress of the first-century church. Though some scholars argue that his reasons had to do with his concerns about the return of Christ, it is possible that he saw the end of the age of the apostles coming.[26] Perhaps Luke wanted a written record of the apostles' work in carrying on the ministry of Jesus.

---

portrait of Paul as presented in Acts when compared with the epistles. See his *New Testament History*, pp. xxvi-xxx.

[25]Robert Maddox, *The Purpose of Luke-Acts* (Edinburgh: T & T Clark, 1982). See also Darryl Palmer, "Acts and the Historical Monograph," *TB* 43 (1992), 373-388.

[26]Maddox, *Purpose*, pp. 100-157.

The immediate purpose of Luke may be indicated in his words in the opening of the gospel. He tells Theophilus that he writes so that this believer will "know the certainty of the things" he had been taught (1:4). This comment may indicate that the two-volume work was meant for Christian instruction.

The apologetic value of Acts has often been noted.[27] Some have wondered if Luke's work was intended to serve as a defense-brief for the Apostle Paul as he stood before Caesar. The problem with this suggestion is that Luke includes so much material that has nothing to do with Paul's defense. Why would he include the birth, ministry, death, and resurrection of the Lord? Why would he focus on the Apostle Peter in the early chapters of Acts? Acts would be very tedious reading if the main purpose were a defense of Paul.

Nevertheless, it is true that much of Acts emphasizes that the believers posed no threat to the Roman empire. When the apostles are summoned before the Jerusalem authorities, their only crime is healing the lame man (see 3:1ff). When Stephen is martyred, his only fault is his zeal for the faith (see 6:8ff). Peter's imprisonment at the hands of Herod Agrippa I is due to no fault of the Apostle (see 12:1ff). Paul's hearing before Gallio is a matter of questions about the Jewish Law (see 18:12-16). The series of trials experienced by Paul repeatedly emphasizes his innocence (see 21:29; 23:29; 24:27; 25:19; 26:31). The cumulative effect of these statements establishes that the church was never any real threat to Caesar.

Beyond these purposes, Acts has a theological purpose. Luke intends to show how the apostles began the work Jesus initiated on the earth. Acts 1:1 describes Luke's Gospel as an account of "all that Jesus began to do and to teach." Acts intends to describe how the apostles continued this work of Jesus. The Gospel begins in Jerusalem and fans out over the whole Roman world to the Imperial City itself.[28] The salvation of the Lord is, in Paul's language, "first for the Jew, then for the Gentile" (Rom. 1:16). Acts records how God used human means to send out the divine message of salvation in Christ.

---

[27]Ibid., pp. 19-30, 91-99. See also Burton Easton, *Early Christianity: The Purpose of Acts and Other Papers*, ed. F.C. Grant (London: SPCK, 1955), pp. 41-57.

[28]Stagg correctly observes, however, that Luke does not tell us how the Gospel came to Rome, but only how Paul came to Rome. See his "The Unhindered Gospel," *RevEx* 71 (1974): 451-462.

THE HISTORICITY OF ACTS

Concerning the historical accuracy of the Book of Acts modern scholarship appears to be at an impasse. Questions have been raised for years about Luke's account of events. Many of the questions have been aimed at the portrait of Paul which is presented in Acts. Since the days of F.C. Baur and the Tübingen school, the issue of how Paul is presented in Acts as compared with the Pauline letters has been prominent among scholars who study Acts.[29] The result has been a series of scholars who cast doubts upon the historical accuracy of Acts.

Drawing much of this attention has been the relationship between Acts and Galatians. Especially important to scholars are such topics as the number of visits Paul made to Jerusalem, the description of the debate about circumcision, the matter of Paul's relationship to the other apostles, the position of Paul regarding the "apostolic decrees" (see 15:19-20), and other matters relating to Paul's association with the Jerusalem leaders. In addition questions have been raised about Paul's portrait in Acts as an apostle who would carry the decrees from church to church when he says nothing of them in his letters to some of the same churches. Also a problem is the fact that Acts is silent with regard to any of these letters Paul was addressing to the churches, even though he wrote during the very time covered in Acts. Beyond this strange silence is the other important event in Paul's ministry about which Acts is so quiet—the collection for the believers in Judea (see 1 Cor 16:1-4; Rom 15:23-33).[30]

These differences have caused some scholars to speak of the "Lucan Paul" in contrast to the "Paul of the epistles."[31] Another scholar explains the difference (in the tradition of Baur) by refer-

---

[29]Gasque documents the conclusions reached by Baur and his followers in his *History*, pp. 55-106.

[30]These are real problems and will be treated as they present themselves in the text of this commentary.

[31]See Haenchen, p. 113. He says that there is "a discrepancy" between the two. As a matter of fact it is standard procedure among New Testament scholars today to establish a firm dichotomy between Paul's epistles as a primary source in Pauline studies while relegating Acts to a secondary (and

ring to the "Paulinism of Acts."[32] Luke is viewed not as a historian recording events in the ministry of Paul, but as a theologian who carefully constructs a historical explanation of Paul even if it is at odds with historical reality. The Pauline speeches of Acts, in particular, are viewed as fabrications of Luke's theological genius, motivated by the need to present Paul in terms which agree with his own theological perspective.

For many scholars, then, Acts is regarded as so preoccupied with theological concerns as to render it suspect as a historical report of events in the life of the first-century church. In the late nineteenth and early twentieth centuries this skepticism was met with a wave of scholars who resisted such a pessimistic assessment of the historicity of Acts. Such scholars as James Smith, Henry Alford, J.B. Lightfoot, F.W. Farrar, R.B. Rackham, William Ramsay, Theodor Zahn, Adolf Harnack, Arthur McGiffert, C.C. Torrey, and H.J. Cadbury found more reasons for confidence in the historical value of Acts.[33] The impact of Martin Dibelius, however, was decisive. His critical studies of Acts produced a significant trend toward the conclusion that Acts should be understood in terms of descriptive theology rather than history. Hans Conzelmann and Ernst Haenchen were instrumental in systematically applying the approach of Dibelius to the text of Acts.[34] Thus a powerful stream of thought continues to influence scholars who study Acts for the purpose of clarifying the theological tendencies of early church teaching, while dismissing the historical contribution of the work.

These trends have been called into question in recent years by such scholars as F.F. Bruce, I.H. Marshall, Martin Hengel, and C.J. Hemer.[35] But no consensus among scholars has been reached. To some extent, then, the study of Acts advances on two entirely different (if not always unrelated) tracks. Work goes on in the effort to

---

far less trustworthy) category as source material. See, for example, Johannes Munck's *Paul and the Salvation of Mankind*, trans. Frank Clarke (Richmond, VA: John Knox, 1959), pp. 79-86.

[32]This is the title of the landmark essay by Philipp Vielhauer. See his "On the 'Paulinism' of Acts," in *Studies in Luke-Acts*, ed. Leander Keck and J.L. Martyn (Philadelphia: Fortress, 1980), pp. 33-50.

[33]See Gasque, *History*, pp. 107-200.

[34]Ibid., p. 235.

[35]See the summary of this debate in Hemer, *Book of Acts*, pp. 1-29.

understand the theological tendencies which shape Luke's production of the Book of Acts. At the same time other scholars look to historical and archaeological studies as potential sources for additional help in comprehending the contribution Acts makes to the historical picture of the emerging church of the first century.

Whenever scholars from the Restoration Movement have engaged in major studies of Acts, the issue of the historicity of the Book has been dominant. Alexander Campbell's *Acts of the Apostles*[36] is largely a grammatical analysis of the text of Acts, but the historicity of Luke's work is assumed throughout. J.W. McGarvey's *New Commentary on Acts of Apostles*[37] not only proceeds on the presupposition that Acts can be trusted as a historical representation of the events it records, but argues the point against such "infidel" scholars as Baur and Zeller. Another commentary was produced in 1896, this time by David Lipscomb.[38] His work makes theology the primary focus, but once again the issue of the historical credibility of Acts is central.

More recent volumes have appeared which offer the same balance. H. Leo Boles produced his commentary in 1941,[39] a study which follows in the same tradition. Don DeWelt's commentary appeared in 1958,[40] and it is stamped with a devotional and didactic quality that makes the message of Acts practical for the believer, yet it never compromises on the assumption that Acts is reliable as a historical account. Finally, the work of Gareth Reese was pivotal. His *New Testament History: A Critical and Exegetical Commentary on the Book of Acts*[41] is from the very start a work which argues the case for

---

[36]Nashville: Gospel Advocate, 1858.

[37]Two volumes in one; Cincinnati: Standard, 1892. This commentary followed an earlier one by McGarvey, which was published in 1863.

[38]*Commentary on Acts of the Apostles* (Nashville: Gospel Advocate, 1896).

[39]*A Commentary on Acts of the Apostles* (Nashville: Gospel Advocate, 1941).

[40]*Acts Made Actual* (Joplin, MO: College Press, 1958). A similar study from an author not associated with the Church of Christ/Christian Churches is Irving Jensen's *Acts: An Independent Study* (Chicago: Moody, 1974). Also a very helpful book of sermons on Acts has been published by Bob Russell, minister with the Southeast Christian Church, Louisville, Kentucky. See his *Making Things Happen: The Power of Christian Leadership* (Cincinnati: Standard, 1987).

[41]Joplin: College Press, 1976.

the historicity of Acts. With full awareness of the challenges from the Bible critics, Reese builds his case for the credibility of Luke's account of these events.

In this commentary our approach is to appreciate the theological motivations of Luke's work while not rejecting this record as the most valuable source we have regarding the developing church. Our confidence does not rest entirely on the fact that Luke's abilities as a historian have proven to be convincing. We also believe in the promise of the Lord to direct his servant into all truth.

OUTLINE

I. THE CHURCH IN JERUSALEM — 1:1–8:1a
A. INTRODUCTION OF THE BOOK — 1:1-3
B. THE COMMISSIONING OF THE APOSTLES — 1:4-8
C. THE ASCENSION OF CHRIST — 1:9-11
D. WAITING FOR THE HOLY SPIRIT — 1:12-14
E. THE REPLACEMENT OF JUDAS ISCARIOT — 1:15-26
F. THE DAY OF PENTECOST — 2:1-47
    1. The Apostles Baptized with the Holy Spirit — 2:1-4
    2. The Amazement of the Crowd — 2:5-13
    3. The Sermon of Peter — 2:14-36
       a. The Promise of Joel — 2:14-21
       b. The Proclamation of Jesus' Resurrection — 2:22-28
       c. Jesus the Lord and Messiah — 2:29-36
    4. The Call to Repentance — 2:37-40
    5. The First Church — 2:41-47
G. THE HEALING OF THE LAME MAN AND ITS CONSEQUENCES — 3:1–4:31
    1. A Cripple Cured — 3:1-10
    2. Peter's Address in Solomon's Colonnade — 3:11-26
       a. The Power of Jesus' Name — 3:11-16
       b. The Call to Repentance — 3:17-21
       c. The Witness of the Prophets — 3:22-26
    3. The Arrest of Peter and John — 4:1-4
    4. Peter and John before the Sanhedrin — 4:5-12
    5. The Debate in the Sanhedrin — 4:13-17
    6. The Prohibition against Preaching Christ — 4:18-22
    7. The Release of Peter and John — 4:23-31
       a. Their Reunion with the Twelve — 4:23
       b. Their Prayer for Boldness — 4:24-30
       c. Their Power from the Holy Spirit — 4:31
H. THE UNITY AND GENEROSITY OF THE EARLY CHURCH — 4:32–5:16
    1. The Sharing of Material Possessions by Believers — 4:32-35
    2. The Example of Barnabas — 4:36-37
    3. The Deceit of Ananias and Sapphira — 5:1-11

4. The Signs and Wonders from the Apostles — 5:12-16
I. **THE ARREST OF THE APOSTLES** — 5:17-42
   1. The Imprisonment of the Apostles — 5:17-26
   2. The Apostles before the Sanhedrin — 5:27-40
   3. The Continued Witness of the Apostles — 5:41-42
J. **THE CHOOSING OF THE SEVEN DEACONS** — 6:1-7
K. **THE ARREST, TRIAL, AND STONING OF
   STEPHEN** — 6:8-8:1a
   1. False Accusations Against Him — 6:8-15
   2. Stephen's Defense — 7:1-53
      a. The Old Testament Patriarchs — 7:1-8
      b. Israel in Egypt — 7:9-19
      c. Early Days of Moses — 7:20-29
      d. The Call of Moses — 7:30-34
      e. The Wilderness Wanderings — 7:35-43
      f. The Tabernacle and the Temple — 7:44-50
      g. The Personal Application — 7:51-53
      h. The Final Witness of Stephen — 7:54-56
      i. The Death of Stephen — 7:57-60
      j. The Consent of Saul — 8:1a

II. **THE CHURCH IN JUDEA AND
   SAMARIA** — 8:1b-12:25
   A. **PERSECUTION AND DISPERSION OF
     THE CHURCH** — 8:1b-3
   B. **MINISTRY OF PHILIP** — 8:4-40
     1. Philip in Samaria — 8:4-8
     2. The Conversion of Simon Magus — 8:9-13
     3. The Visit of Peter and John to Samaria — 8:14-17
     4. Peter's Condemnation of Simon's Offer to
       Pay for the Holy Spirit — 8:18-24
     5. The Return of the Apostles to Jerusalem — 8:25
     6. Philip and the Conversion of the Ethiopian — 8:26-40
   C. **THE CONVERSION OF SAUL OF TARSUS** — 9:1-31
     1. The Expedition of Saul to Damascus — 9:1-2
     2. The Light and the Voice from Heaven — 9:3-7
     3. The Entrance of Saul to Damascus — 9:8-9
     4. The Commissioning of Ananias to Visit Saul — 9:10-16

5. The Visit from Ananias — 9:17-19a

6. The Preaching of Saul in Damascus — 9:19b-22

7. The Escape of Saul from Damascus — 9:23-25

8. The Ministry of Saul in Jerusalem and His Departure
for Tarsus — 9:26-30

D. PEACE AND PROSPERITY FOR THE CHURCH — 9:31

E. PETER'S MINISTRY IN WESTERN JUDEA — 9:32-43

1. The Ministry at Lydda: Healing of Aeneas — 9:32-35

2. The Ministry at Joppa: The Raising of Dorcas — 9:36-43

**F. THE CONVERSION OF THE FIRST
GENTILES** — 10:1–11:18

1. The Ministry of Peter at Caesarea — 10:1-48

   a. The Vision Seen by Cornelius — 10:1-8

   b. The Vision Seen by Peter — 10:9-16

   c. The Arrival at Joppa of Servants Sent
   by Cornelius — 10:17-23a

   d. The Visit of Peter to the House
   of Cornelius — 10:23b-33

   e. The Sermon by Peter — 10:34-43

   f. The Reception of the Holy Spirit
   by Gentiles — 10:44-48

2. The Endorsement of Peter's Ministry
by the Jerusalem Leadership — 11:1-18

   a. The Questioning of the Jerusalem Leaders — 11:1-3

   b. The Defense by Peter — 11:4-17

   c. The Defense Accepted — 11:18

G. THE CHRISTIANS AT ANTIOCH — 11:19-30

1. Evangelism among the Gentiles of Antioch — 11:19-21

2. The Ministry of Barnabas and Saul at Antioch — 11:22-26

3. The Famine Relief Work from Antioch — 11:27-30

**H. THE PERSECUTION OF THE CHURCH
BY HEROD AGRIPPA I** — 12:1-25

1. The Martyrdom of James and
Imprisonment of Peter — 12:1-4

2. The Escape of Peter from Prison — 12:5-11

3. The Report of Peter about the Escape — 12:12-17

4. The Discovery of Peter's Escape — 12:18-19a

5. The Death of Herod Agrippa I — 12:19b-23

6. The Continued Progress of the Gospel — 12:24

7. The Return of Barnabas and Saul to Antioch — 12:25

III. THE CHURCH IN THE ENDS OF THE EARTH — 13:1–28:31

A. THE FIRST MISSIONARY JOURNEY — 13:1–14:28

1. The Commissioning of Barnabas and Saul at Antioch — 13:1-3

2. The Arrival of Barnabas and Saul on Cyprus — 13:4-5

3. The Confrontation at Paphos — 13:6-12

4. The Arrival at Pisidian Antioch — 13:13-15

5. Paul's Address in the Synagogue — 13:16-41

   a. Old Testament Prelude to Christ — 13:16-22

   b. Fulfillment in Christ — 13:23-37

   c. Conclusion and Warning — 13:38-41

6. The Response to Paul's Address — 13:42-43

7. Gentile Interest and Jewish Opposition — 13:44-52

8. The Visit to Iconium — 14:1-7

9. The Healing at Lystra — 14:8-13

10. Paul's Address about the Living God — 14:14-18

11. The Stoning of Paul — 14:19-20a

12. The Visit to Derbe and Return to Lystra, Iconium, and Pisidian Antioch — 14:20b-23

13. Return to Antioch of Syria — 14:24-28

B. THE COUNCIL AT JERUSALEM — 15:1-35

1. The Visit of Judaizers to Antioch — 15:1-2

2. The Journey of Paul and Barnabas to Jerusalem — 15:3-5

3. The Convening of the Council — 15:6

4. The Address of Peter — 15:7-11

5. The Address of Paul and Barnabas — 15:12

6. The Summation by James — 15:13-21

7. The Apostolic Letter to Gentile Christians — 15:22-29

8. The Reception of the Apostolic Letter by the Church in Antioch — 15:30-35

C. THE SECOND MISSIONARY JOURNEY — 15:36–18:22

1. The Proposal and the Debate about John Mark — 15:36-39

2. The Journey through Syria and Cilicia — 15:40-41

3. The Visit to Derbe and Lystra — 16:1-4

4. The Growth of the Churches — 16:5
5. The Journey through Phrygia and Galatia — 16:6-7
6. The Macedonian Vision in Troas — 16:8-10
7. The Visits to Samothrace and Neapolis — 16:11
8. The Visit to Philippi — 16:12-40
    a. The Faith of Lydia — 16:12-15
    b. The Slave Girl with the Spirit of Divination — 16:16-22
    c. The Imprisonment — 16:23-26
    d. The Conversion of the Jailer — 16:27-34
    e. The Departure — 16:35-40
9. The Visits at Amphipolis and Apollonia — 17:1a
10. The Visit at Thessalonica — 17:1b-9
    a. Paul's Preaching in the Synagogue — 17:1b-4
    b. The Backlash from the Jews — 17:5-9
11. The Visit of Paul and Silas in Berea — 17:10-14
12. The Visit at Athens — 17:15-34
    a. Paul's Preaching in Athens — 17:15-17
    b. Paul's Encounter with the Philosophers — 17:18
    c. Paul's Address in the Areopagus — 17:19-31
        1) Paul's Acknowledgement of Their Idols — 17:19-23
        2) God the Creator of Everything — 17:24-26
        3) God Who is Near Enough to Touch — 17:27-29
        4) God Who Judges and Demands
           Repentance — 17:30-31
    d. The Reaction to Paul's Preaching — 17:32-34
13. The Visit at Corinth — 18:1-17
    a. Paul's Arrival and Ministry with Aquila and
       Priscilla — 18:1-4
    b. Resistance from the Jews and Paul's Decision to
       Preach to the Gentiles — 18:5-6
    c. Encouragement in a Night Vision — 18:7-10
    d. Paul's Trial before Gallio — 18:11-17
14. The Visit at Cenchrea — 18:18
15. The Visit at Ephesus — 18:19-21
16. The Journey to Caesarea, Jerusalem,
    and Antioch of Syria — 18:22

D. THE THIRD MISSIONARY JOURNEY — 18:23–21:16
1. The Journey through Galatia and Phrygia — 18:23

2. The Ministry of Apollos in Ephesus
   and Corinth — 18:24-28
3. The Twelve Disciples at Ephesus — 19:1-7
4. Paul's Preaching in the Synagogue
   and the School of Tyrannus — 19:8-10
5. The Conflict with the Exorcists — 19:11-19
6. The Growth of Paul's Ministry — 19:20
7. Paul's Plans to Visit Rome — 19:21-22
8. The Riot of Demetrius and the Silversmiths — 19:23-41
   a. The Anger of the Silversmiths — 19:23-28
   b. The Demonstration in the Theater — 19:29-34
   c. The Calming Words of the Town Clerk — 19:35-41
9. The Journey through Macedonia and Greece — 20:1-6
10. The Visit at Troas — 20:7-12
11. The Visits at Assos, Mitylene, Kios (Chios),
    Samos, and Miletus — 20:13-15
12. The Meeting with the Ephesian Elders — 20:16-38
    a. Paul's Summons of the Ephesian Elders — 20:16-17
    b. Paul's Reflections on His Ephesian Ministry — 20:18-21
    c. Paul's Expectations for the Future — 20:22-24
    d. Paul's Charge to the Ephesian Elders — 20:25-31
    e. Paul's Final Admonition — 20:32-35
    f. The Emotional Parting — 20:36-38
13. The Stops at Cos, Rhodes, and Patara — 21:1-2
14. The Arrival at Tyre — 21:3-6
15. The Arrival at Ptolemais and Caesarea — 21:7-14
    a. The Entrance into the Home of Philip — 21:7-9
    b. The Warning of Agabus and
       Paul's Response — 21:10-14
16. The Arrival at Jerusalem — 21:15-16
E. **PAUL'S VISIT TO THE TEMPLE AND
   HIS ARREST** — 21:17–23:30
    1. Paul's Reception by the Church — 21:17-26
       a. Paul's Report of the Gentile Response
          to the Gospel — 21:17-19
       b. The Proposal of James and the Elders — 21:20-26
    2. The Riot in the Temple — 21:27-30
    3. Paul's Rescue by the Romans — 21:31-36

4. Paul's Request for Permission to Address
the Mob — 21:37-40
5. Paul's Defense to the Jews — 22:1-21
   a. Paul's Early Days — 22:1-5
   b. The Episode on the Damascus Road — 22:6-11
   c. The Visit from Ananias of Damascus — 22:12-16
   d. The Vision in the Temple — 22:17-21
6. The Reaction of the Mob and Paul's
   Imprisonment — 22:22-29
7. The Trial before the Sanhedrin — 22:30–23:10
   a. The Confrontation with the
      High Priest — 22:30–23:5
   b. The Division of the Pharisees and Sadducees over
      the Resurrection Hope — 23:6-10
8. The Word of Encouragement from God — 23:11
9. The Conspiracy Against Paul's Life — 23:12-15
10. The Discovery of the Conspiracy — 23:16-22
11. The Decision to Transfer Paul to Caesarea — 23:23-24
12. The Letter from the Tribune to Felix — 23:25-30
F. **THE IMPRISONMENT AT CAESAREA** — 23:31–26:32
   1. Paul's Transfer to Caesarea — 23:31-35
   2. Paul's Trial before Felix — 24:1-21
      a. The Accusations Against Paul — 24:1-9
      b. The Defense by Paul — 24:10-21
   3. The Postponement of a Verdict by Felix — 24:22-23
   4. Paul's Interviews with Felix — 24:24-26
   5. The Ascension of Festus: Paul's Continued
      Custody — 24:27
   6. The Visit of Festus to Jerusalem — 25:1-5
   7. Paul's Appeal to Caesar — 25:6-12
   8. The Visit of Agrippa II and Bernice to Festus — 25:13-22
   9. Paul's Appearance before Agrippa — 25:23–26:32
      a. The Presentation of Paul to Agrippa
         by Festus — 25:23-27
      b. Paul's Address to Agrippa — 26:1-23
         1) The Introduction — 26:1-3
         2) Paul's Pharisaic Heritage — 26:4-8
         3) Paul's Former Zeal Against Christians — 26:9-11

4) Paul's Experience on the Road
   to Damascus — 26:12-18

5) Paul's Obedience to God — 26:19-20

6) Paul's Arrest — 26:21

7) Paul's Continuing Preaching of Christ — 26:22-23

c. The Interchange Between Festus, Paul, and
   Agrippa — 26:24-29

d. The Agreement Regarding Paul's
   Innocence — 26:30-32

G. PAUL'S VOYAGE TO ROME — 27:1–28:31

1. The Journey from Caesarea to Sidon — 27:1-3

2. The Journey from Sidon to Myra — 27:4-6

3. The Journey from Myra around Crete — 27:7

4. The Arrival at Fair Havens — 27:8-15

   a. Paul's Warning About the Coming
      Danger — 27:8-12

   b. The Storm at Sea — 27:13-15

5. The Difficult Journey around Cauda — 27:16-17

6. The Shipwreck — 27:18-44

   a. The Attempts to Lighten the Ship — 27:18-19

   b. Paul's Words of Encouragement — 27:20-26

   c. The Sighting of Land — 27:27-29

   d. The Attempt of the Sailors to Escape — 27:30-32

   e. Paul's Encouragement of the Crew to
      Eat — 27:33-38

   f. The Running Aground of the Ship — 27:39-41

   g. The Escape to Dry Land — 27:42-44

7. The Winter at Malta — 28:1-10

   a. The Welcome by the Barbarians — 28:1-6

   b. Paul's Ministry of Healing — 28:7-10

8. The Journey to Syracuse — 28:11-12

9. The Journey to Rhegium and Puteoli — 28:13-14

10. The Welcome at Three Taverns — 28:15

11. The Imprisonment at Rome — 28:16-29

    a. The Arrival at Rome — 28:16

    b. Paul's Preaching to the Jews — 28:17-29

       1) Paul's Defense — 28:17-20

       2) The Request for Further Information by
          the Jews — 28:21-22

3) The Interview with the Jews — 28:23
4) The Mixed Response — 28:24-29
12. Paul's Two Years in Rome — 28:30-31

BIBLIOGRAPHY

Commentaries:

Arrington, French. *The Acts of the Apostles: An Introduction and Commentary*. Peabody, MA: Hendrickson, 1988.

Boles, H.L. *A Commentary on Acts of the Apostles*. Nashville: Gospel Advocate, 1941.

Campbell, Alexander. *Acts of the Apostles*. Nashville: Gospel Advocate, 1858.

Conzelmann, Hans. *Acts of the Apostles*, trans. James Limburg, A. Thomas Kraabel, Donald Juel. Philadelphia: Fortress, 1987.

Carter, C.W. and Ralph Earle. *Acts of the Apostles*. Grand Rapids: Zondervan, 1959.

DeWelt, Don. *Acts Made Actual*. Joplin, MO: College Press, 1969.

Foster, Lewis. *"Acts,"* in *The NIV Study Bible*. Grand Rapids: Zondervan, 1985.

Harnack, Adolf. *The Acts of the Apostles*, trans. J.R. Wilkinson. London: Williams & Norgate, 1909.

Haenchen, Ernst. *The Acts of the Apostles: A Commentary*, trans.Bassil Blackwell. Philadelphia: Westminster, 1971.

Harrison, E.F. *Interpreting Acts*. Grand Rapids: Zondervan, 1986.

Lake, Kirsopp and H.J. Cadbury. *The Beginnings of Christianity*, ed. F.J. Foakes-Jackson. Vol. 4. Grand Rapids: Baker, 1979.

Lipscomb, David. *Commentary on Acts of the Apostles*. Nashville: Gospel Advocate, 1896.

McGarvey, J.W. *New Commentary on the Acts of the Apostles*. 2 Vols. in One. Cincinnati: Standard, 1892.

Marshall, I.H. *The Acts of the Apostles*, Tyndale Commentary. Grand Rapids: Eerdmans, 1980.

Munck, Johannes. *The Acts of the Apostles*. The Anchor Bible. Garden City, NY: Doubleday, 1967.

Pesch, Rudolf. *Die Apostelgeschichte*. Teilband I: Apg. 1-12. Zurich: Benziger, 1986.

Polhill, John. *Acts*. The New American Commentary. Nashville: Broadman, 1992.

Stagg, Frank. *The Book of Acts: The Early Struggle for an Unhindered Gospel*. Nashville: Broadman, 1955.

Reese, Gareth. *New Testament History: A Critical and Exegetical Commentary on the Book of Acts*. Joplin, MO: College Press, 1991.

Williams, C.S.C. *A Commentary on the Acts of the Apostles*. Harper's New Testament Commentaries. Peabody, MA: Hendrickson, 1988.

Special Studies:

Arrington, French. *New Testament Exegesis: Examples*. Washington, D.C.: University Press of America, 1977.

Barrett, C.K. *The New Testament Background: Selected Documents*. New York: Harper & Row, 1961.

Bassler, Jouette. *Divine Impartiality: Paul and a Theological Axiom*. Chico, CA: Scholars Press, 1982.

Beasley-Murray, George. *Baptism in the New Testament*. Grand Rapids: Eerdmans, 1974.

Behm, Johannes. *"Glossa,"* in *TDNT*, ed. Gerhard Kittel, Gerhard Friedrich; trans. Geoffrey Bromiley. Vol. 1. Grand Rapids: Eerdmans, 1964.

Beitzel, Barry. *The Moody Atlas of Bible Lands*. Chicago: Moody, 1985.

Blaiklock, E.M. "The Acts of the Apostles as a Document of First-Century History," in *Apostolic History and the Gospel*, ed. Ward Gasque, Ralph Martin. Grand Rapids: Eerdmans, 1970.

Cadbury, H.J. "Roman Law and the Trial of Paul," in *The Beginnings of Christianity*, ed. F.J. Foakes-Jackson. Vol. 5. Grand Rapids: Baker, 1975.

_____. *Style and Literary Method of Luke* Part 1. Cambridge: Harvard University Press, 1920.

_____. *The Making of Luke-Acts*. New York: MacMillan, 1927.

Casson, Lionel. *Ships and Seamanship in the Ancient World*. Princeton: Princeton University Press, 1973.

_____. *The Ancient Mariners*. New York: Macmillan, 1959.

Conzelmann, Hans. *The Theology of St. Luke*, trans. G. Buswell. New York: Harper & Row, 1960.

Cottrell, Jack. *Baptism: A Biblical Study*. Joplin, MO: College Press, 1989.

Dahl, Nils. "The Story of Abraham in Luke-Acts," in *Studies in Luke-Acts*, ed. Leander Keck, J.L. Martyn. Philadelphia: Fortress, 1980.

Davies, W.D. *Paul and Rabbinic Judaism*. London: SPCK, 1958.

_____. *The Gospel and the Land*. Berkeley: University of California, 1974.

_____. *Torah in the Messianic Age and/or the Age to Come*. Philadelphia: SBL, 1952.

Dibelius, Martin. "The Acts of the Apostles in the Setting of the History of Early Christian Literature," in *Studies in the Acts of the Apostles*, trans. M. Ling. London: SCM, 1956.

_____. "Paul on the Areopagus," Ibid.

Dunn, J.D.G. *Baptism in the Holy Spirit*. Philadelphia: Westminster, 1970.

_____. *Jesus and His Spirit*. Philadelphia: Westminster, 1975.

Dupont, Jacques. *The Salvation of the Gentiles: Essays on the Acts of the Apostles*. New York: Paulist, 1967.

_____. *The Sources of Acts: The Present Position*, trans. Kathleen Pond. London: Darton, Longman, & Todd, 1964.

Easton, Burton. *Early Christianity: The Purpose of Acts and Other Papers*, ed. F.C. Grant. London: SPCK, 1955.

Ellis, E.E. *Paul's Use of the Old Testament*. Grand Rapids: Baker, 1985.

Enslin, Morton. *Reapproaching Paul*. Philadelphia: Westminster, 1987.

Esler, Philip. *Community and Gospel in Luke-Acts: The Social and Political Motivations of Lucan Theology*. Cambridge: Cambridge University Press, 1987.

Filson, Floyd. "The Journey Motif in Luke-Acts," in *Apostolic History and the Gospel*, ed. W.W. Gasque and Ralph Martin. Grand Rapids: Eerdmans, 1970.

Fitzmyer, Joseph. *Essays on the Semitic Background of the New Testament*. London: Geoffrey Chapman, 1971.

Flew, R.N. *Jesus and His Church: A Study of the Idea of the Ecclesia in the New Testament*. London: Epworth, 1943.

Gärtner, Bertil. *The Areopagus Speech and Natural Revelation*. Uppsala: Gleerup, 1955.

Gasque, Ward. *A History of the Criticism of the Acts of the Apostles*. Tübingen: Mohr, 1975.

Gaston, Lloyd. *No Stone on Another: Studies in the Significance of the Fall of Jerusalem in the Synoptic Gospels*. Leiden: E.J. Brill, 1970.

Georgi, Dieter. *The Opponents of Paul in Second Corinthians*. Philadelphia: Fortress, 1986.

Goulder, M.D. *Type and History in Acts*. London: SPCK, 1964.

Guthrie, Donald. *New Testament Introduction*. Downers Grove, IL: InterVarsity, 1970.

Hamey, L.A. and J.A. *The Roman Engineers*. Cambridge: Cambridge University Press, 1981.

Harnack, Adolf. *Luke the Physician*, trans. J.R. Wilkinson. New York: Putnam's, 1907.

Harris, J.R. *Testimonies*, I, II. Cambridge: Cambridge University Press, 1916.

Hemer, C.J. *The Book of Acts in the Setting of Hellenistic History*, ed. Conrad Gempf. Winona Lake, IN: Eisenbrauns, 1990.

Hengel, Martin. *Between Jesus and Paul*, trans. John Bowden. Philadelphia: Fortress, 1983.

——————. *Judaism and Hellenism: Studies in Their Encounter in Palestine during the Early Hellenistic Period*, trans. John Bowden. 2 Vols. in One. Philadelphia: Fortress, 1981.

Hobart, W.K. *The Medical Language of St. Luke*. London: Longmans Green, 1882.

Horsley, Richard. *Bandits, Prophets, and Messiahs: Popular Movements in the Time of Jesus*. New York: Harper and Row, 1985.

Horton, Jr., Fred. "Reflections on the Semitisms of Luke-Acts," in *Perspectives on Luke-Acts*, ed. Charles Talbert. Edinburgh: T & T Clark, 1978.

Hubbard, Benjamin. "The Role of Commissioning Accounts in Acts," in *Perspectives on Luke-Acts*, ed. Charles Talbert. Edinburgh: T & T Clark, 1978.

Hurd, John. *The Origin of 1 Corinthians*. London: SPCK, 1965.

Jensen, Irving. *Acts: An Independent Study*. Chicago: Moody, 1974.

Jeremias, Joachim. *Jerusalem in the Time of Jesus*, trans. F.H. and C.H. Cave. Philadelphia: Fortress, 1989.

Jervell, Jacob. *Luke and the People of God: A New Look at Luke-Acts*. Minneapolis: Augsburg, 1979.

Jewett, Paul. *Infant Baptism and the Covenant of Grace*. Grand Rapids: Eerdmans, 1978.

Jewett, Robert. *A Chronology of Paul's Life*. Philadelphia: Fortress, 1979.

Johnson, Luke. *Sharing Possessions: Mandate and Symbol of Faith.* Philadelphia: Fortress, 1981.

Kim, Seyoon. *The Origin of Paul's Gospel.* Tübingen: J.C.B. Mohr, 1981.

Kurz, William. "Luke-Acts and Historiography in the Greek Bible," in SBL *Seminar Papers* 1980, ed. P.J. Achtemeier. Chico, CA: Scholars Press, 1980.

Ladd, George. *A Theology of the New Testament.* Grand Rapids: Eerdmans, 1974.

Lohse, Eduard. *"Pentekoste,"* in *TDNT*, ed. Gerhard Kittel, Gerhard Friedrich; trans. Geoffrey Bromiley. Vol. 6. Grand Rapids: Eerdmans, 1964.

Longenecker, Richard. *Paul, Apostle of Liberty.* Grand Rapids: Baker, 1977.

McRay, John. *Archaeology and the New Testament.* Grand Rapids: Baker, 1991.

Maddox, Robert. *The Purpose of Luke-Acts.* Edinburgh: T & T Clark, 1982.

Manson, T.W. *The Servant-Messiah.* Cambridge: Cambridge University Press, 1953.

Marshall, I.H. *Luke: Historian and Theologian.* Grand Rapids: Zondervan, 1970.

Martin, Ralph. *New Testament Foundations.* 2 Vols. Grand Rapids: Eerdmans, 1978.

Miesner, Donald. "The Missionary Journeys Narrative: Patterns and Implications," in *Perspective on Luke-Acts*, ed. Charles Talbert. Edinburgh: T & T Clark, 1978.

Minear, Paul. *Images of the Church in the New Testament.* Philadelphia: Westminster, 1977.

Moore, G.F. *Judaism in the First Centuries of the Christian Era.* New York: Schocken, 1971.

Moule, C.F.D. "Obligation in the Ethic of Paul," in *Essays in New Testament Interpretation*. Cambridge: Cambridge University Press, 1982.

_____ . "The Christology of Acts," in *Studies in Luke-Acts*, ed. Leander Keck, J.L. Martyn. Philadelphia: Fortress, 1980.

Moulton, J.H., W.F. Howard, and Nigel Turner. *A Grammar of New Testament Greek*. 4 Vols. Edinburgh: T & T Clark, 1963.

Munck, Johannes. *Paul and the Salvation of Mankind*, trans. Frank Clarke. Richmond, VA: John Knox, 1959.

Nickle, K.F. *The Collection*. London: SCM, 1966.

Norden, Eduard. *Agnostos Theos*. Stuttgart: Teubner, 1923.

O'Neill, J.C. *The Theology of Acts in Its Historical Setting*. London: SPCK, 1961.

Plevnik, Joseph. *What Are They Saying about Paul?* New York: Paulist Press, 1986.

Ramsay, William. *Luke the Physician*. London: Hodder and Stoughton, 1908.

_____ . *St. Paul the Traveller and Roman Citizen*. Grand Rapids: Baker, 1978.

Richard, Earl. *Acts 6:1-8:4: The Author's Method of Composition*. Missoula: Scholars Press, 1978.

Rienecker, Fritz. *A Linguistic Key to the Greek New Testament*, trans. Cleon Rogers, Jr. Grand Rapids: Zondervan, 1980.

Rivkin, Ellis. *A Hidden Revolution*. Nashville: Abingdon, 1978.

Robertson, A.T. *Luke the Historian in Light of Research*. Edinburgh: T & T Clark, 1920.

Robinson, J.A.T. *Twelve New Testament Studies*. London: SCM, 1962.

Robbins, Vernon. "By Land and by Sea: The We-Passages and Ancient Sea Voyages," in *Perspectives on Luke-Acts*, ed. Charles Talbert. Edinburgh: T & T Clark, 1978.

Russell, Bob. *Making Things Happen: The Power of Christian Leadership*. Cincinnati: Standard, 1987.

Sanders, E.P. *Paul and Palestinian Judaism*. Philadelphia: Fortress, 1977.

Scharlemann, Martin. *Stephen: A Singular Saint*. Rome: Pontifical Biblical Institute, 1968.

Schürer, Emil. *The History of the Jewish People in the Age of Jesus Christ*, ed. and rev. Geza Vermes, Fergus Millar, and Matthew Black. Edinburgh: T & T Clark, 1979.

Shepard, J.W. *The Life and Letters of the Apostle Paul: An Exegetical Study*. Grand Rapids: Eerdmans, 1956.

Sherwin-White, A.N. *Roman Society and Roman Law in the New Testament*. Oxford: Clarendon, 1963.

Smith, James. *The Voyage and Shipwreck of St. Paul*, 3rd ed. London: Longmans, Green, and Co., 1866.

Spiro, Abram. "Stephen's Samaritan Backgound," in Johannes Munck, *The Acts of the Apostles*, Anchor Bible. Garden City, NY: Doubleday, 1967.

Stagg, Frank. *The Book of Acts: The Early Struggle for an Unhindered Gospel*. Nashville: Broadman, 1955.

Stagg, Frank and Evelyn. *Woman in the World of Jesus*. Philadelphia: Westminster, 1978.

Stendahl, Krister. "The Apostle Paul and the Introspective Conscience of the West," in *Paul among Jews and Gentiles*. Philadelphia: Fortress, 1983.

Swidler, Leonard. *Biblical Affirmations of Woman*. Philadelphia: Westminster, 1979.

Talbert, Charles. *Literary Patterns, Theological Themes and the Genre of Luke-Acts*. Missoula: Scholars Press, 1974.

Tarn, W.W. and G.T. Griffith. *Hellenistic Civilization*. Cleveland: World Publishing, 1969.

Torrey, C.C. *The Composition and Date of Acts*. Cambridge: Harvard University Press, 1916.

Trites, Allison. *The New Testament Concept of Witness*. Cambridge: Cambridge University Press, 1977.

van Unnik, W.C. "Luke-Acts, A Storm Center in Contemporary Scholarship," in *Studies in Luke-Acts*, ed. Leander Keck and J.L. Martyn. Philadelphia: Fortress, 1980.

——————. "Tarsus or Jerusalem: The City of Paul's Youth," trans. G. Ogg, in *Sparsa Collecta*. Part 1. Leiden: E.J. Brill, 1973.

Veltman, Fred. "The Defense Speeches of Paul in Acts," in *Perspectives on Luke-Acts*, ed. Charles Talbert. Edinburgh: T & T Clark, 1978.

Via, E.J. "An Interpretation of Acts 7:35-37 from the Perspective of Major Themes in Luke-Acts," in *Society of Biblical Literature 1978 Seminar Papters*, ed. Paul Achtemeier. Missoula: Scholars Press, 1978.

Vielhauer, Philipp. "On the 'Paulinism' of Acts," in *Studies in Luke-Acts*, ed. Leander Keck, J.L. Martyn. Philadelphia: Fortress, 1980.

Wilson, Stephen. "Law and Judaism in Acts," in *SBL Seminar Papers 1980*, ed. Paul Achtemeier. Chico, CA: Scholars Press, 1980.

——————. *The Gentiles and the Gentile Mission in Luke-Acts*. Cambridge: Cambridge University Press, 1973.

Periodicals:

Acworth, Angus. "Where Was St. Paul Shipwrecked? A Re-examination of the Evidence." *JTS* 24 (1973): 190-193.

Bamberger, Bernard. "The Sadducees and the Belief in Angels." *JBL* 82 (1963): 433-435.

Best, Ernest. "Acts XIII.1-3." *JTS* 11 (1960): 344-348.

Blevins, William. "The Early Church: Acts 1-5." *RevEx* 71 (1974): 463-474.

Bowker, J.W. "Speeches in Acts." *NTS* 14 (1968): 96-111.

Bruce, F.F. "Chronological Questions in the Acts of the Apostles." *BJRL* 68 (1986): 273-295.

Bull, Robert. "Caesarea Maritima: The Search for Herod's City." *BAR* 8 (1982): 24-41.

Cadbury, H.J. "Erastus of Corinth." *JBL* 50 (1930): 42-58.

_____. "Lexical Notes on Luke-Acts: V. Luke and the Horse-Doctors." *JBL* 52 (1933): 55-65.

Catchpole, David. "Paul, James and the Apostolic Decree." *NTS* 23 (1977): 428-444.

Cosgrove, Charles. "The Divine *dei* in Luke-Acts." *NovT* 26 (1984): 168-190.

Clark, David. "What Went Overboard First?" BTr 26 (1975): 144-146.

Culpepper, R.A. "Paul's Mission to the Gentile World." *RevEx* 71 (1974): 487-497.

Daube, David. "On Acts 23: Sadducees and Angels." *JBL* 109 (1990): 493-497.

Davis, J.C. "Another Look at the Relationship between Baptism and Forgiveness of Sins in Acts 2:38." *RestQ* 24 (1981): 80-88.

Downing, F.G. "Common Ground with Paganism in Luke and Josephus." *NTS* 28 (1982): 546-559.

Duncan, G.S. "Paul's Ministry in Asia — The Last Phase." *NTS* 3 (1957): 211-218.

Filson, Floyd. "The Christian Teacher in the First Century." *JBL* 60 (1941): 317-328.

Fitzgerald, Michael. "The Ship of Saint Paul: Comparative Archaeology." *BA* 53 (1990): 31-39.

Fitzmyer, Joseph. "The Ascension of Christ and Pentecost." *TS* 45 (1984): 409-440.

Gilchrist, J.M. "On What Charge Was St. Paul Brought to Rome?" *ExpT* 78 (1967): 264-266.

Goldsmith, Dale. "Acts 13:33-37: A Pesher on II Samuel 7." *JBL* 87 (1968): 321-324.

Goodspeed, E.J. "Gaius Titius Justus." *JBL* 69 (1950): 382-383.

Gordon, Alasdair. "The Fate of Judas according to Acts 1:18." *EQ* 43 (1971): 97-100.

Greenhut, Zvi. "Burial Cave of the Caiaphas Family." *BAR* 18 (1992): 29-36.

Haldane, Douglas. "Anchors of Antiquity." *BA* 53 (1990): 19-24.

Hemer, C.J. "First Person Narrative in Acts 27-28." *TB* 36 (1985): 97-98.

Hirschfield, Nicolle. "The Ship of St. Paul — Part I: Historical Background." *BA* 53 (1990): 19-24.

Hohlfelder, Robert. "Caesarea beneath the Sea." *BAR* 8 (1982): 42-47.

Horsley, G.H.R. "The Inscriptions of *Ephesos* and the New Testament." *NovT* 34 (1992): 105-168.

Kepple, Robert. "The Hope of Israel, The Resurrection of the Dead, and Jesus: A Study of Their Relationship in Acts with Particular Regard to the Understanding of Paul's Trial Defense." *JETS* 20 (1977): 231-241.

Kilgallen, John. "The Function of Stephen's Speech (Acts 7:2-53)." *Biblica* 70 (1989). 173-193.

Kilpatrick, G.D. "Acts XXIII.23 *DEXIOLABOI*." *NTS* 14 (1963): 393-394.

Kodell, Jerome. "'The Word of God grew': The Ecclesial Tendency of *logos* in Acts 1,7; 12,24; 19,20." *Biblica* 55 (1974): 505-519.

Ladouceur, David. "Hellenistic Preconceptions of Shipwreck and Pollution as a Context for Acts 27-28." *HTR* 73 (1980): 435-449.

Lofthouse, W.F. "The Holy Spirit in the Acts and the Fourth Gospel." *ExpT* 52 (1940-41): 334-337.

Malherbe, Abraham. "Gentle as Nurse." *NovT* 12 (1970): 203-217.

Mare, Harold. "Acts 7: Jewish or Samaritan?" *WThJ* 34 (1971): 1-21.

Mastin, B.A. "Scaeva the Chief Priest." *JTS* 27 (1976): 405-412.

Meinardus, Otto. "St. Paul Shipwrecked in Dalmatia." *BA* 39 (1976): 145-147.

Merrill, Eugene. "Paul's Use of 'About 450 Years' in Acts 13:20." *BiblThecSac* 138 (1981): 246-257.

Metzger, Bruce. "The Meaning of Christ's Ascension." *ChrT* 10 (1966): 863-864.

Miles, Gary and Garry Trompf. "Luke and Antiphon: The Theology of Acts 27-28 in the Light of Pagan Beliefs about Divine Retribution, Pollution, and Shipwreck." *HTR* 69 (1976): 259-267.

Nash, Donald. "For the Remission of Sin." *ChrSt* (3-30-75): 270-272.

Palmer, Darryl. "Acts and the Historical Monograph." *TB* 43 (1992): 373-388.

Parrat, J.K. "The Rebaptism of the Ephesian Disciples." *ExpT* (1968): 182-183.

Parker, Pierson. "Once More, Acts and Galatians." *JBL* 36 (1967): 175-182.

Rapuano, Yehudah. "Did Philip Baptize the Eunuch at Ein Yael?" *BAR* (1990): 44-49.

Scott, J.J. "Stephen's Speech: A Possible Model for Luke's Historical Method?" *JETS* 17 (1974): 91-97.

_____ . "The Cornelius Incident in the Light of Its Jewish Setting." *JETS* 34 (1991): 475-484.

Slater, Thomas. "The Possible Influence of LXX Exodus 20:11 on Acts 14:15." *AUSS* 30 (1992): 151-152.

Stagg, Frank. "The Unhindered Gospel." *RevEx* 71 (1974): 451-462.

Stein, Robert. "The Relationship of Galatians 2:1-10 and Acts 15:1-35: Two Neglected Arguments." *JETS* 17 (1974): 239-242.

Stoops, Jr., R.F. "Riot and Assembly: The Social Context of Acts 19:23-41." *JBL* 108 (1989): 73-91.

Talbert, Charles. "The Place of the Resurrection in the Theology of Luke." *Int* 46 (1992): 19-30.

Thornton, T.C.G. "Stephen's Use of Isaiah LXVI.1." *JTS* 25 (1974): 432-435.

Tiede, David. "The Exaltation of Jesus and the Restoration of Israel in Acts 1." *HTR* 79 (1986): 278-286.

Trites, Allison. "The Importance of Legal Scenes and Language in the Book of Acts." *NovT* 16 (1974): 278-284.

Viviano, Benedict and Justin Taylor. "Sadducees, Angels, and Resurrection (Acts 23:8-9)." *JBL* 111 (1992): 496-498.

Walker, William. "Acts and the Pauline Corpus Reconsidered." *JSNT* 24 (1985): 3-23.

Wall, Robert. "Successors to 'the Twelve' according to Acts 12:1-17." *CBQ* 53 (1991): 628-643.

Wilcox, Max. "The 'God-Fearers' in Acts — A Reconsideration." *JSNT* 13 (1981): 102-122.

Workman, W.P. "A New Date Indication in Acts." *ExpT* 11 (1900): 316-317.

ACTS 1

I. THE CHURCH IN JERUSALEM (1:1–8:1a)

A. INTRODUCTION OF THE BOOK (1:1-3)

¹In my former book, Theophilus, I wrote about all that Jesus began to do and to teach ²until the day he was taken up to heaven, after giving instructions through the Holy Spirit to the apostles he had chosen. ³After his suffering, he showed himself to these men and gave many convincing proofs that he was alive. He appeared to them over a period of forty days and spoke about the kingdom of God.

Luke's first words are to his patron, Theophilus. His identity is unknown to us. In Luke's Gospel he is also named and is described as "most excellent" (1:3). This designation suggests that he was a person of some status. Theophilus was a common name in the first century, and the custom of dedicating important literary works to a patron was also common.[1]

He describes his Gospel as "the former book" because he sees in Acts the second volume of his work. Any document which covered more than one roll of papyrus might be referred to as a "book."[2] In

---

[1] Bruce points out that Josephus dedicated his *Jewish Antiquities*, his *Autobiography*, and his two-volume *Against Apion* to one Epaphroditus (pp. 29-30). For a discussion of the prologue of Luke's Gospel see Robert Stein, *Luke* New American Commentary (Nashville: Broadman, 1992), pp. 62-68.

[2] Kirsopp Lake and Henry J. Cadbury, *The Beginnings of Christianity* (Grand Rapids: Baker, 1979), 4:2. Talbert records the close similarities between the prologue of Luke and that of Acts (*Literary Patterns*, pp. 15-18).

this case Luke uses "former" (πρῶτον, *proton*) to mean the first of two volumes.[3] He aptly summarizes the content of the Gospel as "all that Jesus began to do and to teach." Both his miracles and his sayings are recorded there. The word "began" probably does not mean that Acts represents a continuation of this ministry. The phrase is a Hebrew expression implying that the former book deals with what Jesus did and taught "from the beginning."[4]

Events recorded in the Gospel of Luke lead up to the day Jesus was "taken up to heaven." Fittingly enough, the Third Gospel ends where the Book of Acts begins—the ascension of Jesus. The disciples watched Jesus ascend into heaven, but only after he appeared to them over a span of forty days.[5]

During this time, Jesus gave instructions to his disciples "through the Holy Spirit."[6] Jesus had previously testified that the Holy Spirit was working through him (see Luke 4:14-21). Acts continues this theme here by noting that Jesus' final instructions to the Apostles

---

[3]Though William Ramsay presses πρῶτον to mean "the first of three" after the classical sense of the term, this meaning is unlikely here (*St. Paul the Traveller and Roman Citizen*, pp. 27-28,309). See also Gasque, *History*, pp. 144-145,186.

[4]See J.H. Moulton, W.F. Howard, Nigel Turner, *A Grammar of New Testament Greek* (Edinburgh: T & T Clark, 1963), 3:227. Moule, Munck, and Reese agree with this position against Bruce who says that the phrase implies that Acts will be "an account of what Jesus *continued* to do and teach" (p. 30).

[5]The time of the ascension has been questioned because of the mention of the event in Luke 24:50-51 which seems to place the ascension on the same day as the resurrection. See Joseph Fitzmyer, "The Ascension of Christ and Pentecost," *TS* 45 (1984): 409-440. The language in Luke's Gospel cannot be pressed so specifically, however, as to contradict what Luke himself now records in Acts (not to mention that this interpretation of Luke 24:50-51 would put him at odds with other references to the period of his resurrection appearances in such passages as John 20:26; 21:1; 1 Cor 15:5-6). Nevertheless, Fitzmyer correctly observes that Luke is the only one of the sources which "historicized" the ascension, in the sense that he records the event in narrative form (p. 424).

[6]The phrase "through the Holy Spirit" may describe how Jesus chose the apostles rather than how he gave the apostles instructions. Nigel Turner attributes the ambiguity to the unusual word order of the clause. See J.H. Moulton, W.F. Howard, and Nigel Turner, *A Grammar of New Testament Greek* (Edinburgh: T & T Clark, 1963), 3:350.

were delivered under the guidance of the Spirit. Later in Acts the Spirit's role in Jesus' ministry of miracles and healing will be mentioned (see 10:38).

The time of this instruction was a period "after his suffering." During the next forty days after his death and resurrection, Jesus made appearances to the apostles. He would come and go again in such a way that those who saw him were convinced that this was the Jesus whom they had known.[7] The word for "convincing proofs" (τεκμήριον, *tekmērion*) is a term which was used in logic to speak of a demonstration of evidence clinching the case. The sight of the risen Lord and their experiences with him were all the evidence needed to conclude that Jesus was alive again.

Demonstrating that he was alive was not the only reason that Christ appeared to his apostles. He also spent this time telling them things about the Kingdom of God. The term "kingdom" is used to speak of God's reign or rule, whether in heaven or on earth. His subjects include all whose allegiance is to Christ. The Kingdom of God was important in the preaching of Jesus (see Mark 1:15) and continued to be emphasized by his early disciples (see Acts 8:12; 19:8; 20:25; 28:23,31).[8]

B. THE COMMISSIONING OF THE APOSTLES (1:4-8)

[4]On one occasion, while he was eating with them, he gave them this command: "Do not leave Jerusalem, but wait for the gift my Father promised, which you have heard me speak about. [5]For John baptized with[a] water, but in a few days you will be baptized with the Holy Spirit." [6]So when they met together, they asked him, "Lord, are you at this time going to restore the kingdom to Israel?" [7]He said to them: "It is not for you to know the times or dates the Father has set by his own authority. [8]But you will receive

---

[7]Luke's Gospel gives specific examples of Christ's resurrection appearances in 24:13-32, 34, 36-43. A list of those to whom Jesus appeared is given by Paul in 1 Cor 15:5-8. Resurrection appearances are also recorded in Matthew, Mark, and John.

[8]For a discussion of the importance of the resurrection in Jesus' teaching about the Kingdom of God, see George Ladd, *A Theology of the New Testament* (Grand Rapids: Eerdmans, 1974), pp. 332-333.

power when the Holy Spirit comes on you; and you will be my witnesses in Jerusalem, and in all Judea and Samaria, and to the ends of the earth."

ᵃ5 Or *in*

Included among these "things about the Kingdom of God" which Christ taught his disciples was the promise of the Holy Spirit. Jesus used an occasion of eating with his disciples to issue his command.[9] Luke also describes another resurrection appearance which involved a meal (see Luke 24:43). In the present context one particular concern is mentioned by Luke. Jesus wanted his disciples to be ready for the coming of the Holy Spirit.

By commanding them to wait in Jerusalem, Jesus was fulfilling expectations which extended back to the Old Testament prophets. Isaiah 2:3 predicted, "The Law will go out from Zion, the word of the Lord from Jerusalem." His own teaching had confirmed this anticipation. Jesus had told them they would "receive power from on high" (Luke 24:49). Jerusalem would be the place. Though they might be tempted to leave Jerusalem and go back to Galilee or to avoid persecution by returning to their previous way of life, Jesus was telling them to stay in the city.[10]

The "power from on high" of which Jesus had spoken would arrive shortly. As to the specific nature of this power, the only words from Jesus we have are the well-known passages from John 14-16.[11] There Jesus encouraged his disciples not to think of his separation from them as a reason to lose heart. He promised them

---

[9]Besides Luke and Acts, John 21:12-13 is the only other record of a meal in which the risen Lord participated. Benjamin Hubbard has identified seven features of "commissioning accounts" which appear in Luke-Acts, six of which occur here. See his "The Role of Commissioning Accounts in Acts," in *Perspectives on Luke-Acts*, ed. Charles Talbert (Edinburgh: T & T Clark, 1978), pp. 187-198.

[10]W.D. Davies notes that the language used by Jesus implies that the disciples had experienced a temptation to go back to Galilee, perhaps thinking that the destruction of Jerusalem was at hand. See his *The Gospel and the Land* (Berkeley: University of California, 1974), p. 264.

[11]W.F. Lofthouse states that "the emphasis of these five passages is precisely that which underlies the conception of the Spirit in Acts 1-15." See "The Holy Spirit in the Acts and the Fourth Gospel," *ExpT* 52 (1940-41): 336.

that the Father will send "another Counselor" (John 14:16) who would guide them into all truth (John 16:13). Here Jesus was contrasting the coming gift of the Spirit with what was found in the baptism of John. The apostles would experience a power that was unlike anything experienced by those baptized by John.

Luke 3:16 records the testimony of John the Baptist. When baptizing those who came to him, John told the people that the one coming after him would baptize them "with the Holy Spirit and with fire" (see also Matt 3:11 and John 1:33). Now Jesus was reminding the apostles of this promise. John's baptism was performed with water and yet was quite effective. What Jesus was predicting for the apostles would be more than they could imagine. The Holy Spirit was going to be poured out from heaven in a way that would include flames of fire (see Acts 2:3). The days of fulfillment described by the Old Testament prophets were dawning.[12]

It is easy to see what the apostles thought about the coming of the Spirit. Evidently his description of the outpouring of the Spirit caused them to begin thinking about the end of the age.[13] On the day of Jesus' ascension the group was conversing on the Mount of Olives. The apostles saw their opportunity to ask a burning question. Would this time be the moment for the restoration of the kingdom to Israel?

The form of their question indicates that they expected a political reign. "Restore" suggests a return to the national independence enjoyed under former kings.[14] On numerous occasions the apostles had shown that this expectation dominated

---

[12]See, for example, Joel 2:28-32, cited in Acts 2:17-21. Notice that the same contrast between John's baptism and the gift of the Spirit in Christian baptism is the theme of Acts 19:1-6.

[13]For comments on Jewish eschatological expectations associated with the Spirit's coming, see John Polhill, *Acts*, The New American Commentary (Nashville: Broadman, 1992), p. 84. Note that Jesus' presentation of the kingdom of God emphasizes what Rudolf Pesch refers to as its "nicht-politische Charakter," rather than any heightening of nationalistic objectives. See his *Die Apostelgeschichte*, Teilband I: Apg. 1-12 (Zurich: Benziger, 1986), p. 71.

[14]The Greek term ἀποκαθιστάνω (*apokathistanō*) is an eschatological technical term which speaks of God's restoration of the right order in the end time. See Fritz Rienecker, *A Linguistic Key to the Greek New Testament*,

their thinking. They were eager to see the restoration of dominion to Israel and to share positions of authority in the new political order. Even at their last supper with Jesus this issue had surfaced (see Luke 22:24-27; Mark 10:35-45).

Without confronting their misconception directly, Jesus was now reminding them that their position did not permit them such privileged information. They would not be given details about "the times or dates" for the fulfillment of God's purposes.[15] Their concern was not to speculate as to when, but to commit themselves as to what their role would be in the Lord's completing of his divine plans.

"My witnesses" is what Jesus said they would be. With its background in the courtroom, "witness" (μαρτυρία, martyria) implies the act of testifying. They would serve as proclaimers of the earthly ministry, the death, resurrection, and ascension of Jesus. As eyewitnesses they were in the perfect position to do so.

The Old Testament prophet had called on Israel to be God's witnesses in the world (see Isa 43:10; 44:8). Their failure in this mission made the ministry of Jesus even more essential. If Israel would not become the "servant of the Lord," then Jesus, and those whom he commissioned, must take up the task.

The apostles were to become Christ's witness-bearers. The extent of this witnessing would be worldwide. Beginning in Jerusalem they would proclaim the gospel in ever-widening geographical circles.[16] It would be proclaimed also in "all Judea and Samaria, and to the ends

---

trans. Cleon Rogers, Jr (Grand Rapids: Zondervan, 1980), p. 263. David Tiede points out the numerous examples in which Jewish literature reflected the expectation of Jewish repentance which would lead to the restoration of Israel, including such works as *Jubilees*, *The Testament of Moses*, the *Antiquities* of Josephus, *4 Ezra*, *2 Baruch*, and *The Psalms of Solomon*. See his "The Exaltation of Jesus and the Restoration of Israel in Acts 1," *HTR* 79 (1986): 278-286.

[15]Bruce notes that there might be a distinction between "times" (χρόνοι, chronoi) and "dates" (καιροί, kairoi), the former describing the "interval before the consummation of the kingdom of God," and the latter describing the "critical events accompanying its establishment" (p. 35). Jesus had established in previous teaching that the time of these events was not even known by the Son of God, but the Father alone (see Mark 13:32).

[16]The omission of Galilee in this geographical plan is curious. Davies notes that Acts assumes the presence of Christians in Galilee (see 9:31) and

of the earth." Acts 1:8 thus becomes the theme of the entire book. Roughly speaking, Acts 1-7 describes the impact of the gospel in Jerusalem. Then, Acts 8-12 carries the account forward, depicting the effects of the gospel in several places in Judea (the region including Jerusalem) and Samaria (the region immediately north of Judea). Lastly, Acts 13-28 highlights the spread of the gospel to major cities of the whole Roman Empire, the ends of the civilized world. This commentary follows the progression indicated in this verse.

Proclaiming the gospel on such a broad scale was an incredible undertaking. Sufferings and hardships would accompany the apostles on the way. Help from God was vital. Thus Jesus addressed the very real need of the apostles when he reminded them of what the Father had promised for them. They would receive power in the form of the Holy Spirit. Only then could they serve as witnesses. With this power (δύναμις, *dynamis*)—the very power which worked in the ministry of Christ on earth—the apostles would be propelled into the activity of witnessing. Such proclamation of the Christ would lead to a restored Israel in spiritual glory as the kingdom was advanced on a universal scale.

Without the Spirit there could be no witnessing for Jesus. Yet without the focus of witnessing for Jesus the power of the Spirit has no purpose. Wherever disciples of Jesus become distracted from their witness for him, the power is drained away.

C. THE ASCENSION OF CHRIST (1:9-11)

[9]**After he said this, he was taken up before their very eyes, and a cloud hid him from their sight. [10]They were looking intently up into the sky as he was going, when suddenly two men dressed in white stood beside them. [11]"Men of Galilee," they said, "why do you stand here looking into the sky? This same Jesus, who has been taken from you into heaven, will come back in the same way you have seen him go into heaven."**

---

then suggests that Galilee was not evangelized beginning in Jerusalem as were Judea and Samaria, but was converted through the efforts of disciples of Jesus from within Galilee itself. See Davies, pp. 412, 421-422.

The words of Jesus had hardly been spoken before the apostles were witnessing the Lord's being lifted toward heaven. The language indicates that the event occurred before their very eyes. Christ's ascension was unlike his many resurrection appearances to the disciples in which he suddenly appeared and then just as suddenly disappeared (as he did on the road to Emmaus in Luke 24:31). Neither is there any sign of external forces such as a whirlwind or heavenly wonder (as with Elijah in 2 Kgs 2:11). No earthly power assisted in this ascension.[17] Rather, Jesus simply began lifting into heaven in a way that may be described as dignified or majestic.

A cloud appeared after he began to ascend, and hid Jesus from their gaze. The apostles may well have remembered that during the transfiguration of Christ it was a cloud which enveloped them, covering the brilliance of his glory (see Luke 9:34-36).[18] The appearance of such a cloud also sparks memories of Old Testament accounts of the nation of Israel being led in the wilderness by the cloud from which the voice of God was heard (see Exod 40:34) or the temple filled with the cloud of God's glory (see 1 Kgs 8:10-11).

Intently gazing on the unfolding drama in the sky, the apostles were interrupted by two men standing beside them.[19] It was obvious they were angels because of their white garments.[20] The message of the heavenly visitors was filled with rebuke and promise. Addressing the apostles as "men of Galilee," the angels were calling attention to

---

[17]Ernst Haenchen notes that this ascension scene also differs from pagan or Jewish examples of similar ascensions where such forces are a common element of the story. See his *The Acts of the Apostles: A Commentary*, trans. Bassil Blackwell (Philadelphia: Westminster, 1971), p. 149.

[18]Talbert gives details regarding the similarities between Luke's account of Jesus' ascension here and the language of the transfiguration of Christ (*Literary Patterns*, pp. 61-62). The ascension communicated to the disciples Jesus' final departure from his earthly ministry and the moment at which he took his seat at the right hand of God (Eph 1:20; 1 Pet 3:22). See Bruce Metzger, "The Meaning of Christ's Ascension," *ChrT* 10 (1966): 863-864.

[19]The perfect tense of the verb "stood" may indicate that the apostles did not see the two men until they were standing beside them.

[20]White garments were a common feature of the appearance of heavenly beings (see Matt 28:3; John 20:12; Luke 24:4). Such references can also be given from extrabiblical literature (2 Macc 3:26 and 11:8).

the fact that the apostles, except for Judas Iscariot, were not only native Galileans, but they also had spent most of their time with Jesus in Galilee.[21] The question put to the apostles contains a hint of rebuke. Why were they standing there as if Jesus would become visible again? This ascension was not like the transfiguration. Then Jesus was present the moment the cloud was gone. Those days were over. The apostles would have to say good-by to the experience of having Jesus with them in the flesh. But this did not mean he would be far from them when they stood before their persecutors (as with Stephen in Acts 7:56) or when the call came for ministry (as with Paul in Acts 9:5).

More importantly, Jesus Christ would be back again. The words of the two angels also contained a promise. Jesus is coming again. But the promise is quite specific. The one who will come again is "this same Jesus." He is the very one who ministered with them, taught them, performed miracles around them, and was taken from them in the crucifixion, resurrection, and finally, the ascension. His return would be a personal coming (see 1 Thess 4:16).

The ascension of Jesus Christ is, then, a meaningful moment in the purposes of God. It prepares the way for such New Testament doctrines as the exaltation of Christ as heavenly king (see Mark 16:19) and the role of Christ as mediator (see 1 Tim 2:6). Without the ascension of Jesus his existence would be confined to this world. His acceptance into the presence of God assures believers that his mission has been accomplished. His exaltation at the right hand of God means that his new status as Lord and Christ has been confirmed by God (see Luke 22:69; Acts 2:33-36; 5:31).

---

[21]Talbert notes that this address also fits into a larger christological emphasis in Acts, which establishes that the one raised from the dead is the same Jesus who ministered in Galilee with his disciples. See "The Place of the Resurrection in the Theology of Luke," *Int* 46 (1992): 19-30. Another point noted by Talbert is the emphasis here on what the apostles "saw." See his *Literary Patterns*, p. 113.

D. WAITING FOR THE HOLY SPIRIT (1:12-14)

[12]**Then they returned to Jerusalem from the hill called the Mount of Olives, a Sabbath day's walk[a] from the city. [13]When they arrived, they went upstairs to the room where they were staying. Those present were Peter, John, James and Andrew; Philip and Thomas, Bartholomew and Matthew; James son of Alphaeus and Simon the Zealot, and Judas son of James. [14]They all joined together constantly in prayer, along with the women and Mary the mother of Jesus, and with his brothers.**

[a]*12* That is, about ³/₄ mile (about 1,100 meters)

Returning from the Mount of Olives was an uphill climb on a winding road with some spectacular views of Jerusalem to the west and the Dead Sea to the east. This notation by Luke gives the location of the ascension at a place just outside of Jerusalem on the eastern slope of the Mount of Olives. The apostles walked "a Sabbath's day's walk" to get to Jerusalem. This distance was about three-fourths of a mile and was the longest distance one could walk without breaking the Sabbath day regulation established by rabbinic tradition.[22]

When they arrived, the apostles went to "an upstairs room." The term describes a space which was generally found on the third floor of a large Palestinian house. These rooms were normally reached by outside steps and were often used as dining rooms or as places of study. Sometimes they were also sublet to poorer families.[23] No information is given as to the owner of the house, though some suggest that it may have belonged to Mary, mother of Mark (see 12:12). It may have been the same upper room used for Jesus' last supper with his disciples (see Mark 14:15).

At this point the list of apostles is given. The list differs only slightly from similar ones given in the Gospels (Luke 6:14-16; Mark 3:16-19; Matt 10:2-4). The order of the names shows some variation

---

[22]The distance was 2000 cubits and, as Bruce (p. 39) says, was "ingeniously reckoned" by comparing Exod 16:29 ("let no one go out of his place on the seventh day") with Num 35:5 (Levite's pasturelands defined as 2000 cubits in radius from a city of refuge).

[23]Polhill, p. 89.

and Judas Iscariot is, of course, omitted. James son of Alphaeus is probably the same disciple called James the younger (see Mark 15:40). Simon is called "the Zealot" which is likely a reference to his connections with the group of militant Jews fighting for political independence in the latter part of the first century.[24]

Also mentioned here are women who were a part of the fellowship of believers. Included among the women were those who had followed Jesus from Galilee (see Luke 23:49-55). Mary Magdalene, Salome, and Mary the mother of James are mentioned in Mark 15:40-47. In some cases, the women may have been relatives of the apostles, or even their wives (as mentioned in 1 Cor 9:5). Mary the mother of Jesus was there. In addition, the "brothers" of Jesus were present. In Mark 6:3 the names of Jesus' four brothers are given as James, Judas, Joseph, and Simon, and the presence of sisters is also mentioned.[25] These family members were not convinced of Jesus' credibility at first (see John 7:5), but by the time of his ascension, had become believers. Later, James would even become a leader in the church (see 12:17; 15:13; 21:18) and author of the Book of James.

This group of apostles, friends, and family members was continuing in prayer as they waited in Jerusalem for the promise of God. The expression Luke uses is an important one. The disciples "joined together" not just in the sense of being together in the same place. They remained together in the sense of unity of mind and purpose. This expression of oneness (ὁμοθυμαδὸν, homothymadon, in Greek) will appear several more times in Acts (see 2:46; 5:12; 8:6; 15:25). Luke's motive is to show how the believers carried out their ministry and worship with a spirit of harmony. It is no surprise that such unity should follow when Christians are praying and waiting for the Spirit.

---

[24]Though scholars today admit that the evidence for the existence of the Zealots in any organized way prior to A.D. 66 is slight, Josephus dates the beginning of the group to A.D. 6. See Bruce, pp. 40-41; Richard A. Horsley, *Bandits Prophets, and Messiahs: Popular Movements in the Time of Jesus* (New York: Harper and Row, 1985), p. xiv.

[25]See Bruce (*Acts*, p. 41) for details concerning the debate about the brothers and sisters of Jesus. As he says, "the burden of proof lies on those who would understand the term in another than its usual sense" of biological sibling.

E. THE REPLACEMENT OF JUDAS ISCARIOT (1:15-26)

[15]In those days Peter stood up among the believers[a] (a group numbering about a hundred and twenty) [16]and said, "Brothers, the Scripture had to be fulfilled which the Holy Spirit spoke long ago through the mouth of David concerning Judas, who served as guide for those who arrested Jesus—[17]he was one of our number and shared in this ministry." [18](With the reward he got for his wickedness, Judas bought a field; there he fell headlong, his body burst open and all his intestines spilled out. [19]Everyone in Jerusalem heard about this, so they called that field in their language Akeldama, that is, Field of Blood.) [20]"For," said Peter, "it is written in the book of Psalms, "'May his place be deserted; let there be no one to dwell in it,'[b] and, "'May another take his place of leadership.'[c] [21]Therefore it is necessary to choose one of the men who have been with us the whole time the Lord Jesus went in and out among us, [22]beginning from John's baptism to the time when Jesus was taken up from us. For one of these must become a witness with us of his resurrection." [23]So they proposed two men: Joseph called Barsabbas (also known as Justus) and Matthias. [24]Then they prayed, "Lord, you know everyone's heart. Show us which of these two you have chosen [25]to take over this apostolic ministry, which Judas left to go where he belongs." [26]Then they cast lots, and the lot fell to Matthias; so he was added to the eleven apostles.

[a]*15* Greek *brothers*   [b]*20* Psalm 69:25   [c]*20* Psalm 109:8

Peter's ability as a leader among believers became vital at a time when frustration and aimlessness could have overwhelmed the followers of Jesus. These believers had witnessed the cruel death of the Savior, and after a brief, unexpected reunion with him, they had once again been separated from him at the ascension. The small group had been deprived of one of its leaders when Judas Iscariot turned traitor. Under these circumstances Peter stood to address the bewildered group of believers. "In those days" refers to the period between the ascension and the Day of Pentecost. It is appropriate for the NIV to use the term "believers" instead of "brothers" since the word "brothers" here includes both men and women. The number 120 did not include believers elsewhere in Palestine besides Jerusalem.[26]

Addressing the assembly, Peter's first thought was the scriptural authority for taking action. He cited two Old Testament verses— Psalm 69:25 and 109:8. The prophecies of the Old Testament "had to be fulfilled," was Peter's message, and these two Psalms reflected on the present need. Psalm 69:25 is a prayer by the psalmist that the home of his enemy will become deserted. Psalm 109:8 is a prayer that the enemy of the psalmist will die prematurely and be replaced in his position by someone else. Peter thus implied that the abdication of Judas and the opportunity to replace him had been foreseen by God. In stating this, Peter also expressed his confidence in the Scriptures as the very voice of God. The prophetic word had been spoken "by the Holy Spirit through the mouth of" the human spokesman, David. The word of God is authoritative because it originates from God.

Many of the Psalms, especially those which are called "royal" or "coronation," were considered Messianic in the first century. It is possible that lists of such Old Testament references were used by the earliest Christians as they evangelized among the Jews.[27]

Peter's description of the need called attention to what happened to Judas Iscariot. He reminded the apostles that Judas had been a full member of their ministry. Luke adds a parenthetical remark (indicated as such in the NIV) that Judas had used the money to purchase a field (or an estate). Because of the gruesome nature of his death on this property the place became known later as "Field of Blood" (*Akeldama* in Aramaic). The name of the place is translated from the Aramaic for the benefit of Luke's Greek readers. The language indicates that he fell "headlong" and his body "burst open."

Matthew's account of this incident indicates that Judas returned the thirty pieces of silver to the temple, throwing it down, and then went away and hanged himself (see Matt 27:1-5). The best way to harmonize these accounts is to assume that the priests used the

---

[26]Bruce (Ibid., p. 43) notes that 1 Cor 15:6 speaks of one occasion on which the resurrected Jesus appeared to more than 500 of his followers.

[27]J. R. Harris, *Testimonies*, I, II (Cambridge: Cambridge University Press, 1916).

silver to purchase the estate after the death of Judas. This assumes that his death occurred by hanging, and that the body of Judas, having become decomposed, fell from the place where he had committed suicide.[28] Luke's reason for providing such gory details is to remind the reader of the consequences of sin. This point is reinforced in 1:25 where Peter says that Judas abandoned his role "to go where he belongs"—a less than subtle reference to eternal punishment.

After this explanation, the address of Peter resumes. His use of the Psalms argues the need for selecting a new leader. This need was made explicit as Peter explained the qualifications required of the successor of Judas. The position of Judas would not be filled randomly. The field was narrowed to include only those who had "been with us," that is, full participants in the earthly ministry of Jesus.[29] Beyond this requirement, the successor must have been a participant in this ministry for the full period of time beginning from John's baptizing in the Jordan River and including Christ's ascension. This experience would serve to boost the credentials of the new apostle for being a "witness" of Christ's resurrection.

Two candidates, Joseph called Barsabbas and Matthias, were set forth by the apostles. Others may also have been qualified for this role, but these two were placed before the congregation for consideration. Their names are not mentioned again in the New Testament.

---

[28]For a more detailed discussion of the harmonizing of these passages see C.W. Carter and Ralph Earle, *Acts of the Apostles* (Grand Rapids: Zondervan, 1959), pp. 20-21; Alasdair Gordon, "The Fate of Judas according to Acts 1:18," *EQ* 43 (1971): 97-100.

[29]Here some of the criteria for apostleship are described. In Acts it is always the twelve who are called apostles, except in 14:4,6 where Paul and Barnabas are designated as "apostles." Paul's use of the term seems broader, however, and includes not only himself (Gal 1:1), but also Junias and Andronicus (Rom 16:7), and maybe Barnabas (1 Cor 9:6) and James (1 Cor 15:5; Gal 1:19). For a discussion of the origins of this term, see Stephen Wilson, *The Gentiles and the Gentile Mission in Luke-Acts* (Cambridge: Cambridge University Press, 1973), pp. 111-119. See also R.N. Flew, *Jesus and His Church: A Study of the Idea of the Ecclesia in the New Testament* (London: Epworth, 1943), pp. 130-131.

The last step in the process of selection was prayer and the casting of lots. The prayer was simple, but beautiful. God was addressed in a way quite appropriate for the occasion. He is "Lord," but also the one who knows every heart. "Lord" describes his absolute control over circumstances and events. As the one who knows everyone's heart, his assistance was necessary in the selection of a spiritual leader upon whom much would depend. The simple request was that the all-knowing Lord would reveal the proper choice.

Having asked for divine help, the apostles completed the selection with the casting of lots. Lots were usually a collection of marked stones or sticks placed in a jar and then shaken out. The one whose lot fell out was the one chosen.[30] Though this method may seem far too random, we must remember that the Old Testament had already sanctioned the casting of lots for use in some important situations (see Num 26:55; 1 Sam 10:20,21). Now the apostles were using this method in connection with a process that had already narrowed the field of candidates by a rational means, and had brought them down to two perhaps equally qualified men. Thus they prayed for God's choice to be revealed in this final step. They trusted as they did so that the truth of Prov 16:33 would apply: "The lot is cast into the lap, but its every decision is from the Lord."

In this manner, Matthias was "added to the eleven apostles." This is the only instance in the New Testament where an apostle is chosen with human hands. Later, when James was martyred, there was no effort to replace him (see 12:2). The position of apostle was a unique and irreplaceable one (see Eph 2:20; Rev 21:14). As eyewitnesses to the resurrection, their testimony would form the basis for the preaching of the gospel (see 1 Cor 15:1-8).

---

[30]Johannes Munck argues that the casting of lots may refer to a congregational vote. See his *The Acts of the Apostles*, The Anchor Bible (Garden City, NY: Doubleday, 1967), p. 10. J.W. Shepard describes how this passage presents the church taking action through an early form of congregational organization. See his *Life* (Grand Rapids: Eerdmans, 1956), pp. 28-30. Jacob Jervell shows how this passage places emphasis on the fact that an apostle (especially Matthias) was divinely selected for his position among the twelve. See *Luke and the People of God: A New Look at Luke-Acts* (Minneapolis: Augsburg, 1979), pp. 83-89. See also William Beardslee, "The Casting of Lots at Qumran and in the Book of Acts," *NovT* 4 (1960): 245-252.

ACTS 2

F. THE DAY OF PENTECOST (2:1-47)

1. The Apostles Baptized with the Holy Spirit (2:1-4)

[1]When the day of Pentecost came, they were all together in one place. [2]Suddenly a sound like the blowing of a violent wind came from heaven and filled the whole house where they were sitting. [3]They saw what seemed to be tongues of fire that separated and came to rest on each of them. [4]All of them were filled with the Holy Spirit and began to speak in other tongues[a] as the Spirit enabled them.

[a]4 Or *languages*; also in verse 11

Just as Jesus had promised, the Holy Spirit was about to come on the apostles in a dramatic way. The day on which this occurred was the Day of Pentecost. In the Jewish calendar, Pentecost was the second of the three major feasts. It fell fifty days after the Sabbath of Passover week (Lev 23:15-16).[1] In the Old Testament it was also

---

[1]Bruce gives details regarding the debate between the Sadducees and Pharisees as to the exact reckoning of the fifty days (p. 49, n. 3). The Sadducees began counting the fifty days from the next day after the weekly sabbath day, i.e., Sunday (see Lev 23:15). The Pharisees, on the other hand, began their count on the sabbath day of the week-long festival, i.e., on that day of the festival when no work was to be done (see Lev 23:7). As long as the temple stood in Jerusalem, says Bruce, the Sadducean interpretation was prominent for Christians in Jerusalem, though Eduard Lohse argues that the Pharisaic interpretation was followed. See his article on πεντηκοστή in *Theological Dictionary of the New Testament*, eds. Gerhard Kittel, Gerhard Friedrich, trans. Geoffrey Bromiley (Grand Rapids: Eerdmans, 1964) 6:46. Fitzmyer adds to this equation the interpretation of the Essenes, who disagreed with both the Pharisees and the Sadducees. The Essenes at

known as the Feast of Weeks (Deut 16:10), the Feast of Harvest (Exod 23:16), and the Day of Firstfruits (Num 28:26).

More important than the day in the Jewish calendar was what Pentecost came to represent. With the giving of the Spirit, this day became the birthday of the church. As James D.G. Dunn observes, Pentecost was the dividing line between the Old Covenant and the New.[2] The ascension recorded in Acts 1 serves to prepare for the epochal event of Pentecost in Acts 2. Pentecost, says Dunn, "inaugurates the age of the Church."

The place in which they were gathered may have been the upper room referred to in 1:13.[3] The group that was gathered is spoken of as "they." It is not easy to decide whether this pronoun describes only the apostles or also the 120 believers. Grammatically speaking, the nearest antecedent is "the apostles" in 1:26. This reference also seems likely in light of the promise Jesus made to the apostles that they would receive the baptism of the Holy Spirit to become his witnesses (see Acts 1:5,8). Some scholars, however, point to the prophecy of Joel (see Acts 2:18) as an indication that women were included in the group which gathered at this time. They also find in the gathering of the great crowd an indication that the Spirit fell on more than just the twelve apostles.[4]

What was experienced is recorded in some detail. The Holy Spirit was poured out from heaven (v. 17). He arrived in a manner

---

Qumran established a religious calendar in which Pentecost always fell on the same date, 15 Siwan (the third month). Fitzmyer notes that the debate still goes on today. See his "Ascension," 431.

[2]See his *Baptism in the Holy Spirit* (Philadelphia: Westminster, 1970), pp. 41,45-47,49; and his *Jesus and the Spirit* (Philadelphia: Westminster, 1975), pp. 130,135-136. Though Pentecost was for the Jews a celebration of the giving of the law at Sinai, Hans Conzelmann correctly observes that Luke's presentation of the events at Pentecost makes no connection with this event. See his *Acts of the Apostles*, trans. James Limburg, A. Thomas Kraabel, and Donald Juel (Philadelphia: Fortress, 1987), pp. 15-17. See also Ralph Martin, *New Testament Foundations* (Grand Rapids: Eerdmans, 1978), 2:70-82.

[3]Bruce, p. 51. The use of ἐν τῷ with the infinitive is causal, explaining why they were gathered together. See Moulton, Howard, Turner, *Grammar*, 3:145.

[4]Polhill, p. 97; Haenchen, p. 167; Munck, p. 14.

that was both seen and heard.[5] A sound suddenly filled the room, which reminded them of a powerful, roaring wind from heaven. Flames ("tongues;" γλῶσσαι, glōssai) of fire appeared which seemed to shoot out and hover above the head of each one there.

The significance of these elements is first in the fact that they are miraculous displays of divine power. More particularly, the experience was a reminder of the numerous times that the Spirit was compared to the wind. Ezekiel spoke of how the wind blew and God breathed life into the dry bones (see 37:9-14). Jesus told Nicodemus that the Spirit, like the wind, produces results which are obvious though no one sees him (see John 3:8). Fire was the element present when Moses saw the burning bush and heard the voice of God (see Exod 3:2-5). John the Baptist had predicted that Jesus would soon baptize with the Holy Spirit and fire (see Luke 3:16).

Along with these signs of the Spirit's coming there also came the ability to speak with "other tongues." The term for "tongues" (glōssai) is often used to speak of languages used throughout the world, and here the context dictates that this meaning is intended.[6] The crowd was amazed that these Galileans could speak words in so many languages spoken outside of Galilee (see v. 7). Here were twelve men who by a miracle of God were speaking in languages they should not have known.[7]

The explanation of this miracle is included in the narrative. "All of them were filled with the Holy Spirit" in such a way that the Spirit "enabled them" to speak the languages of the audience which had gathered.[8] Little detail is supplied here regarding the mechanics of this miracle of speech. The term "enabled" (ἀποφθέγγομαι,

---

[5]Talbert notes the parallels between this account of the giving of the Spirit and the way in which the Spirit came on Jesus at his baptism. See his *Literary Patterns*, pp. 16,18.

[6]This meaning is discussed by Johannes Behm in his article on γλῶσσα in *TDNT*, 1:719-727.

[7]The exact nature of this language has been discussed by scholars. Bruce takes the language to be "ecstatic utterances" with many words of a foreign dialect included (p. 52). The view of E.F. Harrison is that their speech was presented completely in a foreign language. See his *Interpreting Acts* (Grand Rapids: Zondervan, 1986), pp. 59-62. See also Reese, pp. 51-52.

[8]"All of them" probably refers to the apostles. See the note on this verse in *The NIV Study Bible* (Grand Rapids: Zondervan, 1985).

apophthengomai) does not appear to include the idea of ecstatic speech, though it does carry the idea of speaking in an inspired way.[9] The filling of the Spirit is mentioned in Acts 9:17 in the case of Saul of Tarsus. For the apostles it corresponds to the promise of the baptism of the Spirit. The language of Acts 11:16-17 suggests that the experience of the apostles and that of Cornelius established an expectation that the Spirit, in some form, would be given to all believers. Acts 2:39 reinforces this wide availability of God's Spirit.

The mention of speaking in these languages invites comparisons with Paul's words in 1 Corinthians 12-14. Many commentators argue that what is there referred to as "spiritual gifts" is not the same phenomenon described in Acts. The basis for the distinction is that Paul's language characterizes "speaking in tongues" as a "praise language" addressed only to God and unintelligible to everyone else. By contrast, Acts 2 portrays speaking in tongues as languages understood by those who were visiting in Jerusalem.[10] Both passages, however, use the term *glōssa* in reference to the gift. In 2:11 the content of their speaking in tongues is "declaring the wonders of God," a phrase that bears similarities with Paul's description in 1 Corinthians 14:13-17.[11]

2. The Amazement of the Crowd (2:5-13)

[5]**Now there were staying in Jerusalem God-fearing Jews from every nation under heaven. **[6]**When they heard this sound, a crowd came together in bewilderment, because each one heard them speaking in his own language. **[7]**Utterly amazed, they asked: "Are not all these men who are speaking Galileans? **[8]**Then how is it that each of us hears them in his own native language? **[9]**Parthians, Medes and Elamites; residents of Mesopotamia, Judea and Cappadocia, Pontus and Asia, **[10]**Phrygia and Pamphylia, Egypt and the**

---

[9]Haenchen, p. 168.

[10]Polhill, pp. 98-99.

[11]At stake in this discussion is the modern usefulness of "the gift of tongues." If the gift was a gift in which the Holy Spirit provided the believer with the miraculous ability to speak in foreign languages, then those who claim to speak in tongues must account for this feature of the gift.

parts of Libya near Cyrene; visitors from Rome [11]**(both Jews and converts to Judaism); Cretans and Arabs—we hear them declaring the wonders of God in our own tongues!"** [12]**Amazed and perplexed, they asked one another, "What does this mean?"** [13]**Some, however, made fun of them and said, "They have had too much wine.**[a]**"**

[a]*13 Or sweet wine*

The commotion caused by the Spirit's descent could not be hidden. Whether it was the "sound" of the roaring wind or the noisy speaking from the apostles, a crowd began to gather, probably from the temple area. This location would be the only place where 3000 people could assemble (see 2:41).

Bewilderment was the most appropriate description for the spectators who arrived. Luke spares few adjectives in reporting the astonishment of the crowd. They were bewildered (v. 6), "utterly amazed" (v. 7), "amazed and perplexed" (v. 12). They wondered aloud how these Galileans could be speaking in dialects so foreign to Palestine.

To emphasize the far-reaching nature of these languages, Luke now includes a list of nations represented in the gathering. He reports that in Jerusalem resided devout Jews "from every nation under heaven."[12] Whether these residents were pilgrims to Jerusalem because of the Feast of Pentecost or permanent residents from the communities of Diaspora Jews is not clear. Whichever the case, these Jews were startled to hear the apostles speaking in languages other than Aramaic, Hebrew, or Greek.

The list of nations here is a rough sweep that begins in the eastern part of the Roman world and works its way west. The list begins in present-day Iran (Parthia) and mentions Medes, Elamites, and residents of Mesopotamia, all territories which are located east of

---

[12]The NIV translation is misleading at this point in using the term "God-fearing" for a term which means "devout" (εὐλαβεῖς, *eulabeis*), since the term "God-fearers" in Acts and elsewhere usually refers to Gentiles who associated themselves with the synagogue. Munck observes that the presence of Jews from the Diaspora highlights the universal impact of the gospel. See his *Paul and the Salvation of Mankind*, trans. Frank Clarke (Richmond: John Knox, 1959), pp. 213-214.

the Euphrates River. These areas held large concentrations of Jews since the days of the exiles. The next areas mentioned are located westward and northward. Judea is given, possibly as a substitute for Syria. Then attention swings north to Cappadocia and Pontus, territories in central and northern Turkey. Next comes Asia on the western coast, followed by Phrygia and Pamphylia farther inland. Now a full circle is completed with the mention of territories in North Africa. Egypt and Libya are included at this point in the list. Then comes the mention of Rome,[13] the island of Crete and finally Arabia, the first-century Nabatean kingdom east of the Dead Sea.

Plenty of evidence has been found to establish the presence of Jews in all of these locations sufficient for the account given here by Luke. In addition to Jews, 2:11 suggests that Gentiles were a part of the audience hearing the apostles. "Converts to Judaism" comes from the term for "proselyte" and refers to Gentiles who associated themselves with Judaism through circumcision (for male converts), a self-baptism for purification, and an offering at the temple in Jerusalem.[14] The status that proselytes occupied gave them a more formal participation in Jewish life and worship than did the less formal status of the "God-fearer" (a status mentioned later as held by Cornelius in 10:2).

Such a world-wide representation of nations only serves to amplify the astounding miracle which was witnessed. Luke is emphatic that the miracle which shocked the crowd was that their home dialect[15] was being spoken here in Jerusalem by Galileans. Evidently many in the crowd understood the incident as a sign from God. The question they asked implies this much. They wondered about the meaning of what they were witnessing. Others in the

---

[13]A.N. Sherwin-White comments on this phrase "visitors from Rome," which he thinks indicates "a nice contemporary touch from the Julio-Claudian age" in terms of the distinction between Roman citizens and the provincials. See his Roman Society and *Roman Law in the New Testament* (Oxford: Clarendon, 1963), p. 181.

[14]This self-baptism cannot be established with certainty before the second century.

[15]The Greek word διάλεκτος (*dialektos*) is used in 2:6 rather than γλῶσσα as in 2:4 and 11. Luke's use of *dialektos* is strong evidence that his references to speaking in tongues describe the use of other languages.

crowd dismissed this possibility. They saw nothing spiritual going on here. With stubborn cynicism they explained the whole event as the result of the all too common effects of intoxicating drink.[16] Their rejection of the amazing presence of the Spirit is the first among many such rejections which are chronicled in the Book of Acts.

3. The Sermon of Peter (2:14-36)

The Promise of Joel (2:14-21)

[14]**Then Peter stood up with the Eleven, raised his voice and addressed the crowd: "Fellow Jews and all of you who live in Jerusalem, let me explain this to you; listen carefully to what I say.** [15]**These men are not drunk, as you suppose. It's only nine in the morning!** [16]**No, this is what was spoken by the prophet Joel:** [17]**'In the last days, God says, I will pour out my Spirit on all people. Your sons and daughters will prophesy, your young men will see visions, your old men will dream dreams.** [18]**Even on my servants, both men and women, I will pour out my Spirit in those days, and they will prophesy.** [19]**I will show wonders in the heaven above and signs on the earth below, blood and fire and billows of smoke.** [20]**The sun will be turned to darkness and the moon to blood before the coming of the great and glorious day of the Lord.** [21]**And everyone who calls on the name of the Lord will be saved.'**[a]

[a]*21* Joel 2:28-32

Peter responded to the questions and accusations of the crowd by calling attention to the Old Testament prophet Joel. He would not let stand the uninformed charges of skeptics. With a boldness typical for Peter, he stepped forward to represent the other apostles and addressed the crowd. The term for "addressed" is also used in 2:4 and calls attention to the inspired quality of Peter's speech.

Peter's first words were intended to refute the accusations of drunkenness. With a hint of humor, he calls attention to the early hour. Nine a.m. (the third hour) was usually the hour of prayer,

---

[16]The Greek word is γλεῦκος (*gleukos*) and refers to fresh wine which has not had time to ferment completely (see Rienecker, p. 266).

after which Jews would take their first food.[17] People generally need more time to get drunk.

The true explanation of this event was what Joel had foretold (Joel 2:28-32). At this point Peter launched into a discussion of themes which appear in many of the sermons recorded in Acts. The emphasis on the dawning of the age of the Messiah, the universal appeal of the gospel, and the hope of restoration by a merciful God are themes which appear again and again. Even the structure of Peter's address shows similarities with other sermons in Acts (such as in chapters 3, 10, and 13). His explanation of the sign from God (2:14-21) is followed by an affirmation of the central facts of the gospel, the death, burial, and resurrection of Jesus (2:22-36), and an exhortation to repentance and baptism (2:37-40).[18]

Joel's words were directed toward God's people at a time when God's judgment was being felt. A plague of locusts had ruined the land. Joel called upon the people to repent of their sins and to look expectantly for the restoration of prosperity and the coming age of the Messiah when the Spirit would be poured out upon everybody.

Peter began his sermon by announcing that "this is what was spoken" by Joel. "I will pour out my Spirit in those days," the Lord had promised, and Peter saw in these words the explanation of the events of this Pentecost. "The last days" described in the Old Testament the time when God's purposes would be fulfilled (see Isa 2:2; Hos 3:5; Mic 4:1; also Heb 1:1; 1 Pet 1:20; 1 John 2:18). In the Hebrew quotation the word is "afterward" and the Septuagint has "after these things." Peter was interpreting this phrase to mean "the last days."[19]

The prophecy foretold the giving of the Spirit to all believers. Phrases such as "on all people," "sons and daughters," and "both men and women," vividly make the point. Even the term "pour out" (ἐκχεῶ, ekcheō) implies that God intends for a universal reception of the Holy Spirit in the new age. The wide extent of the reception of the Spirit was just the opposite of the restricted ministry of the Spirit in the Old Testament. What Joel promised would bring to pass the sentiments of Moses who exclaimed, "I wish that all the Lord's people were prophets and that the Lord would put his Spirit on them" (Num 11:29).

---

[17]Polhill, p. 108.
[18]*NIV Study Bible*, note on 2:14-40.
[19]Ibid., note on 2:17.

The mention of "sons and daughters" in v. 17 and "my servants" in v. 18 is meant as a Hebrew parallelism. One group is intended rather than two distinct groups. The sons and daughters are also servants of God. It is significant that the Spirit's ministry would also include women, and Paul later deals with the Corinthian women who exercised spiritual gifts.[20]

In vv. 19-20 several signs are described which may be understood either as figurative or literal. The wonders in heaven may be figurative language which points to a new cosmic order being instituted by God in Christ Jesus. On the other hand, Jerusalem had experienced some of these signs literally on the day Jesus was crucified.[21] It may be, however, that these words are best understood in connection with the final appearing of Jesus and the day of judgment (see 2 Peter 3:7-10).

At any rate, this new age would be dominated by a salvation available to anyone who sought it. Peter's quotation of Joel's prophecy stops with a word about salvation as if to highlight the point. "Lord" here is taken as a reference to Jesus Christ and connects with what follows in Peter's remarks (see 2:36).

The Proclamation of Jesus' Resurrection (2:22-28)

[22]"**Men of Israel, listen to this: Jesus of Nazareth was a man accredited by God to you by miracles, wonders and signs, which God did among you through him, as you yourselves know.** [23]**This man was handed over to you by God's set purpose and foreknowledge; and you, with the help of wicked men,**[a] **put him to death by nailing him to the cross.** [24]**But God raised him from the dead, freeing him from the agony of death, because it was impossible for death to keep its hold on him.** [25]**David said about him: 'I saw the Lord always before me. Because he is at my right hand, I will not be shaken.** [26]**Therefore my heart is glad and my tongue rejoices; my body also will live in hope,** [27]**because you will not abandon me to the grave, nor will you let your Holy One see decay.** [28]**You have made known to me the paths of life; you will fill me with joy in your presence.'**[b]

[a]*23* **Or** *of those not having the law* **(that is, Gentiles)**   [a]*28* **Psalm 16:8-11**

---

[20]See 1 Cor 12-14.
[21]See Luke 23:45; Polhill, p. 109.

After giving adequate attention to why the miracle of the languages had occurred, Peter moved to the central theme of his message—the death and resurrection of Jesus Christ. Peter placed blame for the crucifixion of Jesus on his audience, but argued that God counteracted the deed with the raising of Jesus from death. This balance is seen in later sermons in Acts (see 3:15; 4:10; 5:30; 10:39-40; 13:28-30).

The distinction between human decision and the purposes of God is maintained throughout Peter's address. Jesus was a man "accredited by God" by miracles he performed among them.[22] They saw the deeds, knew that they were from God, and still they, "with the help of wicked men, put him to death by nailing him to the cross." There was no escaping the responsibility. Some in this audience probably were present on the day the crowd was shouting "Crucify him!" Blame should go to the Jews who were in a position to prevent this injustice, but also to the "wicked men" who helped in the crucifixion (i.e., the Romans).[23]

God was not caught by surprise in all of this. Peter insisted that while Christ was crucified by human hands, he was "handed over" to them by "God's set purpose."[24] The crucifixion was also God's decision. His decision predated that of the Jews and Romans. While they had intended to do away with Jesus in the crucifixion, God foiled their plans by raising him from death.

The language used to describe the liberation of Jesus from death is vivid here. In raising Jesus from the dead, God freed him "from the agony of death" (2:24). The term for "agony" is ὠδίν (ōdin) and usually speaks of the pain of childbirth. Death is thus portrayed as a

---

[22]The Greek word is ἀποδείκνυμι (apodeiknymi) and means "to appoint, designate, or authenticate." The term had special application to office holders (see Polhill, p. 111). Dunn points out that the working of miracles in the ministry of Jesus was the sure sign of him as "a man of the Spirit." See his Jesus, pp. 70,164. The contents of the "witness" offered by the apostles can be seen by examining the speeches which follow in the Book of Acts. See Allison Trites, The New Testament Concept of Witness (Cambridge: Cambridge University Press, 1977), pp. 136,142-143,149-150.

[23]Some see in Peter's words a rejection of all that the old Israel represented. See Flew, Jesus, p. 122.

[24]The Greek phrase is ὡρισμένη βουλῇ (hōrismenē boulē) and refers to God's predetermined will.

fearful infliction of misery which attempted to "keep its hold on" Jesus. From death's unwelcome clutches Jesus was released since God's power could not be resisted.

Turning to the Psalms, Peter established the point from Scripture. Reproducing the Septuagint version of Psalm 16:8-11, he began by noting David's authorship and the fact that he could not have been speaking of himself. The Psalm was originally an expression of David's confidence in escaping "the grave" (ᾅδης, *hadēs*). The term is not to be confused with the word for "hell."[25]

Jesus the Lord and Messiah (2:29-36)

[29]"Brothers, I can tell you confidently that the patriarch David died and was buried, and his tomb is here to this day. [30]But he was a prophet and knew that God had promised him on oath that he would place one of his descendants on his throne. [31]Seeing what was ahead, he spoke of the resurrection of the Christ,[a] that he was not abandoned to the grave, nor did his body see decay. [32]God has raised this Jesus to life, and we are all witnesses of the fact. [33]Exalted to the right hand of God, he has received from the Father the promised Holy Spirit and has poured out what you now see and hear. [34]For David did not ascend to heaven, and yet he said, 'The Lord said to my Lord: "Sit at my right hand [35]until I make your enemies a footstool for your feet."'[b] [36]Therefore let all Israel be assured of this: God has made this Jesus, whom you crucified, both Lord and Christ."

[a]31 Or *Messiah*. "The Christ" (Greek) and "the Messiah" (Hebrew) both mean "the Anointed One"; also in verse 36.   [b]35 Psalm 110:1

David's words, Peter contended, must be a reference to the Messiah, the "Holy One" of God. David's own death and burial were a matter of public record. "His tomb is here to this day," undisturbed in Jerusalem, and thus stood as testimony that no

---

[25]The Greek word for "hell" is *gehenna* as in Luke 12:5, or *tartarus* as in 2 Pet 2:4. See the special study on *hadēs* in Reese, pp. 135-144. Dunn observes that this text was used by the Pharisees as a prooftext in their argument against the Sadducees regarding the doctrine of the resurrection before the Christians began using it in connection with Christ. See *Jesus*, pp. 118-119.

resurrection from death had occurred with this most famous of
Israel's kings.[26] The Psalm had to refer to the Messiah.

As Peter noted, David's words pointed to "one of his descendants." David had spoken as a prophet inspired by God and one
trusting in God's solemn ("on oath") promise to place one of his
descendants on the throne of Israel after himself. Such Old
Testament promises as 2 Samuel 7:12-13 and Psalm 132:11 come to
mind.[27] Since no other descendant of David had ever risen from
death, this reference must be to the Messiah.[28] If the Scripture foretold that the Messiah would rise from death and the apostles were
witnesses to the fact that Jesus rose from death, Jesus must then be
the Messiah spoken of by David.

A similar line of reasoning occurs in verses 34-36. This time the
Scripture reference Peter used was Psalm 110:1 and David's words
again provided the evidence. This Psalm may have been an
enthronement Psalm used in connection with the king of Israel. It is
used often in the New Testament (see 1 Cor 15:25; Heb 1:13;
10:13). Peter called attention to the fact that once again David
described someone other than himself—someone invited by the
Lord to sit at the right hand of the heavenly throne. Peter's interpretation of Psalm 110:1 was "the Lord God" said to "my Lord" (the
Messiah), "sit at my right hand." This invitation to sit at God's right
hand could not have applied to David because he "did not ascend to
heaven." But the apostles had seen one raised from death and taken
up to heaven.

Scripture and eyewitness testimony were, then, the foundation
of Peter's proclamation. The Old Testament prophecies described

---

[26]Bruce notes that half a century earlier King Herod had built a white
marble entrance to the tomb of David (p. 66).

[27]The Apostle Paul acknowledges Jesus' Davidic descent in Rom 1:3 and
15:12.

[28]The Greek word for Christ is *Christos* and means "anointed one." The
Hebrew parallel is "Messiah" which also means "anointed one." Flew argues
that the disciples would not have concluded that *Jesus* was Messiah on the
basis of his resurrection had he not accepted this honor during his ministry.
See *Jesus*, p. 116. This conclusion has many detractors. See R.F. Zehnle, *Peter's
Pentecost Discourse: Tradition and Lukan Reinterpretation in Peter's Speeches of
Acts* (Nashville: Abingdon, 1971). For a discussion of the significance of the
term "Lord" and "Christ," see Ladd, *Theology*, pp. 170-171; 331-341.

what the Messiah would accomplish. The apostles saw with their own eyes how Jesus fulfilled these expectations in his resurrection. Though Peter's audience was not present to witness the resurrection of Jesus, they had been given the privilege of seeing some of its results. "The promised Holy Spirit" had been given to Jesus and he had "poured out" the visible effects of the Spirit's presence.

On this basis Peter proclaimed Jesus as "both Lord and Christ." Directing his remarks to his Jerusalem audience, he reminded them that they were guilty of rejecting the very one God had set forth as Messiah. Jesus was "Lord" (κύριος, *kyrios*) in the same sense that the Old Testament (Septuagint) used the term of the only living God.[29] Jesus was "Messiah" in the sense that he was anointed by God for the purpose of saving people from their sins.

This Lord and Christ is the one Peter urged his audience to confess. Thus the early church did not "just preach what Jesus preached." The church "preached Jesus himself,"[30] and that to him belongs our allegiance.

4. The Call to Repentance (2:37-40)

[37]When the people heard this, they were cut to the heart and said to Peter and the other apostles, "Brothers, what shall we do?" [38]Peter replied, "Repent and be baptized, every one of you, in the name of Jesus Christ for the forgiveness of your sins. And you will receive the gift of the Holy Spirit. [39]The promise is for you and your children and for all who are far off—for all whom the Lord our God will call." [40]With many other words he warned them; and he pleaded with them, "Save yourselves from this corrupt generation."

The reaction of the crowd was swift and obvious. They were "cut to the heart." The rare term κατανύσσομαι (*katanyssomai*) describes a piercing, or a stinging pain. Peter's charge that his audience bore

---

[29]See Gen 12:8; Exod 9:16; Deut 5:11; Luke 11:2. See also Blevins, "Early Church," 463-474.
[30]Blevins, ibid., 467.

responsibility for the crucifixion of Christ hit them hard. Their question sought relief from the painful jolt of recognizing how wrong they had been about Jesus. Naturally, they wondered what they could do to rectify this wrong and remove their guilt.

Peter's response presents the very core of the Gospel—the kernel of the Good News. Something can be done about sin and guilt, even guilt as serious as the crucifixion of Jesus Christ. Two imperatives are given, "repent and be baptized." The Greek term for repentance (μετανοέω, *metanoeō*) carries the idea of turning from sin to God. Repentance incorporates a change of heart about unrighteousness and a desire to be reoriented toward the will of God.

The second imperative is baptism. Peter's response makes both of these actions equally necessary. He said "repent and be baptized" — not "repent or be baptized." During the ministry of John the Baptist, believers participated in "a baptism of repentance for the forgiveness of sins" (Mark 1:4; Luke 3:3). Now Peter instructed his audience to follow a similar course, except this baptism would be "in the name of Jesus Christ."[31] They would be baptized now as a response of allegiance to the risen Lord. This repentance and baptism would also bring forgiveness of sins and the gift of the Holy Spirit.

A number of commentators seek to diminish the force of the phrase "for the forgiveness of sins" at this point, apparently seeking to safeguard the doctrine of salvation by grace.[32] They take the preposition "for" (εἰς, *eis*) to mean "because of" rather than "in order to." Peter, they say, meant be baptized because of the forgiveness of sins, implying that such forgiveness had already been granted by the time baptism was administered.

---

[31]As George Beasley-Murray observes, "baptism in Acts is always administered 'in the name of Jesus Christ' or 'in the name of the Lord Jesus.'" He cites 2:38; 8:16; 10:48; 19:5. See his *Baptism in the New Testament* (Grand Rapids: Eerdmans, 1974), p. 100. See also Flew, *Jesus*, pp. 119-120.

[32]See Polhill, p. 117; Bruce correctly observes that "the idea of an unbaptized believer does not seem to be entertained in the New Testament" (p. 70). Beasley-Murray says, "God's gracious giving to faith belongs to the context of baptism, even as God's gracious giving in baptism is to faith." Likewise he quotes the words of K.K. Rasmussen who says, "Where baptism is spoken of faith is presumed, and where faith is spoken of baptism is included in the thought" (*Baptism*, pp. 272, n. 2; p. 273).

This position disregards the very common use of *eis* in the New Testament to mean "for the purpose of, in order to."[33] In Matthew 26:28 where this exact phrase appears, Jesus says his blood is poured out" for (*eis*) the forgiveness of sins. It would be absurd to argue that the phrase means "because of" and that Jesus' blood was poured out because sins had already been forgiven. Beyond this, the command to be baptized is only one of the imperatives Peter gave. "Be baptized" is joined to "repent" with "and." Whatever Peter says about the forgiveness of sins follows from both imperatives. Just as repentance is needed "for the purpose of" the forgiveness of sins, so is baptism. This position need not rob the plan of salvation of its basis in the grace of God. Both imperatives expect action to be taken on the part of the sinner. Yet Peter considered neither to be a work which merits salvation, but merely the response of faith dictated by the prophecy he had already cited—"everyone who calls on the name of the Lord will be saved" (2:21).

---

[33]The preposition is used more than 1700 times in the New Testament, very often with the meaning "for the purpose of." See Donald Nash, "For the Remission of Sin," *ChrSt* (3-30-75): 270-272, and the chart included by H. Leo Boles, *A Commentary on Acts of the Apostles* (Nashville: Gospel Advocate, 1941), p. 47. See also the excellent article by J.C. Davis, "Another Look at the Relationship between Baptism and Forgiveness of Sins in Acts 2:38," *RestQ* 24 (1981): 80-88; McGarvey, pp. 243-262. Among other things, Davis surveys the grammars to find that the vast majority give the meaning of this preposition as "purposive" (i.e. "for the purpose of," or "into"). He also notes that "in every place in the New Testament where 'baptism' and 'salvation' or 'baptism' and 'washing away of sins' are mentioned in the same passage, the order is always the same: first, 'baptism,' then, 'forgiveness' (or 'salvation' or 'washing away of sins')." This includes such passages as Mark 1:4; Luke 3:3; Acts 22:16; Mark 16:15,16; 1 Pet 3:20,21. Beasley-Murray compares the phrase εἰς ἄφεσιν (*eis aphesin*) to the corresponding use of the preposition in Rom 10:10: "for with the heart faith is exercised for righteousness (εἰς δικαιοσύνην, *eis dikaiosynēn*)" and "with the mouth confession is made for salvation (εἰς σωτηρίαν, *eis sōtērian*)." He lists forgiveness of sins and possession of the Spirit as only two of the numerous God-given graces. See *Baptism*, pp. 103, 264. Dunn says that v. 38 is the only verse in Acts "which directly relates to one another the three most important elements in conversion-initiation: repentance, water-baptism, and the gift of the Spirit" (*Baptism*, p. 91).

One more distinction which separated this baptism from that of
John was the gift of the Holy Spirit. He did not promise "the gifts of
the Spirit" to everyone (see 1 Cor 12:1), but "the gift of the Spirit"—
that is, the Holy Spirit himself. He also repeated the universal availability of this gift for "you and your children and for all who are far
off." The last phrase even embodies Gentiles.[34]

5. The First Christian Church (2:41-47)

[41]**Those who accepted his message were baptized, and about three
thousand were added to their number that day. [42]They devoted
themselves to the apostles' teaching and to the fellowship, to the
breaking of bread and to prayer. [43]Everyone was filled with awe,
and many wonders and miraculous signs were done by the apostles. [44]All the believers were together and had everything in
common. [45]Selling their possessions and goods, they gave to
anyone as he had need. [46]Every day they continued to meet
together in the temple courts. They broke bread in their homes
and ate together with glad and sincere hearts, [47]praising God and
enjoying the favor of all the people. And the Lord added to their
number daily those who were being saved.**

Beginning with 3000 conversions, the apostles founded a permanent fellowship of believers in Jerusalem. The language of these
verses emphasizes the continuing nature of this fellowship. "They
devoted themselves to" all of the defining elements of Christian
living. They "continued to meet together" daily, even enjoying their
meals at home in a spirit of oneness.[35]

"The apostles' teaching" provided the foundation of their faith.
As is evident in the New Testament documents, this teaching was
always Christ-centered, yet relevant to life. "The fellowship" (κοινωνία,
koinōnia) should be connected with the following activities which
describe believers in their life together. It probably includes the

---

[34]Paul Jewett shows how untenable it is to make this phrase an argument
for infant baptism. See his *Infant Baptism and the Covenant of Grace* (Grand
Rapids: Eerdmans, 1978), pp. 119-120.
[35]See the note on 12:24.

idea of sharing one's resources with others.[36] These believers felt a closeness which extended even to their personal possessions. Many of them sold property so that they had money to share with needy believers.[37]

Included in their oneness were the spiritual activities of the Lord's Supper and prayer. "Breaking of bread" in v. 42 probably refers to the observance of communion in congregational worship. This conclusion seems likely because of its association with the other elements mentioned. The last element is given in its plural form in the Greek text. They devoted themselves to "the prayers." Since the believers continued to make the temple central to their gatherings, it is not surprising that they continued to recognize the times for prayer.

---

[36]Compare Heb 13:16; Rom 15:26; 2 Cor 8:4. See Shepard, *Life*, p. 34. Robert Karris notes how unusual it was for Greeks or Romans to engage in alms-giving. See his "Poor and Rich: The Lukan Sitz im Leben," *Perspectives in Luke-Acts*, ed. Charles Talbert (Edinburgh: T & T Clark, 1978), pp. 112-125. Flew takes it as a reference to a kind of spiritual fellowship (pp. 109-110).

[37]Dunn draws the distinction between this voluntary sharing and communism. See *Jesus*, p. 161. Examples of communistic groups can be found in ancient literature. See Conzelmann, p. 24. For a description of the forced communism of Qumran see Joseph Fitzmyer, *Essays on the Semitic Background of the New Testament* (London: Geoffrey Chapman, 1971), pp. 284-288.

ACTS 3

G. THE HEALING OF THE LAME MAN AND ITS CONSEQUENCES (3:1–4:31)

1. A Cripple Cured (3:1-10)

[1]One day Peter and John were going up to the temple at the time of prayer—at three in the afternoon. [2]Now a man crippled from birth was being carried to the temple gate called Beautiful, where he was put every day to beg from those going into the temple courts. [3]When he saw Peter and John about to enter, he asked them for money. [4]Peter looked straight at him, as did John. Then Peter said, "Look at us!" [5]So the man gave them his attention, expecting to get something from them. [6]Then Peter said, "Silver or gold I do not have, but what I have I give you. In the name of Jesus Christ of Nazareth, walk." [7]Taking him by the right hand, he helped him up, and instantly the man's feet and ankles became strong. [8]He jumped to his feet and began to walk. Then he went with them into the temple courts, walking and jumping, and praising God. [9]When all the people saw him walking and praising God, [10]they recognized him as the same man who used to sit begging at the temple gate called Beautiful, and they were filled with wonder and amazement at what had happened to him.

The healing of the lame man follows the paragraph which describes the "many wonders and miraculous signs" done by the apostles (2:43).[1] Acts continues to focus on the conversions of those

---

[1]Shepard comments on Luke's wisdom in choosing this episode to demonstrate this turning point in the young life of the church (*Life*, p. 35).

who might be considered unlikely prospects for God's favor — first
the crowd in Jerusalem, which was responsible for the crucifixion of
Jesus, and now a lame man whose life seemed to be hopelessly
ruined. Many Jews probably considered the man as suffering from
the punishment of God.[2] But the apostles were ready to proclaim
the gospel to all who would hear them.

Peter and John walked "up to the temple," since the temple was
located on a highly elevated stone platform in Jerusalem. As was
mentioned in 2:46 the believers continued to meet in the temple
courts. The word for "temple" is ἱερόν (*hieron*) and describes the
temple precincts rather than suggesting that the apostles went into
the holy place itself.

Going to the temple at the time of prayer was not unusual for
the early Christians. Three times for prayer had been established.
The first was at the time of sacrifice in the early morning and then
again at about 3 p.m. The last time for prayer was at sunset.[3] Peter
and John were present for the afternoon prayer time.

Entering through the large gateway to the temple courts, they
arrived about the same time that a man was being carried to a place
beside the entrance. Their location was at a "gate called Beautiful,"
a name unknown in any Jewish literature from the time. It is usually
identified with the gate called Nicanor located on the eastern wall
of the temple court. This gate may be the one Josephus described as
being made not of silver and gold overlays, but of "Corinthian
bronze" which "far exceeded in value those plated with silver and
set in gold."[4]

The lame man was placed here because Jewish worshipers would
be extremely conscious of their duty to obey the law, to worship
God, and to show charity to the needy. His friends and family
brought him here "every day to beg." It was well known that his
affliction had been present since birth. Those Jews entering through

---

Talbert discusses the parallels here between this healing of the lame man
followed by Jewish opposition and the beginning of Jesus' ministry as
described in Luke 5:17–6:11 (*Literary Patterns*, pp. 16,19).

[2]See John 9:1-5.

[3]Josephus, *Antiquities*, 14.65.

[4]Josephus, *War*, 5.201. See the discussion of Conzelmann on the identification of this gate (p. 26).

the gateway would pass by him on their way from the court of Gentiles up the steps and past the barrier which warned Gentiles not to go further on pain of death. There he sat conspicuously, repeating over and over, "alms, alms." No doubt many other beggars were seen around the temple courts as well.

The lame man noticed Peter and John and quickly directed his request to them. Peter and John "looked straight at him," as if to emphasize the pointed significance of this communication. Peter commanded the same attention from the beggar when he said, "Look at us." The man responded with his full attention, thinking this might be the day he would receive a significant contribution from such interested worshipers.

Peter's unexpected admission must have caught the lame man by surprise. Not to have silver or gold meant disappointment for a beggar. Peter quickly assured the man that he possessed something more valuable and then commanded the lame man to walk. To give this command in the name of "Jesus Christ of Nazareth" refers to something done in the power and authority of Christ. This point will be important later in this account (see 4:17).

The cure was miraculous and instantaneous. The affliction carried by the lame man for years was removed in an instant. His joy and gratitude expressed themselves in his "walking and jumping, and praising God," actions which the Greek tense portrays as going on continuously.[5] He went with the apostles as they moved through the court of women to the court of Israel. Other worshipers saw him and realized that this was the man who "used to sit begging" at the temple gate. They could not believe their eyes.

2. Peter's Address in Solomon's Colonnade (3:11-26)

The Power of Jesus' Name (3:11-16)

[11]**While the beggar held on to Peter and John, all the people were astonished and came running to them in the place called Solomon's Colonnade. **[12]**When Peter saw this, he said to them:**

---

[5]Each is a present participle, denoting continuous action.

"Men of Israel, why does this surprise you? Why do you stare at us as if by our own power or godliness we had made this man walk? **13**The God of Abraham, Isaac and Jacob, the God of our fathers, has glorified his servant Jesus. You handed him over to be killed, and you disowned him before Pilate, though he had decided to let him go. **14**You disowned the Holy and Righteous One and asked that a murderer be released to you. **15**You killed the author of life, but God raised him from the dead. We are witnesses of this. **16**By faith in the name of Jesus, this man whom you see and know was made strong. It is Jesus' name and the faith that comes through him that has given this complete healing to him, as you can all see.

As worshipers came streaming from all directions, Peter began his address.[6] His first objective was to interpret the miracle which had been witnessed by this Jewish crowd. He emphasized that only by the power of Jesus' name could such a remarkable thing occur. His second objective was to move the Jews toward sincere repentance of their rejection of Christ and a willingness to accept him as God's appointed servant.

Passing from the court of Israel back again through the court of women and the Beautiful Gate, Peter and John came with the healed man to the court of Gentiles. On the eastern side of the court of Gentiles was located Solomon's Colonnade. It was a porch along the inside of the wall with rows of stone columns twenty-seven feet high supporting a cedar roof. Evidently the Christians met here frequently (see Acts 5:12). The Jewish tradition which credited the porch to Solomon was inaccurate.

Peter met the astonishment of the crowd with an explanation of what they had seen. No human virtue could explain the healing. Instead the credit should go to "the God of Abraham, Isaac and Jacob," the patriarchal formula for God that was important in the

---

[6]Trites identifies in this speech six themes also found in Peter's Pentecost address (2:14-36), as well as his sermon at the home of Cornelius in 10:34-43. Each of them mentions the appointment of Jesus by God; his signs, wonders, and mighty works; his death and resurrection; the harmony of all these details with Scripture; Christ's exaltation in heaven; and the position of the apostles as eyewitnesses (*Witness*, p. 143).

Old Testament and in Judaism.[7] This is the same God who "glori-fied his servant Jesus." The "servant" (παῖς, *pais*) described in Isaiah's "servant psalms" (52:13–53:12) was Jesus.[8] Through the ministry of God's appointed servant the lame man was now walking around.

God's initiative, however, had been met with opposition from the citizens of Jerusalem. As Peter had done in his Pentecost address (2:23,36), he laid blame at the feet of the Jews in Jerusalem. "You handed him over to be killed, and you disowned him before Pilate," Peter charged. These were the historical facts. Luke records them in his gospel (23:13-25).

On a higher plane, however, they had "disowned the Holy and Righteous One." They had resisted the action of God as witnessed

---

[7]Philip Esler sees in this formula the beginning of the "recurrent motif in Acts" in which Christianity is spoken of as "intrinsically connected with the fathers or ancestors of Israel." See also 5:30; 15:10; 22:14; 26:6; 28:25. He argues that this theme serves to legitimize Christianity in the eyes of the Romans who already viewed Judaism as legitimate. See his *Community and Gospel in Luke-Acts: The Social and Political Motivations of Lucan Theology* (Cambridge: Cambridge University Press, 1987), pp. 215-219.

[8]The titles used to describe Jesus in this address differ from those used in Peter's address in 2:36. J.A.T. Robinson suggests that the titles in this address are more primitive and that the Christology here conflicts with that in Peter's address in 2:22-36. See his *Twelve New Testament Studies* (London: SCM, 1962), pp. 139-153. J.C. O'Neill rejects this argument based on the fact that the titles "the holy and just one" and "the author of life" can scarcely be called pre-messianic. He also doubts that the evidence will show that the phrase about the suffering Messiah is a Lukan insertion. See his *The Theology of Acts in Its Historical Setting* (London: SPCK, 1961), pp. 127-128. Ladd believes that these titles were used of Jesus during his ministry and that Robinson's suggestion makes Luke guilty of carelessness in his placing contradictory doctrines of Christ side-by-side. He suggests that the idea that the Messiah would suffer arose from Jesus' own sufferings as the παῖς (servant) of the Lord, and then later these sufferings were also associated with the Messiah (*Theology*, pp. 229-334). C.F.D. Moule argues against Robinson that there is no reason to interpret the phrase "Christ, who has been appointed for you" as meaning that in the first advent Christ was only designated as Christ, but not sent as Christ. Moule argues that Peter's words here mean that Christ had been "*previously* predestined Christ" and sent as that Christ. See his "The Christology of Acts," in *Studies in Luke-Acts*, ed. Leander Keck and J. Louis Martyn (Philadelphia: Fortress, 1980), pp. 159-185.

by even the demons who acknowledged Jesus as "the Holy One of God" (Mark 1:24). They managed to murder the "author of life," but God thwarted their wickedness by raising him from the dead. To this event the apostles were eyewitnesses, and Peter repeated this fact.[9]

Thus the Jewish worshipers should not wonder about the cause of the miracle. The power came through "faith in the name of Jesus." Though Peter did not specify whose faith — the lame man's or the apostles' — his words drew attention to a risen Lord whose spiritual activity continued to be obvious among believers.

The Call to Repentance (3:17-21)

[17]"Now, brothers, I know that you acted in ignorance, as did your leaders. [18]But this is how God fulfilled what he had foretold through all the prophets, saying that his Christ[a] would suffer. [19]Repent, then, and turn to God, so that your sins may be wiped out, that times of refreshing may come from the Lord, [20]and that he may send the Christ, who has been appointed for you—even Jesus. [21]He must remain in heaven until the time comes for God to restore everything, as he promised long ago through his holy prophets.

[a]18 Or Messiah; also in verse 20

In the same way that Peter had called the Pentecost crowd to repentance, he said to this crowd, "Repent, then, and turn to God." Though the verb "turn" does not have the object "to God" in the Greek text, the thought is true to the idea of repentance. Repentance is a turning away from sin. Turning to God completes the transformation.[10] The results which would follow, declared Peter, were the forgiveness of sins ("your sins may be wiped out") and "times of refreshing" from the Lord. The verb "wiped out" (ἐξαλείφω, exaleiphō) was sometimes used of the canceling of a debt.[11] The "refreshing" (or "cooling") would be like

---

[9]Trites observes that "the eye-witness character of apostolic testimony" is here (as in 2:32) of utmost importance. See his Witness, pp. 137-138.

[10]The passive voice of this verb implies that the "wiping out" is accomplished by God. See French Arrington, New Testament Exegesis: Examples (Washington, D.C.: University Press of America, 1977), p. 38.

[11]Ibid., pp. 44-45.

a breeze which brings relief from scorching heat. The term corresponds to the "restoration of all things" in 3:21 and includes the new world order established eternally by the Messiah.

One difference in this sermon and Peter's Pentecost sermon is his mention of the ignorance of the Jews. From the cross Jesus prayed, "Father, forgive them for they do not know what they are doing" (Luke 23:34). Peter attributed their actions in the crucifixion to ignorance on their part and on the part of their national leaders. Meanwhile, he again drew the contrast between the misguided decisions of the Jews and the powerful action of God.

In addition, Peter noted that this event had been "foretold through all the prophets." Later passages in Acts will point to these prophecies again and again.[12] The substance of the prophecies was that the Messiah would suffer, but that God would establish through him a kingdom of righteousness.

The demand of God was that Israel repent. Then God would send the Messiah in order "to restore (ἀποκαταστάσις, apokatastasis) everything," a term used in 1:6 when the disciples asked Jesus about the restoration of the kingdom. Here Peter reflects on the return of the Christ from his position in heaven, an event which will be followed by the fulfillment of God's promise "through his holy prophets."[13]

The Witness of the Prophets (3:22-26)

22"For Moses said, 'The Lord your God will raise up for you a prophet like me from among your own people; you must listen to everything he tells you. 23Anyone who does not listen to him will be completely cut off from among his people.'ᵃ 24Indeed, all the prophets from Samuel on, as many as have spoken, have foretold these days. 25And you are heirs of the prophets and of the covenant God made with your fathers. He said to Abraham,

---

[12]For example, Acts 3:22 points to Deut 18:15,18; Acts 8:32-33 points to Isa 53:7-8 and Acts 4:25-26 points to Ps 2:1-2.

[13]See Paul's reference to the salvation of the Jews in Rom 11:25-26. Dunn sees this statement as an expression of the apocalyptic hope "brought to a new pitch of expectation" because of the pouring out of the Holy Spirit. See his *Jesus*, p. 194. Also see Matt 19:28.

'Through your offspring all peoples on earth will be blessed.'[b]
[26] When God raised up his servant, he sent him first to you to
bless you by turning each of you from your wicked ways."

[a]*23* Deut. 18:15,18,19   [b]*25* Gen. 22:18; 26:4

Peter concluded his message with specifics regarding the prophecies. Turning attention to Deuteronomy 18:15-19, Peter pointed out
that Moses had described the prophet whom God would raise up
among the people. God had fulfilled this promise by sending Jesus
Christ.[14]

Moses was not the only prophet, Peter insisted, who spoke of the
coming Messiah. From the prophet Samuel on there had been an
unbroken succession of God's spokesmen promising that the Messiah
was coming. These promises were the possession of Israel and thus
Peter called his Jewish audience "heirs of the prophets and of the
covenant" God had made with their forefathers.

Peter then referred to the specific promise repeated to Abraham
and recorded in Genesis (12:2-3; 22:18; and 26:4). "Offspring" here, as
in Paul's discussion in Galatians 3:16, is singular rather than plural.
Paul contended in that discussion that "offspring" refers to Christ.
Peter made the same point to the audience in the temple. The Messiah
came "first" to the Jews when God "raised him up," a phrase which
hints at the resurrection of Christ.

Peter's conclusion speaks of repentance. Christ's mission included
the repentance of the Jews. But the Jews were not his only target. The
word "first" implies that the gospel had a wider objective than just the
Jews, and events later in Acts will make this point again and again.[15]

---

[14]Polhill cites evidence that this prophecy was understood as Messianic
even before the time of Jesus (p. 136). See also the evidence from 1 and 2
Maccabees in W.D. Davies, *Torah in the Messianic Age and/or the Age To Come*
(Philadelphia: SBL, 1952), p. 44.

[15]See, for example, 13:46. Peter's use of Gen 22:18 seems to correspond to
15:14-19 where the inclusion of the Gentiles is viewed as the fulfillment of
God's promise to Abraham. Israel's role in this drama is first to repent, a
conversion which would grant them a share in the "messianic salvation" and
ratify their place in the covenant of Abraham. Then the Jews could participate in the mission to the Gentiles. See Jervell, *People of God*, pp. 58-60.

ACTS 4

3. The Arrest of Peter and John (4:1-4)

[1]The priests and the captain of the temple guard and the Sadducees came up to Peter and John while they were speaking to the people. [2]They were greatly disturbed because the apostles were teaching the people and proclaiming in Jesus the resurrection of the dead. [3] They seized Peter and John, and because it was evening, they put them in jail until the next day. [4]But many who heard the message believed, and the number of men grew to about five thousand.

Peter's sermon before the temple crowd caught the attention of the temple leaders. The excitement caused by the healing of the lame man and the explanation given by Peter raised concerns among the religious authorities. Thus the account continues with a description of the apostles' hearing before the Sanhedrin, as well as their release and reception by the church.

The religious authorities are identified as the "priests," the "captain of the temple guard"[1] and "the Sadducees." By the time of Jesus the Sadducean sect controlled the operation of the temple. They are described by Josephus as one of the three "schools of thought" found in Judaism, along with the Pharisees and Essenes.[2] They differed from the Pharisees in doctrinal matters. The Sadducees did not consider the oral law authoritative, as did the

---

[1]Martin Hengel describes the independence of this office in relation to that of the high priest. See his *Judaism and Hellenism: Studies in Their Encounter in Palestine during the Early Hellenistic Period*, trans. John Bowden (Philadelphia: Fortress, 1981), 1:25.

[2]*Antiquities*, 13.171.

Pharisees. For the Sadducees, the written law was the only authority. In addition, they rejected the Pharisaic concept of angels[3] and the resurrection.

Because the Sadducees had responsibility for the temple, they took a more cooperative attitude toward the Romans. Sensing that accommodation was better than confrontation, they did everything possible to remain on peaceful terms with the Romans. Any disturbance in the temple was considered a dangerous situation. For this reason a "temple guard" was posted to prevent any rioting or turmoil. The captain of the guard was an important enough position that one who occupied this office was viewed as having the advantage in reaching the position of high priest.

They approached Peter and John while "they" were speaking to the people.[4] What disturbed the Sadducees was the message of the apostles. Key words in Peter's address could well become inflammatory. Phrases like "times of refreshing," the sending of "the Christ," resurrection, and the new Moses could foster rebellion among the temple crowd. For the Sadducees this disturbance was intolerable. The apostles had to be taken into custody, as far as they were concerned. The late afternoon hour made it impossible to hold the hearing until the next day, so Peter and John spent the night in confinement.

Luke's note about the growth of the church, though seemingly out of place, serves to note how the church's progress was not hindered by resistance from the authorities. When many "believed" (a term used to describe the response of conversion) this meant that they belonged to the fellowship of believers. The number of believers had grown from 120 (1:15) to more than 3,000 (2:41) to 5,000 with the addition of these converts. This calculation includes "the number of men." Women and children were not included in the number.

4. Peter and John before the Sanhedrin (4:5-12)

[5]**The next day the rulers, elders and teachers of the law met in Jerusalem. [6]Annas the high priest was there, and so were Caiaphas, John, Alexander and the other men of the high priest's**

---

[3]See comments on 23:8.
[4]John evidently was involved in the addressing of the crowd.

**family. ⁷They had Peter and John brought before them and began
to question them: "By what power or what name did you do this?"
⁸Then Peter, filled with the Holy Spirit, said to them: "Rulers and
elders of the people! ⁹If we are being called to account today for
an act of kindness shown to a cripple and are asked how he was
healed, ¹⁰then know this, you and all the people of Israel: It is by
the name of Jesus Christ of Nazareth, whom you crucified but
whom God raised from the dead, that this man stands before you
healed. ¹¹He is 'the stone you builders rejected, which has become
the capstone.'ᵃᵇ ¹²Salvation is found in no one else, for there is no
other name under heaven given to men by which we must be
saved."**

ᵃ*11* Or *cornerstone*   ᵇ*11* Psalm 118:22

The day after the arrest of Peter and John they were brought
before the "rulers, elders and teachers of the law." This phrase
designates the Sanhedrin (see 22:5; Luke 22:66). The Sanhedrin was
the Jewish high court, the ruling council of Jerusalem. The Romans
permitted the council to exercise authority over the civic life of the
Jews.

Membership of the court consisted of seventy-one men from
both the Sadducees and the Pharisees (though the Pharisees were
probably always a minority). The presiding officer was the high
priest. Included among the members were the ruling priests, landed
aristocrats, and experts in the law of Moses. Their meeting place
may have been just west of the temple precincts.[5]

Annas is mentioned as high priest, though officially he was priest
only from A.D. 6-15. He was appointed to the position by Quirinius,
legate of Syria. By the early 30s when Peter and John stood before
the Sanhedrin he did not occupy the position in any formal sense.
But since his son-in-law, Caiaphas, held the position from A.D. 18-
36, Annas was often referred to as high priest by the Jews.[6] Such

---

[5]Josephus, *Wars*, 2.344; 5.144; 6.354.
[6]In a very recent archaeological discovery outside of Jerusalem, the family
burial place and ossuary box of Caiaphas appears to have been located and
identified. See Zvi Greenhut, "Burial Cave of the Caiaphas Family," *BAR* 18
(1992): 29-36.

respect for him may be due to the fact that his presence continued to be felt in major decisions during the years after his term had ended.

In addition to Annas and Caiaphas, a man named John is mentioned as holding an official role in the proceedings. Some suggest that this John may have been the son of Annas who was appointed high priest in A.D. 36, but no certainty is possible on this point.[7] Alexander cannot be identified.

Rabbinic literature indicates that the Sanhedrin sat in a semi-circle.[8] Peter and John thus stood before (or in the midst) of the Council. Questioning focused on their authority to "do this." Perhaps the high priest had heard the report of the healing and that the name of the resurrected Christ was used to explain it. At any rate, the court was interested in the claims of the apostles.

Peter's address was the fulfillment of Christ's prediction. The apostles would not have to plan their defense in these situations because they would be given words to speak (Luke 12:11-12; 21:14-15). Peter was "filled with the Holy Spirit" as the apostles were on the Day of Pentecost (see 2:4). His address repeats many of the themes he had already announced to the temple crowd.

The source of power for this miracle, Peter contended, was the name of Jesus of Nazareth. This name is the one in which "salvation" may be found. The word "saved" is used in two senses here. The first refers to the lame man's healing in v. 9 ("healed" is the Greek σῴζω, sōzō, "to save"). The second refers to salvation from sin in v. 12.

As Peter had done before (2:23-24; 3:15) he now contrasts what the Jewish leaders did with Jesus and what God did with Jesus. They had crucified him, but God raised him from death. He then cited Psalm 118:22, identifying Jesus as "the stone you builders rejected."[9] God made him the "capstone" in the resurrection.[10] Salvation, both of body and spirit, could be found only in him.

---

[7]Bruce, p. 92.

[8]*M. Sanh* 4.3.

[9]Eph 2:20 and 1 Pet 2:7 also cite this Psalm.

[10]The Greek word γωνία (*gōnia*) can mean either "the highest corner-stone right under the roof or the cornerstone under the building" (Rienecker, p. 270).

5. The Debate in the Sanhedrin (4:13-17)

[13]**When they saw the courage of Peter and John and realized that they were unschooled, ordinary men, they were astonished and they took note that these men had been with Jesus.** [14]**But since they could see the man who had been healed standing there with them, there was nothing they could say.** [15]**So they ordered them to withdraw from the Sanhedrin and then conferred together.** [16]**"What are we going to do with these men?" they asked. "Everybody living in Jerusalem knows they have done an outstanding miracle, and we cannot deny it.** [17]**But to stop this thing from spreading any further among the people, we must warn these men to speak no longer to anyone in this name."**

The Sanhedrin was in a quandary. Healing a man in the temple courts was not illegal. No charge could be made against the apostles.[11]

They duly noted the courage of Peter and John in speaking so boldly before this august body of authorities. This astonishment was increased by the fact that these were simple men. They were "unschooled" (ἀγράμματος, *agrammatos*) as far as rabbinic training was concerned and not considered professional interpreters (ἰδιώτης, *idiōtēs*) of the law. The rulers took note, however, that "these men had been with Jesus." Such an observation would have been important to many members who remembered the hearings only weeks before, which sent the one called Jesus to the cross.

Dismissing the defendants was a normal practice for the Sanhedrin, allowing private deliberation of the facts of the case. Their conclusion shows that they found no way to refute the basic claim of the apostles. Had it been possible to produce the body of Jesus, they could have easily disposed of the testimony of the apostles. They could not do it. They had to be satisfied with giving a warning to the apostles not to speak any more in the name of Jesus.

---

[11]F. Lamar Cribbs notes the similarities between their question about what to do with Peter and John and the question in John about what to do about Jesus. See his "The Agreements that Exist between John and Acts," in *Perspectives on Luke-Acts*, ed. Charles Talbert (Edinburgh: T & T Clark, 1978), pp. 52-53.

6. The Prohibition against Preaching Christ (4:18-22)

[18]Then they called them in again and commanded them not to speak or teach at all in the name of Jesus. [19]But Peter and John replied, "Judge for yourselves whether it is right in God's sight to obey you rather than God. [20]For we cannot help speaking about what we have seen and heard." [21]After further threats they let them go. They could not decide how to punish them, because all the people were praising God for what had happened. [22]For the man who was miraculously healed was over forty years old.

After summoning Peter and John, the Sanhedrin revealed their conclusion. The apostles were ordered not to speak or teach in the name of Jesus. Peter and John replied in terms that may be traced back to Socrates and his reply to the authorities in Athens.[12] Truth cannot be chained by civil authorities. The apostles repeated this well-known axiom to their adversaries. They were duty-bound to heed God's will when any authority placed themselves in the way of the gospel.

As a matter of fact, the apostles indicated that even if they wanted to, they could not hold their tongues. Once again they emphasized that they were eyewitnesses to these things. They were merely reporting on what they had "seen and heard."

Since punishing the apostles seemed out of the question, they resorted to further threats before releasing them. In view of the Jerusalem crowd which had witnessed the miracle, persecuting Peter and John could have been disastrous.

The note about the age of the lame man indicates the length of his malady. The miracle did not involve someone engaged in a fraudulent claim. For forty years the Jerusalem community had known about the tragedy of the lame man's condition. There could be no doubt that the healing was a sign from God.

---

[12]Plato, *Apology*, 29d.

7. The Release of Peter and John (4:23-31)

Their Reunion with the Twelve (4:23)

²³On their release, Peter and John went back to their own people and reported all that the chief priests and elders had said to them.

After their release, Peter and John "went back," perhaps to the same upper room in which the church had been meeting. They communicated to the other apostles and believers what the Sanhedrin said.

Their Prayer for Boldness (4:24-30)

²⁴When they heard this, they raised their voices together in prayer to God. "Sovereign Lord," they said, "you made the heaven and the earth and the sea, and everything in them. ²⁵You spoke by the Holy Spirit through the mouth of your servant, our father David: 'Why do the nations rage and the peoples plot in vain? ²⁶The kings of the earth take their stand and the rulers gather together against the Lord and against his Anointed One.ᵃᵇ ²⁷Indeed Herod and Pontius Pilate met together with the Gentiles and the peopleᶜ of Israel in this city to conspire against your holy servant Jesus, whom you anointed. ²⁸They did what your power and will had decided beforehand should happen. ²⁹Now, Lord, consider their threats and enable your servants to speak your word with great boldness. ³⁰Stretch out your hand to heal and perform miraculous signs and wonders through the name of your holy servant Jesus."

ᵃ26 That is, Christ or Messiah   ᵇ26 Psalm 2:1,2   ᶜ27 The Greek is plural.

The reaction of the believers took the form of a prayer.[13] Using

---

[13]Talbert discusses the striking parallels between 4:24–5:42 and 1:12–4:23, which include prayer together, filling with the Spirit, speaking the word with boldness, fear coming on the church, signs and wonders done by the apostles, healings by Peter, and gathering together at Solomon's Porch. See his *Literary Patterns*, pp. 35-37.

an address for God that is unusual in the New Testament, they asked God for divine protection in their witnessing. "Sovereign Lord" (δεσπότης, *despotēs*) is the address that was used. It appears frequently in the Septuagint and calls attention to the supreme authority of the Lord as ruler of the universe.[14] The address is significant here in view of the threats from the Sanhedrin. Powers and authorities of this earth are nothing compared to the God who is sovereign.

Polhill notes the similarities between this prayer and that of Hezekiah in Isaiah 37:16-20. In that prayer the address of God also includes his role as Lord and Creator. In addition that prayer contains a reference to the enemies of Israel and a prayer for deliverance.[15]

In this prayer, however, the new element is the reference to Psalm 2. In its original context Psalm 2 was probably a royal psalm, referring to the enthronement of Israel's king and the conspiracies of surrounding enemies. Bruce notes that Psalm 2 was recognized to be Messianic at least as early as the middle of the first century B.C.[16] The reference to the Lord's anointed was understood as an indication that God's chosen servant would bring deliverance to his people.[17]

As these believers prayed, it was obvious that the "Anointed One," the "holy servant," in this Psalm was a reference to Jesus Christ. Those conspiring against him, the "rulers" and "kings of the earth," were Herod and Pontius Pilate. The "peoples" and the "nations" raging against him were the Jews and the Gentiles. Their plotting was an attempt to hinder the gospel. For this reason, they prayed along the same lines as the apostles' stance before the Sanhedrin. Refusing to give up preaching in the name of Jesus, the believers petitioned God to go on healing and performing "miraculous signs and wonders through the name" of Jesus.

Their confidence was firm in the God who had absolute control

---

[14]See Exod 20:11; Neh 9:6; Ps 146:6; Isa 42:5. In the NT see Luke 2:29 and Rev 6:10.

[15]Polhill, p. 148.

[16]Bruce, p. 98. He cites Ps Sol 17:26, where this Psalm refers to the expected Son of David, the "anointed lord."

[17]At the baptism of Jesus the words from heaven echoed this Psalm: "You are my Son" (Matt 3:17).

over these actions by the Sanhedrin. As a matter of fact, God was not caught by surprise. The "Sovereign Lord" knew that these leaders would oppose the gospel. The rulers had acted only in terms of what God's "power and will had decided beforehand" would happen.

For this reason they requested "boldness" for their preaching. As Hezekiah had taken the blasphemous letter from the Assyrian king to the temple and prayed to God, the believers prayed that God would once again overrule authorities who resisted God's will.

Their Power from the Holy Spirit (4:31)

[31]After they prayed, the place where they were meeting was shaken. And they were all filled with the Holy Spirit and spoke the word of God boldly.

God's immediate response to their prayer was a fresh filling of the Holy Spirit. The verb "filled" (ἐπλήσθησαν, from πίμπλημι, *pimplēmi*) is the same word as in 2:4 where the events of Pentecost are described. The filling here is not identical to the one in Acts 2 and this filling does not imply that the experience of Pentecost was repeated here. The apostles already had received the baptism of the Spirit and it was the Spirit which empowered them as they stood before the Sanhedrin. Thus it is best to understand this filling as a renewal of the Spirit's presence with the apostles and believers.

Accompanying this activity of the Spirit was a display of power. On the day of Pentecost these indications of power had been present (see 2:2). Now the place was "shaken," whether from an earthquake, a miraculous tremor, or from some inner sense of God's power.[18]

Along with these signs of God's presence came a renewed enthusiasm for the proclamation of the gospel. As they sensed the power of the Spirit among them, they "spoke the word of God boldly," a phrase which captures the spirit of courage with which the apostles preached.[19]

---

[18]Dunn considers 4:29-31 to be one of the clearest expressions of the "atmosphere of these early days" in which the believers experienced "the assurance and confidence in God, the almost physical presence of God's power, and the enthusiastic ecstatic speaking." See his *Jesus*, p. 188.

[19]Trites notes that this "boldness is an outstanding characteristic" of the

H. THE UNITY AND GENEROSITY
OF THE EARLY CHURCH (4:32-5:16)

1. The Sharing of
Material Possessions by Believers (4:32-35)

[32]All the believers were one in heart and mind. No one claimed that any of his possessions was his own, but they shared everything they had. [33]With great power the apostles continued to testify to the resurrection of the Lord Jesus, and much grace was upon them all. [34]There were no needy persons among them. For from time to time those who owned lands or houses sold them, brought the money from the sales [35]and put it at the apostles' feet, and it was distributed to anyone as he had need.

Once again Luke supplies a summary to describe the progress of the church (see 2:42-47). In this case, however, the summary points ahead rather than behind. Luke gives these words to prepare for the accounts which follow—the generosity of Barnabas and the hypocrisy of Ananias and Sapphira.

"One in heart and mind" describes the spiritual unity of the believers. This sense of oneness extended to a concern for the practical needs of one another. A spirit of voluntary sharing dominated the church. Possessions were shared so that "there were no needy persons among them." Polhill notes that the ideal of such communal sharing can be found as early as the Greeks.[20] Certainly the Old Testament required that needy members of the congregation be cared for (Deut 15:4; 14:29; Lev 25:35).[21]

---

testimony of the early church. He lists such examples as Peter on the Day of Pentecost (2:23,29); Peter and John before the Sanhedrin (4:9-10,13); Barnabas and Paul in their missionary work at Antioch and Iconium (13:46; 14:3); Stephen (7:2-53); Philip (8:30-35); and Apollos (18:26). Add to these the examples of boldness in the preaching of the Apostle Paul (see 9:27-28; 19:8; 28:31). See his *Witness*, pp. 151-152.

[20]Polhill, pp. 151-152.

[21]Karris thinks that Luke includes these verses (as well as 2:41-47) in order to challenge his Gentile Christian community who, because of cultural conditioning, "have little or no concern for love of neighbor and almsgiving." See his "Sitz im Leben," pp. 114-116.

Every indication in the text is that this sharing was not the kind which characterized the Jewish sect at Qumran. There communal living was enforced in writing.[22] In the Jerusalem church those who had possessions determined in what way they might assist the needs of other believers. "From time to time those who owned land or houses sold them," implying that the rest of the time the rule of private ownership prevailed. Money from the sale of these properties was placed at "the apostles' feet" because these church leaders were active in the distribution to needy households.

Meanwhile the apostles continued their testifying. The content of their message was "the resurrection of the Lord Jesus."[23] To this event they were eyewitnesses. "God's grace was upon them" so that the powerful voice of the gospel continued to have success.

2. The Example of Barnabas (4:36-37)

[36]Joseph, a Levite from Cyprus, whom the apostles called Barnabas (which means Son of Encouragement), [37]sold a field he owned and brought the money and put it at the apostles' feet.

In the context of this sharing of possessions the example of Barnabas is presented by Luke. He voluntarily sold a field "he owned" and donated the money to the ministry for those in need. The implication is that he brought the entire amount as a contribution. He laid it at the apostles' feet as evidence of his submission to their leadership and cooperation with their ministry.

The exact derivation of the name Barnabas is uncertain, but for those who knew him he was a "Son of Encouragement." He was a

---

[22]See 1QS 1.12; 5.2; 6.17-25. For a discussion of the practices of the Qumran community see Fitzmyer, *Essays*, pp. 284-288. Luke Johnson calls attention to the diversity of practices with regards to possessions reflected in Acts. See his *Sharing Possessions: Mandate and Symbol of Faith* (Philadelphia: Fortress, 1981), pp. 21-23. Shepard notes that this sharing of possessions was encouraged by the idea of "God's ownership of everything" (*Life*, p. 40).

[23]Turner notes that this phrase could also be understood to say "the apostles of the Lord Jesus witnessed to the resurrection." The ambiguity is due to unusual Greek word order in this clause. See Moulton, Howard, Turner, *Grammar*, 3:350.

Jew from Cyprus, the island in the eastern Mediterranean Sea. A Jewish presence was found on Cyprus since Maccabean times.

Barnabas was a Levite. By this time in the first century Levites occupied a secondary role in the operation of the Temple, often serving as gatekeepers or enforcement officials. The Levitical background of Barnabas is added without further comment by Luke. The Old Testament restrictions which prohibited a Levite from owning property may not have been observed in the first century or Barnabas may have owned the property through marriage.

Luke introduces Barnabas into the Book of Acts in his characteristic way. He mentions him here quite briefly only to return to a much fuller description of his contributions to the spread of the gospel (see 9:27; 11:22,25; 13:1-4; 15:37-39).

ACTS 5

3. The Deceit of Ananias and Sapphira (5:1-11)

[1]Now a man named Ananias, together with his wife Sapphira, also sold a piece of property. [2]With his wife's full knowledge he kept back part of the money for himself, but brought the rest and put it at the apostles' feet. [3]Then Peter said, "Ananias, how is it that Satan has so filled your heart that you have lied to the Holy Spirit and have kept for yourself some of the money you received for the land? [4]Didn't it belong to you before it was sold? And after it was sold, wasn't the money at your disposal? What made you think of doing such a thing? You have not lied to men but to God." [5]When Ananias heard this, he fell down and died. And great fear seized all who heard what had happened. [6]Then the young men came forward, wrapped up his body, and carried him out and buried him. [7]About three hours later his wife came in, not knowing what had happened. [8]Peter asked her, "Tell me, is this the price you and Ananias got for the land?" "Yes," she said, "that is the price." [9]Peter said to her, "How could you agree to test the Spirit of the Lord? Look! The feet of the men who buried your husband are at the door, and they will carry you out also." [10]At that moment she fell down at his feet and died. Then the young men came in and, finding her dead, carried her out and buried her beside her husband. [11]Great fear seized the whole church and all who heard about these events.

In contrast to Barnabas' example of sincere generosity, Luke adds an example of the opposite. Ananias and Sapphira represent the spirit of selfishness and personal ambition. But Luke does not describe this unusual event merely for the purpose of urging a higher standard of morals. Both cases advance Luke's primary concern of demonstrating how the witness of the apostles through the Spirit continued. They also show the unity of the church in placing a high priority on ministering to the needy among them.[1]

The link between 5:1 and 4:37 is strong. "Now" in the NIV is the Greek particle δέ (*de*) and continues the chain of comments from 4:35-36 where *de* is also used.

The names Ananias and Sapphira have no meaning outside this context. We meet them here and here alone. Little is said of them on a personal note. They were wealthy enough to own property. Evidently they were also interested in associating themselves with the ministry of benevolence in the Jerusalem church.

Their sin is described in 5:2. They "kept back" part of the profits gained from selling their property. The verb νοσφίζομαι (*nosphizomai*) carries the idea of embezzling. Apparently they had previously pledged that whatever money the sale of the land brought would be donated to the church.[2] Perhaps this was the procedure being used with all those involved with the giving described in 4:34-37.

This arrangement would explain Peter's words in 5:4: "Didn't it belong to you before it was sold?" Of course it did, and Peter was suggesting that Ananias and Sapphira were not forced to make the original pledge to contribute the money from the sale of the land. His second question followed: "And after it was sold, wasn't the money at your disposal?" Of course it was, since Ananias and Sapphira could simply have explained that they could not give all of the money to the church after all.

---

[1]Talbert's analysis of the consistency of Luke's account is somewhat negative here. He finds Luke to contradict his own picture of the unity of the Jerusalem church by introducing the account of Ananias and Sapphira. Surely Luke's account in Acts 1-5, however, must be viewed as a whole. His inclusion of Ananias and Sapphira is intended to depict the flaws in this unity, as well as the way in which the church moved to meet such problems (see also 6:1-7). See Talbert, *Literary Patterns*, p. 101.

[2]Some precedent for this existed in Judaism. See Lake and Cadbury, p. 50. In another example of communal living among the Jews, members of the Qumran community were required to surrender their property, giving it to the community. Those who failed to do so were refused a place at the common meal for a year and denied a quarter of their regular rations (Polhill, p. 161).

Luke is careful to note that both husband and wife were involved in this business. They both knew what the sale price was and they both knew that some of it had been withheld from the church while the rest was put "at the feet of the apostles." This descriptive phrase implies the authority held by the apostles in supervising the ministry of benevolence in the Jerusalem church. We can imagine the apostles sitting in their places, surrounded by contributions for the needy.

What happens next reminds us of the sin of Achan, who stole the dedicated wedge of gold (Josh 7:1ff); Nadab and Abihu, who offered "unauthorized fire" in the tabernacle; or Uzzah, who touched the teetering ark of the covenant (2 Sam 6:6-7). Peter questioned Ananias concerning his gift. His question assumes that Ananias was withholding money and that in doing so he was sinning. Peter's insight into the heart of Ananias is one of the reasons this event is recorded.[3] In 4:31 it is said that the Holy Spirit filled the believers again. With that filling of the Spirit active in Peter, he assumed the role of a prophet who could perceive thoughts and intentions in others.[4]

Peter's question also assumed that Ananias was influenced by Satan in this affair. Rather than operating by the filling of the Holy Spirit, Ananias had allowed Satan to fill his heart. Such an act was equal to rebellion against the Spirit and his work. The lie that Ananias had spoken to the apostles was really a lie spoken to God. Peter, as a prophet speaking the will of God, was in a position to render the verdict on the guilt of Ananias.

As soon as Peter pronounced these words, Ananias fell dead. It seems useless to ask about the cause of death. Whether from a heart attack or from fright, the text clearly implies that the death was punishment from God.

The abrupt manner in which the story is told reinforces this

---

[3]Dunn sees the punishment of Ananias and Sapphira in the context of the charismatic qualities of the early church. In this sense he compares the event here to Paul's judgment of the Corinthian offender (see 1 Cor 5:3-5). See his *Jesus*, p. 166.

[4]This ability may be similar to the spiritual gift described in 1 Cor 12:10 as "distinguishing between spirits." See also the reaction of the Samaritan woman when Jesus perceived hidden truths about her (John 4:17-19).

conclusion. No details are given about any of the usual procedures associated with death. Even the burial is presented without ceremony. Ananias' body was attended to by "the young men," a phrase which does not refer to any official position. His body was wrapped, probably with a death shroud and linens wrapped around the body to hold the shroud in place. Often spices would be placed inside the wrapping. The young men "carried him out" because burials took place outside the city walls of Jerusalem.

Though it is true that burials in first-century Palestine often took place the same day as the death, this burial seems particularly unceremonious. There is no mention of a funeral procession, no mourning, and apparently no effort to contact Sapphira. As a matter of fact, Sapphira came to the place where Peter was about three hours later unaware of what had happened to her husband. The lack of sympathy in this tragedy implies that the event was understood as God's judgment upon sin.

Peter's question to Sapphira followed the same line as with Ananias. Her response reflected her commitment to the scheme she had entered into with her husband. Since Peter already knew about the hoax they had perpetrated, he went straight to the verdict. She had decided to "test the Spirit of the Lord," a phrase which means seeing how far he would go in his tolerance.[5] Her guilt would bring the judgment of God. Only now did Peter reveal that her husband had also been discovered, and he did it at the same moment he pronounced her own disastrous end. "The feet of the men" is a Hebrew expression which uses one part of the body to refer to the whole person.[6]

When Sapphira heard these words she fell dead. The young men carried her to the place of her husband's grave and buried her there. Peter's role as prophet had been carried out with sudden drama. He delivered judgment which was not his own, but that of God. He could do nothing less. The impact on the church was immediate. Fear (φόβος, *phobos*) gripped the church as believers sensed the presence of the Spirit in this affair and perceived the urgency of their ministry.

---

[5]Polhill, p. 159.
[6]See Isa 52:7; Rom 10:15.

One further note should be added. Here in 5:11 is the first appearance of the term "church" (ἐκκλησία, *ekklēsia*) in Acts. Acts will use the term frequently, sometimes of city assemblies whether legal or illegal (19:32,39), sometimes of a local congregation of believers (8:1; 11:22; 13:1), and sometimes of the universal church (20:28). In the Septuagint (Greek translation of the OT) *ekklēsia* was often used to denote the Old Testament people of God (see Deut. 9:10).

4. The Signs and Wonders from the Apostles (5:12-16)

[12]**The apostles performed many miraculous signs and wonders among the people. And all the believers used to meet together in Solomon's Colonnade. [13]No one else dared join them, even though they were highly regarded by the people. [14]Nevertheless, more and more men and women believed in the Lord and were added to their number. [15]As a result, people brought the sick into the streets and laid them on beds and mats so that at least Peter's shadow might fall on some of them as he passed by. [16]Crowds gathered also from the towns around Jerusalem, bringing their sick and those tormented by evil[a] spirits, and all of them were healed.**

[a]*16* Greek *unclean*

Luke now adds a third summary statement concerning the progress of the church. His previous statement in 4:32-35 reflected the unity of the believers and their willingness to share their material goods. The present statement comments on the continuing ministry of the apostles and the increasing numbers of believers.

The Spirit's work in the apostles resulted in miraculous actions which had a doubled-edged effect. Fear caused some not to join the group of believers as they continued to meet in Solomon's Colonnade in the court of the temple. On the other hand, "more and more men and women" became believers and "were added to the number." Though these details seem to be contradictory, the implication seems to be that only those who were completely committed to the Lord were courageous enough to enter the fellowship.

The miracles were "signs and wonders" which pointed the way to faith in the Lord. They were performed by "the apostles." Evidently the power to work these miracles was limited to the twelve. In some cases sick people were brought on beds and mats to Peter so that, at the least, his "shadow might fall on some of them." Because the shadow was often understood as the extension of the person, people came expecting even this nearness to the apostles to bring healing. The text does not say whether they actually found healing by contacting Peter's shadow. Luke's Gospel does record, however, the case of the woman who came to Jesus and found healing by touching the fringe of his garment (8:44).

Nevertheless, many found healing through their contact with the apostles. The witness of the apostles began to reach even into "towns around Jerusalem." The power of the Spirit had filled them (4:30-31) and the evidence was being felt by many.

I. THE ARREST OF THE APOSTLES (5:17-42)

1. The Imprisonment of the Apostles (5:17-26)

[17]Then the high priest and all his associates, who were members of the party of the Sadducees, were filled with jealousy. [18]They arrested the apostles and put them in the public jail. [19]But during the night an angel of the Lord opened the doors of the jail and brought them out. [20]"Go, stand in the temple courts," he said, "and tell the people the full message of this new life." [21]At daybreak they entered the temple courts, as they had been told, and began to teach the people. When the high priest and his associates arrived, they called together the Sanhedrin—the full assembly of the elders of Israel—and sent to the jail for the apostles. [22]But on arriving at the jail, the officers did not find them there. So they went back and reported, [23]"We found the jail securely locked, with the guards standing at the doors; but when we opened them, we found no one inside." [24]On hearing this report, the captain of the temple guard and the chief priests were puzzled, wondering what would come of this. [25]Then someone came and said, "Look! The men you put in jail are standing in the temple courts teaching the people." [26]At that, the captain went with his officers and brought

the apostles. They did not use force, because they feared that the people would stone them.

Once again the anger of the high priest and Sadducees burned against the apostles. As the believers were filled with the Spirit, the Jewish leaders were also "filled," but in their case it was with jealousy. Caiaphas, the high priest, and Annas, his father-in-law (see notes on 4:6), were determined to stop this threat to their authority.

Earlier it was Peter and John who were taken into custody. Now all of the apostles were placed in "the public jail" as a measure to make known to everyone that the temple authorities considered the teaching of the apostles to be dangerous. From there they could be brought for a hearing the next day.

They could not, however, keep the apostles there. During the night an "angel of the Lord"[7] set them free and commanded them to go to the temple courts and preach about "this new life."[8] The Jewish attempts to lock up the gospel were once again thwarted, this time by direct intervention from God.

How ironic that when the Jewish authorities arrived the next day the apostles were in "the temple courts" where they were teaching the people! The temple authorities could not even protect their own precincts from the message of Christ. As the Sanhedrin gathered for the day's session their intention was the questioning of the apostles. But when the officials went to the jail to get the prisoners they found them gone. The doors were locked and the guards still in place. Apparently, the angel had kept the guards from seeing the escape. Immediately the officials reported the news to the full body. While they were puzzling about this development, someone came with the news that the apostles were in the temple courts. Now the "captain" decided to take charge.[9] Since he was second in command

---

[7]Polhill notes the irony here if the Sadducees did not believe in angels (p. 166). See, however, the comments on 23:8. Four more times in Acts the "angel of the Lord" will be mentioned (7:30-38; 8:26; 12:7-10; 12:23).

[8]Hubbard categorizes 5:17-21a among the "commissioning accounts" of Acts (which include 1:1-14; 8:26-30; 9:1-9,10-19; 10:1-8,9-23,30-33; 11:4-12; 12:6-12; 13:1-3; 16:8-10; 18:7-11; 22:6-11,12-16,17-21; 23:11; 26:12-20; 27:21-26). See "Commissioning Accounts," pp. 195-198.

[9]See the note on 4:1.

to the high priest, his reputation was at stake. He went to the temple courts and found the apostles. Because the people respected the apostles so much, the captain "did not use force," but gently persuaded the apostles to come with him.

2. The Apostles before the Sanhedrin (5:27-40)

[27]Having brought the apostles, they made them appear before the Sanhedrin to be questioned by the high priest. [28]"We gave you strict orders not to teach in this name," he said. "Yet you have filled Jerusalem with your teaching and are determined to make us guilty of this man's blood." [29]Peter and the other apostles replied: "We must obey God rather than men! [30]The God of our fathers raised Jesus from the dead—whom you had killed by hanging him on a tree. [31]God exalted him to his own right hand as Prince and Savior that he might give repentance and forgiveness of sins to Israel. [32]We are witnesses of these things, and so is the Holy Spirit, whom God has given to those who obey him." [33]When they heard this, they were furious and wanted to put them to death. [34]But a Pharisee named Gamaliel, a teacher of the law, who was honored by all the people, stood up in the Sanhedrin and ordered that the men be put outside for a little while. [35]Then he addressed them: "Men of Israel, consider carefully what you intend to do to these men. [36]Some time ago Theudas appeared, claiming to be somebody, and about four hundred men rallied to him. He was killed, all his followers were dispersed, and it all came to nothing. [37]After him, Judas the Galilean appeared in the days of the census and led a band of people in revolt. He too was killed, and all his followers were scattered. [38]Therefore, in the present case I advise you: Leave these men alone! Let them go! For if their purpose or activity is of human origin, it will fail. [39]But if it is from God, you will not be able to stop these men; you will only find yourselves fighting against God." [40]His speech persuaded them. They called the apostles in and had them flogged. Then they ordered them not to speak in the name of Jesus, and let them go.

Now came the moment for all of the apostles to stand before the Sanhedrin. Both Sadducees and Pharisees would be present to hear the facts of the case. This time the apostles would have some explaining to do. In the previous hearing (4:5ff) Peter and John had not been guilty of any infraction of the Sanhedrin's orders. But now they would have to admit they had disregarded the Sanhedrin's command to cease preaching in the name of Jesus (4:18).

The high priest began the questioning. On his mind was why the apostles had disobeyed the first injunction against preaching in the name of Jesus. He reminded the apostles that they had been warned previously. Why had they "filled Jerusalem"[10] with their teaching and, more specifically, why did their teaching seek to make the temple authorities guilty of Jesus' death?

Peter spoke up for the apostles with a statement much like the one made in the first hearing (4:19). He courageously insisted that their first obligation was still to God. He then launched into a sermon about Jesus. To the dismay of the Sanhedrin, Peter's words demonstrated he would not back down. Once again the theme of his sermon was that the Jewish leaders had put Jesus to death, but God raised him back to life. This theme had been used earlier (2:23-24; 3:15; 4:10).

The phrase "God of our fathers" reminded the Sanhedrin that the preaching of Jesus had its roots in the identity of Old Testament Israel. The religious authorities had been guilty of resisting the will of the God of Abraham, Isaac, and Jacob. They killed[11] Jesus by "hanging him on a tree." Such a description of the crucifixion is possible because the term for "tree" (ξύλον, *xylon*) can also refer to a stake, a beam, a pole, or a cross. Deuteronomy 21:22-23 spoke to the Israelites about procedures for execution which included "hanging on a tree," and this verse was thought by Christians to speak of the suffering of Christ.[12]

Peter also included the ascension and exaltation of Christ. He not only was raised from death, but sits at God's "own right hand," a position of prestige and authority. His titles included both

---

[10]The verb is put in the perfect tense to indicate the deed has been done but the impact is still being felt.

[11]The Greek verb is διεχειρίσασθε (*diecheirisasthe*). See the note on 26:21.

[12]See 1 Pet 2:24; Gal 3:13; Acts 10:39; 13:29.

"Prince" and "Savior." But his intent was to give repentance and forgiveness to Israel. Once again Peter reminded his audience that the apostles were eyewitnesses of these events,[13] and he added that the Holy Spirit also was a witness who should be considered.

The reaction of the Sanhedrin was immediate. They were furious and were ready to resort to the death penalty. But a Pharisee named Gamaliel saved the day. Luke describes him as "a teacher of the law"[14] and one who "was honored by all the people." Jewish tradition speaks of him as the grandson of Hillel and the finest example of Pharisaism. According to Rabbinic tradition his son, Simeon, and his grandson, Gamaliel II, followed him as leaders of the high court. In this situation he spoke words of caution to the council.

After having the apostles removed from the chamber, Gamaliel presented his argument. He emphasized God's role in directing the events of history and the need for patience in allowing God's will to be done. Two historical examples were used to build his case—Theudas and Judas.

Some difficulties arise at this point with the words of Gamaliel. His mention of Theudas causes two chronological problems. Is this Theudas the same one mentioned by Josephus in *Antiquities* 20.97-98? Secondly, did this Theudas arrive on the scene before or after Judas?

To answer the first question we must note that the Theudas mentioned by Josephus did not appear until about A.D. 45. This date is more than 10 years after Gamaliel's speech would have occurred. For this reason Luke is often accused of making a historical blunder.

The description Josephus gives of Theudas, however, does not seem to match the one given in Acts. Josephus speaks of how Theudas went to the Jordan River and claimed that he could divide

---

[13]See the note on 3:26. As Trites notes here, Peter's words about the Spirit's serving as a witness reflect the Old Testament requirement that testimony be established on the basis of two or three witnesses. Peter claims in 5:32 that the "two sources of testimony" are himself as an eyewitness and the Holy Spirit. See his *Witness*, pp. 135,167-168.

[14]Ellis Rivkin points out that the term "teacher of the law" was always associated with the Pharisees. See his *A Hidden Revolution* (Nashville: Abingdon, 1978), p. 120.

it. He also states that Theudas attracted "the majority of the masses" in this endeavor. The Theudas in Acts rallied only about 400 men to himself and nothing is said about his trip to the Jordan River.

Besides this problem, Gamaliel mentioned that Judas appeared "in the days of the census." It seems clear that the census he meant was the one taken by Quirinius in A.D. 6.[15] This means that Gamaliel placed the uprising of Theudas before that of Judas, and thus before A.D. 6, some 40 years before the Theudas described by Josephus.[16]

These inconsistencies imply that another historical figure was on the mind of Gamaliel when he made his speech to the Sanhedrin. Some other Theudas must have led a rebellion, perhaps in the turmoil after the death of Herod the Great in 4 B.C.[17] Gamaliel's reference to Judas also has a parallel in Josephus. Two of Josephus' larger works describe a major rebellion which occurred as a response to the census and the anticipated taxation.[18] Decades later the sect which sprang from this rebellion was known as the Zealots and they instigated the rebellion which led to the destruction of Jerusalem. This time it would seem that Gamaliel and Josephus are in agreement.

Advising the Sanhedrin to allow God to determine what historical movements rise and fall, Gamaliel closed his address. He concluded that the apostles should not be persecuted. The Jewish authorities did not want to place themselves in opposition to God if the movement was of divine origin.

Gamaliel's argument won the day. The Sanhedrin decided to release the apostles, but only after inflicting punishment as a warning against further infractions. Flogging was the usual punishment and consisted of thirty-nine lashes from a leather strap. As Polhill notes, the beating was given on the bare back and chest of the

---

[15]This census is not the one described in Luke 2:1-2 which must have been taken around 4 B.C.

[16]The unlikelihood that Luke consulted Josephus for this information is discussed by Arrington, *Exegesis*, pp. 25-26.

[17]Bruce, p. 116.

[18]*Antiquities* 18.4-10; 18.23; 20.102; *War* 2.433; 7.253. Josephus says that Judas was from Gamala in Gaulanitis. See G.F. Moore, *Judaism in the First Centuries of the Christian Era* (New York: Schocken, 1971), 2:375.

victim, and at times might even cause death.[19] The number thirty-
nine came from Deuteronomy 25:3, which authorized forty stripes.
But since the Jews were determined not to transgress the Law, the
number was kept at "forty less one" (see 2 Cor 11:24). With the
beating came also the repetition of the earlier warning not to
preach in the name of Jesus.

3. The Continued Witness of the Apostles (5:41-42)

[41]**The apostles left the Sanhedrin, rejoicing because they had
been counted worthy of suffering disgrace for the Name. [42]Day
after day, in the temple courts and from house to house, they
never stopped teaching and proclaiming the good news that Jesus
is the Christ.[a]**

[a]*42 Or Messiah*

Rather than suffering fearful intimidation, the apostles became
even bolder. They considered it an honor to suffer "for the Name"
of Jesus.[20] Before long the temple courts were once again echoing
with the preaching of Jesus — not just on one occasion in order to
test the determination of the Sanhedrin. They preached and taught
"day after day" both in the temple courts and "from house to
house." Their message contained one constant theme — "that Jesus
is the Christ."

---

[19]Polhill, 174.

[20]The expression "for the sake of the Name" (ὑπὲρ τοῦ ὀνόματος, *hyper
tou onomatos*) also appears in 3 John 7 in reference to Christ.

ACTS 6

J. THE CHOOSING OF
THE SEVEN DEACONS (6:1-7)

[1]In those days when the number of disciples was increasing, the Grecian Jews among them complained against the Hebraic Jews because their widows were being overlooked in the daily distribution of food. [2]So the Twelve gathered all the disciples together and said, "It would not be right for us to neglect the ministry of the word of God in order to wait on tables. [3]Brothers, choose seven men from among you who are known to be full of the Spirit and wisdom. We will turn this responsibility over to them [4]and will give our attention to prayer and the ministry of the word." [5]This proposal pleased the whole group. They chose Stephen, a man full of faith and of the Holy Spirit; also Philip, Procorus, Nicanor, Timon, Parmenas, and Nicolas from Antioch, a convert to Judaism. [6]They presented these men to the apostles, who prayed and laid their hands on them. [7]So the word of God spread. The number of disciples in Jerusalem increased rapidly, and a large number of priests became obedient to the faith.

Until now the record of Acts has shown a sense of unity in the church which by modern standards can only be called remarkable. The believers "were together and had everything in common" (2:44). They were "one in heart and mind" and "shared everything they had" (4:32). Their numbers had grown from eleven (1:2) to about 120 (1:15) to over 3,000 (2:41) and then to more than 5,000 (4:4).

Now for the first time internal division made its appearance.[1] At a time when "the number of disciples was increasing" the problem

---

[1]Shepard puts this internal division into perspective with the following words: "In primitive Christianity, which we see pictured in the first chapters

surfaced. Here is the first time the term "disciple" (μαθητής, *mathētēs*) is used of believers in Acts. So rapidly were the converts coming that the church's desire to minister to needy members was becoming more and more difficult.[2] It was inevitable that someone would inadvertently be left out.

When the problem finally became obvious it raised some divisions among segments of the church which had known friction for years. Within Judaism those who had a Grecian background were quite distinct from those with a Hebraic background. The first and most obvious difference was language. Greek was the language of choice for the former segment, while the latter preferred Hebrew. In addition, the Grecian Jews quite likely had a background in the Diaspora—Jews scattered throughout the Roman world. Hebraic Jews had grown up in the Judaism of Palestine.[3]

These linguistic and cultural differences did not disappear when Grecian and Hebraic Jews became Christians. In the Jerusalem church the tensions arose in connection with the "daily distribution of food" for needy widows. In the ancient world the neediest people were often widows. The loss of a husband meant severe economic hardships for many, especially in cases where families had moved to Jerusalem from far-flung areas of the Roman Empire. Jews were familiar with the Old Testament commands regarding caring for widows.[4] The Jewish practice of benevolence was continued by the church in Jerusalem.[5]

---

of Acts, we find the nearest approach to the purity of the Christ, in conduct and doctrine," despite the abuses seen in such examples as Ananias and Sapphira. See his *Life*, p. 48. See also Arrington, pp. 64-65. Earl Richard argues for the structural unity of Acts 6:1–8:4, viewing 6:1-7 as an introduction to the speech by Stephen in that it "introduces the reader fully into a community quarrel." See his *Acts 6:1–8:4: The Author's Method of Composition* (Missoula: Scholars Press, 1978), pp. 215; 267-274. Johnson sees in this account Luke's preparation for the second stage of the prophecy of 1:8. See *Literary Function*, pp. 211-212.

[2]Jacques Dupont calls attention to the way this account highlights the generosity of the early church, advancing a theme found consistently in Acts. See his *The Salvation of the Gentiles: Essays on the Acts of the Apostles* (New York: Paulist, 1967), p. 94.

[3]For a discussion of the identification of the Hellenists see Fitzmyer, *Essays*, pp. 277-279.

[4]Exod 22:22; Deut 10:18; 14:29; Ps 146:9.

[5]The care of widows is also discussed in such passages as 1 Tim 5:3-16 and James 1:27.

Two forms of benevolence were practiced by the Jews. Every Friday relief officers would collect money for the poor in a box (*kupah*) and distribute enough for fourteen meals to those resident poor in the community. The second form was for poor strangers whose presence was temporary. The relief officers would go house to house to fill a tray (*tambuy*) with food and drink from which they would distribute to the poor.[6] The description Luke gives here implies that the church had adopted a combination of these methods for "daily" distribution of food to widows.

Trouble began when some of the Grecian widows were neglected. As a result complaints came against the Hebraic Jews and old suspicions were reopened. The "Twelve" took action. They gathered together all of the disciples and explained that it would be wrong for the apostles to neglect preaching the word of God in order to "wait (διακονεῖν, *diakonein*) on tables." The apostles should rather be engaged in "prayer and the ministry (διακονία, *diakonia*) of the word." The implication is that all gifts and ministries within the church are subservient to "the supremacy of the ministry of the Word."[7]

Polhill's observation is helpful at this point. Modern preachers who use this verse "as a biblical warrant for refusal to do the mundane administrative tasks in the church" are overlooking one important distinctive about the Jerusalem situation. The apostles occupied a unique role. "They alone in all of Christian history were the witnesses to the life, death, and resurrection of Jesus," he argues. "Their witness was unique, unrepeatable, and absolutely foundational for the Christian movement," and thus should not be limited by preoccupation with tasks which could be performed by others.[8]

For this reason the apostles encouraged the congregation to become involved in the solution to the problem. "Choose seven men from among you" so that this ministry may be continued. Though the apostles had the authority to appoint these men themselves, they carefully provided for the involvement of the whole

---

[6]Haenchen, p. 261. He cites the study of Joachim Jeremias, translated in *Jerusalem in the Time of Jesus*, trans. F.H. and C.H. Cave (Philadelphia: Fortress, 1989), pp. 131-133.

[7]Flew, *Jesus*, p. 140.

[8]Polhill, p. 180.

church. No details are given as to what method was used for the selection.

Emphasis was placed, however, on the quality of men to be chosen. By now the language of "filling" is familiar in Acts (see 2:4; 4:8,31; 5:3). The apostles instructed the believers to choose seven men known to be "full of the Spirit and wisdom." This phrase suggests a lifestyle in which the Holy Spirit's presence was obvious to fellow believers. They were men of faith, boldness, and holiness. The term "wisdom" indicates that they also were men who had skills in ministry and, perhaps, problem-solving.

The congregation was satisfied with the proposal of the apostles. The words "they chose" refer to the nearest antecedent, the "whole group." The choice of these leaders was left to the church, but the apostles also had a role. Their job was to "turn (καθίστημι, *kathistēmi*) this responsibility over" to the new leaders. The Greek word includes the idea of "appoint" or "approve." In addition the apostles completed the process of selection when they "prayed and laid their hands on" the new leaders.[9] Though the text does not call the seven "deacons," the use of the verb διακονεῖν (*diakonein*) to describe their work may imply that these were the first deacons.[10]

Seven names are given for the men chosen. That all of them are Greek names does not imply that they were Gentiles or Hellenistic Jews from outside of Palestine. Jewish residents of Palestine often had Greek names.[11] The names do suggest, however, that these men were on the Grecian side of the present dispute.

Of the seven, only Stephen and Philip will be heard from again

---

[9]The laying on of hands in a situation like ordination occurs also in 13:3, as well as 1 Tim 4:14 and 2 Tim 1:6.

[10]Flew gives arguments against the conclusion that the seven were the first "deacons," as the role was later understood. He notes that the term διάκονος is not used to identify these men. He also points to the ambiguity of the term χρεία (*chreia*), translated "responsibility" in the NIV. The term, he says, does not necessarily mean "office." See his *Jesus*, pp. 138-140. Flew's second point appears to be influenced by a perception of the role of deacon which comes only later in the history of the church.

[11]Lake and Cadbury, pp. 65-66. Johannes Munck, however, speaks of the improbability that seven names of Palestinian Jews would all be Greek. He thinks the seven were a mix of Palestinian and Diaspora Jews. See his *Paul* pp. 226-228. See also Wilson, *Gentile Mission*, pp. 129-130.

in Acts.[12] Nicholas was "from Antioch" and "a convert to Judaism." This mention of Antioch, a city that became a center for Christian activity, introduces for Luke an interest that will appear again in Acts (11:19-21). To call Nicholas a convert was to say that he was not Jewish by birth, but from a pagan background. His conversion to Judaism had occurred before his conversion to Christianity.

Luke adds at this point a summary of the church's progress. The word of God "spread" in the sense that its proclamation reached farther and farther. Luke uses the imperfect tense ("was growing") to indicate a continuous growth during this period.[13] The same is true with the next two verbs—"increased" and "became obedient." The numbers "were increasing" continuously and at the same time many priests "were becoming" obedient to the faith.[14] Believers were witnessing growth in the church almost moment by moment.

K. THE ARREST, TRIAL, AND STONING OF STEPHEN (6:8–8:1a)

1. False Accusations against Him (6:8-15)

[8]Now Stephen, a man full of God's grace and power, did great wonders and miraculous signs among the people. [9]Opposition arose, however, from members of the Synagogue of the Freedmen (as it was called)—Jews of Cyrene and Alexandria as well as the provinces of Cilicia and Asia. These men began to argue with Stephen, [10]but they could not stand up against his wisdom or the

---

[12]Stephen appears in 6:8–7:60 and Philip in 8:5-40 and 21:8-9.

[13]Jerome Kodell suggests that the terminology used by Luke is an application of Jesus' parable of the sower (Luke 8:1-15). His conclusion is that the growth of the seed is used as a metaphor for the growth of the church. See his "'The Word of God grew:' The Ecclesial Tendency of logos in Acts 1,7; 12,24; 19,20," *Biblica* 55 (1974): 505-519. Ward Gasque refers to the attention these summary statements in Acts received beginning with the commentary of Thomas Page in 1886. See his *History*, pp. 125-126.

[14]Evidently those closest to the operation of the temple were open to the message of the Gospel in many cases.

Spirit by whom he spoke. [11]Then they secretly persuaded some men to say, "We have heard Stephen speak words of blasphemy against Moses and against God." [12]So they stirred up the people and the elders and the teachers of the law. They seized Stephen and brought him before the Sanhedrin. [13]They produced false witnesses, who testified, "This fellow never stops speaking against this holy place and against the law. [14]For we have heard him say that this Jesus of Nazareth will destroy this place and change the customs Moses handed down to us." [15]All who were sitting in the Sanhedrin looked intently at Stephen, and they saw that his face was like the face of an angel.

Stephen's story is resumed with a description of his provocative ministry. He was "full of God's grace" (see 6:3) and powerfully proclaimed the gospel.[15] The Spirit made himself known through Stephen's ministry in the form of "great wonders and miraculous signs." Here is the first instance in Acts where miracles are mentioned in connection with the ministry of someone other than an apostle. It is not a coincidence that in 6:6 is the statement that the apostles "laid their hands" on Stephen and the other men chosen by the church.[16]

Opposition once again surfaced as a result of the church's ministry. Unlike previous resistance, this opposition came from Jews who were not connected with the Sadducees and the temple leaders. The "Synagogue of the Freedmen" was the source of the antagonism. Out of the many synagogues in Jerusalem, this one was attended by Hellenistic Jews from the Diaspora.

The synagogue was usually a center for the social, the educational, and the religious life of the Jewish community. Originally synagogues were houses of prayer. They were influenced more by the Pharisees than by the Sadducees, whose major interest was in the operation of the temple.

"Freedmen" in the first century were slaves or descendants of slaves who had gained their release. The name of this synagogue

---

[15]Richard discusses in detail the stylistic and factual parallels between 6:8–7:53 and both 3:1-12 and 5:17-34. See his *Acts 6:1–8:4*, pp. 223-224.

[16]In 8:6 the same power will be seen working in Philip's ministry.

implies that the freedmen were Jews who previously had lived in Cyrene or Alexandria in Northern Africa, or in the provinces of Cilicia and Asia. Quite frequently Jews moved from these areas around the Roman Empire and took up residence in Jerusalem. The Apostle Paul, for example, was a Cilician Jew who may well have participated with this synagogue. The Jews in this synagogue found Stephen's message highly offensive. From the charges they brought to the Sanhedrin it appears that their objections centered on whether the temple and the law were relevant in light of the gospel of Jesus. They took Stephen's message to imply that "this holy place" and the law of Moses were no longer valid components in God's dealings with his people.[17] Stephen had probably emphasized that salvation is to be found in Christ alone, not in the Old Testament system of sacrifices. His message may well have carried a universalistic theme.[18]

When their arguments failed to adequately refute Stephen's message, these Jews resorted to stirring up "the people and the elders and the teachers of the law." Here for the first time opposition to the Christians came from the people, as well as the temple authorities.[19] The Sanhedrin became involved and brought Stephen in for a hearing. Staring at Stephen, the Sanhedrin detected a man unafraid of the powers opposing the gospel. Something about his appearance seemed to say that his witness had come from the realm of the angels themselves. Stephen looked like a man who had been in the presence of God.

---

[17]These accusations contain echoes of the words of Jesus (see Mark 14:58; Matt 26:60; John 2:19; Mark 13:2). See Flew, *Jesus*, p. 40. O'Neill thinks that these points in Stephen's theology imply that the destruction of the temple had already occurred by the time Acts was written, thus requiring a date after A.D. 70. But the role of the temple was already an issue with Jesus during his ministry. See his *Theology*, pp. 89-91. See also Wilson, *Gentile Mission*, p. 132.

[18]Shepard, *Life*, p. 54.

[19]Contrast, for example, 2:47.

ACTS 7

2. Stephen's Defense (7:1-53)

The Old Testament Patriarchs (7:1-8)

[1]Then the high priest asked him, "Are these charges true?" [2]To this he replied: "Brothers and fathers, listen to me! The God of glory appeared to our father Abraham while he was still in Mesopotamia, before he lived in Haran. [3]'Leave your country and your people,' God said, 'and go to the land I will show you.'[a] [4]"So he left the land of the Chaldeans and settled in Haran. After the death of his father, God sent him to this land where you are now living. [5]He gave him no inheritance here, not even a foot of ground. But God promised him that he and his descendants after him would possess the land, even though at that time Abraham had no child. [6]God spoke to him in this way: 'Your descendants will be strangers in a country not their own, and they will be enslaved and mistreated four hundred years. [7]But I will punish the nation they serve as slaves,' God said, 'and afterward they will come out of that country and worship me in this place.'[b] [8]Then he gave Abraham the covenant of circumcision. And Abraham became the father of Isaac and circumcised him eight days after his birth. Later Isaac became the father of Jacob, and Jacob became the father of the twelve patriarchs.

[a]3 Gen. 12:1   [b]7 Gen. 15:13,14

Caiaphas, who was high priest until A.D. 36, was handling still another case associated with the followers of Christ. He had been determined to rid Jerusalem of Jesus (Matt 26:57-66) and had strictly warned Peter and John not to preach in the name of Jesus

(4:18). He had supervised the hearing in which all of the apostles were punished for preaching in this name (5:40). Now he directed his questions to Stephen.

Stephen's address is a defense of himself only indirectly.[1] The two points he emphasized were that God's presence could not be confined to a place, whether to a particular land or material building.[2] Secondly, Stephen established the record of Jewish hostility to the leaders appointed by God over the nation. To the extent that his preaching had stirred up controversy on these issues, Stephen's address was a defense of his message.

He began by tracing the Old Testament account of God's dealings with the patriarchs.[3] God's[4] calling of Abraham in Meso-

---

[1]This fact has caused scholars to puzzle over the authenticity of this speech. Davies notes that scholars have used two lines of approach with regard to the speech. The more recent one has been to argue that Luke borrowed material used in the Jewish synagogue for inserting here, and that the picture of Stephen delivering these comments before the Sanhedrin has been fabricated. Davies names Dibelius and Haenchen as representatives of this approach. The second approach sees a close connection between the charges brought against Stephen in 6:13 (i.e., his historical context as given in Acts) and his comments in this speech. See his *Land*, pp. 267-268. Nils Dahl represents the latter approach. He argues that Stephen's statements about the temple should be understood in much the same way as the argument in Heb 4:3-11 where the author discusses the fulfillment of God's promises relating to Joshua. If Joshua had given the people rest, then God would not have promised another rest. Similarly, says Dahl, Stephen's point is that if Solomon had fulfilled David's prayer about a house for God, then the prophet would not have said, "What house will you build for me?" See his "The Story of Abraham in Luke-Acts," in *Studies in Luke-Acts*, ed. Leander Keck and J.L. Martyn (Philadelphia: Fortress, 1980), pp. 139-158. See also J.J. Scott, "Stephen's Speech: A Possible Model for Luke's Historical Method?" *JETS* 17 (1974): 91-97, and Wilson, *Gentile Mission*, pp. 133-134. Wilson finds "at least a general thematic connection between the charges brought against Stephen and his speech in vv. 35f."

[2]Flew sees implications for the church in Stephen's points. The rejection of Joseph by his brothers foreshadows the rejection of the Messiah by the Jews. The "supersession of the Temple" is about to occur. Also, the resistance of the Jews to the mission of the Holy Spirit follows from Stephen's remarks. See his *Jesus*, pp. 126-127.

[3]Dahl points out the selectivity of Stephen in his survey of Old Testament history ("Story of Abraham," pp. 139-158).

[4]See Psalm 28:3 for the expression "the God of glory."

potamia to travel to Palestine established the presence of God with
the patriarchs even though "He gave them no inheritance" in
Palestine, "not even one foot of ground." As a matter of fact,
Stephen focused attention on the promise which was given to
Abraham in word only, at a time when the patriarch "had no child"
or anyone to call an heir. His implication was that the presence of
God had been evident even though no temple or sacred location
was established. God's people will always "live loose to any particularly earthly spot."[5]

Stephen also mentioned the covenant of circumcision given to
Abraham (Gen 17:10-11). The essential elements of God's relationship with Israel were thus established before any location had been
chosen for the temple.

Two historical problems present themselves at this point in
Stephen's address. The first has to do with the time of Abraham's
calling. Stephen places God's call of Abraham "in Mesopotamia,
before he lived in Haran." The call recorded in Genesis 12:1,
however, comes after Abraham's arrival in Haran. But this problem
seems to disappear when Genesis 15:7 is taken into account, a
passage which has the Lord saying to Abraham "I am the Lord, who
brought you out of Ur of the Chaldeans."

The second problem is also connected with chronology.
Stephen's address has Abraham leaving for Canaan "after the death
of his father." Genesis 11 and 12 imply that Abraham's father,
Terah, was 145 years old at the time Abraham left Haran, some sixty
years before his death. Some have solved this problem by suggesting
that the list of Terah's sons in Genesis 11:27 does not mean that
Abraham was the oldest and that his birth came later in Terah's life.[6]
Another possibility which is just as likely, however, is that Stephen's
speech follows the Samaritan Pentateuch where the Genesis account
has Abraham leaving for Canaan after his father's death.[7]

---

[5]Bruce, p. 134. Scott says that Stephen's speech "demonstrates that God's
promise to Abraham was not primary [sic] territorial" ("Stephen's Speech,"
p. 93). Interesting also is the way in which Stephen's address corresponds to
the charges brought against him. See John Kilgallen, "The Function of
Stephen's Speech (Acts 7:2-53)," *Biblica* 70(1989): 173-193.
[6]See *NIV Study Bible*, note on 7:4.
[7]Abram Spiro, "Stephen's Samaritan Background," in Johannes Munck,

The number 400 (7:6) in connection with the bondage years in
Egypt can be understood as an approximation of the time reported
in Genesis 15:13. Paul uses the number 430 in Galatians 3:17.

Stephen made his major points by citing Abraham's call by God
and the divine promises which God made to him. For this reason he
only briefly summarized the lives of Isaac and Jacob.

Israel in Egypt (7:9-19)

9"Because the patriarchs were jealous of Joseph, they sold him
as a slave into Egypt. But God was with him 10and rescued him
from all his troubles. He gave Joseph wisdom and enabled him to
gain the goodwill of Pharaoh king of Egypt; so he made him ruler
over Egypt and all his palace. 11Then a famine struck all Egypt and
Canaan, bringing great suffering, and our fathers could not find
food. 12When Jacob heard that there was grain in Egypt, he sent
our fathers on their first visit. 13On their second visit, Joseph told
his brothers who he was, and Pharaoh learned about Joseph's
family. 14After this, Joseph sent for his father Jacob and his whole
family, seventy-five in all. 15Then Jacob went down to Egypt, where
he and our fathers died. 16Their bodies were brought back to
Shechem and placed in the tomb that Abraham had bought from
the sons of Hamor at Shechem for a certain sum of money. 17As
the time drew near for God to fulfill his promise to Abraham, the

The Acts of the Apostles, Anchor Bible (Garden City, NY: Doubleday, 1967),
pp. 285-300. Also arguing that Stephen's theology about the temple was
influenced by Samaritan views concerning the temple is Martin Scharlemann in Stephen: A Singular Saint (Rome: Pontifical Biblical Institute, 1968).
His thesis is that Stephen's concern was the evangelizing of the Samaritans.
See also Lloyd Gaston, No Stone on Another: Studies in the Significance of the
Fall of Jerusalem in the Synoptic Gospels (Leiden: E.J. Brill, 1970). Gaston also
sees a Samaritan influence in Stephen's position which he did not learn
from Jesus (p. 150). Gaston says, "The opposition of Stephen to the temple
is really without parallel within Judaism or the church in the period before
A.D. 70" (p. 158). Harold Mare, however, disputes the notion that Stephen's
speech shows any connections with the Samaritan Pentateuch. See his
"Acts 7: Jewish or Samaritan?" WThJ 34 (1971): 1-21.

number of our people in Egypt greatly increased. [18]Then another king, who knew nothing about Joseph, became ruler of Egypt. [19]He dealt treacherously with our people and oppressed our forefathers by forcing them to throw out their newborn babies so that they would die.

Stephen now began to introduce the second major theme of his address—the pattern of Jewish resistance to those leaders God raised up. His summary of the patriarchs called attention to the friction between those God used to accomplish his will and those who opposed them.

Jealousy provoked "the patriarchs" (he does not say "his brothers") to sell Joseph into slavery. These leaders whom the Jews revered set themselves against Joseph, even though "God was with him." The evidence of God's presence was Joseph's rise to power in Egypt.

Regarding the famine, Stephen mentioned the two visits of the brothers to Egypt. Though this item may seem unimportant, Stephen's point may have been a subtle reference to the two comings of Christ. In the first one he was not recognized, but in the second he will be seen for who he is.[8]

In citing the number of Joseph's family who traveled to Egypt, Stephen's number was not the same number used in the Hebrew Old Testament. The number seventy-five probably comes from the Septuagint where the number given is seventy-five, rather than the number seventy given in the Hebrew Bible (Gen 46:27; Exod 1:5; Deut 10:22). The difference of five resulted from the Septuagint's addition of two sons of Manasseh, two of Ephraim, and one grandson of Ephraim.

Stephen's comments on the location of the tomb of the patriarchs presents an example of compressing of the narrative. Genesis describes two purchases of burial plots—one by Abraham at Hebron (Gen 23:17-18) and the other by Jacob at Shechem (Gen 33:19). Abraham, Isaac, and Jacob were buried at Hebron, while Joseph was buried later at Shechem (Josh 24:32). Stephen compressed these accounts into one story in his statement that the patriarchs were buried "in the tomb that Abraham had bought" at Shechem. The

---

[8]Polhill, p. 192.

Sanhedrin would have understood his summary completely. The burial of the patriarchs was also outside of the "holy" land in the "hated Samaritan territory."[9]

Drawing this stage of Israel's history to a close, Stephen summarized the period of bondage by noting the increasing numbers of Hebrews in Egypt. The turning point for their fortunes came with the rise of a new pharaoh (see Exod 1:8). At this point Stephen had set the stage for his reflections on the leadership of Moses.

Early Days of Moses (7:20-29)

[20] "At that time Moses was born, and he was no ordinary child.[a] For three months he was cared for in his father's house. [21]When he was placed outside, Pharaoh's daughter took him and brought him up as her own son. [22]Moses was educated in all the wisdom of the Egyptians and was powerful in speech and action. [23]When Moses was forty years old, he decided to visit his fellow Israelites. [24]He saw one of them being mistreated by an Egyptian, so he went to his defense and avenged him by killing the Egyptian. [25]Moses thought that his own people would realize that God was using him to rescue them, but they did not. [26]The next day Moses came upon two Israelites who were fighting. He tried to reconcile them by saying, 'Men, you are brothers; why do you want to hurt each other?' [27]But the man who was mistreating the other pushed Moses aside and said, 'Who made you ruler and judge over us? [28]Do you want to kill me as you killed the Egyptian yesterday?'[b] [29]When Moses heard this, he fled to Midian, where he settled as a foreigner and had two sons.

[a]20 Or was fair in the sight of God   [b]28 Exodus 2:14

The Sanhedrin continued listening as Stephen emphasized his two dominant themes. Moses was an example of a leader chosen by God but resisted by his own people.[10] He was also an example of

---

[9]Polhill, pp. 192-193.

[10]Zehnle calls attention to the parallels between this part of Stephen's address and Acts 3. He believes that a "Moses-Jesus typology" underlies the

one who served in the power of God, yet without a homeland.

Following the Old Testament account from Exodus 2:11-15 closely, Stephen interpreted the record by drawing out particular points along the way, beginning with the first forty years of Moses' life. As an infant his parents realized he was "no ordinary child," a phrase which reads literally "fair to God." The phrase fits with Stephen's emphasis on Moses as one chosen by God.

After reviewing the details of Moses' escape from Pharaoh's decree, Stephen mentioned the accomplishments of Moses in Egypt.[11] At forty years of age, he "decided to visit (ἐπισκέψασθαι, *episkepsasthai*) his fellow Israelites." Polhill notes that this term is used "throughout Luke-Acts for God or his emissaries overseeing and caring for his people."[12] The implication is that Moses was being used by God to "look out for" the people while in bondage. God had chosen Moses to deliver the people from slavery.

Stephen, however, focused on the lack of acceptance of Moses. After Moses had defended and even delivered his Hebrew brother from the Egyptian, the Israelites refused to accept him. When Moses found two Hebrew brothers quarreling and tried to reconcile them, they rejected his help with the question, "Who made you ruler and judge over us?" Not so subtle in Stephen's address was the conclusion that God had made Moses ruler and deliverer over them and they did not know it nor were they prepared to accept it. Moses was, like Christ, sent from God to deliver and reconcile his people, but the people to whom he came rejected him.

Because of the danger he now faced, Moses fled to Midian (Exod 2:15). Located in southeastern Sinai along either side of the eastern arm of the Red Sea (known as the Gulf of Aqabah), Moses was now settling in a foreign land. Stephen's point was reinforced. Those whom God has invested with his presence have often been pilgrims without a home. The Lord has a history of dealing with his chosen leaders apart from any sacred plot of ground. The implication is that the temple is not necessary for God's purposes.

---

text at this point. See his *Pentecost Discourse*, pp. 75-94.

[11]Bruce notes that some Hellenists described Moses as the father of science and culture and the founder of the Egyptian civilization (p. 139).

[12]Polhill, p. 195.

The Call of Moses (7:30-34)

[30]"After forty years had passed, an angel appeared to Moses in the flames of a burning bush in the desert near Mount Sinai. [31]When he saw this, he was amazed at the sight. As he went over to look more closely, he heard the Lord's voice: [32]'I am the God of your fathers, the God of Abraham, Isaac and Jacob.'[a] Moses trembled with fear and did not dare to look. [33]Then the Lord said to him, 'Take off your sandals; the place where you are standing is holy ground. [34]I have indeed seen the oppression of my people in Egypt. I have heard their groaning and have come down to set them free. Now come, I will send you back to Egypt.'[b]

[a]32 Exodus 3:6   [b]34 Exodus 3:5,7,8,10

Moses' exile in Midian closed with another major turning point in his life. The forty years in Egypt were followed by forty years in Midian. Then he witnessed the burning bush which was not burned up, an experience in which the voice of God spoke to him, calling him to fulfill a mission by going back to Egypt.

Again Stephen's theme was emphasized as he recounted how Moses experienced the presence of God in a foreign land. The same God who had revealed himself to the patriarchs when they were foreigners was the God who spoke to Moses. Ironically, this spot became "holy ground"—a place far from the sacred precincts of the temple and the Sanhedrin. Removal of his sandals was a way of demonstrating respect for the presence of God and of avoiding any possibility of defiling the ground through contact with something defiled on the foot.[13]

The Wilderness Wanderings (7:35-43)

[35]"This is the same Moses whom they had rejected with the words, 'Who made you ruler and judge?' He was sent to be their ruler and deliverer by God himself, through the angel who appeared to him in the bush. [36]He led them out of Egypt and did

---

[13]Lake and Cadbury, p. 77.

wonders and miraculous signs in Egypt, at the Red Sea[a] and for forty years in the desert. [37]This is that Moses who told the Israelites, 'God will send you a prophet like me from your own people.'[b] [38]He was in the assembly in the desert, with the angel who spoke to him on Mount Sinai, and with our fathers; and he received living words to pass on to us. [39]But our fathers refused to obey him. Instead, they rejected him and in their hearts turned back to Egypt. [40]They told Aaron, 'Make us gods who will go before us. As for this fellow Moses who led us out of Egypt—we don't know what has happened to him!'[c] [41]That was the time they made an idol in the form of a calf. They brought sacrifices to it and held a celebration in honor of what their hands had made. [42]But God turned away and gave them over to the worship of the heavenly bodies. This agrees with what is written in the book of the prophets: 'Did you bring me sacrifices and offerings forty years in the desert, O house of Israel? [43]You have lifted up the shrine of Molech and the star of your god Rephan, the idols you made to worship. Therefore I will send you into exile'[d] beyond Babylon.

[a]*36* That is, Sea of Reeds   [b]*37* Deut. 18:15   [c]*40* Exodus 32:1
[d]*43* Amos 5:25-27

The final forty years of Moses' life now became the focus of Stephen's speech. His theme was clearly in view at this juncture. Examples of resistance to the leader chosen by God were prominent. The Israelites had asked, "Who made you ruler and judge?" They had no inclination to follow Moses' leadership, even though it was God who made Moses "ruler and deliverer" when He appeared to Moses at the burning bush.

In spite of this resistance, it was Moses who led the Israelites out of Egyptian bondage and across the Red Sea. God's presence was evident in these events, especially in the "wonders and miraculous signs in Egypt," a reference to the plagues inflicted on pharaoh and his people.

---

[14]Whereas Stephen speaks of "our fathers" through most of this address, at the end of his speech he changes the pronoun to "your fathers." E.J. Via makes this point and also discusses how the themes in Stephen's address relate to themes enunciated throughout Luke-Acts. See her "An Interpretation of Acts 7:35-37 from the Perspective of Major Themes in Luke-Acts," in *Society of Biblical Literature 1978 Seminar Papers*, ed. Paul Achtemeier (Missoula: Scholars Press, 1978), pp. 209-233.

Even still, Stephen pointed out, their "fathers" did not honor him with their cooperation.[14] They "refused to obey him." The best example of their resistance was their insisting that Aaron help them construct an idol at the foot of Sinai. Rather than honoring what God had instituted among them, they preferred to worship "what their hands had made." Even here, Stephen appeared to be making subtle references to the temple made with human hands, to which the Sadducees had become so attached. God's condemnation of Israel was severe. He "gave them over" to their idolatry, a judgment upon idolaters which Paul describes in Romans 1:24-28. The idea is that he consigned them to the wickedness their hearts determined to achieve.

The idolatry of Israel was also the subject of warnings from later prophets. When Amos confronted the Israelites about their wickedness, he foretold of the Assyrian captivity which was coming upon them. Stephen found in these words the appropriate reference to the rebellious spirit of idolatry which continued to live in Israel. Following the Septuagint, Stephen quoted Amos 5:25-27, replacing the destination of "Damascus" with "Babylon" since that city had been the ultimate captivity. The quotation highlighted Israel's idolatry in the wilderness where the "sacrifices and offerings" they brought were not to the Lord, but to other gods.[15] Bruce notes that both Molech and Rephan appear to be references to planetary deities in the time of Amos.[16]

Moses predicted that God would raise up another prophet like himself (Deut 18:15). If Israel was determined to resist the leadership of Moses, God would send another leader. The subtle references to Christ are evident in Stephen's words at this point. Jesus was the new Moses. Stephen's contention remained consistent. The temple authorities were standing in the way of the chosen leader of God whose story was being proclaimed by his disciples.

The Tabernacle and the Temple (7:44-50)

44"Our forefathers had the tabernacle of the Testimony with them

---

[15]Dupont notes that by Stephen's "selection and presentation of the details from the exodus story, the superstitious attachment of the Jews to their temple is made to appear as a continuation of their idolatry in the desert." See his *Salvation*, p. 134.

[16]Bruce, p. 145, n. 70.

in the desert. It had been made as God directed Moses, according to the pattern he had seen. ⁴⁵Having received the tabernacle, our fathers under Joshua brought it with them when they took the land from the nations God drove out before them. It remained in the land until the time of David, ⁴⁶who enjoyed God's favor and asked that he might provide a dwelling place for the God of Jacob.ᵃ ⁴⁷But it was Solomon who built the house for him. ⁴⁸"However, the Most High does not live in houses made by men. As the prophet says: ⁴⁹'Heaven is my throne, and the earth is my footstool. What kind of house will you build for me? says the Lord. Or where will my resting place be? ⁵⁰Has not my hand made all these things?'ᵇ

ᵃ46 Some early manuscripts *the house of Jacob*   ᵇ50 Isaiah 66:1,2

In the wilderness the "forefathers" had the "tabernacle of Testimony." It was not considered a house in the sense of the temple, but Stephen pointed to its construction as an effort conforming to the will of God. To this point in Israel's history, he implied, the nation had not fixed a sacred site as the place for God. Even during the time of Joshua the tabernacle was in use and continued to be used through the period of the judges until the time of David.

At this juncture, Stephen suggested, a change occurred. David "enjoyed God's favor" and wanted to build a permanent dwelling place for God. His wish was fulfilled by Solomon. But now Stephen turned to the words of Isaiah 66:1-2 to impress upon the Jewish audience that God cannot be confined to temples made by human hands.[17] God is far too big for such houses. If heaven is his throne and earth his footstool, who can construct an edifice to hold Him? If everything was created by his hand, how can people build him a house as if he had need of such assistance?

---

[17]T.C.G. Thornton calls attention to evidence from the Jewish Targum that Isa 66:1 was understood to warn the Jews about overconfidence because of the temple. See his "Stephen's Use of Isaiah LXVI.1," *JTS*, 25 (1974): 432-435. This evidence may explain why Stephen quotes Isaiah in answer to the charges about his preaching against the temple. Conzelmann demonstrates that criticism of the temple began in late Judaism, but usually it included the "concern to justify the existence of the Temple" (p. 56).

Stephen's quotation of these words was enough to hint at the problem in Jerusalem. The Sanhedrin was engaged in false worship built on the false premise that God needed the Jerusalem temple. No such help was needed by God. He had a history of making his presence known to his chosen people when they were far removed from the sacred precincts of this plot of ground in Jerusalem.

As to the charges leveled against Stephen (6:11-14), his message had no hint of blasphemy. But in regard to the temple, Stephen had perhaps echoed the prediction of Jesus that "not one stone here will be left on another; every one will be thrown down" (Matt 24:2). Even this quotation could have brought the wrath of the leaders of the temple.

The Personal Application (7:51-53)

[51]"You stiff-necked people, with uncircumcised hearts and ears! You are just like your fathers: You always resist the Holy Spirit! [52]Was there ever a prophet your fathers did not persecute? They even killed those who predicted the coming of the Righteous One. And now you have betrayed and murdered him—[53]you who have received the law that was put into effect through angels but have not obeyed it."

As Stephen came to the conclusion of his address, he drove the message home. The Jewish leaders were the guilty ones. They were "stiff-necked" and had "uncircumcised hearts and ears," charges that had already been made in Old Testament times.[18] They were always resisting the Holy Spirit, that is, they were standing in the way of the Spirit's work.[19]

Bertil Gärtner also traces this polemic to Jewish tradition. See his The Areopagus Speech and Natural Revelation (Uppsala: Gleerup, 1955), p. 208. Kilgallen also discusses the reasons for Stephen's opposition to the temple. See his The Stephen Speech: A Literary and Redactional Study of Acts 7,2-53 (Rome: Biblical Institute Press, 1976), pp. 91-92. Davies thinks that the larger issue in Acts 6 and 7 is the land rather than the temple (Land, pp. 271-273).

[18]See Exod 33:3,5; 34:9; Deut 9:6,13; Lev 26:41; Jer 4:4; 6:10; 9:26.

[19]Richard notes that "the intended contrast is clear: Stephen and the other appointees are full of the Spirit, but the early Hebrews and the present generation of Jews are not and indeed 'resist' Him" (Acts 6:1–8:4, p. 138).

As if these accusations from Stephen were not serious enough, he also charged them with persecuting and killing the prophets. The Old Testament speaks of the sufferings of some of the prophets, but Jewish tradition has more to say about such incidents as the sawing in two of Isaiah in the reign of Manasseh and the stoning of Jeremiah before he was forced to go to Egypt with the people.[20]

Stephen climaxed his address by accusing the religious authorities of crucifying the Messiah. Following in the footsteps of their fathers who "killed those who predicted the coming of the Righteous One," they "betrayed and murdered him." This nation so favored by God that they received the law "put into effect through angels" was guilty of rejecting the chosen servant of God.[21]

The Final Witness of Stephen (7:54-56)

[54]When they heard this, they were furious and gnashed their teeth at him. [55]But Stephen, full of the Holy Spirit, looked up to heaven and saw the glory of God, and Jesus standing at the right hand of God. [56]"Look," he said, "I see heaven open and the Son of Man standing at the right hand of God."

Stephen's accusations hit home with the members of the Sanhedrin.[22] They were outraged. They were "cut to the heart" (διεπρίοντο, *dieprionto*) with anger. Even their teeth showed anger as they were ground together at Stephen.

Stephen's reaction to their outburst was to look into heaven and witness the Lord Jesus standing at the right hand of God. His words described the scene and his accusers were even angrier. Stephen's vision of Jesus contradicted their position. If the vision was true, God was giving a sign of his approval of Stephen.[23] They could not

---

[20]Bruce, p. 152. He cites *The Ascension of Isaiah* 5:1-14 and the Christian writer Tertullian in *Remedy against Scorpions* 8.

[21]Jewish tradition held that the law was given to Moses through the mediation of angels (see Gal 3:19; Heb 2:2). See Bruce, p. 153 (n. 99).

[22]Hengel notes the intolerance of Palestinian Judaism to any "critical consideration of their own history and especially the giving of the law." See his *Judaism and Hellenism*, 1:309.

[23]Stephen's use of "Son of Man" to identify Christ is a rare example

believe this was possible. Stephen must be further blaspheming the Lord. They placed their hands over their ears to shut out the sound and they rushed toward him to silence him. He deserved to be stoned as far as they were concerned.

His testimony that Jesus was standing at the right hand of God is curious. Usually references to the ascended Christ picture him seated at the right hand of God (see Mark 16:19; Matt 26:64; Luke 22:69). Was he standing in order to welcome the first Christian martyr? Was his stance before the throne seen to conform to the vision recorded in Daniel 7:14-15 where the Son of Man was pictured?[24] It is impossible to say for certain, but his presence at the Lord's right hand communicates his divinity and authority.

The Death of Stephen (7:57-60)

[57]At this they covered their ears and, yelling at the top of their voices, they all rushed at him, dragged him out of the city and began to stone him. Meanwhile, the witnesses laid their clothes at the feet of a young man named Saul. [59]While they were stoning him, Stephen prayed, "Lord Jesus, receive my spirit." [60]Then he fell on his knees and cried out, "Lord, do not hold this sin against them." When he had said this, he fell asleep.

---

outside of the words of Jesus of the use of this title to speak of Christ (see Mark 8:31; Matt 25:31; Ladd, *Theology*, p. 146). The title can be traced to Dan 7:13-14. W.F. Howard takes the title as a literal translation from the Aramaic, and "quite unintelligible except on Palestinian soil." See J.H. Moulton and W.F. Howard, *A Grammar of New Testament Greek* (Edinburgh: T & T Clark, 1979), 2:441. Hengel sees in Stephen's being "full of the Holy Spirit" a reference to the contrast between this martyr (and all believers) and "the satanic hostility" of those resisting the Gospel. See his *Between Jesus and Paul*, trans. John Bowden (Philadelphia: Fortress, 1983), pp. 22-23.

[24]Dupont, *Salvation*, p. 114. Wilson speaks of Stephen's vision as Luke's attempt to deal with the delayed Parousia, claiming that in this vision Stephen saw "a private, personal Parousia" (*Gentile Mission*, p. 78). This conclusion is hardly necessary in light of the many times in Acts where God's servants receive Divine encouragement in times of danger (see 4:31; 18:9-10; 22:17,21; 23:11; 27:23-26). Also this interpretation contradicts the promise of 1:11 in which the angel says that Jesus will come back in the same manner as the disciples saw him go.

Stoning as a form of execution involved throwing the victim over a small cliff. The first witness then rolled a heavy stone down the precipice, intending that the weight of the stone should crush the victim to death. If the first stone did not accomplish this task, the second witness rolled down a second stone until the objective was accomplished.[25]

In Stephen's case it seems as if the Sanhedrin's members resorted to more of a mob action than the organized procedure called for by Jewish law.[26] Stephen had time before his death to pray and ask forgiveness for his persecutors. This note implies that the mob was throwing stones at him in those last few moments of his life. Also the note that they "laid their clothes" at the feet of the young man Saul implies that they wanted freedom of movement for throwing stones. Saul of Tarsus will become one of the prominent characters in the rest of Acts. Whether this mention of Paul indicates that he was in charge of the execution is unclear. No one can doubt, however, that he gave his consent to the action. Luke thus introduces one new personality which he wants to describe more fully in the chapters to come.

The Consent of Saul (8:1a)

[1]And Saul was there, giving approval to his death.

Luke's final comment with regard to the martyrdom of Stephen has to do with the disposition of Saul. He was "giving approval" (συνευδοκῶν, *syneudokōn*) to the action against Stephen. The participle in the present tense indicates more than just a momentary enthusiasm on the part of Saul. His very condition gave evidence of an ongoing determination to oppose any example of this new teaching.

---

[25]Lake and Cadbury, p. 85.

[26]Martin refers to Stephen's execution as a "lynching." See his *Foundations*, 1:88. For a discussion on Jewish regulations in such cases see Moore, *Judaism*, 2:180-197.

ACTS 8

II. THE CHURCH IN
JUDEA AND SAMARIA (8:1b-12:25)

A. PERSECUTION AND
DISPERSION OF THE CHURCH (8:1b-3)

On that day a great persecution broke out against the church at Jerusalem, and all were scattered throughout Judea and Samaria. [2]Godly men buried Stephen and mourned deeply for him. [3]But Saul began to destroy the church. Going from house to house, he dragged off men and women and put them in prison.

A new division in Luke's material begins at this point. The previous seven chapters of Acts described the success of the gospel in Jerusalem, largely focusing on the ministry of Peter and the other apostles. With the beginning of chapter eight comes a new focus. Now Luke describes the successes of the gospel in areas around Jerusalem, especially in Judea and Samaria, in conformity to his theme statement in 1:8. Now the people carrying the gospel are not just the apostles, but other believers, including Philip, Barnabas, and Paul.

The effects of Stephen's trial and martyrdom were felt in the church immediately. Luke ties together the scattering of the church very closely with the Sanhedrin's action against Stephen. He mentions the persecution and scattering of the church[1] and in the next sentence reports the burial of Stephen. Everyone was dispersed

---

[1]Hengel sees the persecution of the Hellenistic Christians by the Jews as a part of larger developments within Judaism itself. See his *Judaism and Hellenism*, 1:312-313.

"except the apostles." Commentators often puzzle about this exception, but most solve the problem by suggesting that the persecution
focused on the Hellenistic Christians (from which Stephen came),
and this permitted the apostles to remain untouched by persecution.[2] Beyond this possibility, however, is the suggestion that the
apostles may have sensed the need to maintain a presence in
Jerusalem, perhaps in obedience to the command of Jesus (1:4).

The term "scattering" (διασπείρω, *diaspeirō*) is a word used of
the scattering of seeds. Believers were distributed in all directions
from Jerusalem.

Meanwhile, "godly men" took care of the burial of Stephen, a task
that would have placed them at risk for their lives. The persecution of
Christians had begun. One of the chief instigators was Saul who
began to "destroy" (λυμαίνομαι, *lymainomai*) the church—a powerful
figure of speech which pictures a wild animal tearing at its prey.
Saul's method included going from house to house in search of
people who had confessed Jesus as Messiah. When he found them, he
"dragged" them away to prison, whether they were men or women.

B. MINISTRY OF PHILIP (8:4-40)

1. Philip in Samaria (8:4-8)

**[4]Those who had been scattered preached the word wherever
they went. [5]Philip went down to a city in Samaria and proclaimed
the Christ[a] there. [6]When the crowds heard Philip and saw the
miraculous signs he did, they all paid close attention to what he
said. [7]With shrieks, evil[b] spirits came out of many, and many para-
lytics and cripples were healed. [8]So there was great joy in that city.**

[a]5 Or *Messiah*   [b]7 Greek *unclean*

Persecution accomplished the further spread of the gospel.
Believers went everywhere in Judea and Samaria carrying the good

---

[2]See Bruce, pp. 162-163; Lake and Cadbury, p. 87; Polhill, p. 211.
[3]Flew observes that the use of the term "word" in 8:4 corresponds to
Paul's descriptions of the preaching of the word (*Jesus*, p. 154).

news of Jesus.[3] In this scattering another of the seven men from Jerusalem takes center stage. Luke has reported on the ministry of Stephen in chapters six and seven. Now he focuses on Philip.

Philip traveled north to "a city in Samaria," which may be a reference to the old capital city renamed Sebaste, or more likely the city of Shechem at the foot of Mt. Gerizim. His ministry included performing miracles of healing, as well as the preaching of Christ. Luke places the preaching and miracles in their proper relationship by noting that the miracles drew attention to the message so that the Samaritans "paid close attention (προσεῖχον, *proseichon*) to what he said."[4]

The importance of this evangelistic thrust should not be missed. Jesus had promised that the apostles would be witnesses first in Jerusalem, and then in "all Judea and Samaria." At this point Luke shows how the gospel began to leave Jerusalem and expand its influence into ever-widening territories.[5]

Samaritans were hated by the Jews. They were descendants of the northern tribes of Israel and had remained in the land after the Assyrian captivity had removed much of the nation. Partly because of their intermarrying with the Canaanites, they were looked upon with suspicion. Jews frequently avoided any contact with Samaritans.

The gospel, however, shows no favoritism. Salvation is intended for all nations. The cross of Christ is long enough to bridge any chasm between people.

2. The Conversion of Simon Magus (8:9-13)

[9]Now for some time a man named Simon had practiced sorcery in the city and amazed all the people of Samaria. He boasted that

---

[4]The verb is used as a synonym of believing, in spite of Haenchen's reservations on the point (p. 302). The use of πιστεύω (*pisteuō*) in v. 12 confirms the point. See Dieter Georgi, *The Opponents of Paul in Second Corinthians* (Philadelphia: Fortress, 1986), p. 226, n. 541. See also Rienecker, p. 278; Lake and Cadbury, p. 89.

[5]For a discussion of the importance in Acts of the mission to the Samaritans as distinct from the Gentiles see Jervell, *People of God,* pp. 113-132. He argues that Luke does not characterize the Samaritans as Gentiles, but as Jews.

he was someone great, [10]and all the people, both high and low, gave him their attention and exclaimed, "This man is the divine power known as the Great Power." [11]They followed him because he had amazed them for a long time with his magic. [12]But when they believed Philip as he preached the good news of the kingdom of God and the name of Jesus Christ, they were baptized, both men and women. [13]Simon himself believed and was baptized. And he followed Philip everywhere, astonished by the great signs and miracles he saw.

When Philip arrived in the Samaritan city he found a man who had been practicing "sorcery" and had "amazed" the citizens. Simon was his name and his following was large and enduring. His "magic" (μαγεία, *mageia*) impressed people of all ranks and resulted in his being considered a man of "divine power" (ἡ δύναμις τοῦ θεοῦ, *hē dynamis tou theou*).[6] Even the details mentioned here are enough to suggest the status given people in the ancient world who knew about magic. In Persia a magician (μάγος, *magos*) was someone with a reputation for having a very intimate relationship with the deity. Often the magician engaged in astrology, divination, magic formulas, and potions. Usually kings in the ancient world had magi in the palace to give them counsel about important events. In the Gospel of Matthew (2:1) the magi knew enough about the constellations to notice the star which informed them of Jesus' birth. Other references to magicians in the New Testament are more negative, including this case of Simon and that of Elymas in 13:6-12.[7]

In spite of the influence of Simon, the preaching of Philip was effective. Those who formerly had given their attention to the magical arts of Simon now heard Philip's message about the "kingdom of God" and "the name of Jesus Christ." Those who received the word were baptized. Even Simon believed and was also baptized. But the final note in v. 13 sets the stage for what is to come with Simon's act of

---

[6]It is possible that Simon was claiming for himself the position of "the Son of God," something parallel to the title used for Jesus (Rom 1:3; compare Mark 14:62).

[7]Early church tradition made this Simon the founder of the Gnostic sect known as the Simonians (Justin Martyr, *Apology* 26:3; Irenaeus, *Against Heresies* 1.16).

greed. Simon, the magician who was astonishing the multitudes, was himself astonished by the miracles performed by Philip in his ministry.

3. The Visit of Peter and John to Samaria (8:14-17)

[14]**When the apostles in Jerusalem heard that Samaria had accepted the word of God, they sent Peter and John to them. [15]When they arrived, they prayed for them that they might receive the Holy Spirit, [16]because the Holy Spirit had not yet come upon any of them; they had simply been baptized into[a] the name of the Lord Jesus. [17]Then Peter and John placed their hands on them, and they received the Holy Spirit.**

[a]*16* Or *in*

News of Samaritan conversions reached the apostles in Jerusalem. The response of the twelve was to send Peter and John, not to exercise control over the new believers so much as to impart to them the power of the same Spirit which empowered the apostles. Such an action by the apostles demonstrated the unity of Jerusalem believers with Samaritan believers. The barriers were coming down. Jews and Samaritans could be one in Christ.

Peter and John "prayed for them" and "placed their hands on them." The Samaritans had believed the gospel (see vv. 6,12,14) and become genuine converts. But "the Holy Spirit had not yet come upon any of them," and the apostles were present to fulfill this need. Much discussion has been generated by this passage. If the Holy Spirit was promised in connection with Christian baptism (2:38), why had these disciples not received the Spirit?

They had been baptized, but "had simply been baptized into the name of the Lord Jesus." This cannot imply that their baptism was inadequate because of the name, as if to say "they had only been baptized in the name of the Lord Jesus."[8] Peter's command on the Day of Pentecost was that the believers be baptized "in the name of Jesus Christ" and they would receive the Spirit (2:38). In addition it

---

[8]The phrase "into the name of" appears to be related to the formula "believe in" (πιστεύω εἰς, *pisteuō eis*), a phrase original to Christianity. See Ladd, *Theology*, pp. 272-273. See also Beasley-Murray, *Baptism*, pp. 100-102.

is doubtful that any significance is intended in the different preposi-
tions used. Here the phrase is they had only been baptized "into"
(εἰς, *eis*) the name, rather than "in" (ἐπί, *epi*) the name (2:38).

The contrast intended in 8:16 puts the emphasis on baptism
versus the laying on of hands. "They had simply been baptized," but
had not received the laying on of hands. The next verse states that
the apostles laid their hands on them, praying that the Spirit would
be given to them.

Various suggestions have been made as to why the laying on of
hands was necessary in addition to baptism. Had the Samaritans
been authentic converts?[9] Was the reception of the Spirit sometimes
the result of baptism and sometimes the result of the laying on of
the apostles' hands?[10] Was the Spirit's activity so unpredictable that
it was impossible to limit the reception of the Spirit to baptism?[11]
Or did the Samaritans receive the Spirit's indwelling presence when
they were baptized, but had not received any outward manifestations of the Spirit?[12]

It would seem that the language of the text indicates it was the
Holy Spirit himself (rather than spiritual gifts) which the Samaritans
had yet to receive. The apostles, we are told, went to Samaria so
that the converts "might receive the Holy Spirit." Yet it is obvious
that outward manifestations were involved in view of Simon's aston-

---

[9]See Dunn, *Baptism*, pp. 55-72. He suggests that the Samaritans were not
Christians because they had not received the Spirit (p. 68). He also lists five
ways of understanding the reception of the Spirit by the Samaritans when
Peter and John laid hands on them: 1) they had already received the Spirit,
but were now receiving the spiritual gifts, 2) they experienced a second
reception of the Spirit, 3) the reception of the Spirit came only because of
the laying on of hands, 4) the distinction between receiving the Spirit
through baptism and through laying on of hands was Luke's, but was
contrary to the facts, and 5) God's sovereignty determined that sometimes
the Spirit was withheld from Christians. He points out the difficulty of each
interpretation, finally settling on a modification of number five. He argues
that the Samaritans were at a unique moment in the history of the church
and at a major turning point in the mission efforts of the church. Thus
God's decision was that the Spirit be given in a way which departed from
the usual pattern.

[10]Lake and Cadbury, p. 93.

[11]Polhill, pp. 217-218.

[12]Reese, pp. 323-324.

ished reaction (8:18). As a matter of fact, the outward manifestations described here sound very similar to the activities on the Day
of Pentecost (2:2ff), prompting some to refer to this event as the
"Samaritan Pentecost."

The explanation which best harmonizes with the data in Acts, as
well as other New Testament references,[13] is that the believers
received the Spirit when they were baptized. Then the apostles went
to Samaria to lay hands upon the new converts so that the spiritual
gifts might be conferred upon them.[14] But it is important for believers to remember the words of Jesus about the Holy Spirit—"the
wind blows wherever it pleases . . . so it is with everyone born of the
Spirit" (John 3:8).

4. Peter's Condemnation of Simon's Offer
to Pay for the Holy Spirit (8:18-24)

[18]When Simon saw that the Spirit was given at the laying on of
the apostles' hands, he offered them money [19]and said, "Give me
also this ability so that everyone on whom I lay my hands may
receive the Holy Spirit." [20]Peter answered: "May your money
perish with you, because you thought you could buy the gift of
God with money! [21]You have no part or share in this ministry,
because your heart is not right before God. [22]Repent of this
wickedness and pray to the Lord. Perhaps he will forgive you for
having such a thought in your heart. [23]For I see that you are full of
bitterness and captive to sin." [24]Then Simon answered, "Pray to
the Lord for me so that nothing you have said may happen to me."

Simon couldn't believe his eyes. His professional instincts as a
magician immediately were piqued. He could only imagine what a

---

[13]Acts 9:17-18; 19:1-7; 1 Cor 6:11; 12:13; John 3:5; Titus 3:5; 1 Tim 4:14;
2 Tim 1:6.

[14]The laying on of hands is found in the Old Testament when the patriarch Jacob blessed his grandsons (Gen 48:13-20) and when Joshua became
the successor of Moses (Num 27:23). In the New Testament the laying on
of hands is found in connection with the reception of the gifts of the Spirit,
but also the ordination or commissioning of leaders (Acts 6:6; 13:3).

boost to his reputation this power to pass along the gifts of the Spirit might be. If only he had the ability to lay his hands on someone and transfer to them such wonderful power, it would be worth a fortune. ·

Simon offered Peter money to purchase what he may have considered a trade secret. Peter was not amused. He responded with one of the harshest replies ever directed toward a Christian by an apostle. His words may be understood either as a pronouncement (in the form of a curse)[15] or as a prediction that such an attitude would lead Simon to condemnation and destruction. After all, greed had been the downfall of such New Testament people as Judas (1:18), and Ananias and Sapphira (5:1-11).

Peter was not concerned only with condemning Simon's behavior. He also commanded him to repent. Simon was "full of bitterness," a phrase translated "bitter poison" in Deuteronomy 29:18, and a "captive to sin." Though Peter does not say that this means Simon was never converted in the first place, he leaves no doubt that in the present condition Simon had "no part or share (κλῆρος, klēros) in this ministry." The latter phrase seems to exclude Simon from the hope of any inheritance among the saints.[16]

Peter's words do not necessarily imply that Simon will have trouble getting God to grant him forgiveness. The NIV translates the phrase "perhaps" God will forgive. This expression, while indicating that God's forgiveness cannot be taken for granted, implies nonetheless that even this serious sin can be pardoned. Simon's response may represent a repentant spirit, though such an interpretation is not demanded.

5. The Return of the Apostles to Jerusalem (8:25)

[25]When they had testified and proclaimed the word of the Lord, Peter and John returned to Jerusalem, preaching the gospel in many Samaritan villages.

---

[15]See Moulton, Howard, Turner, *Grammar*, 3:122.
[16]See Deut 12:12; 14:27; Acts 20:32; Rom 8:17; 1 Pet 1:4.

Luke's account of the apostles' work in Samaria comes to an end with this summary statement. Their service as "witnesses" (1:8) is again alluded to here. They "testified" and "proclaimed" the gospel. On the way back to Jerusalem, Peter and John even continued the ministry to the Samaritans by preaching in their villages. No longer would there be any barriers to having these people reached with the gospel.

This mention of John is the final one by name in Acts. The focus shifts from the twelve and Jerusalem to the ministries of other key servants in the spread of the gospel, including Philip, Barnabas, Paul, and others.

6. Philip and the Conversion of the Ethiopian (8:26-40)

[26]Now an angel of the Lord said to Philip, "Go south to the road—the desert road—that goes down from Jerusalem to Gaza." [27]So he started out, and on his way he met an Ethiopian[a] eunuch, an important official in charge of all the treasury of Candace, queen of the Ethiopians. This man had gone to Jerusalem to worship, [28]and on his way home was sitting in his chariot reading the book of Isaiah the prophet. [29]The Spirit told Philip, "Go to that chariot and stay near it." [30]Then Philip ran up to the chariot and heard the man reading Isaiah the prophet. "Do you understand what you are reading?" Philip asked. [31]"How can I," he said, "unless someone explains it to me?" So he invited Philip to come up and sit with him. [32]The eunuch was reading this passage of Scripture: "He was led like a sheep to the slaughter, and as a lamb before the shearer is silent, so he did not open his mouth. [33]In his humiliation he was deprived of justice. Who can speak of his descendants? For his life was taken from the earth."[b] [34]The eunuch asked Philip, "Tell me, please, who is the prophet talking about, himself or someone else?" [35]Then Philip began with that very passage of Scripture and told him the good news about Jesus. [36]As they traveled along the road, they came to some water and the eunuch said, "Look, here is water. Why shouldn't I be baptized?"[c] [38]And he gave orders to stop the chariot. Then both Philip and the eunuch went down into the water and Philip

baptized him. [39]**When they came up out of the water, the Spirit of the Lord suddenly took Philip away, and the eunuch did not see him again, but went on his way rejoicing. [40]Philip, however, appeared at Azotus and traveled about, preaching the gospel in all the towns until he reached Caesarea.**

[a]*27 That is, from the upper Nile region.*   [b]*33 Isaiah 53:7,8*   [c]*36 Some late manuscripts baptized?" [37]Philip said, "If you believe with all your heart, you may." The eunuch answered, "I believe that Jesus Christ is the Son of God."*

After concluding his preaching to the Samaritans, Philip now heard from "an angel of the Lord." Another occasion for preaching was about to take place, this time with a foreigner from far to the south. Philip was commanded by the Spirit[17] to go south to the road which ran from Jerusalem to Gaza, a road that Luke notes was "a desert (ἔρημος, *erēmos*) road," meaning that it was not heavily traveled. Two such roads are possible references here—one which ran south out of Jerusalem to Hebron and Birosaba and on to Gaza, and the other one which ran southwest to Eleutheropolis and then to Gaza.

When Philip reached this road he met an Ethiopian who was an official in the court of Candace. Ethiopia was the ancient Nubian empire, located on the Nile River, just south of the first cataract at Aswan in Northern Africa. The name Candace was a dynastic title used frequently of the queen mother who was placed in charge of the secular duties of the king. Thus the man met by Philip held an important position.

The Ethiopian is also described as a "eunuch." Such a description does not necessarily amount to a comment on his physical condition. The use of actual eunuchs for palace duties was so common in the ancient world that even those officials of normal physical condition could be called eunuchs.

On the other hand, the fact that Luke calls the Ethiopian both a eunuch and "an important official in charge of all the treasury" may be an indication that the man was a eunuch physically. Such a conclusion is strengthened by the fact that Luke frequently notes the physical condition of those introduced into the record.[18] The

---

[17]Shepard discusses the Spirit's role in directing Philip's preaching in this situation (*Life*, pp. 83-85).

[18]See Luke 5:12; 9:39; 13:11; Acts 3:2,7; 28:8.

condition of the eunuch would have served as a barrier of sorts in his worship at the temple.[19] He would have been quite ready to hear of a Jesus who was humiliated in Jerusalem, but opened the door of fellowship for all believers.

Whether the Ethiopian was a Jew or Gentile, Luke does not say.[20] Northern Africa had a wealth of Jewish communities whose religious life was centered around the synagogue. In Acts 10 Cornelius will be introduced into the account as a man who was "God-fearing" (φοβούμενος τὸν θεὸν, *phoboumenos ton theon*). This technical term for a Gentile loosely connected to the Jewish synagogue is not used of the Ethiopian, a point which would have clearly defined him as Gentile.

Philip found the Ethiopian sitting in his "chariot" (ἅρμα, *harma*), a vehicle which looked more like an ox cart or covered wagon. It was a form of travel that averaged only ten to fifteen miles a day, allowing plenty of time for reading. Philip overheard him reading from a scroll of Isaiah[21] and drew near at the command of the Spirit.

Exhibiting an eagerness unusual for Jewish men, Philip ran to the side of the wagon to ask the Ethiopian if he understood the passage. Receiving an invitation to explain the Scripture, Philip began "with that very passage" and told the Ethiopian "the good news about Jesus." The Ethiopian's question focused on the identity of the one suffering.

The passage came from the Septuagint version of Isaiah 53:7-8 and described the suffering Servant of the Lord. He would be humiliated and treated unjustly, yet would not speak out in his own defense. The difficult words "Who can speak of his descendants?" probably have reference to the fact that his life would be taken

---

[19]Deut 23:1 placed restrictions on anyone "who has been emasculated by crushing or cutting." Bruce notes that the removal of this ban may be foreshadowed in Isa 56:3-5 (p. 175).

[20]Polhill takes the eunuch to be a Gentile (p. 224). Hubbard thinks that Luke deliberately leaves the eunuch's religious background ambiguous so as not to preempt the conversion of Cornelius in Acts 10. See his "Commissioning Accounts," *Perspectives on Luke-Acts*, p. 196.

[21]Reading was often done aloud in the ancient world (Polhill, p. 224). The fact that the Ethiopian possessed a scroll of Isaiah may also indicate that he was Jewish rather than Gentile.

prematurely, leaving him with no possibility of producing descendants — a point which may have spoken directly to the Ethiopian in his condition. Bruce states that there is no evidence that the Suffering Servant of Isaiah 53:7-8 had been identified with the Davidic Messiah before the time of Jesus.[22] Philip's contact with the Ethiopian is a demonstration that the apostles and early Christians saw a definite connection and spoke of it in their efforts in evangelism.

As they were traveling, they came to a place with water and the Ethiopian asked about being baptized. Evidently Philip's way of preaching Jesus included the need for baptism. As is noted in the NIV text, the response of Philip and the confession of the Ethiopian recorded in 8:37 lack solid manuscript support, though the conversation may well accord with the dynamics of the situation.

The orders of the Ethiopian that the vehicle be stopped indicate that an attendant was driving, and suggest a royal retinue of servants was probably at hand. Nevertheless, the Ethiopian got out of his wagon and "went down into the water" with Philip. This language gives the picture of an immersion, a method of baptism which also suits the meaning of the verb βαπτίζω (baptizō, to immerse). Several suggestions have been made concerning the location of this baptism, among which are the site known as "the spring of Philip" at Ein Dirweh north of Hebron, the Wadi el Hasi north of Gaza, or Ein Yael.[23]

When they came up out of the water, the Spirit again took control of the situation. The language describes a supernatural removal of Philip from the presence of the Ethiopian who went on his way rejoicing. Philip later continued his ministry twenty miles north in Azotus, the Old Testament city of Ashdod, working his way toward Caesarea, Herod's lavish city by the sea.

---

[22]Bruce, p. 176.
[23]See Yehudah Rapuano, "Did Philip Baptize the Eunuch at Ein Yael?" BAR (1990): 44-49.

ACTS 9

C. THE CONVERSION OF SAUL OF TARSUS (9:1-31)

1. The Expedition of Saul to Damascus (9:1-2)

[1]Meanwhile, Saul was still breathing out murderous threats against the Lord's disciples. He went to the high priest [2]and asked him for letters to the synagogues in Damascus, so that if he found any there who belonged to the Way, whether men or women, he might take them as prisoners to Jerusalem.

Luke now continues the story of Saul, which began in his introductory words in 8:3: "Saul began to destroy the church." So crucial is Paul's conversion to the story of the early church and the spread of the gospel, that Luke repeats the full record of Saul's conversion three times in Acts. No event is given more attention.

This account of Saul's conversion appears also in 22:3-21 and 26:4-20. Differences in the accounts are obvious, though the major facts of the event are present in each of the them.[1] In each case

---

[1]The reason for the variations will be discussed in later chapters. Munck reflects on the variations in *Paul*, pp. 13-20. He also compares the details in Acts with those in Gal 1. The differences are not limited to wording. In some cases the substance of the accounts also varies. As far as the sources used by Luke for these accounts, A.T. Robertson thinks that Luke received information from Paul himself. See his *Luke the Historian in Light of Research* (Edinburgh: T & T Clark, 1920), pp. 80-85. Other scholars have proposed a variety of sources. See Dupont, *Sources*, pp. 26-28; 53-71. Some scholars argue that Luke inserts some of this material between 8:4 and 11:19 in order to impose a scheme by which the gospel is preached first in Jerusalem and then to the Gentiles (see 1:8). Other scholars see Luke's

Luke presents the story in a way which suits the purpose of the situation. All three passages, however, tell the story of a Jewish leader[2] whose mind and heart were filled with a rage against Christians which drove him to great lengths in crushing the life from this new movement.

The persecutor's condition is described as "breathing out (ἐμπνέων, *empneōn*) murderous threats," a phrase which means that "threatening and murder were the atmosphere which he breathed and by which and in he lived."[3] This rage had already been evident in his consent in Stephen's death. Now he was pursuing new targets for his wrath, not necessarily to commit murder, but to bring prisoners who might have to face death.

One avenue available to him was hunting down Christians who had fled to other cities from Jerusalem (see 8:1). To gain authority for this pursuit, Saul went to the high priest, probably still Caiaphas, and received letters addressed to the synagogues in Damascus. Scholars have spent much time debating the issue of these letters. The question is whether any evidence supports a situation in which the Sanhedrin had authority over synagogues so far from home.[4]

The point may be moot, however, in view of the fact that Luke does not say that the letters were papers of extradition. The letters may simply have been letters introducing Paul and his mission, as well as recommendations that such Jews be handed over to him. Such letters would carry no official authority to enforce the arrests.

Believers are referred to as "the Way," a designation which may be traced to the words of Jesus (see Matt 7:13; John 14:6).[5] The

description as an accurate representation of events (see Wilson, *Gentile Mission*, pp. 151-153).

[2]Munck notes that in this account no "description of Paul as a Jew" is given (such as in 22:3), though it is mentioned that he was zealous in persecuting Christians (*Paul*, pp. 13-14).

[3]Rienecker, p. 280.

[4]For a summary of the debate see Haenchen, pp. 320-321.

[5]This designation for Christians is found in Acts 16:17; 18:25-26; 19:9,23; 22:4; 24:14,22. Paul Minear traces this concept back to Jesus and then to such Old Testament references as Deut 20:19 and Jer 21:8. See his *Images of the Church in the New Testament* (Philadelphia: Westminster, 1977), p. 148. See also Flew, *Jesus*, pp. 113-115. Conzelmann notes that the analogies from Qumran are not quite parallel (p. 71).

irony is that Saul was about to see the Christ while "on the way" to the city of Damascus.

2. The Light and Voice from Heaven (9:3-7)

[3]**As he neared Damascus on his journey, suddenly a light from heaven flashed around him. [4]He fell to the ground and heard a voice say to him, "Saul, Saul, why do you persecute me?" [5]"Who are you, Lord?" Saul asked. "I am Jesus, whom you are persecuting," he replied. [6]"Now get up and go into the city, and you will be told what you must do." [7]The men traveling with Saul stood there speechless; they heard the sound but did not see anyone.**

Saul was not far from the city gates of Damascus when the event occurred which changed his life.[6] Damascus was a six-day journey on foot from Jerusalem (about 150 miles). As the small group of travelers walked nearer the city, a brilliant light flashed from the sky, shining all around (περιήστραψεν, *periēstrapsen*) Saul. The suddenness and the overwhelming brightness of the light forced him to his knees. At the same moment a voice from heaven addressed Saul.[7] It was the voice of Christ which challenged him to account for his actions, especially in view of the fact that the persecuting of Christians amounted to the persecuting of Christ.

It may well be that this moment finds expression later in Paul's letter to the Corinthians: "God, who said, 'Let light shine out of darkness,' made his light shine in our hearts to give us the light of the glory of God in the face of Christ'" (2 Cor 4:6).[8] At any rate,

---

[6]For the view that Saul was converted in this moment on the Damascus Road see the discussion by Dunn, *Baptism*, pp. 73-78. Dunn argues that the revelation on the Damascus Road, the three days of fasting and prayer, and the appearance of Ananias to administer baptism should all be viewed as a single event.

[7]Munck notes that this brief exchange between Paul and the Lord are the only words in the story that show verbatim agreement in all three accounts (*Paul*, p. 15).

[8]Shepard describes Paul as a man in spiritual vacillation. He was "in a disturbed state of mind," and after "seven days of reflection upon the bloody scene of Stephen's martyrdom," nothing could "bring rest to his

Paul was convinced that he had been permitted to see the resurrected Christ, just as the other apostles had seen him (1 Cor 15:3-8).

Luke makes it clear that Saul was the only one of the travelers to experience this manifestation of Christ. Saul's response to the heavenly vision was to ask, "Who are you, Lord (κύριε, *kyrie*)?" As Bruce notes, the use of "Lord" in this context may not be more than a respectful "sir."[9] But Saul quickly discovered that he was being confronted by one with more authority than he had ever met in his life. Those traveling with Saul did not understand any of this conversation, a point which fits quite well with the language in 22:9.

3. The Entrance of Saul into Damascus (9:8-9)

[8]Saul got up from the ground, but when he opened his eyes he could see nothing. So they led him by the hand into Damascus. [9]For three days he was blind, and did not eat or drink anything.

Though Saul's companions did not see the vision of Christ, they could certainly verify its effects. The immediate effects were on Saul's physical condition. He was blind. Humbled and helpless, his traveling friends led him by the hand the rest of the way to the city. Beyond blindness, he was "three days" in fasting, indicating how completely devastated was his spirit. This period was likely a time for much reflection on what he had witnessed and what it meant regarding his place among the people of God.

---

soul." Even the words of Gamaliel that he might be "fighting against God" (5:39) were weighing heavily upon his heart and soul (*Life*, p. 62). Not only is there no evidence for this kind of psychoanalytical picture of Saul, several points in the text contradict it (see 23:1; 24:16; Phil 3:6). See also the essay by Krister Stendahl, "The Apostle Paul and the Introspective Conscience of the West," in *Paul among Jews and Gentiles* (Philadelphia: Fortress, 1983), pp. 78-96.

[9]Bruce, pp. 182-183.

4. The Commissioning of
Ananias to Visit Saul (9:10-16)

[10]In Damascus there was a disciple named Ananias. The Lord called to him in a vision, "Ananias!" "Yes, Lord," he answered. [11]The Lord told him, "Go to the house of Judas on Straight Street and ask for a man from Tarsus named Saul, for he is praying. [12]In a vision he has seen a man named Ananias come and place his hands on him to restore his sight." [13]"Lord," Ananias answered, "I have heard many reports about this man and all the harm he has done to your saints in Jerusalem. [14]And he has come here with authority from the chief priests to arrest all who call on your name." [15]But the Lord said to Ananias, "Go! This man is my chosen instrument to carry my name before the Gentiles and their kings and before the people of Israel. [16]I will show him how much he must suffer for my name."

The next servant whom the Lord calls is Ananias. From the information given here it appears that Ananias was not one of the believers who had fled Jerusalem when the persecution of Christians began (8:1). He "had heard many reports," but apparently had not experienced the crisis directly.

Nevertheless, Ananias was well informed about the conditions in Jerusalem. He knew that believers were being persecuted and that Saul had been given "authority from the chief priests" to arrest Christians who had fled from Jerusalem to Damascus. It is not surprising that he hesitated in going to see Saul.

God's will overruled Ananias. He commanded him to go to the place in Damascus where Saul was staying—a place on "Straight Street" at the house of a man named Judas, unknown anywhere else in the New Testament. In ancient times Straight Street ran east and west through the city and was lined with colonnades on both sides with large gates at either end. The street is still visible today, though its modern site is farther north. The objective of Ananias was to lay his hands on Saul so that he could receive his sight.

The reluctance of Ananias disappeared when God told him that Saul would serve as a chosen instrument in taking the gospel to the Gentiles, as well as the people of Israel. The mention of "kings" of the Gentiles foreshadows accounts coming in Acts in which the Apostle was arrested and forced to defend himself before royal tribunals. Later in Galatians, the Apostle reflected on the fact that he had received a call directly from God to preach the gospel (1:15). His service would bring on him the same kind of suffering he had inflicted on others.

5. The Visit from Ananias (9:17-19a)

[17]Then Ananias went to the house and entered it. Placing his hands on Saul, he said, "Brother Saul, the Lord—Jesus, who appeared to you on the road as you were coming here—has sent me so that you may see again and be filled with the Holy Spirit." [18]Immediately, something like scales fell from Saul's eyes, and he could see again. He got up and was baptized, [19]and after taking some food, he regained his strength.

Perhaps reluctantly (but still obediently), Ananias went to the house to find Saul. He placed his hands on Saul and spoke to him in the name of the Lord Jesus. He began by referring to Saul as "brother," a term that surely has no implication for Saul's spiritual condition since it is used in several contexts where such an implication would be out of place (see 2:29; 22:1; 23:1).[10]

Two objectives were now stated for the arrival of Ananias. He had been sent by the "Jesus who appeared" on the road. His purpose was that Saul would be able to see again and also that he might receive the Holy Spirit. If these were the objectives of Ananias it speaks to the importance of baptism in the reception of the Spirit. The first objective was accomplished when Ananias placed his hands on Saul and "something like scales" fell from his eyes. This scale-like or flaky substance may have been similar to fish scales.

The second objective, the reception of the Holy Spirit, is not described. Rather, the next action described is that Saul got up and "was baptized." Apparently it was in his baptism that Saul received the Spirit.[11]

---

[10]Dunn, *Baptism*, p. 74.
[11]See notes on 8:16.

The conversion of Saul has been the subject of much discussion in the past few decades. Was he reacting against the Judaism he came to see as legalistic and ritualistic? Was he experiencing guilt with regard to his ability to live up to the Law of Moses? Or was he simply convinced that in God's sending of Christ was the message that salvation cannot come through any means other than Christ?[12]

6. The Preaching of Saul in Damascus (9:19b-22)

[19]**Saul spent several days with the disciples in Damascus. [20]At once he began to preach in the synagogues that Jesus is the Son of God. [21]All those who heard him were astonished and asked, "Isn't he the man who raised havoc in Jerusalem among those who call on this name? And hasn't he come here to take them as prisoners to the chief priests?" [22]Yet Saul grew more and more powerful and baffled the Jews living in Damascus by proving that Jesus is the Christ.[a]**

[a]*22 Or Messiah*

What Saul did next demonstrated the depth of his conversion. After spending several days with the disciples in Damascus, he took his new faith to the synagogues. The content of his preaching was that "Jesus is the Son of God." Here, in the only use in Acts of the title "the Son of God," is the summary of Saul's message.[13] Quite probably his method included calling attention to Old Testament passages which described the work of the Messiah.

Astonishment was the response of the crowd. The message was not as shocking as the one delivering it. Those who heard Saul were very much aware of his former hatred of Christians. To them it was inconceivable that he was now preaching it with enthusiasm. It was obvious to them that something very unusual had taken place in his life.

In Galatians 1:15 the Apostle comments on this period of his new Christian life. In defending himself against those who argued

---

[12]For a discussion of this debate see Joseph Plevnik, *What Are They Saying about Paul?* (New York: Paulist, 1986), pp. 5-27.

[13]This summary of the Apostle's doctrine suits the language of such Pauline passages as Gal 1:16.

that he was not a true apostle, but got his authority from Jerusalem, he contended that he did not go to Jerusalem as soon as he was converted. Rather, he went into Arabia—a point which Luke does not mention here. Nothing that Luke says here about the early period of Saul's life in Christ stands in direct conflict with the account in Galatians.

7. The Escape of Saul from Damascus (9:23-25)

[23]After many days had gone by, the Jews conspired to kill him, [24]but Saul learned of their plan. Day and night they kept close watch on the city gates in order to kill him. [25]But his followers took him by night and lowered him in a basket through an opening in the wall.

Saul's ministry became so controversial that he was driven out of Damascus. "After many days" leaves room for Paul's own description of this period of time in Galatians 1:17-18. In that passage he explained that he spent a total of three years in Damascus and Arabia immediately after his conversion. The kingdom of Arabia (also known as Nabatea) extended north and east as far as Damascus and southward as far as the Arabian Gulf. As the Apostle mentioned in 2 Corinthians 11:32, Aretas IV was king during this time (9 B.C. to A.D. 40).

When Saul returned to Damascus, Aretas IV sought to have him arrested.[14] The arrest would have led to his execution, perhaps by mob action, at the hands of the Jews of Damascus. Saul's only escape was to get help from friends who lived on the city wall. They lowered him down in a basket one night through an opening in the wall and he escaped to Jerusalem.

---

[14]The problem of the jurisdiction of Aretas IV over Damascus has generated some discussion over this verse. Arguments have been made by Lake (*Beginnings* 5:193) and Haenchen (330-336) which suggest that Aretas IV did not control Damascus at this time. Even so, however, he could have deployed forces (possibly even covertly) to take Paul captive. Robert Jewett discusses the best date for this event and arrives at a date of between A.D. 37 and 39. See his *A Chronology of Paul's Life* (Philadelphia: Fortress, 1979), pp. 30-33. See also the comments by Polhill, p. 242.

8. The Ministry of Saul in Jerusalem
and His Departure for Tarsus (9:26-30)

[26]When he came to Jerusalem, he tried to join the disciples, but they were all afraid of him, not believing that he really was a disciple. [27]But Barnabas took him and brought him to the apostles. He told them how Saul on his journey had seen the Lord and that the Lord had spoken to him, and how in Damascus he had preached fearlessly in the name of Jesus. [28]So Saul stayed with them and moved about freely in Jerusalem, speaking boldly in the name of the Lord. [29]He talked and debated with the Grecian Jews, but they tried to kill him. [30]When the brothers learned of this, they took him down to Caesarea and sent him off to Tarsus.

The period of time covered in this part of Luke's account is mentioned by the Apostle Paul in Galatians 1:13–2:10.[15] Finding the harmony in the two accounts presents some problems. Doing so requires that the purpose of both Luke and Galatians be kept in mind.

Luke's summary of Saul's days in Jerusalem is quite brief and very general. When Saul arrived in Jerusalem, he wanted to be a part of the fellowship of believers, but they were, quite naturally, afraid of him. Could his "conversion" be a hoax which would give him just the opportunity he needed to arrest them?

Barnabas, true to his name ("Son of Encouragement"), intervened and convinced the believers that Saul's conversion was authentic. How Barnabas came by his information is not mentioned. At any rate, he showed himself very well informed concerning the events on the Damascus Road and the subsequent ministry of Saul in Damascus. Remarkably, these saints, who had suffered as a result of Saul's rage against the church, opened their hearts and welcomed him into their fellowship.

Luke's abbreviated comment on this period is to say that Saul

---

[15]The fact that Luke's summary bears similarities to Paul's in Galatians causes Morton Enslin to conclude that Luke used Paul's letters as one of his sources for Acts. See his *Reapproaching Paul* (Philadelphia: Westminster, 1987), pp. 40-43.

stayed with them in Jerusalem and "moved about freely," conducting his ministry in the name of the Lord. Such a summary would seem to indicate that Saul got very well acquainted with the apostles in Jerusalem.

The account in Galatians intends to show, however, that this was not the case. The Apostle states emphatically that he did not become acquainted with the other apostles during this period. He says that besides Peter, he "saw none of the other apostles—only James, the Lord's brother" (1:18-19). In addition he says, "I was personally unknown to the churches of Judea that are in Christ" (1:23).

Though these accounts seem to contradict each other, what must be remembered is that Luke's description is intentionally general. He was not concerned with the details of Saul's relationship with the other apostles. He does not even mention the matter directly. On the other hand, in Galatians Paul's objective is to refute accusations from the Judaizers that he was merely a pawn in the hands of the other apostles. For this reason, he writes in specific detail about his limited contacts with Jerusalem.

Beyond this observation, the details in both accounts which correspond argue for the credibility of both accounts. Both mention the visit, and place it early in the ministry of the Apostle. Both mention contact with the believers in Jerusalem. Both note that Saul was known for his persecution of the believers. It seems unfair to accuse Luke of historical inaccuracy at this point.[16]

Saul's preaching apparently picked up where Stephen's left off— debating with the "Grecian Jews." Once again they were offended at the teaching, and once again sought to bring to an end the life of the preacher. This time, however, Saul's brothers in the faith responded to their attempts at murder by moving Saul to Caesarea (by the Sea) and placing him on a ship headed for Tarsus, his hometown. Here the record leaves him until Barnabas will bring him back to Antioch (11:25f), some ten years later.

---

[16]For a discussion of scholars who have found reasons here for doubting Luke's accuracy, see Haenchen, pp. 333-336. Munck, for example, writes "when Acts 9:26-30 speaks of Paul's first visit to Jerusalem after the Damascus call, and describes how Barnabas brings him into touch with the apostles, that description contradicts Paul's own account in Gal. 1.18f" (*Paul*, p. 80).

D. PEACE AND PROSPERITY FOR THE CHURCH (9:31)

³¹**Then the church throughout Judea, Galilee and Samaria enjoyed a time of peace. It was strengthened; and encouraged by the Holy Spirit, it grew in numbers, living in the fear of the Lord.**

Luke now adds a summary statement about the progress of the church in the region[17] on which he focuses in chapters eight through twelve. The persecution which had begun after the martyrdom of Stephen now came to a close (see 8:1), as Bruce says, "with the conversion and departure of the leading persecutor."

The singular "church" is used to speak of the body of Christ as a whole in this region, a body consisting, of course, of individual congregations. Only here and possibly in 20:28 does such an application of "church" occur in Acts.[18]

E. PETER'S MINISTRY IN WESTERN JUDEA (9:32-43)

1. The Ministry at Lydda: Healing of Aeneas (9:32-35)

³²**As Peter traveled about the country, he went to visit the saints in Lydda. ³³There he found a man named Aeneas, a paralytic who had been bedridden for eight years. ³⁴"Aeneas," Peter said to him, "Jesus Christ heals you. Get up and take care of your mat." Immediately Aeneas got up. ³⁵All those who lived in Lydda and Sharon saw him and turned to the Lord.**

Now the spotlight turns to ministry accomplished in western Judea. Peter was mentioned last in 8:25 when he went back to Jerusalem after visiting Samaria with John. Now that the persecution of the church in this region had ceased, Peter's ministry picked

---

[17]Davies notes the absence of references to Galilean Christianity in Acts and gives some attention to the origins of the church in this region (*Land*, pp. 421-425). These summaries appear frequently in Acts. See the note on 12:24.

[18]Bruce, p. 196.

up again. Lydda was some twenty-five miles northwest of Jerusalem. How the church was established there is unclear, but Luke refers to them as "saints" (ἁγίους, *hagious*), a rare term for Christians in Acts (see 9:13, 32, and 41 where it is translated "believers" in the NIV).[19]

Peter's preaching tour brought him into contact with a man named Aeneas who had been paralyzed for eight years. He was probably one of the Christians in Lydda, and Peter may well have been invited to his home for the purpose of prayer and healing. At any rate, Peter spoke the command to Aeneas, which was not unlike the command Jesus had spoken to the paralyzed man lowered through the roof of the house in Capernaum (Mark 2:11). Peter first made it clear that the healing came from the Lord when he said, "Jesus Christ heals you." Then Peter told him to "get up and take care of his mat," a command which probably meant that he should fold it up and put it away. After eight years Aeneas got up immediately and did just that.

The news traveled far and wide, reaching throughout Lydda and also Sharon, the fifty-mile plain stretching along the coast from Joppa to Mt. Carmel. Anyone who saw him was convinced that the claims of the gospel were valid and "turned to the Lord."[20]

2. The Ministry at Joppa:
The Raising of Dorcas (9:36-43)

[36]**In Joppa there was a disciple named Tabitha (which, when translated, is Dorcas[a]), who was always doing good and helping the poor. [37]About that time she became sick and died, and her body was washed and placed in an upstairs room. [38]Lydda was near Joppa; so when the disciples heard that Peter was in Lydda, they sent two men to him and urged him, "Please come at once!" [39]Peter went with them, and when he arrived he was taken upstairs**

---

[19]Paul, however, uses the term often for believers (see Rom 1:7; 8:7; 1 Cor 6:2; Eph 1:15,18; 6:18; Phlm 7). The term's basic meaning is one set apart for the Lord or made holy.

[20]Dupont notes that this phrase was employed by early Christians "to describe what happens at the conversion of pagans." It is an "older Jewish expression" which carries the idea of forsaking idols in favor of the Lord. See his *Salvation*, pp. 70-72.

to the room. All the widows stood around him, crying and showing him the robes and other clothing that Dorcas had made while she was still with them. ⁴⁰Peter sent them all out of the room; then he got down on his knees and prayed. Turning toward the dead woman, he said, "Tabitha, get up." She opened her eyes, and seeing Peter she sat up. ⁴¹He took her by the hand and helped her to her feet. Then he called the believers and the widows and presented her to them alive. ⁴²This became known all over Joppa, and many people believed in the Lord. ⁴³Peter stayed in Joppa for some time with a tanner named Simon.

ᵃ36 Both *Tabitha* (Aramaic) and *Dorcas* (Greek) mean *gazelle*.

Peter's ministry stretched closer to Caesarea as events unfolded rapidly. A "female disciple" (μαθήτρια, *mathētria*) named Tabitha (Aramaic; Dorcas in Greek) fell ill in Joppa, the main port city of Judea, located about ten miles northwest of Lydda. When she died, her body was washed in preparation for burial (as was customary among Jews) and was placed in an upstairs room. Often in Palestine, burial took place the same day as the death. On this occasion it seems that the family and friends delayed the burial so that Peter could be summoned.

The messengers were sent to Lydda, a journey which would take most of a day. They found Peter and he accompanied them to Joppa and went immediately to the house where Tabitha's body lay.

Her reputation for helping the poor was demonstrated by the pathetic scene in which the widows of the town[21] wept at the side of the body, and showed the robes and garments they wore, which had been made by Tabitha. Widows in first-century Palestine were often the most helpless of citizens. Evidently the ministry of Tabitha had furnished for them even their necessary clothing.

Just as Jesus had raised the daughter of Jairus (Luke 8:49-56; Mark 5:35-43), Peter approached the body of Tabitha with the same objective. Sending the spectators out of the room as Jesus had done, Peter got on his knees to pray. He then gave the command to

---

[21]Leonard Swidler thinks that Tabitha may have been the leader of an "order" or "society" of widows. See his *Biblical Affirmations of Woman* (Philadelphia: Westminster, 1979), pp. 304-305.

Tabitha's body in words so similar to those of Jesus, the difference is only one letter. Jesus had commanded the little girl in Aramaic, "Little girl, arise" (*Talitha koum*). Peter's words were *Tabitha koum*. Those who were readers of Luke's two volumes would not have missed the similarity.[22]

At the sound of his command she came back to life and he presented her to the believers alive. This news could not help but draw attention, and Peter's ministry continued there for some time.

Peter lived with a tanner named Simon whose house was by the sea. Such a location would be helpful to tanners since their work involved sea water. The location was also helpful to the townspeople since a tanner's work involved the defilement of dead animals and the presence of skins created an odor that could not be hidden. Beyond these things, the mention of this house as Peter's temporary residence is important in that it may indicate that Peter was already becoming receptive to the abrogation of the Jewish laws of uncleanness. Living with one who earned his living by handling dead animals was a radical step for a rigid observer of the laws of purity.

---

[22]Acts also contains a resurrection performed by Paul near the end of his ministry. See 20:7-12. For further parallels with Luke's Gospel see Talbert, *Literary Patterns*, pp. 16,19. Compare also Old Testament resurrections, such as those of Elijah and Elisha (1 Kgs 17:17-24; 2 Kgs 4:32-37).

ACTS 10

F. THE CONVERSION OF
THE FIRST GENTILES (10:1–11:18)

1. The Ministry of Peter at Caesarea (10:1-48)

The Vision Seen by Cornelius (10:1-8)

[1]At Caesarea there was a man named Cornelius, a centurion in what was known as the Italian Regiment. [2]He and all his family were devout and God-fearing; he gave generously to those in need and prayed to God regularly. [3]One day at about three in the afternoon he had a vision. He distinctly saw an angel of God, who came to him and said, "Cornelius!" [4]Cornelius stared at him in fear. "What is it, Lord?" he asked. The angel answered, "Your prayers and gifts to the poor have come up as a memorial offering before God. [5]Now send men to Joppa to bring back a man named Simon who is called Peter. [6]He is staying with Simon the tanner, whose house is by the sea." [7]When the angel who spoke to him had gone, Cornelius called two of his servants and a devout soldier who was one of his attendants. [8]He told them everything that had happened and sent them to Joppa.

Luke now focuses attention on one of the most significant events in all of Acts—the conversion of the first Gentile.[1] Though some

---

[1]Wilson proposes that the mention of Gentile converts in 11:19 should be understood as occurring after the conversion of Cornelius. See his *Gentile Mission*, pp. 151-152. In this way Luke may be seen carrying out his theme

identify the Ethiopian as the first Gentile convert in Acts,[2] the language used of Cornelius sets him apart for this honor.[3] Caesarea was predominantly a Gentile city and the position of Cornelius in the Roman army betrays his Gentile background. The term "God-fearing" (φοβούμενος, *phoboumenos*) also denotes a Gentile because of its technical application to non-Jews who had not become full proselytes.

The issues raised by this event were far-reaching for the church. Would Christianity continue to be a largely Jewish phenomenon, confined for the most part to Palestine? Would believers continue to be dominated by the Jewish notion that salvation must include circumcision and the laws of separation in matters of table fellowship? Luke points to the preaching by Peter to the household of Cornelius as the resounding answer to these questions. As a matter of fact, reference will be made to this event at the conference in Jerusalem (15:6-11) where these very issues will be discussed in detail.

Cornelius lived in Caesarea, a city considered by the Roman administration to be the capital of Judea. Located about thirty miles north of Joppa, this city on the coast had previously been called

---

as presented in 1:8, but also showing accurately the historical progress of the Gospel. Munck emphatically objects to the attempt by Martin Dibelius to distinguish between "the original harmless 'legend' about Cornelius' baptism by the Apostle Peter, and its editing by Luke, who lifts the story into the realm of principles" (*Paul*, p. 228). See also Conzelmann, p. 80. Martin, showing sympathy to the position of Munck, notes nevertheless that this passage highlights "the novelty of grace" which is extended to Gentiles, a point which consists of "the deeper fulfilment [*sic*] of what Peter had barely hinted at in 2:39." This passage demonstrates that "there is no 'most favored nation' clause in God's covenant with his people." See his *Foundations*, 2:101-103. Dunn finds it difficult to believe that Luke could have fabricated such an account (*Jesus*, pp. 152-156). Dupont describes how important this event is in the story of Acts, especially in the development of the theme that salvation is intended for the Gentiles. See his *Salvation*, pp. 24-27.

[2]Polhill, p. 249; Bruce, p. 175.

[3]Haenchen argues that the term "God-fearer" (φοβούμενος) indicates that Cornelius was a Gentile (pp. 313-314,346). Max Wilcox, however, disputes that the Greek term must carry this meaning. See his "The 'God-Fearers' in Acts—A Reconsideration," *JSNT* 13 (1981): 102-122.

Strato's Tower, but was rebuilt by Herod the Great in honor of Augustus Caesar.[4]

As a centurion, Cornelius was considered commander over about a sixth of a regiment. Each Roman legion had about 6,000 men and was divided into ten regiments, sometimes called "cohorts." Cohorts were subdivided into groups of 100. Thus a centurion commanded about 100 men. As Bruce observes, the centurions were considered "the backbone of the Roman army."[5] It was not unusual for a regiment to maintain its individual identity and in the case of "the Italian Regiment,"[6] some inscriptional evidence suggests that this force was an auxiliary division.[7]

His spiritual qualities are described in terms of Jewish piety. He was "devout" (εὐσεβής, eusebēs) and "God-fearing," including such acts of mercy as giving to the needy and also regular prayer.[8] His regular prayers meant that he was in prayer at "three in the afternoon," a customary time for prayer (see 3:1). During this time of prayer Cornelius saw "an angel of God," who spoke his name. The response of Cornelius imitated that of Paul on the road to Damascus (9:5), and the angel continued by explaining that the prayers and acts of benevolence from Cornelius had ascended as a "memorial offering" (μνημόσυνον, mnēmosynon) to God (Lev 2:2). By the standards of some, Cornelius was not a man who needed to be saved.

The command of the angel was that Cornelius send messengers to Joppa and bring Simon Peter to Caesarea. The messengers Cornelius called were trusted attendants. Their means of travel is not specified.

---

[4]For a thorough discussion of the features of the city of Caesarea see Robert Bull, "Caesarea Maritima: The Search for Herod's City," BAR 8 (1982): 24-41; Robert Hohlfelder, "Caesarea beneath the Sea," ibid., 42-47.

[5]Bruce, p. 202. Whether such a division would have been located in Caesarea during the reign of Herod Agrippa (A.D. 41-44) in Palestine is still a matter for debate. Haenchen argues that Luke has read back into the story a situation which existed later in the first century (p. 346, n. 2). But this argument ignores the possibility that this event could be dated before A.D. 41 or that Cornelius may have been a retired centurion living in Caesarea.

[6]Other regiments were known as "the Imperial" or "the Augustan" (27:1). See NIV Study Bible note on Acts 10:1.

[7]Bruce, p. 202.

[8]The only act of Jewish piety not included here is fasting (Polhill, p. 252).

The Vision Seen by Peter (10:9-16)

⁹**About noon the following day as they were on their journey and approaching the city, Peter went up on the roof to pray. ¹⁰He became hungry and wanted something to eat, and while the meal was being prepared, he fell into a trance. ¹¹He saw heaven opened and something like a large sheet being let down to earth by its four corners. ¹²It contained all kinds of four-footed animals, as well as reptiles of the earth and birds of the air. ¹³Then a voice told him, "Get up, Peter. Kill and eat." ¹⁴"Surely not, Lord!" Peter replied. "I have never eaten anything impure or unclean." ¹⁵The voice spoke to him a second time, "Do not call anything impure that God has made clean." ¹⁶This happened three times, and immediately the sheet was taken back to heaven.**

Peter's role in this event began on the roof of Simon's house in Joppa.⁹ He had no idea that the messengers of Cornelius were at that moment drawing near his location. About noon (an hour not usually designated for prayer by the Jews) he was praying. Flat rooftops in Palestine often had awnings for shade, allowing for a peaceful place for meditation, and Peter may have desired such a time and place in view of his ongoing ministry in Joppa. Whether the cloth in this awning had anything to do with Peter's vision is unclear.

While Peter was there he became hungry¹⁰ and a vision from heaven engaged his attention. He "fell into a trance" (ἔκστασις, *ekstasis*) and watched as heaven opened and something like "a large sheet" was being dropped from heaven, held by its four corners. On the sheet Peter saw all kinds of creatures, described in the typical Jewish categories of "four-footed animals," "reptiles of the earth," and "birds of the air" (see Gen 6:20).

Then a voice from heaven commanded Peter to "kill and eat." At once he objected that he could never do such a thing, since he had always observed the laws of purity. Even the mixture of these

---

⁹Hubbard sees in Peter's vision many of the same elements found in other "commissioning accounts" in Luke-Acts. See his "Commissioning Accounts," in *Perspectives*, ed. Talbert, pp. 188-191.

¹⁰The Jews normally ate a light meal in the middle of the morning and a full meal in the later afternoon. Perhaps Peter had missed the first meal.

unclean animals with the clean presented an abomination to him.[11] But the voice persisted with the primary lesson of the vision. He was not to consider anything unclean which had been cleansed.

This vision brings to mind the teaching of Jesus as recorded in Mark 7:14-19. In his debate with the scribes and Pharisees, Jesus had taught that it was not foods taken into the body that caused defilement, but thoughts and words which proceed from the heart and mouth. Mark then adds the comment, "In saying this, Jesus declared all foods 'clean.'" Peter's vision reinforced this teaching of Jesus. But even in Mark 7 the words of Jesus are brought into close connection with attitudes toward people. Just after Jesus made these comments, he healed the daughter of a Gentile woman. Purity regulations about eating were associated with purity regulations in associations with people.[12]

The Arrival at Joppa of Servants Sent by Cornelius (10:17-23a)

[17]**While Peter was wondering about the meaning of the vision, the men sent by Cornelius found out where Simon's house was and stopped at the gate. [18]They called out, asking if Simon who was known as Peter was staying there. [19]While Peter was still thinking about the vision, the Spirit said to him, "Simon, three[a] men are looking for you. [20]So get up and go downstairs. Do not hesitate to go with them, for I have sent them." [21]Peter went down and said to the men, "I'm the one you're looking for. Why have you come?" [22]The men replied, "We have come from Cornelius the centurion. He is a righteous and God-fearing man, who is**

---

[11]The distinction between clean and unclean is given in Lev 11 and concerned itself with those animals which could be used for sacrifice or eating. Domesticated animals were considered clean if they had a divided hoof and chewed their cud.

[12]Bruce thinks the connection came because Gentiles were considered by the Jews to be unclean largely because of what they ate (p. 206). J.J. Scott thinks that the conclusion was reached with a "lesser-to-greater" rationale, which was famous in Rabbinic circles. If God pronounced certain foods unclean, he must also take the same approach to people. See his "The Cornelius Incident in the Light of Its Jewish Setting," *JETS* 34 (1991): 475-484.

respected by all the Jewish people. A holy angel told him to have
you come to his house so that he could hear what you have to
say." [23]Then Peter invited the men into the house to be his guests.

^a*19* One early manuscript *two*; other manuscripts do not have the number.

As if frozen by the vision, Peter remained on the roof "wondering about the meaning" of what he had seen. As the messengers
from Cornelius were arriving, Peter was being instructed by the
Holy Spirit to go down and meet them.

Whether the Spirit spoke to him audibly or with an inner voice
we are not told. What matters is that the Holy Spirit was directing
Peter to welcome Gentiles into the home in which he was staying.
Peter's obedience to the Spirit permitted him to take the first steps
in fulfilling the lesson of the vision.

Descending by the outside stairs, Peter welcomed the messengers. After he asked why they had come, they explained the vision
of Cornelius the day before. As Polhill notes in this section, Luke
may easily have abbreviated his report by simply summarizing the
details here of Cornelius' vision. But each time the details of the
vision and other aspects of the event are repeated their significance
is underscored once again.[13]

The Visit of Peter to the House of Cornelius (10:23b-33)

[23]The next day Peter started out with them, and some of the
brothers from Joppa went along. [24]The following day he arrived in
Caesarea. Cornelius was expecting them and had called together
his relatives and close friends. [25]As Peter entered the house,
Cornelius met him and fell at his feet in reverence. [26]But Peter
made him get up. "Stand up," he said, "I am only a man myself."
[27]Talking with him, Peter went inside and found a large gathering
of people. [28]He said to them: "You are well aware that it is against
our law for a Jew to associate with a Gentile or visit him. But God
has shown me that I should not call any man impure or unclean.
[29]So when I was sent for, I came without raising any objection.

---

[13]Polhill, p. 257.

May I ask why you sent for me?" [30]**Cornelius answered: "Four days ago I was in my house praying at this hour, at three in the afternoon. Suddenly a man in shining clothes stood before me** [31]**and said, 'Cornelius, God has heard your prayer and remembered your gifts to the poor.** [32]**Send to Joppa for Simon who is called Peter. He is a guest in the home of Simon the tanner, who lives by the sea.'** [33]**So I sent for you immediately, and it was good of you to come. Now we are all here in the presence of God to listen to everything the Lord has commanded you to tell us."**

The day after the messengers arrived (two days after the vision of Cornelius), Peter started for Caesarea with both the messengers from Cornelius and several believers from Joppa.[14] The journey took the whole day, requiring a stop overnight. They arrived in Caesarea on the third day after the original vision (or the fourth day if the day of the vision is counted).

Peter's entrance into the house was met with a reverent greeting from Cornelius,[15] which indicates that he understood Peter's arrival to be part of the divine direction related to the vision. Peter was horrified at the gesture, seeing in it too much reverence for a mere man. It may well have been going through his mind that Cornelius' actions represented the spirit of idolatry which Gentiles were all too accustomed to participating in.

When Peter saw the large group of "relatives and close friends" of Cornelius gathered at his house, he immediately raised the issue which stood at the heart of the lesson from his vision in Joppa. Jews considered it unlawful "to associate with a Gentile or visit him." But Peter answered his own observation by recalling the vision of the animals on the sheet. He demonstrated that he had understood the point of the vision when he said that God showed him he should not call "any man impure or unclean." For Peter the summons from Cornelius was the divine invitation to apply directly the truth of the vision.

Cornelius responded by giving Peter the details of his own vision, which Luke again repeats in detail. Then Cornelius offered

---

[14]Acts 11:12 says the number was six.
[15]See other references to this form of greeting in Matt 8:2; 9:18; 15:25; 18:26; 20:20; Luke 8:41; Acts 9:4; 22:7.

his own conclusion of the purposes of God. They were gathered because God had a message to deliver through Peter.

The Sermon by Peter (10:34-43)

[34]Then Peter began to speak: "I now realize how true it is that God does not show favoritism [35]but accepts men from every nation who fear him and do what is right. [36]You know the message God sent to the people of Israel, telling the good news of peace through Jesus Christ, who is Lord of all. [37]You know what has happened throughout Judea, beginning in Galilee after the baptism that John preached—[38]how God anointed Jesus of Nazareth with the Holy Spirit and power, and how he went around doing good and healing all who were under the power of the devil, because God was with him. [39]We are witnesses of everything he did in the country of the Jews and in Jerusalem. They killed him by hanging him on a tree, [40]but God raised him from the dead on the third day and caused him to be seen. [41]He was not seen by all the people, but by witnesses whom God had already chosen—by us who ate and drank with him after he rose from the dead. [42]He commanded us to preach to the people and to testify that he is the one whom God appointed as judge of the living and the dead. [43]All the prophets testify about him that everyone who believes in him receives forgiveness of sins through his name."

Peter now made clear his understanding of the vision. God does not show favoritism (προσωπολήμπτης, *prosōpolēmptēs*). The word literally speaks of an "acceptor of faces"[16] and was used by Peter to refer to a God who did not show preference among nationalities. The particular context of this statement was the Jewish prejudice against Gentiles. God does not show favoritism among nations, though he does favor those "who fear him and do what is right."

---

[16]Rienecker, p. 285. This theme surfaces throughout the Old Testament and Judaism, as well as in such New Testament passages as Rom 2:11; Gal 2:6; Eph 6:9; Jas 2:1. For a thorough study of this important theme see Jouette Bassler, *Divine Impartiality: Paul and a Theological Axiom* (Chico, CA: Scholars Press, 1982).

Peter thus began his sermon by tracing the ministry of Jesus from the baptism by John, to his acts of mercy, healings, and exorcisms, his crucifixion and resurrection. In mentioning the anointing of Jesus with the Holy Spirit, Peter made reference to the Holy Spirit's descending at Jesus' baptism (Luke 3:21-22) and to the words of Jesus himself when he read to the worshipers in the synagogue at Nazareth.[17] Jesus read from Isaiah 61 (see Luke 4:18f) and then applied the passage to himself. The passage begins with the words, "The Spirit of the Sovereign Lord is on me."

The crucifixion is described as "hanging him on a tree." This expression is traced back to Deuteronomy 21:23 and carries with it the idea of suffering under the curse of God.

Again as in previous sermons, Peter presented the two sides of Jesus' crucifixion. Concerning the human side, "they (the Jews in Jerusalem) killed him," but God "raised him from the dead."[18] Beyond the facts about Jesus' ministry, death, and resurrection, Peter also emphasized that the apostles were witnesses of all of these events. As witnesses, Peter focused on the experience of eating and drinking with the risen Lord (see Luke 24:30f; John 21:13-14). These experiences not only stayed in the memories of the apostles, but demonstrated that Jesus was resurrected in bodily form.

Peter also made it clear that the ministry of the apostles was a work of divine origin. They were "commanded" to preach. This explained Peter's visit to the house of Cornelius. God commanded the apostles to preach "to the people,"[19] that is the Jews. But the wider reach of the gospel message included all the living and the dead over whom Jesus has been "appointed as judge."

---

[17]Dupont thinks that Peter's reference to "forgiveness" (ἄφεσις, *aphesis*) may be derived from this quotation from Isaiah which speaks of the "release (ἄφεσις) of captives." See his *Salvation*, p. 143.

[18]See 2:23-24; 3:15; 4:10; 5:30-32. Trites notes that many of the elements found in other addresses by the apostles are found here, including Jesus' appointment by God; his signs, wonders and mighty works; his death and resurrection; the harmony of all these things with Scripture; Christ's exaltation in heaven; and the authority of the apostles as witnesses (*Witness*, p. 143).

[19]Jervell cites this point in Peter's address—a point which seems out of place to a Gentile audience—as an indication of the perception that the mission to Gentiles must begin with the Jews. See his *People of God*, p. 57.

What an exalted position obtained by Christ! He had gone from the cursed cross in Jerusalem to the right hand of God as judge over all the earth. Such authority was his that sinners could find "forgiveness of sins" only through his name.

The Reception of the Holy Spirit by Gentiles (10:44-48)

[44]While Peter was still speaking these words, the Holy Spirit came on all who heard the message. [45]The circumcised believers who had come with Peter were astonished that the gift of the Holy Spirit had been poured out even on the Gentiles. [46]For they heard them speaking in tongues[a] and praising God. Then Peter said, [47]"Can anyone keep these people from being baptized with water? They have received the Holy Spirit just as we have." [48]So he ordered that they be baptized in the name of Jesus Christ. Then they asked Peter to stay with them for a few days.

[a]*46 Or other languages*

Peter did not get to finish this sermon. He had just spoken of the forgiveness of sins which comes through Christ when suddenly he was interrupted. He watched as the Gentiles before him, Cornelius, his family, friends, and servants, began "speaking in tongues" (λαλούντων γλώσσαις, *lalountōn glōssais*).[20] Peter recognized immediately that this event was a repetition of the Day of Pentecost, and that the Gentiles had received the Holy Spirit "just as (ὡς καί, *hōs kai*) we have."[21] Later Peter will state the case even stronger in his statement before the apostles in Jerusalem: "the Holy Spirit came on them as (ὥσπερ, *hōsper*) he had come on us at the beginning" (11:15). He saw no difference in the Spirit's gift when he compared

---

[20]The phrase is not exactly the same as in 2:4 (*lalein heterais glōssais*), but certainly similar enough to describe this outpouring of the Spirit to include the same type of gift as at Pentecost. See Polhill for the view that this gift of the Spirit was not the same as Pentecost, but more like the spiritual gifts of 1 Cor 12-14.

[21]Dunn argues that this text will not support the modern Pentecostal contention that Cornelius was born again and received the Spirit as distinct and separate acts of God. See his *Baptism*, pp. 79-82.

it with the Day of Pentecost. Apparently, the Spirit's outpouring on Cornelius also included speaking in other (known) languages as was true at Pentecost.[22]

Those Jewish Christians who had traveled with Peter from Joppa were also amazed. The gift of the Spirit had been "poured out" (ἐκκέχυται, *ekkechytai*) on Gentiles. The verb appears in the perfect tense, and places the emphasis on the effects of the "pouring out." All doubt was removed because they could see them speaking in tongues and praising God.

After seeing what was surely the work of the Spirit on this Gentile audience, Peter concluded that these people were truly believers, accepted by God. If the Lord had determined to give them the Spirit, how could anyone argue that they should not be baptized into Christ, just as Peter had commanded on the Day of Pentecost?[23]

Whether this mention of the outpouring of the Spirit included the indwelling of the Spirit as well cannot be determined from the language of the text. Bruce points out that the sequence at Pentecost for the believers was conviction of sin, repentance and faith, baptism into Christ for the forgiveness of sins and the reception of the Spirit.[24] In the case of Cornelius this order was interrupted. The reception of the Spirit came first. God poured out the Spirit in a way unlike anything since the Day of Pentecost.

Peter's question about baptizing these believers points again to the connection between the reception of the Spirit and baptism. Had no connection been expected, there would have been no reason to ask how anyone could object to the baptism of these Gentiles. Had baptism not been understood as the moment for believers to receive the Spirit, Peter would never have asked the question. But after asking the question, Peter commanded them to submit themselves to baptism, and they did so. They showed their gratitude by asking Peter to stay on, perhaps for further instruction in the gospel.

---

[22]It does not seem that Luke sees any difference either.

[23]That this "household baptism" is not the object of appeal for many who defend infant baptism is perhaps because the text speaks of them as believers and as people who received the evidences of the Spirit's outpouring. See Jewett, *Infant Baptism*, p. 48.

[24]Bruce, pp. 217-218.

ACTS 11

2. The Endorsement of Peter's Ministry by the Jerusalem Leadership (11:1-18)

The Questioning of the Jerusalem Leaders (11:1-3)

[1]The apostles and the brothers throughout Judea heard that the Gentiles also had received the word of God. [2]So when Peter went up to Jerusalem, the circumcised believers criticized him [3]and said, "You went into the house of uncircumcised men and ate with them."

The news of the baptism of the Gentile Cornelius spread throughout Judea. By using the term "brothers" here Luke refers not only to Jews (as in 2:29 and 7:2), but to Jewish Christians (as in 6:3). In Jerusalem was also a group Luke labels "the circumcised believers" (literally "those from the circumcision") who raised objections to the action of Peter. This group seems to be distinct from the apostles and the rest of the church, or at least a faction of the church. Peter was criticized not for baptizing Gentiles, but for eating with them.

Some scholars have doubted that the question of table fellowship was original to the story. They argue that the issue which animated this story was the issue of Gentiles being admitted to the church, and that the matter of eating with Gentiles was connected with the account at a later time.[1] But the question of how the Jewish

---

[1]See Bruce's comments on this debate on p. 220. Martin Dibelius is one critic who has taken this position. I.H. Marshall points out some of the

purity laws coming from the Old Testament should apply to the Gentiles coming into the church was bound to raise controversy on a number of levels. There is no reason to doubt that this account accurately reflects the very real issues which would have been raised by the conversion of Gentiles.

At any rate the disputing was sharp and prolonged. Luke uses the imperfect tense (διεκρίνοντο, *diekrinonto*; literally "were disputing") to describe the give and take of the controversy.

The Defense by Peter (11:4-17)

[4]Peter began and explained everything to them precisely as it had happened: [5]"I was in the city of Joppa praying, and in a trance I saw a vision. I saw something like a large sheet being let down from heaven by its four corners, and it came down to where I was. [6]I looked into it and saw four-footed animals of the earth, wild beasts, reptiles, and birds of the air. [7]Then I heard a voice telling me, 'Get up, Peter. Kill and eat.' [8]I replied, 'Surely not, Lord! Nothing impure or unclean has ever entered my mouth.' [9]The voice spoke from heaven a second time, 'Do not call anything impure that God has made clean.' [10]This happened three times, and then it was all pulled up to heaven again. [11]Right then three men who had been sent to me from Caesarea stopped at the house where I was staying. [12]The Spirit told me to have no hesitation about going with them. These six brothers also went with me, and we entered the man's house. [13]He told us how he had seen an angel appear in his house and say, 'Send to Joppa for Simon who is called Peter. [14]He will bring you a message through which you and all your household will be saved.' [15]As I began to speak, the Holy Spirit came on them as he had come on us at the beginning. [16]Then I remembered what the Lord had said: 'John baptized with[a] water, but you will be baptized with the Holy Spirit.' [17]So if God gave them the same gift as he gave us, who believed in the Lord Jesus Christ, who was I to think that I could oppose God?"

[a]16 Or *in*

weaknesses in his case in *The Acts of the Apostles* (Grand Rapids: Eerdmans, 1980), pp. 181-183, 196.

Peter had evidently heard about the controversy before going to Jerusalem. He began his defense by merely repeating what had happened in Joppa and then in Caesarea. The word "precisely" (καθεξῆς, *kathexēs*) echoes the objective of the entire Luke-Acts material as the author states it in Luke 1:3 ("write an orderly account"). Peter spoke in precise terms about the events, relating one detail after the other.

The report given by Peter is an abbreviation of Acts 10. His list of the animals added "wild beasts" to the list in 10:12. He also mentioned that the number of brothers who accompanied him to Caesarea was six, and then alluded to them as present in the audience, having come up to Jerusalem to attest to Peter's story. In addition to these items, Peter adds that the angel's message to Cornelius was that Peter would bring him the message "through which you and all your household will be saved." These incidental differences in the accounts demonstrate the flexibility of historical reporting by Luke, yet with accuracy.

Peter commented that the Holy Spirit came upon those gathered with Cornelius "as I began (ἄρχομαι, *archomai*) to speak."[2] His emphasis was that the Gentiles received the same Spirit in the same manner as the apostles on the Day of Pentecost.[3] The Holy Spirit, said Peter, fell on them "as he had on us at the beginning." God gave them "the same (ἴσην, *isēn*) gift as he gave us," he argued.

Peter's language draws attention to the unique character of the event at Pentecost. By this time Peter was looking backwards in time perhaps as much as ten years. As far as he was concerned, nothing like it had been seen since. The Spirit had come on them as upon the apostles "at the beginning," that is, the Day of Pentecost. Peter did not say the Spirit came as had been the case in many conversions in recent memory. He did not use recent outpourings of the Spirit with the Samaritans (8:17f) or the Jerusalem church (4:31) as the standard by which to compare. He looked all the way back to

---

[2]Dibelius saw in this comment from Peter an unavoidable contradiction between this report and Acts 10. How could Peter say the Spirit fell as "he began to speak?" Was he not well into his message when the Spirit came? As Bruce points out, such an objection reads too much into the word "began," which in Semitic use may be merely an auxiliary verb (p. 222).

[3]See also 10:44-48; 15:8.

Pentecost, and concluded that what he saw in Cornelius was exactly what he had seen then.

Also significant in Peter's remarks is his reference to the words of Jesus. When he saw the Spirit come down on the Gentiles, Peter said he remembered that the Lord Jesus said John would baptize with water, but Jesus himself would baptize with the Holy Spirit.[4] Peter next argued, in effect, that baptism by the Spirit is superior to baptism in water. Therefore, if God gave the superior gift, how could anyone oppose the lesser action? Nevertheless, Peter did not conclude that baptism in water was irrelevant, even though the Spirit had been poured out on these Gentiles. He commanded them to be baptized to fulfill the gospel's requirements for the response of faith.

The Defense Accepted (11:18)

[18]When they heard this, they had no further objections and praised God, saying, "So then, God has granted even the Gentiles repentance unto life."

Luke gives the final summary of this discussion by describing the approval of the Jerusalem church. They were convinced that Peter's testimony meant God was at work among the Gentiles. Though the battle over the requirements for Gentiles coming into the church was not over (see Acts 15), the believers had agreed in principle that the gospel must go to the Gentiles. The church would not be confined within the framework of Judaism, but would become an expanding kingdom of universal proportions.

The last glimpse of the leaders at this meeting has them praising God for the success among the Gentiles. All nations of the world would now have the opportunity of repentance that leads to life.

---

[4]See note on 10:44.

G. THE NEW CHRISTIANS AT ANTIOCH (11:19-30)

1. Evangelism among the
Gentiles of Antioch (11:19-21)

[19]Now those who had been scattered by the persecution in connection with Stephen traveled as far as Phoenicia, Cyprus and Antioch, telling the message only to Jews. [20]Some of them, however, men from Cyprus and Cyrene, went to Antioch and began to speak to Greeks also, telling them the good news about the Lord Jesus. [21]The Lord's hand was with them, and a great number of people believed and turned to the Lord.

Those scattered by the persecution resulting from Stephen's martyrdom in Jerusalem come into Luke's picture once again. Acts 8:1 describes how they were driven from Jerusalem and 9:1-2 notes that Saul's mission involved bringing them back from Damascus for prosecution. Now Luke gives us still another glimpse into the faithfulness of these believers.[5]

These Christians traveled northward to Phoenicia, Cyprus, and Antioch.[6] The Phoenician plain ran some 125 miles north from the plain of Dor (south of Mt. Carmel) to the Eleutheros River. On its west was the Mediterranean Sea and Phoenicia reached inland only about fifteen miles to the mountains of Lebanon and Galilee. Chief cities in Phoenicia included Tyre, Sidon, Ptolemais, and Zarephath. The island of Cyprus lay about 100 miles off the Syrian coast in the Mediterranean.

Antioch was the third largest city of the Empire (behind Rome

---

[5]Goulder sees in these verses the prelude to another example of the charity of the church. The believers were scattered after Stephen's martyrdom, which leads ultimately to the prophecy of Agabus and the benevolence of the church at Antioch (11:29-30). See M.D. Goulder, *Type and History in Acts* (London: SPCK, 1964), p. 25. Also, see note on 10:1.

[6]Hengel points to these verses as evidence for an active Greek-speaking element within Palestinian Judaism. He notes that the use of the Greek language among Palestinian Jews was not always considered in negative terms since speaking Greek was associated with "a higher social standing, better education and stronger contacts with the world outside." See his *Judaism and Hellenism*, 1:105.

and Alexandria), boasting a population of 500,000. Because of its location as the hinge which joined together the eastern and western Roman empire, Antioch was truly a cosmopolitan city.

Here the believers fled, who were escaping the persecution, and they found a receptive population, first among the Jews. Then some believers from Cyprus and some from Cyrene (in Northern Africa) even preached among the Gentile population. What connection this evangelism had with the conversion of Cornelius is not stated in the text, but the results were immediate. "The Lord's hand" was evident in the work, a phrase which is used frequently to describe the power and blessing of God.[7] The preaching brought a plentiful harvest of converts who "believed and turned to the Lord."[8]

As Polhill notes, these Christians of the Jewish dispersion had grown up in a Gentile environment and did not have the same geographical and social confinements as the Jewish Christians of Palestine. They preached with a "sensitivity to Gentile concerns." They "did not preach Jesus as the Messiah (Christ) but rather as Lord, a title far more familiar to Gentiles" than Jewish ideas of the Messiah.[9]

2. The Ministry of Barnabas and Saul at Antioch (11:22-26)

[22]**News of this reached the ears of the church at Jerusalem, and they sent Barnabas to Antioch.** [23]**When he arrived and saw the evidence of the grace of God, he was glad and encouraged them all to remain true to the Lord with all their hearts.** [24]**He was a good man, full of the Holy Spirit and faith, and a great number of people were brought to the Lord.** [25]**Then Barnabas went to Tarsus to look for Saul,** [26]**and when he found him, he brought him to**

---

[7]See Exod 8:19 9:3; 1 Sam 5:6; 6:9; Isa 59:1; 66:14; Ezek 1:3; Luke 1:66; Acts 4:30; 13:11.

[8]This statement serves to summarize the response of conversion in terms of "faith" and "repentance." In other instances the response is summarized as faith and baptism (see 8:13; 16:31,33; 16:14-15; 18:8), repentance and baptism (2:38), just faith (8:17; 9:42; 13:12,48; 17:4, 12), just repentance (9:35), or just baptism (8:38; 9:18; 10:47).

[9]Polhill, p. 271. See also the note on 9:35; Flew, *Jesus*, pp. 118-119.

Antioch. So for a whole year Barnabas and Saul met with the church and taught great numbers of people. The disciples were called Christians first at Antioch.

"The ears of the church at Jerusalem" heard about the conversions.[10] Luke uses this Hebraic expression to describe how the news traveled to the apostles and leaders who had given their blessing to the events with Cornelius. Whether this evangelizing among Gentiles had occurred before or after the conversion of Cornelius is not specifically stated. It appears, however, that the news did not reach Jerusalem until sometime after the discussion of Cornelius.

The response of the church in Jerusalem was to send a representative to see the work, much as they had done with Philip's ministry among the Samaritans (8:14). Their reason for doing so was not so much to exercise authority as to bless and encourage this work in view of the conclusions reached regarding Cornelius.

Barnabas was the appointed delegate. His credentials for the role included the fact that he was also from Cyprus (4:36) and thus would have a natural understanding of the Hellenists working in Antioch. Known as "a good man, full of the Holy Spirit," Barnabas had also demonstrated his generosity in the contributions to the needy (4:36f). He was instrumental, as well, in the acceptance of Saul of Tarsus by the Jerusalem church (9:27). He had exhibited the capability of seeing the good in people who might otherwise be rejected.

Such an ability was essential now in Antioch, and Barnabas was able to see "the evidence of the grace of God." Whether the evidence appeared in the form of the Spirit's obvious working or in

---

[10]O'Neill remarks on the centrality of Jerusalem in the unfolding events throughout Acts. He detects five divisions in Acts (1:9–8:3; 8:4–11:18; 11:19–15:35; 15:36–19:20; 19:21–28:31), each of which makes Jerusalem the hub of activity. This activity includes the springboard for launching evangelistic efforts after Stephen's martyrdom, the supervision of the apostles over missionary efforts in Samaria, and the sending of Barnabas to Antioch. Of course, Jerusalem is also the location of Peter's defense after baptizing Cornelius, of the Jerusalem conference, and the place of Paul's arrest before his journey to Rome. The role of Jerusalem is also an important theme in Luke's Gospel. See O'Neill, *Theology*, pp. 66-67.

lives that were transformed by the power of God, Barnabas was thrilled by what he saw. He responded by encouraging them, as his name implied that he would (4:36).

Feeling the need for a ministry on an expanded basis, Barnabas went to Tarsus, some 150 miles away, "to look (ἀναζητέω, *anazēteō*) for Saul." The verb carries the idea of searching high and low until, with great difficulty, the person is found. Bruce thinks this term may suggest that Saul, who had gone to Tarsus years earlier (9:30), had been disinherited.[11] This could explain the difficulty of the search by Barnabas.

"For a whole year" represents one of the few times in Acts where Luke gives a definite period of time.[12] Saul and Barnabas continued a ministry of teaching and preaching which produced such results that the believers gained the attention of the society of Antioch. Luke notes that it was here that the believers were first known (χρηματίζω, *chrēmatizō*) as "Christians."[13] The name "Christian" means "belonging to Christ," and appears to have been given by those outside of the church. It is not clear, however, that it was given to the believers as a derogatory term. Only two other times does the designation appear in the New Testament (Acts 26:28; 1 Pet 4:16). In the writings of Ignatius (early second century), however, the name was used extensively.

---

[11]Bruce, p. 227, n. 30.

[12]See also 18:11; 19:8,10; 24:27; 28:30.

[13]Bruce notes that this use of the verb has the idea of "to be publicly known" rather than any idea of a divine oracle (p. 228). Martin suggests that the name was given to the believers by the people of Antioch. The ending of the word (*-ianos*) is the Greek equivalent of the Latin *-ianus*. It describes possession, and thus carries the idea "people who belong to Christ," possibly even as slaves. See Martin, *Foundations*, 1:104. Conzelmann sees the verb as a statement of what was commonly known among the population of Antioch about the believers (p. 88). Ladd thinks that the name "Christ" was understood in the Gentile world as a proper name rather than a Hebrew title meaning "anointed." See his *Theology*, pp. 135, 409. The debate over the time when the title "Lord" was first attached to Jesus has been lively (see Ladd, *Theology*, p. 340).

3. The Famine Relief Work from Antioch (11:27-30)

[27]**During this time some prophets came down from Jerusalem to Antioch. [28]One of them, named Agabus, stood up and through the Spirit predicted that a severe famine would spread over the entire Roman world. (This happened during the reign of Claudius.) [29]The disciples, each according to his ability, decided to provide help for the brothers living in Judea. [30]This they did, sending their gift to the elders by Barnabas and Saul.**

During the time that the mission to the Gentiles was taking place, some "prophets came down" from Jerusalem. Often the terminology of "coming down" is used when travelers leave Jerusalem, largely because of its elevation. A "prophet" was one who had the gift of the Holy Spirit which permitted the sharing of inspired messages from the Lord.[14] Thus they delivered their message "through the Spirit" (see 2 Pet 1:21).

The prophet Agabus was among those who came to Antioch. Later in Acts this prophet will foretell the imprisonment of Saul (21:10). Now his message focused on economic and agricultural conditions. A famine was coming, the kind of conditions that are documented in the time of Claudius.[15]

The response of the church was to collect contributions to send to churches in Judea which would be affected. They did this "each according to his ability," a phrase which sounds very much like the procedure used later when the Corinthians were asked to participate in the collection (1 Cor 16:2; 2 Cor 8:11-12). Barnabas and Saul were appointed as representatives from Antioch to carry the gift. They accomplished their mission by taking the money to the elders of the Jerusalem church. This verse is the first in Acts to mention the role of elders in the church. One wonders about the absence of any mention of the apostles here, but perhaps this verse represents

---

[14]Paul ranks the gift of prophecy second only to that of the apostle in 1 Cor 12:28.

[15]Historians who described the famines in the reign of Claudius were Dio Cassius (*History* 60.11), Suetonius (*Claudius* 18.2), and Tacitus (*Annals* 12.43). Hengel finds some parallels between Agabus and the Essene prophets (*Judaism and Hellenism* 1:240).

a transition in the leadership of the Jerusalem church. At any rate, by the time of the Jerusalem conference (15:6) the elders were playing an important part in crucial decisions in the church.

One problem which cannot be avoided in this text is Paul's own listing of his visits to Jerusalem in Galatians 1-2.[16] In his reflections on his contacts with the other apostles, he describes just two visits to Jerusalem. Acts records three during the same period. Paul first came to Jerusalem after his escape from Damascus (9:26). The visit recorded here would thus be the second visit; the third comes at the time of the Jerusalem Conference (15:2).

In Galatians the first visit Paul describes is placed three years after his conversion (Gal 1:18). His second visit occurred fourteen years later (Gal 2:1). Paul says he went on this journey with Barnabas and Titus. He adds that this visit was made "in response to a revelation" and that on this visit he "set before them the gospel that I preach among the Gentiles."

Two problems surround these facts. Why did Paul report two visits, while Luke reports three? Secondly, which journeys described by Paul are recorded in Acts? The answer to the first question has to do with the purpose of both Acts and Galatians. Paul's purpose in Galatians is to demonstrate how limited were his contacts with the apostles.[17] Luke, on the other hand, seems content with a general summary of the events of these years, except for the details of the Jerusalem Conference itself in Acts 15.

Because Galatians 2:1-10 seems to describe Paul's visit for the Jerusalem Conference, the visit Luke describes in Acts 15 can be equated with Galatians 2:1-10. This leaves two more visits in Acts to work with.[18] Paul's description in Galatians 1:18-20 of a visit just

---

[16]This problem is also discussed in the comments on 15:1.

[17]This emphasis begins in Gal 1:1 when Paul declares that he was "sent not from men nor by man." He gets more explicit about this point in 1:16 when he says that after his conversion he "did not consult any man," nor "go up to Jerusalem to see those who were apostles" before he was. See comments on 9:28.

[18]Some scholars think that the visits of Acts 11 and 15 are really one and the same. Among these is Pesch (*Apostelgeschichte*, 1:356). Others take Gal 2:1-10 and Acts 11:27-30 to refer to the same visit—the second one. These scholars contend that the visit for the Jerusalem conference (Acts 15) is not mentioned in Galatians because Galatians was written before it occurred.

three years after his conversion would seem to fit Acts 9:26-29. Thus if Acts 9:26-29 corresponds to Galatians 1:18-20, and Acts 15 seems to correspond with Galatians 2:1-10, then Galatians omits any reference to Paul's visit in this text (11:27-30). This explanation seems to best suit the available evidence.

Examples of those taking this position are Bruce (p. 282-284) and Marshall (pp. 204-205). Robert Jewett discusses the problem of dating the famine alluded to in this text. See his *Chronology*, p. 34. Robertson objects to any attempt in this discussion to cast doubt on Luke's accuracy. See his *Luke the Historian*, pp. 170-173. See also Polhill, p. 275, n. 136; Gasque, *History of Criticism*, p. 141.

ACTS 12

H. THE PERSECUTION OF THE CHURCH BY HEROD AGRIPPA I (12:1-25)

1. The Martyrdom of James and Imprisonment of Peter (12:1-4)

[1]It was about this time that King Herod arrested some who belonged to the church, intending to persecute them. [2]He had James, the brother of John, put to death with the sword. [3]When he saw that this pleased the Jews, he proceeded to seize Peter also. This happened during the Feast of Unleavened Bread. [4]After arresting him, he put him in prison, handing him over to be guarded by four squads of four soldiers each. Herod intended to bring him out for public trial after the Passover.

Luke next turns attention from the famine-relief work of the church of Antioch to describe how the church was met with persecution at the hands of the king. Some have questioned the significance of chapter twelve in the Book of Acts as a whole.[1] Nevertheless, the events described here serve to demonstrate how the early church coped with opposition to the faith, as well as how the gospel overcame every obstacle in conquering the Roman world. In

---

[1]Robert W. Wall, "Successors to 'the Twelve' according to Acts 12:1-17," *CBQ* 53 (1991): 628-643. See also Jervell, *People of God*, pp. 185-207. Dunn speaks of the difficulty of thinking of this account as historical, though it is obvious that Luke himself presents this event as such (Jesus, pp. 166-167). The account itself distinguishes between a "visionary" experience and an external historical event (12:9).

addition, this story accounts for the rise of James to a position of influence in the church of Jerusalem.

"About this time" is an indefinite way of referring to the occasion of the famine-relief effort with the churches in Judea. Whether the events of this chapter took place before, during, or after this work is not specified from the text. The death of Herod (12:23) can be accurately dated at A.D. 44, and thus these events may well have occurred during A.D. 43.

"King Herod" is a reference to Herod Agrippa I, the grandson of Herod the Great (who played such a prominent role in the birth of Jesus recorded in Matt 2). Herod the Great had his son executed because he might be a threat to gain the throne. This son, Aristobulus, had fathered Agrippa, and the boy's mother made sure that when the order for the execution came, young Agrippa would be far from the reach of Herod the Great. So Agrippa was raised and educated in Rome. Here he grew up with the Roman aristocracy, becoming friends with Claudius and Gaius.

When Gaius (Caligula) succeeded Tiberius as emperor in A.D. 37, he gave Agrippa the title "king" and authority over the tetrarchies of Philip and Lysanias in southern Syria, which included lands in the Transjordan and the Decapolis. In A.D. 39 this authority was extended to Galilee and Perea, territories formerly ruled by his uncle, Antipas (who was exiled). Then in A.D. 41 when Agrippa's former schoolmate, Claudius, came to power in Rome, the authority was again extended to include Judea and Samaria. By now Agrippa's authority was approximately the same as that which his grandfather, Herod the Great, had enjoyed.

Now Herod Agrippa used this authority to arrest (ἐπέβαλεν . . . χεῖρας, *epebalen . . . cheiras;* "lay [violent] hands on") some "who belonged to the church." His objective was persecution of the Jerusalem church, and to this end he even executed James, the "brother of John." James and John are mentioned frequently in the Gospels and are described as the sons of Zebedee (Matt 4:21). Now, some thirteen years after the crucifixion of Jesus, James also paid the ultimate price for his faith, just as Jesus had predicted he would (Matt 20:23). To be "put to death with the sword" usually meant beheading in the Roman system, but if Jews were in charge, a method was preferred which did not desecrate the body. In such cases the sword was used to thrust through the body.[2]

Herod's interest in pleasing the Jews extended to cruelty where necessary. Perhaps as a result of tensions produced by the reports of the conversion of Cornelius, the Jewish leaders were more than happy to use force to crush the Christian movement. Herod's participation served to strengthen his position as ruler of the Jews (see 12:11).

The seven-day "Feast of Unleavened Bread" (Passover; Nisan 14-21 in the Jewish calendar) was the occasion chosen by Herod to move against another prominent leader of the church—Peter. The trial and sentence could be concluded after the holy days. Herod's action placed Peter in prison under "four squads of four soldiers each." The location of the prison is not stated, but a good guess is the Fortress of Antonia on the northwest corner of the Temple complex (where Jesus had no doubt been taken thirteen years before at Passover time). The heavy guard of soldiers indicates that Peter would be under constant watch, since the four squads represented the four watches of the night. Did Herod use such security because of Peter's habit of escaping confinement (see 5:17ff)? At any rate, such attention to Peter as prisoner implies how certain was his fate in the hands of Herod and how hopeless was his future without the direct intervention of God.

2. The Escape of Peter from Prison (12:5-11)

[5]So Peter was kept in prison, but the church was earnestly praying to God for him. [6]The night before Herod was to bring him to trial, Peter was sleeping between two soldiers, bound with two chains, and sentries stood guard at the entrance. [7]Suddenly an angel of the Lord appeared and a light shone in the cell. He struck Peter on the side and woke him up. "Quick, get up!" he said, and the chains fell off Peter's wrists. [8]Then the angel said to him, "Put on your clothes and sandals."And Peter did so. "Wrap your cloak around you and follow me," the angel told him. [9]Peter followed him out of the prison, but he had no idea that what the angel was

---

[2]Polhill, p. 278.

doing was really happening; he thought he was seeing a vision.
[10]They passed the first and second guards and came to the iron
gate leading to the city. It opened for them by itself, and they went
through it. When they had walked the length of one street,
suddenly the angel left him. [11]Then Peter came to himself and
said, "Now I know without a doubt that the Lord sent his angel
and rescued me from Herod's clutches and from everything the
Jewish people were anticipating."

Peter's dangerous predicament is underscored with the contrast
in 12:5—Peter was guarded in prison, but the church was in earnest
prayer. The Greek construction indicates that the prayer was continuous.[3] As far as the believers knew, Peter was about to suffer the
same end as James had.

Meanwhile, Peter was "sleeping between two soldiers." This
statement suggests that Peter was being held in the typical Roman
fashion in which prisoners were chained to the soldiers who
guarded them. Apparently these soldiers were also asleep. Two
other soldiers stood guard, one at each gate of the prison.

Luke describes Peter as sleeping on the night before he was to
die. Is this a look at how assured he was of God's deliverance? Was
Peter's faith giving him such peace of mind that sleep was the
natural condition for this man of courage? Certainly with other
saints under pressure in the Book of Acts attention is given to the
courage of the faithful (see 4:21; 5:41; 6:15; 16:25; 20:24; 23:11;
27:25; 28:31).

At the same time, Haenchen points to the way this observation
dramatizes Peter's complete passivity in the deliverance. He was
asleep when it began, and the effects of the sleep lingered throughout the whole scene inside the prison. When the angel appeared he
"struck Peter on the side," as if punching him in the ribs to wake
him up. Even as the chains were falling miraculously from his wrists,
Peter's sleepy grogginess made it necessary for the angel to tell him
a step at a time how to get dressed to leave the prison. The comic
elements of this account cannot be ignored.

---

[3]The construction ἦν ...γινομένη (ēn ... ginomenē) is periphrastic and
expresses ongoing action.

Peter "put on (his) clothes," that is, he tightened up his tunic with the wide belt that was loosened for sleep. During the night the tunic thus became "a long-flowing undergarment."[4] His sandals were tied on and his outer garment wrapped around himself.

The appearance of the "angel of the Lord" came with a light that "shone in the cell." This language reminds the reader of the "glory of the Lord that shone around" the shepherds when the "angel of the Lord" appeared to them, telling them of the birth of Jesus (Luke 2:9).

Peter followed the angel as they passed by two guards to the outer gate of the prison. He was still having trouble comprehending what was happening as they moved along. Whether the guards were asleep when the angel and Peter went by is not stated. But the supernatural influence of the Lord was obvious at the iron gate. It opened for them "by itself" (αὐτομάτῃ, *automatē*), and the two of them passed through to street level.[5] It was only then that Peter realized that he was, in fact, being rescued from Herod by the Lord.

3. The Report of Peter about the Escape (12:12-17)

[12]**When this had dawned on him, he went to the house of Mary the mother of John, also called Mark, where many people had gathered and were praying. [13]Peter knocked at the outer entrance, and a servant girl named Rhoda came to answer the door. [14]When she recognized Peter's voice, she was so overjoyed she ran back without opening it and exclaimed, "Peter is at the door!" [15]"You're out of your mind," they told her. When she kept insisting that it was so, they said, "It must be his angel." [16]But Peter kept on knocking, and when they opened the door and saw him, they were astonished. [17]Peter motioned with his hand for them to be quiet and described how the Lord had brought him out of prison. "Tell James and the brothers about this," he said, and then he left for another place.**

---

[4]Rienecker, p. 289.

[5]Polhill lists other places in Greco-Roman literature where miraculous openings of gates occur (p. 281, n. 151). Compare also Acts 16:26.

Peter now knew what had happened to him, and he quickly went to the place where he knew he would find believers. Apparently Mary's large home was a meeting place for Christians.[6] She is identified by Luke as the mother of John Mark (Col 4:10 makes her the aunt of Barnabas). This note reminds us that by the time Luke was writing Acts many first-generation Christians were being remembered because of their relationship to second-generation Christians. Perhaps Luke's readers were more familiar with John Mark than with Mary herself.[7] This John Mark will appear again in the next chapter as a missionary companion of Barnabas and Saul (13:5).

When Peter arrived he knocked on the door of the courtyard. Mary's house was a splendid one which included the typical gate leading from the street to the front door. A servant girl named Rhoda (meaning "rose") was charged with the responsibility of keeping the gate, and when Peter arrived she quickly recognized his voice. She could not believe her ears. She rushed toward the house without even taking time to let him in.

The reaction to her news indicates one of the beliefs held by many Jews—that each believer had a guardian angel (compare Matt 18:10) and that at death the angel might appear in the form of the person who died. In other words, the believers took Rhoda's message to mean either that the slave girl was crazy or that Peter had been executed already, permitting his guardian angel to appear.

Meanwhile, Peter was standing outside at the gate, continuing to knock. Would the soldiers from the prison come after him? Would he be permitted entrance before being detected?

Finally, they went out to open the door. They were amazed. It was Peter. The buzzing of surprised voices began immediately, and Peter gestured with his hand so as to quiet them. He then explained what had happened, giving full credit to the Lord for delivering him.

---

[6]Mary belongs to a lengthy list of women who used their homes for the gathering place for Christians, including Chloe (1 Cor 1:11), Lydia (Acts 16:14-15,40), Phoebe (Rom 16:1-2), Nympha (Col 4:15), and Prisca, or Priscilla (Rom 16:3,5; 1 Cor 16:19). See Swidler, *Biblical Affirmations*, pp. 296-297.

[7]The same appears to be true with the mention of Simon of Cyrene who is identified in Mark 15:21 as the father of Alexander and Rufus.

The next matter Peter mentioned is significant. He instructed the believers to give the news to James (the Lord's brother; Mark 6:3) and "the brothers." "The brothers" could be a reference to the other elders who were taking more authority in the Jerusalem church. Peter's reference to James implies that this leader was becoming prominent in the church at Jerusalem. The Apostle Paul addressed the Galatians later and referred to James as one of the "pillars" (2:9). Once again Luke is introducing a character into the record who will play an important role in his history of the church (see 15:13-21; 21:18).

Then Peter quickly left Jerusalem for "another place." With this ambiguous reference, the story of Peter breaks off. Peter will not be heard from again in the Book of Acts until the Jerusalem Conference (15:7).

4. The Discovery of Peter's Escape (12:18-19a)

[18]In the morning, there was no small commotion among the soldiers as to what had become of Peter. [19]After Herod had a thorough search made for him and did not find him, he cross-examined the guards and ordered that they be executed.

Unfortunately for the soldiers guarding Peter, Herod ordered an investigation into Peter's disappearance. When no explanation could be found, Herod commanded that they be executed for failing to keep Peter in the prison. Such a sentence was not uncommon for Roman guards.[8]

5. The Death of Herod Agrippa I (12:19b-23)

[19]Then Herod went from Judea to Caesarea and stayed there a while. [20]He had been quarreling with the people of Tyre and

---

[8]Bruce notes that according to the Code of Justinian, the guard was to suffer the same sentence the prisoner would have suffered (p. 240). The Philippian jailer's concern in 16:27 reflects how common it was for guards to fear for their life if a prisoner escaped.

Sidon; they now joined together and sought an audience with him. Having secured the support of Blastus, a trusted personal servant of the king, they asked for peace, because they depended on the king's country for their food supply. ²¹On the appointed day Herod, wearing his royal robes, sat on his throne and delivered a public address to the people. ²²They shouted, "This is the voice of a god, not of a man." ²³Immediately, because Herod did not give praise to God, an angel of the Lord struck him down, and he was eaten by worms and died.

Now Luke brings to a close the story of Herod. The chapter opens with Herod's active persecution of the believers, but Luke intends to show how the judgment of God finished Herod's haughtiness.

The king left Jerusalem and traveled to Caesarea, the city which was considered the capital of Judea as far as Romans were concerned. Luke's language depicts graphically a dispute of Herod with the cities of Tyre and Sidon.[9] These cities had sent a delegation headed by one Blastus of whom we know nothing more than what is mentioned here. His position as "a trusted personal servant"[10] would put him in a powerful position to represent the interests of these northern cities. It is probable that the delegation paid for his services. With Blastus as their spokesman, they petitioned for peace because their food supply depended on it.

Fortunately, Josephus also describes Herod's appearance on an occasion where the king stood before the people of Caesarea.[11] The occasion seems to describe this one in Acts. His account of the death of Herod corresponds quite closely to Luke's.

Though Josephus does not mention the dispute with Tyre and Sidon, he describes the extravagance of Herod's royal robes. Josephus says that Herod entered the theater on the second day of the feast in honor of Caesar wearing robes made of silver and extravagant weaving. His clothing glistened radiantly as the first rays of the

---

[9]The word is θυμομαχέω (thymomacheō), "to fight desperately," or "be furious," or "exasperated" (Rienecker, p. 290).

[10]His position is called literally the "one over the king's bedroom" (τὸν ἐπὶ τοῦ κοιτῶνος τοῦ βασιλέως, ton epi tou koitōnos tou basileōs), a most trusted position.

[11]Antiquities, 19.343-52.

morning sun fell on them. When his admirers saw this they called out to him as if he were a god, urging him to be gracious to them. Before then, they said, he had been reverenced as a human being, but from then on he would be confessed as an immortal deity.

This description of Josephus parallels Luke's language in that the crowd shouted that they were hearing "the voice of a god, not of a man." As in Luke's account, Josephus notes that Herod did not rebuke them for their flattery. Luke says he "did not give praise to God."

Both historians record Herod's death as being the direct result of his presumption. Luke says that "an angel of the Lord struck him down." Josephus says that soon afterward Herod looked up and saw an owl. Apparently on an earlier occasion an owl had appeared as a harbinger of good, but he was warned on that occasion that the next time an owl appeared it would mean he had but five days to live.[12]

Josephus says that a "pang of grief" pierced his heart and he was seized with "a severe pain in his bowels." He was carried to his bed where he suffered for the next five days until he died. Luke says that he was "eaten by worms."[13] God had rendered judgment on the king only months after he persecuted the church of God.

6. The Continued Progress of the Gospel (12:24)

[24]But the word of God continued to increase and spread.

For the third time in Acts (see also 6:7 and 9:31) Luke adds a brief summary of the progress of the church.[14] Here it is given in direct contrast to the downfall of Herod. The persecutor was destroyed, but the word of God "continued to increase and spread." Luke uses the imperfect tense with these verbs to emphasize that the gospel was daily expanding its reach.

---

[12]*Antiquities*, 18.200.

[13]Polhill notes the attempts which have been made to give a medical identification to the malady which killed Herod (p. 285, note 162). It is interesting that "eaten by worms" is also a feature of the deaths of Antiochus IV and Herod the Great. See also Conzelmann, pp. 96-97.

[14]Gasque reviews some of the attention scholars have given to these summary statements. See his *History of Criticism*, pp. 125-129. Six of these

7. The Return of Barnabas and Saul to Antioch (12:25)

[25]When Barnabas and Saul had finished their mission, they returned from[a] Jerusalem, taking with them John, also called Mark.

[a]*25 Some manuscripts* to

The mention of Barnabas and Saul finishes the account which Luke began in 11:30. Their mission to Jerusalem had been completed; the gift from Antioch had been delivered. They returned to Antioch from Jerusalem. Some commentators note the grammatical problem here. Some manuscripts have "to Jerusalem," rather than "from Jerusalem." This reading would not make sense if it means that Barnabas and Saul returned "to Jerusalem," since in 11:30 they had already gone to Jerusalem. On the other hand, the phrase "to Jerusalem" may well be accepted if Luke means to describe the "ministry" of Barnabas and Saul "to Jerusalem" from Antioch.[15]

summaries, reflecting on the growth of the church, appear in Acts (6:7; 9:31; 12:24; 16:6; 19:20; 28:30-31).

[15]See Bruce, p. 243 (n. 45); Polhill, p. 286.

ACTS 13

III. THE CHURCH IN
THE ENDS OF THE EARTH (13:1–28:31)

A. THE FIRST MISSIONARY JOURNEY (13:1–14:28)

1. The Commissioning of Barnabas and Saul at Antioch (13:1-3)

¹In the church at Antioch there were prophets and teachers: Barnabas, Simeon called Niger, Lucius of Cyrene, Manaen (who had been brought up with Herod the tetrarch) and Saul. ²While they were worshiping the Lord and fasting, the Holy Spirit said, "Set apart for me Barnabas and Saul for the work to which I have called them." ³So after they had fasted and prayed, they placed their hands on them and sent them off.

With this chapter of Acts a new division begins in this book. Luke has recorded the witness of the gospel in Jerusalem (chapters one through seven), as well as in Judea and Samaria (chapters eight through twelve).[1] Now the spotlight swings toward the progress of the gospel as it reaches to the wider targets of the

---

[1]Talbert comments on the many parallels between the two major divisions of Acts, 1-12 and 13-28. These are parallels not only in content, but also in sequence of material. See his *Literary Patterns*, pp. 23-25. Gasque documents the history of scholarly attention to this point in his *History of Criticism*, pp. 25,33,36,79,88. Trite also notes the parallel between events now recorded about Paul and those previously recorded about Peter. He says, "This parallelism between the 'Acts of Peter' and the 'Acts of Paul' has long been noted" and Luke was guided to choose those incidents which showed

Roman world.[2] Thus Luke is fulfilling his theme as recorded in 1:8 in the quotation of Jesus.

Luke does not, however, move into this division of his book without preparation. At several points along the way he has included glimpses of the outreach of the gospel into the non-Jewish world. The conversion of Cornelius in chapter ten foreshadowed a successful mission to the Gentiles. In 11:20-21 the Antioch church's evangelism among Gentiles prefigured the thrust by the church into brand new regions of mission endeavor.

From this point in the record of Acts, then, Saul (Paul) and his companions will depart from Antioch for the West on three different occasions. Led by the Holy Spirit, these gospel pioneers will accumulate thousands of miles in the interest of proclaiming the message of Christ.[3]

They will visit many of the most important cities of the Roman Empire. The term "missionary journeys" should not be understood in the sense of established itineraries with brief stops in every case. In some instances a city like Corinth or Ephesus will become the headquarters for the missionaries' work for extended periods of time.

Acts 13:1 begins by drawing attention away from the events with Herod in Caesarea and focuses on what was happening in the church in Antioch. This congregation had already shown itself to be very active in evangelism (see 11:19-30) and it is not surprising that the earliest efforts to spread the gospel on a worldwide scale began with this congregation.

The "prophets and teachers" who were present in this church

---

that Paul's apostleship was confirmed by the same signs and wonders by which Peter's was confirmed. See his *Witness*, p. 134.

[2]Martin notes that this division of Acts can be appropriately entitled "The Church Breaks Barriers." See his *Foundations*, 2:104. Goulder states that the "book of Acts is like a road stretching from the mount of Olives to the city of Rome" (*Type and History*, p. 203). He thinks that Acts 13-28 has the earmarks of actual history rather than a narrative reporting an idealized version of events in the earliest church.

[3]One estimate says that the total number of miles covered was at least 13,400 when all of the journeys are taken into account. See Barry Beitzel, *The Moody Atlas of Bible Lands* (Chicago: Moody, 1985), p. 176.

made it similar to many first-century congregations.[4] These roles are mentioned in connection with the Ephesian church (Eph 4:11), the Roman church (Rom 12:6), and the Corinthian church (1 Cor 12:10, 28), among the congregations of Paul. The gift of prophecy was known in the Old Testament (Deut 18:18-20; 2 Pet 1:21), but was promised for the New Testament age, as well (2:17-18).

"Prophets" (προφῆται, prophētai) were those believers to whom God revealed his will so that it might be communicated to the church. Together with teachers they took the responsibility of instructing the congregation in matters of doctrine and practical Christianity.

The names of these prophets and teachers, except for Barnabas and Saul, are unfamiliar to the New Testament. Though the name Simeon is Jewish, the term "Niger" (Latin for "black") may suggest a dark complexion. Lucius is not likely a reference to Luke, our author. Manaen was "brought up with" (σύντροφος, syntrophos) Herod Antipas (Luke 3:1; Acts 4:27). This advantage would have given Manaen a social standing of high importance.

The dramatic story began to unfold "while they were worshiping," a phrase indicating a habitual practice among the Antiochian disciples. The word for "worship" (λειτουργέω, leitourgeō) was used in the Old Testament of the service rendered by priests in the temple. Its use here shows that the church understood that believers had become a priesthood before God (see 1 Pet 2:5).

Worth noting also is that the Spirit spoke to the church (probably through one of the prophets in the church) while they were already active in serving him.[5] God rarely speaks his will to those not fully engaged in some manner of service. "Fasting" was frequently practiced by the Jews as an expression of single-minded worship (see Luke 18:12; Matt 9:14).

When God did speak it was "the Holy Spirit" who revealed the Divine will. So by God's initiative this work was brought about, not by human imagination. "Set apart" describes an appointment for

---

[4]See Floyd Filson, "The Christian Teacher in the First Century," *JBL* 60 (1941): 317-328.

[5]Talbert observes the parallels between the Spirit's activity here and his work with the apostles on the Day of Pentecost. See his *Literary Patterns*, p. 23. Hubbard discusses this passage with the other "commissioning accounts" in Acts (see his "Commissioning Accounts," pp. 190-197).

fulfilling a specific task, but the work envisioned is not fully defined.[6] Only in reading the following verses does one understand the scope of this "work" to which they were called.

The formal commissioning of Barnabas and Saul was accompanied by prayer and fasting. Then, probably in a public assembly, they "placed hands on them" as a symbol of their designation for service (see 14:23,26).[7] Finally, they sent them on their way.

2. The Arrival of Barnabas and Saul on Cyprus (13:4-5)

[4]The two of them, sent on their way by the Holy Spirit, went down to Seleucia and sailed from there to Cyprus. [5]When they arrived at Salamis, they proclaimed the word of God in the Jewish synagogues. John was with them as their helper.

Barnabas and Saul were missionaries "sent on their way by the Holy Spirit," a reference to the fact that their calling and even the nature and extent of their work would be directed by the Spirit (see 13:9, 52; 15:12; 16:6-7).[8]

About a day's walk toward the coast (sixteen miles) stood the port city of Seleucia. The two missionaries used this city as a place to board a ship which would take them to Cyprus. The island of Cyprus was about 100 miles off the coast in the Mediterranean Sea. It was the birthplace of Barnabas (4:36) and had belonged to the Roman Empire since 57 B.C. In 22 B.C. it became a senatorial province and a proconsul began to govern it. Luke notes that

---

[6]Shepard notes, "This positive and urgent order was not directed to the church, to constitute these men apostles. Paul was already an apostle from his conversion . . . . It was a special consecration of these missionaries for a work they would do in the Gentile world. . ." (*Life*, p. 97).

[7]Ernest Best takes this laying on of hands as a commissioning to a ministry on behalf of the church. See his "Acts XIII.1-3," *JTS* 11 (1960): 344-348.

[8]Alexander Campbell has a lengthy note on this verse regarding the Greek formula for "the Holy Spirit." In many cases the phrase appears with the Greek article (as is true in this verse) and in other cases the phrase lacks the Greek article. He points out that in both cases the phrase describes the same Holy Spirit. See his *Acts of the Apostles* (Nashville: Gospel Advocate, 1858), pp. 85-86.

Sergius Paulus (13:7) was the proconsul at the time Barnabas and Saul arrived, and he uses the correct term for proconsul (ανθυπάτος, *anthypatos*).

One of the major cities of Cyprus was Salamis. Located on the eastern coast of the island, it was the nearest Cyprian city from their point of departure. They immediately visited "in the Jewish synagogues." The presence of Jews on Cyprus is a historical point also established by both Philo and Josephus.[9] The missionary message is summarized with the phrase "the word of God" (τὸν λόγον τοῦ θεοῦ, *ton logon tou theou*) — a description of the gospel, as becomes obvious when the content of the speeches of Acts 13–14 is studied.

Here Luke also notes that John Mark, a cousin of Barnabas, was present (see 12:25; Col 4:10). Possibly Luke waits to mention him now in order to distinguish between his role as "helper" (ὑπηρέτης, *hypēretēs*, which means "assistant") from that of Barnabas and Saul who were called by the Holy Spirit to lead in the work.

3. The Confrontation at Paphos (13:6-12)

[6]**They traveled through the whole island until they came to Paphos. There they met a Jewish sorcerer and false prophet named Bar-jesus, [7]who was an attendant of the proconsul, Sergius Paulus. The proconsul, an intelligent man, sent for Barnabas and Saul because he wanted to hear the word of God. [8]But Elymas the sorcerer (for that is what his name means) opposed them and tried to turn the proconsul from the faith. [9]Then Saul, who was also called Paul, filled with the Holy Spirit, looked straight at Elymas and said, [10]"You are a child of the devil and an enemy of everything that is right! You are full of all kinds of deceit and trickery. Will you never stop perverting the right ways of the Lord? [11]Now the hand of the Lord is against you. You are going to be blind, and for a time you will be unable to see the light of the sun." Immediately mist and darkness came over him, and he groped about, seeking someone to lead him by the hand. [12]When the proconsul saw what had happened, he believed, for he was amazed at the teaching about the Lord.**

[9]See Philo, *Embassy to Caius* 282 and Josephus, *Antiquities* 13.284-287.

Traveling the entire width of Cyprus would be about ninety miles. The word for "traveled" is διέρχομαι (*dierchomai*) and in Acts frequently means "to travel while preaching."[10]

Paphos was located on the western end of Cyprus. This city was considered important enough by the Romans to become the seat of governmental administration. Barnabas and Saul came into contact with the proconsul Sergius Paulus here and were making progress with him in their witness for the gospel. This particular Roman official has left no definite record in history other than this mention in Acts, though two inscriptions found in Pisidian Antioch may refer to him.[11]

A Jewish sorcerer, however, sought to obstruct their progress.[12] Luke describes him as a "false prophet named Bar-Jesus," a description which distinguishes him from the prophets in Antioch (13:1). Beyond the label false prophet, he is also called a sorcerer (μάγος, *magos*), a term which invites comparisons with Simon the Sorcerer (8:9ff). In addition, his name was Bar-Jesus ("son of Jesus" or "son of Joshua" in Aramaic), and he apparently had taken the name "Elymas," which probably comes from an Arabic word meaning "sage," but in this case had the practical reference to a court magician.

It was quite common for Roman officials to consult magicians. In the case of Elymas, he may have felt that his position would be threatened if Sergius Paulus took seriously the claims of the gospel.

Just as Peter had denounced Simon the Sorcerer, so Saul did in this case. It is at this very point that Luke chooses to note the change in his identification of Saul. He notes that he was also called Paul. The significance of this item has nothing to do with the name of the proconsul or of any heavenly revelation. Rather, the use of the Roman name Paul begins just at that point where the apostle

---

[10]See Acts 16:4,6; 18:23.

[11]Bruce gives details concerning these inscriptions, one to L. Sergius Paullus and another to a female Sergia Paulla. See his "Chronological Questions," 279-280. Proconsuls were appointed to Roman provinces which were controlled by the Roman Senate. When a province was controlled by the emperor directly, a legion was stationed there and it was administered by a legate (or governor). R. Jewett discusses the difficulty of using this data to establish any concrete dates for Paul's visit to Cyprus (*Chronology*, p. 36).

[12]Dunn comments on how Luke avoids embellishing this account (*Jesus*, pp. 168-169).

launches into his mission to the Greco-Roman world. Perhaps Paul felt the need to identify more closely with his non-Jewish audience. Luke's sensitivity to the realities of the Mediterranean world are also obvious in this gesture.[13]

Besides the change in Paul's name, another fascinating development in the record begins at this point. Until now, references to the two missionaries were always "Barnabas and Saul," in that order (see 13:1,7; 11:30; 12:25). From here on the references will be "Paul and Barnabas" or "Paul and his companions" (see 13:13,42,46).[14] This change in order implies that Paul's role was becoming more prominent in the work.

Thus it was Paul, "filled with the Holy Spirit," who looked at Elymas and called him a "child of the devil." This sorcerer was no true son of Jesus as his name might suggest (*bar* means "son" in Aramaic). His actions placed him totally at odds with the ways of the Lord. Such an indictment would be a serious blow to one who promoted himself as having intimate contact with the Divine will, as did all court magi.

The sentence pronounced by Paul was ironic. Just as the apostle had experienced blindness on the way to Damascus (9:9), so now he describes for Elymas what he will experience. In pronouncing this sentence from God, Paul was fulfilling the role of a prophet. He was filled with the Spirit, and thus possessed Divine authority to speak words of condemnation in regard to Elymas.

For the proconsul the effects were immediate. He "believed" in the sense that he was converted. The miracle confirmed what he had already heard regarding "the teaching about the Lord."

4. The Arrival at Pisidian Antioch (13:13-15)

[13]From Paphos, Paul and his companions sailed to Perga in Pamphylia, where John left them to return to Jerusalem. [14]From

---

[13]Polhill explains that as a Roman citizen Paul would have three names—a praenomen, a nomen, and a cognomen. "Paul" was probably the Apostle's cognomen. His first two names are lost to us (p. 295).

[14]The only exceptions are 14:12,14 and 15:12,25 where the perspective of the people of Lystra and the Jerusalem conference determines the priority of Barnabas.

**Perga they went on to Pisidian Antioch. On the Sabbath they
entered the synagogue and sat down. [15]After the reading from the
Law and the Prophets, the synagogue rulers sent word to them,
saying, "Brothers, if you have a message of encouragement for the
people, please speak."**

After the episode in Paphos, the missionaries sailed on toward
the city of Perga in the province of Pamphylia. They journeyed
northwest to reach the harbor city of Attalia where they disem-
barked. Getting to Perga meant sailing some seven miles up the
Cestrus River and then walking about five miles west.[15] Pamphylia
was made a separate province by the Romans from 25 B.C. to A.D.
43, and then was merged with Lycia to become Pamphylia-Lycia
from A.D. 43-68. Perga's history predated the Hellenistic period,
and by the time Paul visited it was the capital of Pamphylia.
Apparently the missionaries did no preaching here until their next
visit (14:25), but used the city as a springboard for their push
toward Pisidian Antioch.

At Perga, however, John Mark decided to abandon the journey.
No reasons are give by Luke for this decision. Did he resent Paul's
becoming the leader of the mission effort? Did he oppose the plan
to travel the long distance to Antioch of Pisidia? Did he become ill
and need to return home? Did he reject something in the content of
Paul's message? All of these questions have been asked, but there is
little evidence to answer them.[16]

At any rate, Paul and Barnabas moved on some 110 miles northwest to Pisidian Antioch. To do so meant a climb across the Taurus
Mountain Range to an elevation of 3,600 feet. They traveled
through barren land which sometimes became dangerous with
flooded streams and criminals waiting in ambush. Antioch itself was
a Roman colony and populated with large numbers of retired military men.

---

[15]This was true unless the Cestrus River was not navigable by the time of
Paul's visit, in which case the whole distance was covered on foot. See Lake
and Cadbury, p. 147.

[16]William Ramsay speculates that Paul caught malaria in the lowlands and
John Mark did not want to travel into the highlands with Paul. See his *St.
Paul the Traveller and Roman Citizen* (London: Hodder & Stoughton, 1897),

After making the long journey (which Luke passes over with a phrase), they "entered the synagogue." Antioch had a substantial Jewish population, and Paul and Barnabas again chose to begin their work here. Doing so would allow Paul to speak the gospel first to the people to whom the Messiah came (see Rom 1:16; 9-11). At the same time he would be reaching Gentiles who were the "God-fearers" in the synagogue.

"After the reading from the Law and the Prophets" the missionaries were asked to speak. According to the best evidence, synagogues in the Diaspora used a pattern for worship involving specific activities. These included the recitation of the Shema, followed by prayer, the reading from the Torah (Law), the reading from the prophets, preaching, and the priestly benediction. Often competent visitors were asked to deliver the sermon.[17]

5. Paul's Address in the Synagogue (13:16-41)

Old Testament Prelude to Christ (13:16-22)

[16]Standing up, Paul motioned with his hand and said: "Men of Israel and you Gentiles who worship God, listen to me! [17]The God of the people of Israel chose our fathers; he made the people prosper during their stay in Egypt, with mighty power he led them out of that country, [18]he endured their conduct[a] for about forty years in the desert, [19]he overthrew seven nations in Canaan and gave their land to his people as their inheritance. [20]All this took

---

pp. 89-97. Perhaps the best suggestion is that of Martin who suggests that John Mark never envisioned the extent to which the missionary journey would take them into Gentile territory (*Foundations*, 2:105). See also Polhill, 296-297; R.A. Culpepper, "Paul's Mission to the Gentile World," *RevEx* 71 (1974): 487-497. Whatever the reason, Luke's mention of this incident serves to demonstrate his willingness to report events honestly without giving in to the temptation to embellish his characters beyond what the facts will allow. See also 15:36-40.

[17]For a full description of worship in the synagogue see Emil Schürer, *The History of the Jewish People in the Age of Jesus Christ*, ed. and rev. Geza Vermes, Fergus Millar, and Matthew Black (Edinburgh: T & T Clark, 1979), 2:447-454.

about 450 years. After this, God gave them judges until the time of Samuel the prophet. [21]Then the people asked for a king, and he gave them Saul son of Kish, of the tribe of Benjamin, who ruled forty years. [22]After removing Saul, he made David their king. He testified concerning him: 'I have found David son of Jesse a man after my own heart; he will do everything I want him to do.'

[a]*18* Some manuscripts *and cared for them*

Paul's opening remarks[18] took stock of the make-up of his audience. Two groups were represented in the synagogue. "Men of Israel" was Paul's phrase to acknowledge the Jewish hearers and "you Gentiles who worship God" paid respect to the non-Jewish listeners.

Paul then launched into a brief summary of Old Testament history (much as Stephen had done in 7:2-53). Throughout this address, however, Paul's emphasis was on the gracious dealings of God with the people of Israel. Polhill draws attention to the verbs used by Paul.[19] God "chose" (ἐκλέγομαι, *eklegomai*, "elected") the patriarchs. He "made the people prosper" in Egypt (ὑψόω, *hypsoō*, "exalted"). He "led them out" (ἐξάγω, *exagō*) of Egypt. Beyond all this, he "endured their conduct," and "overthrew" their enemies.

---

[18]This speech of Paul is one of those used by Philipp Vielhauer to call into question the authenticity of the speeches of Acts. He contends a close examination of Paul's letters shows the speeches of Paul in Acts to be different in both form and substance. See his "'Paulinism' of Acts," in *Studies in Luke-Acts*, pp. 33-50. Though it may be admitted that Luke in some cases reproduces the speeches of Paul from a distance, and often in his own terminology, the objections of Vielhauer are not insurmountable obstacles to seeing the speeches in Acts as at least summaries of Paul's own words. Some of the problem arises because of a misunderstanding of Paul's doctrine of justification by faith, a topic which has received much scholarly attention in recent years. See Marshall, *Historian and Theologian* (Grand Rapids: Zondervan, 1971), pp. 190-192; Bruce, p. 262; Gasque, *History of Criticism*, pp. 196,220,231. See also E.P. Sanders, *Paul and Palestinian Judaism* (Philadelphia: Fortress, 1977). A.T. Robertson saw no problem with the correlation between Acts and the Pauline letters. He states that "Acts rightly understood is the best commentary of the letters of Paul, and the letters on the Acts." See his *Luke the Historian*, p. 83. Hemer has no problem putting together an entire list of correlations between Acts and the Epistles. See his *Book of Acts*, pp. 181-190. J.W. Bowker analyzes Paul's address in the synagogue to see if he can find links to what is known about

He then "gave their land to his people as their inheritance" (κατα-κληρονομέω, *kataklēronomeō*), "gave them judges," and at their request "gave them Saul" as their king. Finally, he "made (literally "raised up") David" as their king.[20] All of these verbs argue for the kindnesses of God as demonstrated to Israel.

David's reign was characterized by righteousness because of David's own sense of loyalty to the Lord, especially as contrasted with Saul. When God announced that Saul would be replaced, the king was told that the Lord had "sought out a man after his own heart" (1 Sam 13:14).[21]

Paul's approach in covering this period of Old Testament history stands in contrast to that of Stephen. When Stephen addressed the Sanhedrin, his point was how rebellious the fathers had always been in matters of fulfilling God's will. Paul's purpose differed from Stephen's and so Paul's approach built a foundation for demonstrating that Christ was the ultimate fulfillment of God's gracious care over Israel.

Paul's mention of "450 years" presents some problems only if we try to make the number apply to the period of the judges. But Paul's reference is to the 400 years of Egyptian bondage, plus the forty years of wilderness wanderings and ten years for the conquest of Canaan.[22]

Fulfillment in Christ (13:23-37)

[23]**"From this man's descendants God has brought to Israel the Savior Jesus, as he promised. [24]Before the coming of Jesus, John**

---

the style of Jewish sermons from the synagogue. He finds some elements in common, but the picture is ambiguous. See his "Speeches in Acts," *NTS* 14 (1968): 96-111. Meanwhile, Dale Goldsmith finds some parallels in Qumran. See his "Acts 13:33-37: A *Pesher* on II Samuel 7," *JBL* 87 (1968): 321-324.

[19]Polhill, p. 300.

[20]Dupont observes the parallel between Paul's mention of the "raising up" of David as king and the "raising up" of the Savior to serve as the new king. See his *Salvation*, pp. 125,136-137.

[21]Paul's quote also draws from Ps 89:20 and Isa 44:28.

[22]Eugene Merrill, on the other hand, takes Paul's language to refer to the total sum of years for the judges plus the years that Eli was judge — a total of 447 years. See his "Paul's Use of 'About 450 Years' in Acts 13:20," *BiblThecSac* 138 (1981): 246-257.

preached repentance and baptism to all the people of Israel. [25]As John was completing his work, he said: 'Who do you think I am? I am not that one. No, but he is coming after me, whose sandals I am not worthy to untie.' [26]Brothers, children of Abraham, and you God-fearing Gentiles, it is to us that this message of salvation has been sent. [27]The people of Jerusalem and their rulers did not recognize Jesus, yet in condemning him they fulfilled the words of the prophets that are read every Sabbath. [28]Though they found no proper ground for a death sentence, they asked Pilate to have him executed. [29]When they had carried out all that was written about him, they took him down from the tree and laid him in a tomb. [30]But God raised him from the dead, [31]and for many days he was seen by those who had traveled with him from Galilee to Jerusalem. They are now his witnesses to our people. [32]We tell you the good news: What God promised our fathers [33]he has fulfilled for us, their children, by raising up Jesus. As it is written in the second Psalm: 'You are my Son; today I have become your Father.'[a],[b] [34]The fact that God raised him from the dead, never to decay, is stated in these words: 'I will give you the holy and sure blessings promised to David.'[c] [35]So it is stated elsewhere: 'You will not let your Holy One see decay.'[d] [36]For when David had served God's purpose in his own generation, he fell asleep; he was buried with his fathers and his body decayed. [37]But the one whom God raised from the dead did not see decay.

[a]33 Or *have begotten you*   [b]33 Psalm 2:7   [c]34 Isaiah 55:3   [d]35 Psalm 16:10

The epitome of God's goodness to Israel, declared Paul, was his choice of David to be king. Behind these words stands the promise made to David in 2 Samuel 7:12-16. God promised David that he would raise up his offspring to succeed him on the throne and establish his throne forever.

Paul announced to the worshipers at Antioch that this promise had been fulfilled in Christ. "From this man's descendants," that is, from the royal line of David himself God "brought to Israel the Savior" (see Matt 1:1-17; Luke 3:23-38; Rom 1:3).

Pointing to John's baptism, Paul described how God had prepared the way for the Savior's arrival. The quotation from John is found in all four gospels (Matt 3:11; Mark 1:7; Luke 3:15; John 1:27). John insisted that he was not the one coming (possibly a reference to the Messianic prophecy of Mal 3:1), and was unworthy to perform even the slave's duty of untying the sandals of the one coming. The influence of John's baptism of repentance was still being felt in communities as far away as Ephesus (see 19:1-7).

Paul's concern was to get to the core of the gospel—the crucifixion and resurrection of Jesus. As in previous apostolic addresses, the blame for the crucifixion was placed on the people of Jerusalem, especially the leaders (see 2:23; 3:17; 4:27; 10:39). In this sermon Paul even referred to Pilate's conclusion that Jesus was innocent (see Luke 23:4; Acts 3:13). In spite of the Jews' actions, Paul insisted, God used the event to fulfill every Scripture which spoke of him.

Paul used the word "tree" to speak of the cross, probably to show the connection between Jesus' death and the words of Deuteronomy 21:23: "anyone who is hung on a tree is cursed" (see also 5:30; 10:39; and Gal 3:13). Of course, the reference to their taking him down from the cross fits the Gospel narratives which name Joseph of Arimathea and Nicodemus as the ones who performed this act of mercy (Luke 23:53; John 19:38-42).

Christ could not, however, be kept in the tomb. "God raised him from the dead," Paul announced. He also referred to the witnesses who saw him after the resurrection.

So Paul came to the climax of his discourse about Christ. He is the fulfillment of "what God promised our fathers." His resurrection is the fulfillment of such passages as Psalm 2:7, Isaiah 55:3, and Psalm 16:10 which Paul strung together in this sermon. "You are my Son" was a Messianic Psalm based on the promise of 2 Samuel 7.[23] Paul was arguing that Jesus is the "Son" whom the Father claimed as his own. "Today" refers to the event of the resurrection of Jesus (see Rom 1:4).

---

[23]Dupont shows how the linking of these Old Testament references functions in Heb 1:3-5 in much the same way as here. See his *Salvation*, pp. 115-117. Dunn discusses the importance of the resurrection in the establishment of Jesus as the Son of God. See his *Christology in the Making: A New Testament Inquiry into the Origins of the Doctrine of the Incarnation* (Philadelphia: Westminster, 1980), pp. 35-36.

The "holy and sure blessings promised to David" also referred to the promise of 2 Samuel 7. Paul insisted that it was in Christ's resurrection that these blessings were offered, largely because of the statement in Psalm 16:10 that God's "Holy One" would not see decay. Paul argued that this promise could not apply to David, since this famous king was dead and buried (compare 2:31). The promise could only refer to Jesus, who was raised from the dead.

Conclusion and Warning (13:38-41)

[38]"Therefore, my brothers, I want you to know that through Jesus the forgiveness of sins is proclaimed to you. [39]Through him everyone who believes is justified from everything you could not be justified from by the law of Moses. [40]Take care that what the prophets have said does not happen to you: [41]'Look, you scoffers, wonder and perish, for I am going to do something in your days that you would never believe, even if someone told you.'[a]"

[a]41 Hab. 1:5

Now Paul was driving to his final point. If Jesus was sent as God's Holy One, then "forgiveness of sins" can be found only in him. Furthermore, Paul summarized the doctrine of justification through faith in Christ, for which he is so famous in such letters as Romans and Galatians. "Everyone who believes" may find forgiveness, and that not by obedience to "the law of Moses," since by that means one "could not be justified" (δικαιόω, dikaioō; compare Rom 3:20-26).

Paul's last word was a quotation of Habakkuk 1:5, a passage which served originally as a warning to Israel about King Nebuchadnezzar's rise to world dominion. Paul indicated that God was about to bring these words to fulfillment again, and this time in Antioch of Pisidia. God would do something they never would have believed—he turned to the Gentiles with salvation.[24]

---

[24]Polhill, p. 305.

6. The Response to Paul's Address (13:42-43)

[42]As Paul and Barnabas were leaving the synagogue, the people invited them to speak further about these things on the next Sabbath. [43]When the congregation was dismissed, many of the Jews and devout converts to Judaism followed Paul and Barnabas, who talked with them and urged them to continue in the grace of God.

The response of the synagogue audience was positive. Many were impressed enough to ask for further discussion of the message Paul had preached. Evidently from among both "Jews and devout converts to Judaism," the two groups represented in the synagogue (see comments above on 13:16), came interested listeners. Some were serious enough that they "followed Paul and Barnabas" as they left the synagogue, seeking more information. For these listeners the missionaries expressed encouragement to continue their eagerness for "the grace of God."

7. Gentile Interest and Jewish Opposition (13:44-52)

[44]On the next Sabbath almost the whole city gathered to hear the word of the Lord. [45]When the Jews saw the crowds, they were filled with jealousy and talked abusively against what Paul was saying. [46]Then Paul and Barnabas answered them boldly: "We had to speak the word of God to you first. Since you reject it and do not consider yourselves worthy of eternal life, we now turn to the Gentiles. [47]For this is what the Lord has commanded us: 'I have made you[a] a light for the Gentiles, that you may bring salvation to the ends of the earth.'[b] [48]When the Gentiles heard this, they were glad and honored the word of the Lord; and all who were appointed for eternal life believed. [49]The word of the Lord spread through the whole region. [50]But the Jews incited the God-fearing women of high standing and the leading men of the city. They stirred up persecution against Paul and Barnabas, and expelled them from their region. [51]So they shook the dust from

**their feet in protest against them and went to Iconium. [52]And the
disciples were filled with joy and with the Holy Spirit.**

[a]*47* **The Greek is singular.**   [b]*47* **Isaiah 49:6**

As Paul fully intended, the Gentiles were captivated by the idea
that salvation also included them. One Sabbath later, "almost the
whole city" was present to hear what they could of the preaching of
Paul and Barnabas. Even if this phrase is intended as hyperbole, the
crowd was large enough that the Jews "were filled with jealousy"
and began opposing Paul's proclamation of the gospel.

Paul's reaction was decisive. The Jews were showing their rejection of the message bringing eternal life. Paul announced that the
gospel mission would now turn to the Gentiles. He reinforced this
principle by quoting Isaiah 49:6, a passage which Paul applied to
what Jesus Christ did. He came to serve as a "light for the Gentiles."
So to the Gentiles Paul would go.

This principle will be followed throughout the rest of Acts. We
should not understand that Paul abandoned the idea that Jews
could still be converted to Christ. Neither did he quit preaching to
them whenever the opportunity came (see 14:1). His practice of
beginning with the local synagogue continued. But he now considered his primary mission to be one to the Gentiles (see Rom 11:13;
Eph 3:8).

Paul's principle was met with enthusiasm by the Gentiles of
Antioch. They "were glad and honored the word of the Lord."
Besides this, "many believed," meaning that they became converts.
Luke clarifies his mention of this group with the description "all who
were appointed for eternal life." As Bruce notes, the participle
"appointed" comes from the Greek word τάσσω (*tassō*), which carries
the idea of being "enrolled" or "inscribed," and seems to refer to the
book of life (Exod 32:32-33; Ps 69:28; Isa 4:3; Dan 12:1; Luke 10:20;
Rev 13:8).[25] The phrase implies the initiative of God in the matter of
personal salvation, but does not contradict the role of free will when
a person comes to Christ. God can "work in" us to accomplish our
salvation, but we must also "work out" our salvation (Phil 2:12-13).

---

[25]Bruce, p. 267, n. 111.

While the Gentiles were rejoicing, however, the Jewish element of the city was enraged. "The word of the Lord spread," and the Jews decided to do what they could to derail its progress, even enlisting the help of women of high social status who came from the ranks of the God-fearers. Evidently these women had enough influence among the political forces in Antioch that a persecution of the apostles was initiated. They saw to it that Paul and Barnabas were expelled "from their region," which would include the area around Antioch.

In response the apostles "shook the dust from their feet." This practice was used by the Jews to indicate their disgust at being defiled by even the clinging earth from Gentile lands they visited. In the case of the apostles a reversal of this implication was given. They were ridding themselves of the remnants of these antagonistic Jews. Meanwhile, these disciples who were largely Gentiles, were filled with "joy and with the Holy Spirit" (see 2:4; 4:31).

ACTS 14

8. The Visit to Iconium (14:1-7)

¹At Iconium Paul and Barnabas went as usual into the Jewish synagogue. There they spoke so effectively that a great number of Jews and Gentiles believed. ²But the Jews who refused to believe stirred up the Gentiles and poisoned their minds against the brothers. ³So Paul and Barnabas spent considerable time there, speaking boldly for the Lord, who confirmed the message of his grace by enabling them to do miraculous signs and wonders. ⁴The people of the city were divided; some sided with the Jews, others with the apostles. ⁵There was a plot afoot among the Gentiles and Jews, together with their leaders, to mistreat them and stone them. ⁶But they found out about it and fled to the Lycaonian cities of Lystra and Derbe and to the surrounding country, ⁷where they continued to preach the good news.

Paul and Barnabas arrived "at Iconium" after journeying some ninety miles to the southeast from Pisidian Antioch. They followed the Sebastian Way to the ancient region of Phrygia. Entrance to the city meant a climb of 3,370 feet to a plateau on which the city rested. Iconium was thoroughly hellenized, but by the time of Paul also showed Roman influences. After A.D. 41 one of the names for the city was "Claudiconium," a name worn to show the city's relationship to Claudius Caesar. For a city to wear the name of an emperor was considered a high honor.

"As usual," Paul and Barnabas began their efforts in the Jewish synagogue. Luke's language here might raise a question concerning Paul's statement in 13:46 that he was turning to the Gentiles. But that statement did not rule out any attempt at winning his Jewish countrymen (see Rom 10:1; 11:1-2).

Besides his concern for the Jews, Paul knew that the synagogue was a fruitful place to begin evangelizing a new area. Here he could find Jews with a sufficient understanding of the Old Testament to hear how Jesus fulfilled the Scriptures. Also, the presence of Gentile proselytes and other Gentiles gave Paul immediate access to those Gentiles most likely to hear the gospel claims.

The efforts of Paul and Barnabas produced encouraging results in that "a great number of Jews and Gentiles believed" (πιστεύω, *pisteuō*). By contrast some of the Jews "refused to believe" (οἱ ... ἀπειθήσαντες, *hoi . . . apeithēsantes*) and sponsored opposition to the gospel. The contrast of these two words for "believe" probably indicates that the first verb carries with it the idea of obedience, as well as believing.

While these antagonistic Jews fomented distrust among the Gentile population, Paul and Barnabas remained firm in their commitment to preach. As a matter of fact, the word "so" creates a bit of a problem in the text. We would expect something like "the apostles spent considerable time in spite of the opposition of the Jews." The Greek phrase μὲν οὖν (*men oun*) can carry the idea of "even though," and the sense is that "the apostles spent considerable time there" even though they endured persecution from the Jews.

Some scholars, however, solve this problem by suggesting that two waves of persecution occurred with a period of peace between them. If this is the case, v. 2 would represent the first wave and v. 5 the second.[1]

During this extended stay in Iconium the apostles were able through the power of God to perform a number of miracles which "confirmed the message of his grace." Throughout the ministries of the apostles supernatural actions served not as a curiosity piece, but as a witness to the divine character of the gospel (see Heb 2:4; Mark 16:15-18).

As time went on the evidence of mixed opinions became pronounced. The "people of the city were divided" in their feelings about this new ministry, some siding with the Jews and others with the apostles. But such a scenario was described by Jesus when he

---

[1]See the note on this verse in the *NIV Study Bible*.

brought the truth which would set "a man against his father, a daughter against her mother, a daughter-in-law against her mother-in-law" (Matt 10:34).

Interesting here is Luke's use of the term "apostle" to describe both Paul and Barnabas (also in 14:14).[2] The word literally means "one who is sent" and is used of the twelve apostles in Acts (1:26; 2:37, etc.). The verses in this chapter are exceptions to the rule. Elsewhere in the New Testament the term is used of James, the brother of the Lord (Gal 1:19; 1 Cor 15:7), Adronicus and Junias (Rom 16:7), and a group who saw the resurrected Jesus distinct from the twelve apostles (1 Cor 15:7; cf. 15:5). Here Paul and Barnabas may be described as apostles because of their commissioning from Antioch.

The resistance faced by Paul and Barnabas now took the form of mob action. Leaders from both the Jewish and Gentile communities worked through elements within the public at large to oppose the preaching of the gospel. For this reason the apostles were forced to flee Iconium, demonstrating that even courageous servants must know when it is wise to step out of the way of oncoming persecution.

In 14:6 Luke's sense of geographical and political realities shines through. The apostles "fled" from Iconium "to the Lycaonian cities of Lystra and Derbe." The phrase suggests that Iconium was not one of the Lycaonian cities. But some ancient writers seem to disagree, placing Iconium in Lycaonia.[3] Further literary and inscriptional evidence shows, however, that Luke is correct here. Iconium was a Phrygian city in the mid-first century. In A.D. 41 Lycaonia was divided into two areas: one eastern and the other to the west. Iconium was referred to as Phrygian because it was in the eastern territory, closer to Phrygia than Lycaonia.[4]

---

[2]See the note on 1:21.

[3]Cicero in *Letters to Friends* 15.4.2 and Pliny the Elder in *Natural History* 5.25.

[4]See the note in the *NIV Study Bible*. Also see Ramsay, *Traveller*, pp. 110-113.

9. The Healing at Lystra (14:8-13)

[8]**In Lystra there sat a man crippled in his feet, who was lame from birth and had never walked. [9]He listened to Paul as he was speaking. Paul looked directly at him, saw that he had faith to be healed [10]and called out, "Stand up on your feet!" At that, the man jumped up and began to walk. [11]When the crowd saw what Paul had done, they shouted in the Lycaonian language, "The gods have come down to us in human form!" [12]Barnabas they called Zeus, and Paul they called Hermes because he was the chief speaker. [13]The priest of Zeus, whose temple was just outside the city, brought bulls and wreaths to the city gates because he and the crowd wanted to offer sacrifices to them.**

"In Lystra" the apostles found the crippled man.[5] Lystra was a city whose ruins were discovered in 1885. When Paul arrived it was a small country town, used by the Romans as a military outpost. It was made a Roman colony in 6 B.C. A military road connected it with Pisidian Antioch, which was also a Roman colony located ninety miles away.

The man they found was "crippled in his feet," "lame from birth," and "had never walked." Luke gives a very full description which prepares the way for the dramatic miracle he is about to relate.

The similarities between Paul's healing of this man and Peter's healing of the lame man in the temple (3:2-10) will be obvious. Like the lame man in the temple, this man's disability began from birth. In the same way Peter did, Paul "looked directly at him." Whether Paul "saw that he had faith" because of supernatural insight is unclear. Also, this lame man responded to the healing in the same way as the man in the temple. When Paul told him to stand on his feet, the man "jumped up and began to walk."

Immediately the crowd responded with amazement. Their reaction included the perception that they were in the presence of powerful deities (compare 28:6).[6] The miracle caused them to conclude that

---

[5]Goulder notices the parallels between the healing here and that of the lame man in the temple (3:1-11). See his *Type and History*, p. 85.

[6]F.G. Downing discusses some of the parallels between this account and

Zeus and Hermes had descended in the human form of Barnabas and Paul. The identification of Paul with Hermes had to do with Paul's being "the chief speaker," a role assigned to Hermes in the Greek pantheon. If Paul was Hermes the next assumption was that Barnabas must be Zeus, since Zeus was usually attended to by Hermes.[7]

Prompting the Lycaonians to these conclusions was perhaps an ancient legend connected with Lystra. Ovid reports that Lystrans felt they had once been visited by these two gods. An impoverished couple showed them hospitality, but the city as a whole was punished for failing to show this kindness.[8] The existence of this legend is confirmed by inscriptions which link these deities in the mythology of Lystra.[9]

The people of Lystra quickly moved to celebrate this visit with a reverence they considered appropriate. "The priest of Zeus" even brought bulls for the sacrifice.[10] This gesture was carried out not in a hasty way, but with "wreaths" that carefully prepared a garlanded sacrifice, a very elaborate expression of worship. The temple was located "just outside the city," suggesting the positioning of the temple to Zeus as divine protection for the city.

But Paul and Barnabas were apparently unaware of the intentions of these people. The reason was the language barrier. Though Paul and Barnabas could communicate with them in the Greek language, they probably could not understand the Lystrans as they communicated with one another in "the Lycaonian language." This language was a dialect in the hill-country which has left few literary remains. Even with the guidance of the Spirit, Paul and Barnabas did not have the ability to interpret this dialect.

---

passages from Josephus regarding the bestowal of divine honors on such Jewish personalities as Abraham, Moses, Daniel, and the Jewish high priest. See his "Common Ground with Paganism," *NTS* 28 (1982): 546-559.

[7]Hermes was also considered the inventor of speech. The Roman equivalent for Hermes was Mercury; for Zeus was Jupiter.

[8]Ovid, *Metamorphoses* 8.620-724. See also Shepard, *Life*, p. 110.

[9]Polhill, p. 314.

[10]The actions of the priest here cause O'Neill to reject the account as historical (*Theology*, p. 150). Shepard, on the other hand, sees no problem with this point in the story (*Life*, p. 110). See also Bruce, p. 275.

10. Paul's Address about the Living God (14:14-18)

[14]**But when the apostles Barnabas and Paul heard of this, they tore their clothes and rushed out into the crowd, shouting:** [15]**"Men, why are you doing this? We too are only men, human like you. We are bringing you good news, telling you to turn from these worthless things to the living God, who made heaven and earth and sea and everything in them.** [16]**In the past, he let all nations go their own way.** [17]**Yet he has not left himself without testimony: he has shown kindness by giving you rain from heaven and crops in their seasons; he provides you with plenty of food and fills your hearts with joy."** [18]**Even with these words, they had difficulty keeping the crowd from sacrificing to them.**

Again the term "apostles" (as in 14:4) is used to designate the role of both Paul and Barnabas. They were messengers "sent" from God and commissioned by the church at Antioch. When Paul and Barnabas understood what was being planned, "they tore their clothes" in the Jewish manner of extreme protest. The practice of tearing one's clothes may be traced back to Old Testament times where it was done to express grief (Gen 37:29), show deep distress (Josh 7:6), or to protest against blasphemy (Mark 14:63).

In this case the apostles realized how inappropriate it was to treat them as beings deserving of worship. Tearing their clothes expressed their horror. But they also used the incident to launch into the gospel. Insisting that they were not deities, but mere human beings (ὁμοιοπαθεῖς, *homoiopatheis*, "human like you"),[11] they rejected the proposals of the crowd to worship them. Instead, they began their message concerning the true and living God.

Parallels between this address and Paul's later sermon on the Areopagus (17:22-31) have often been cited. The setting was similar, since this sermon at Lystra is the first one in Acts addressed to a purely pagan audience. Even with Cornelius and the Ethiopian there was a connection with the Jewish synagogue. The pagan context influenced the approach used by the apostles here. Rather than speaking

---

[11]The word also occurs in James 5:17. Rejecting such attempts to deify a mere man is exactly what King Herod failed to do (12:23).

of the law of Moses or Old Testament personalities and promises (such as in 2:25-34; 7:2-47; 13:17-23), Paul spoke to the people of Lystra as if they knew nothing about Jewish history and religion.

He began by emphasizing the emptiness of worshiping "these worthless things." His reference was to the worship of idols (see 1 Sam 12:21), and he drew a sharp contrast between these things and the goodness of the living God. This God is the one who created the universe.[12] He is a personal God, for he not only created "heaven and earth and sea and everything in them," but he also has plans for the nations. In all of this God can be understood not as some impersonal force or power, but as an intelligent, personal God who conducts himself rationally.

The core of Paul's sermon, however, is God's kindness and patience. God has shown himself forbearing when it comes to punishing sin. He "let all nations go their own way," a phrase that is best understood in light of Paul's statement on the Areopagus where he said that "in the past God overlooked such ignorance, but now he commands all people everywhere to repent" (17:30).

God also gave them "rain from heaven and crops in their seasons," as well as "plenty of food" to fill their "hearts with joy." Provisions of divine providence were thus a testimony to God's goodness.[13] In Romans 1:20 Paul makes a similar statement and then concludes that humanity has no excuse for ignoring God. Though he did not in this context argue to that same conclusion (as far as the record shows), he implied that God's kindnesses impose demands upon his creatures. Luke does not provide the conclusion to the remarks by Paul and Barnabas, which surely included a call to repentance directed at the audience. Even with these words, says Luke, the apostles "had difficulty keeping the crowd from sacrificing to them." The comment implies, though, that they did indeed get the sacrifice stopped.

---

[12]Thomas Slater believes that Paul's quotation of Exod 20:11 from the LXX serves as an implicit validation of the Gentile mission. See his "The Possible Influence of LXX Exodus 20:11 on Acts 14:15," *AUSS* 30 (1992): 151-152.

[13]Polhill notes that such ideas of divine providence would not have been strange to the Lystrans, since pagan writers often reflected on the "benevolence of the gods" (p. 316).

11. The Stoning of Paul (14:19-20a)

[19]Then some Jews came from Antioch and Iconium and won the crowd over. They stoned Paul and dragged him outside the city, thinking he was dead. [20]But after the disciples had gathered around him, he got up and went back into the city.

Trouble would not stay away from the apostles. Though the word "then" may imply some time lapse in which Paul and Barnabas ministered in Lystra, the work was cut short. The mention of "disciples" in 14:20, however, suggests that they did see results from their work.

"Some Jews came from Antioch and Iconium," as far as 130 miles away (a journey of six or seven days on foot) in order to stir up trouble for the apostles. The ties between Lystra and Antioch of Pisidia were close, as is demonstrated by the "statue of Concord" dedicated by the citizens of Lystra in Antioch. But the zeal of Jewish leaders from Antioch explains their willingness to go to such lengths in order to counter the progress of the gospel.

The Jews succeeded in that they "won the crowd over," managing to convince them that Paul and Barnabas were a threat to their community. How they may have accomplished this is not stated, but among the crowd were those who were more than willing to take matters into their own hands. "They stoned Paul," pelting him with rocks so that even as they "dragged him outside the city," they assumed he was dead. Because of their concern for him, "the disciples" gathered around him. Perhaps they were praying for him. Maybe they laid hands on him or sought to bind up his wounds. It may be that they were grieving because they also assumed he was dead. Whether Paul really was dead or in a state of unconsciousness is unclear. Luke's language that they dragged him out "thinking he was dead" may indicate that the latter was the case until sometime after the mob departed.

At any rate, he then "got up" (whether by resurrection or by resuscitation) and went back into the city. Quite possibly this event was what Paul has in mind years later when he describes his hardships to the Corinthian believers and says that once he was stoned (2 Cor 11:25). Besides this, he told the Galatians that he bore on his body "the marks of Jesus" (6:17), which in the physical sense of the word could certainly be produced by experiences like the one at Lystra.

12. The Visit to Derbe and Return to Lystra, Iconium, and Pisidian Antioch (14:20b-23)

[20]The next day he and Barnabas left for Derbe. [21]They preached the good news in that city and won a large number of disciples. Then they returned to Lystra, Iconium and Antioch, [22]strengthening the disciples and encouraging them to remain true to the faith. "We must go through many hardships to enter the kingdom of God," they said. [23]Paul and Barnabas appointed elders[a] for them in each church and, with prayer and fasting, committed them to the Lord, in whom they had put their trust.

[a]*23* Or *Barnabas ordained elders*; or *Barnabas had elders elected*

A day after Paul's stoning the mission team was on the road bound for Derbe. Even if what happened to him was not a resurrection from the dead, it is nothing short of miraculous that he had been restored to the point of traveling the sixty miles to Derbe. The journey would take several days on foot.

Derbe was a border town in the southeastern corner of the Lycaonian region of the province of Galatia.[14] Here the apostles preached "the good news" and saw "a large number of disciples" won for the Lord. The summary is brief, but shows that even after the discouragements of Antioch, Iconium, and Lystra, the missionaries continued to preach faithfully the good news of Jesus. Their endurance was rewarded richly.

At this point the decision was made to return to these cities. As Polhill notes, from Derbe the apostles might have traveled some 150 miles southeast through the Cilician Gates to Tarsus, and then on to Antioch of Syria. They could have preferred the comforts of Paul's hometown or the city which had provided encouragement for their mission. Instead they felt the obligation to revisit the churches they

---

[14]An inscription discovered recently establishes the site of Derbe as thirty miles east of what was previously believed to be the location of the city.

had established. Though it is possible that new magistrates were in position by the time Paul and Barnabas returned,[15] going back to places where they had met such hostility demanded a high degree of courage.

Their desire was the "strengthening" of the disciples and "encouraging them to remain true to the faith." This work included instruction about coping with the trials which would come. The implication is that the resistance faced earlier by Paul and Barnabas had carried over to other believers once the apostles were gone. The theme of suffering for Christ is very characteristic of Paul's letters (Rom 8:17; 2 Thess 1:4; 2 Tim 2:12). Those waiting for the return of the King must be prepared to endure hardships.[16]

Included with this instruction also was the need for leaders. Paul and Barnabas "appointed elders (πρεσβύτερος, presbyteros) for them in each church." The word "appointed" (χειροτονέω, cheirotoneō) carries a wide range of meanings. The question arises as to who did the choosing of the elders. In Acts 6:3 the congregation chose their leaders. Here the verb cheirotoneō may mean "to appoint by a show of hands" or "to appoint or elect without regard to the method."[17] On the other hand, it may also mean simply "to appoint" or "ordain." This last meaning would imply that Paul and Barnabas selected the elders. Given the pattern established in 6:3, however, it is probable that the apostles would have provided the congregations here some voice in the matter.

"Elders" is a term describing a leadership role which is prominent in the letters of Paul. Though the term "elder" is not always used (see 1 Cor 16:15-18; Gal 6:6; Phil 1:1; 2:29; 1 Thess 5:12-13), it is clear that Paul's congregations typically included mature believers in this role (see Acts 20:17-31; 1 Tim 3:1-13; Titus 1:5-9). The term "elder" was used of spiritual leaders in the Jewish synagogue, as well.

---

[15]Ramsay, Traveller, p. 120.

[16]Rabbinic comments may be found which echo this theme. See Moore, Judaism, 2:254-255.

[17]NIV Study Bible. That Paul could find men of sufficient maturity for these positions is probably due to the fact that they had been associated with the Jewish synagogue. See McGarvey, 2:50.

13. Return to Antioch of Syria (14:24-28)

[24]After going through Pisidia, they came into Pamphylia, [25]and when they had preached the word in Perga, they went down to Attalia. [26]From Attalia they sailed back to Antioch, where they had been committed to the grace of God for the work they had now completed. [27]On arriving there, they gathered the church together and reported all that God had done through them and how he had opened the door of faith to the Gentiles. [28]And they stayed there a long time with the disciples.

Luke only briefly summarizes the concluding stops in the mission tour. From Pisidian Antioch they descended into the lowlands of Pamphylia. They stopped to preach in Perga before going to Attalia, which was the main seaport of the region. From Attalia they set sail for Syrian Antioch, their beginning point. The circuit was now complete.

Their return to Antioch is best explained in light of the words that it is this church "where they had been committed to the grace of God for the work they had now completed." This phrase calls attention to the events of 13:2-3, and puts a period on this initial mission endeavor.

They "gathered the church" for the purpose of reviewing their progress. After all, the sponsoring church would wish to know of the victories of the gospel. But the credit went not to Paul or Barnabas, but to God and what he had "done through them and how he had opened the door," a reference especially to the entrance of Gentiles into the kingdom of Christ. This theme will figure prominently in Acts 15.

ACTS 15

B. THE COUNCIL AT JERUSALEM (15:1-35)

1. The Visit of Judaizers to Antioch (15:1-2)

¹Some men came down from Judea to Antioch and were teaching the brothers: "Unless you are circumcised, according to the custom taught by Moses, you cannot be saved." ²This brought Paul and Barnabas into sharp dispute and debate with them. So Paul and Barnabas were appointed, along with some other believers, to go up to Jerusalem to see the apostles and elders about this question.

Luke now reports on the event which paves the way for the rest of the Book of Acts. The conference at Jerusalem makes it possible for the mission efforts of Paul. These efforts dominate the rest of Luke's report on the spread of the gospel. He has related how the interest in converting Gentiles began with the conversion of Cornelius (10:1–11:18) and the outreach of Antioch (11:19-24). Then came the first missionary journey with its concentration on Gentiles (13:1–14:28). Appropriately enough, Luke now turns to some of the dissension caused by the entrance of Gentiles into the church and how it was handled.

Thus Acts 15 is central, not only because of its position in the book, but because of its role in the story of the early church. What should be done about Gentile converts and their relationship to the Law of Moses? Should they be circumcised? Should they enter the church in the same way that Jewish proselytes entered the synagogue? Once accepted as believers, should they be taught to keep the regulations in the Law? Finally, should Jewish Christians eat with Gentile Christians?

Though these questions seem alien to modern theological concerns, they were burning questions in the first century. The Gentile
mission had shown no inclination to force converts to be circumcised or to keep the regulations of the Law. Now questions were
being raised about this policy.

Acts 15 has become the most controversial chapter in the book.
New Testament scholars have spent reams of paper comparing Acts
15 with what Paul writes in Galatians 2:1-10. The traditional view is
that the two passages discuss the same conference in Jerusalem. But
differences between the passages have forced many to doubt that
they are the same conference (details of which will be noticed later).
In some cases scholars have used the differences to indict Luke's
accuracy.[1] But the similarities between the passages seem to out-

---

[1]For a full discussion of these issues see Marshall, pp. 242-247; Haenchen,
pp. 455-472. Acts records five visits for Paul after his conversion: his acceptance by the Jerusalem believers (9:26ff), the famine visit (11:27-30), the
visit for the Jerusalem Conference (15:2ff), the visit at the conclusion of the
second missionary journey (18:22), and his arrest in the temple (21:17).
Galatians, however, mentions but two visits. The first of these (Gal 1:18ff)
seems to correspond to the visit of Acts 9:26ff. The traditional view has
been that Paul's visit to Jerusalem in Acts 15 for the Jerusalem Conference
is to be identified with his description in Gal 2:1-10, an interpretation which
means that Paul omits any reference to the famine visit (Reese, pp. 425, n.
53; 527, n. 1). But the accounts do not correspond in every detail. Gal 2:2
implies a private meeting, while Acts 15 describes a public one. Gal 2 says
nothing about the apostolic decrees, while Acts 15 makes these the primary
outcome of the meeting. Because of these problems, some commentators
have equated Gal 2 with the famine visit in Acts 11:27-30 (Marshall, p. 245),
a view which was adopted by Ramsay. Others take the position that Acts 15
is not a historically reliable account of the event, and that Paul's description
of this event in Gal 2 is to be preferred (Haenchen, pp. 462-463). Another
position which has been advocated is that Acts 15:1-19 is a doublet of Acts
11:27-30, and that Gal 2 corresponds to both. David Catchpole argues this
position in his "Paul, James and the Apostolic Decree," *NTS* 23 (1977): 428-
444. He believes that the decrees came some time after the Jerusalem
Conference. Though all of these interpretations have come in response to
problems with the traditional view, the fact remains that both Acts 15 and
Gal 2 describe a meeting concerning Gentiles and circumcision. Not one
word is spoken about this issue in Acts 11:27-30. Whatever problems associated with Paul's omission of the famine visit in Gal 2, it seems better to take
his comments as his own perspective of the meeting in Acts 15. He writes

weigh the differences, and it is not necessary to conclude that Luke has reported the incident inaccurately.[2]

The trouble began when "some men" arrived in Antioch from Judea. Luke's language here carefully keeps us from assuming that the view of these teachers represented the Jerusalem apostles in any official way.[3] Their position took issue with the policy of evangelism in Antioch. Gentiles must be taught to be "circumcised according to the custom taught by Moses."[4] For them the conversion of Cornelius was not the final word as it had been for Peter and the apostles (see 10:47; 11:17-18). They insisted that the issue was more than a matter of table fellowship; unless Gentiles were circumcised they "cannot be saved."

Not only was this perspective a rejection of the conversion of Cornelius, it was also a direct attack on the mission efforts of the church in Antioch through Paul and Barnabas in Acts 13-14. Perhaps these teachers hoped to convince the church, Paul, and Barnabas to alter their approach in future evangelistic efforts. These teachers may be the ones Paul refers to when he speaks of "false brothers" who "infiltrated our ranks to spy on the freedom we have in Christ Jesus and to make us slaves" (Gal 2:4).

Paul and Barnabas came into "sharp dispute and debate with them." Paul's position was that this teaching amounted to an enslavement of believers who had been set free in Christ (see Gal 5:1). He refused to "give in to them for a moment" (Gal 2:5). The gospel was meant for the Gentiles, as well as the Jews. Imposing the Jewish Law would mean excluding Gentiles from salvation.[5]

---

to the Galatians about the meeting for the purpose of arguing for his independence from the other apostles in terms of the authority of his ministry. See Robert Stein, "The Relationship of Galatians 2:1-10 and Acts 15:1-35: Two Neglected Arguments," *JETS* 17 (1974): 239-242.

[2]Pierson Parker solves the problem by contending that Luke was wrong about Paul's first journey to Jerusalem (9:26). See his "Once More, Acts and Galatians," *JBL* 36 (1967): 175-182.

[3]Munck argues emphatically that Paul's opponents were never the Jerusalem apostles. He thinks that much of the account in Gal 2:1-10 refers to opposition Paul experienced away from Jerusalem. See *Paul*, pp. 96-100.

[4]The unusual use of the dative case in this clause should be understood to connote cause. See Moulton, Howard, Turner, *Grammar*, 3:242.

[5]This seems to be Paul's argument in Rom 3:21-31 when he argues that

Thus Paul and Barnabas "were appointed" by the church at
Antioch to go with "some other believers" to Jerusalem, a delegation which may have included Titus (Gal 2:3). The issue of circumcision would not be settled until the whole church, including the
apostles in Jerusalem, met to consider the matter.

2. The Journey of Paul and Barnabas to Jerusalem (15:3-5)

**[3]The church sent them on their way, and as they traveled
through Phoenicia and Samaria, they told how the Gentiles had
been converted. This news made all the brothers very glad. [4]When
they came to Jerusalem, they were welcomed by the church and the
apostles and elders, to whom they reported everything God had
done through them. [5]Then some of the believers who belonged to
the party of the Pharisees stood up and said, "The Gentiles must
be circumcised and required to obey the law of Moses."**

On this journey of some 250 miles to Jerusalem it was natural for
Paul and Barnabas to visit churches in "Phoenicia and Samaria."[6]
This is the first time the presence of Christians in Phoenicia is
revealed, and reminds us of how much evangelism occurred which
is not recorded in Acts.

Paul and Barnabas described for them "how the Gentiles had
been converted," a reference no doubt to their mission tour (Acts
13-14), and this news "made all the brothers very glad." These
believers were the result of mission efforts by the Hellenists who
fled Jerusalem after the martyrdom of Stephen (11:19). Their
sympathy to the Gentile mission emphasizes that those who came to
Antioch (15:1) did not represent everyone in the vicinity.

When Paul and Barnabas arrived in Jerusalem they were greeted
warmly by "the church and the apostles and elders." The conference

---

justification comes apart from the law because God is a God "of Gentiles,
too."

[6]Jervell observes that the presence of Christians in Samaria represents a
fulfillment of the mandate given in 1:8. He contends that Acts portrays the
conversion of the Samaritans as part of the task of evangelizing the Jews.
See his *People of God*, pp. 113-132.

in Jerusalem would include a wide representation of the church. As Paul and Barnabas had done in Antioch (14:27), in Phoenicia and Samaria, they also did in Jerusalem. God had worked "through them" to open the door of salvation to the Gentiles.

Yet this report was not met with universal happiness. Those who "belonged to the party of the Pharisees" were not pleased. Because of their connections with Pharisaic doctrine, they insisted on the role of circumcision, even among Gentiles. These Jewish Christians argued that Gentiles must add something more to their conversion to Christ. They must also become Jews in terms of obedience to the Law, beginning with circumcision.

Some commentators see 15:4 as the first of two meetings on the question. This position has the advantage of harmonizing with Paul's statement in Galatians 2:2 that he met "privately" with the apostles. In this view the private meeting is reflected in 15:4 and the public meeting in 15:6-29.[7]

Paul disagreed with the Pharisaic element not because he promoted permissive morals among the Gentiles, but because the law could never inspire holiness among the Gentiles anyway. Indeed, he argues in Romans 6:1-14 that believers have every motivation to eject sin out of their lives. But he also argues in Romans 7:1-25 that the law could not eradicate sin in the lives of believers. As far as Paul was concerned, when the Gentiles were baptized "into Christ" they could fulfill "the righteous requirements of the Law" (Rom 8:4) without being circumcised or living by the regulations of the law.

3. The Convening of the Council (15:6)

[6]The apostles and elders met to consider this question.

As leaders of the church, "the apostles and elders" served as moderators of the conference. Though the apostles were the recognized authorities in matters of doctrine in the church, their practice was to include other recognized leaders in important decisions of the church.

---

[7]See *NIV Study Bible*; Shepard, *Life*, pp. 116-124.

The convening of this council marks the final achievement in Acts of the apostles in Jerusalem as a group. From this point on, the focus will shift away from Jerusalem to the missionary journeys in the far stretches of the Roman world.[8] The apostle who will get Luke's attention from now on will be Paul.

It must be remembered that Luke's summary of the discussion is quite abbreviated. The number and the content of the speeches are not given in their entirety, but only a rough outline of remarks is given.

4. The Address of Peter (15:7-11)

[7]**After much discussion, Peter got up and addressed them: "Brothers, you know that some time ago God made a choice among you that the Gentiles might hear from my lips the message of the gospel and believe. [8]God, who knows the heart, showed that he accepted them by giving the Holy Spirit to them, just as he did to us. [9]He made no distinction between us and them, for he purified their hearts by faith. [10]Now then, why do you try to test God by putting on the necks of the disciples a yoke that neither we nor our fathers have been able to bear? [11]No! We believe it is through the grace of our Lord Jesus that we are saved, just as they are."**

A lively discussion by all the participants kept the crowd buzzing at the beginning of the conference. "After much discussion" the leaders brought the meeting to order.

Peter was first to speak in presenting the case for rejecting the effort to impose circumcision on the Gentile converts. To some modern scholars this portrait of Peter has seemed unlikely.[9] But his experience with Cornelius had left an impression on him.[10]

---

[8]The only exception is when Paul is arrested and tried in Jerusalem in Acts 21–23.

[9] The Tübingen scholars in the middle of the nineteenth century argued that Peter represented a staunch Judaizing Christianity in opposition to the Gentile mission of Paul. But the truth is there is no evidence to support the figure of a Judaizing apostle Peter.

[10] This is true in spite of his lapse at Antioch (Gal 2:11), a confrontation

This experience was what Peter called attention to when he said "you know that some time ago." The time lapse might have been as much as ten years. Peter's understanding of the event was that "God made a choice among us" in that the Holy Spirit directed Peter to the house of Cornelius. After reading Acts 10 this interpretation of the event is obvious. God decided that from the lips of Peter the Gentiles were to hear the gospel.

God "who knows the heart," and therefore the spiritual condition, accepted the Gentiles. The language Peter used at this point corresponds closely to the language used in Acts 10–11. Phrases like "giving the Holy Spirit," "just as he did to us," and "purified their hearts" came directly from Peter's encounter with Cornelius (see 10:15,47; 11:8,9,17). God determined to make "no distinction between us (Jewish believers) and them (the Gentile believers),"[11] said Peter, a conclusion which he drew immediately from his visit to Cornelius (see 10:34-35). No other verdict was possible for him than to say that the Gentiles had been purified "by faith."

If this was so, Peter argued there was no reason to add to their obligations. In fact, said Peter, to do so would be "to test God," since it would mean calling into question matters already settled by the Lord's hand.

Peter's argument was that the council should not seek to put on the "necks of the disciples a yoke that neither we nor our fathers have been able to bear." Peter's point is not that the fathers considered the law to be burdensome. Indeed the words of the Psalmist rang in the ears of first-century Jews: "Oh, how I love your law! I meditate on it all day long. Your commands make me wiser than my enemies, for they are ever with me" (119:97-98). Peter's rejection of the law had to do with its necessity for salvation, especially among the Gentiles. "Neither we nor our fathers," he says, were able to count on our obedience to the law as a means for salvation.

The "yoke" did not refer to an intolerable burden. The "yoke of

---

which is dated by some as occurring before the conference of Acts 15, and thus representing a point on which Peter changed his mind.

[11] Dunn notes that the two statements are parallel. "God showed that he accepted them by giving the Holy Spirit to them" is defined by "He made no distinction between us and them, for he purified their hearts by faith." See his *Baptism*, p. 81.

the law" was a common rabbinic phrase to speak of becoming a child of the covenant. Thus the expression "taking up the yoke of the kingdom of heaven" had a very positive connotation because a believer who had the yoke of the law was closely bound to the will of the Lord.[12]

Rather than the law, said Peter, it is "through the grace of our Lord Jesus that we are saved." Nothing could sound more like Paul (see 13:38ff; Eph 2:8-10). Peter's point was that if salvation comes through the grace of Jesus, why should the council impose on the Gentile converts the regulations of the law?

5. The Address of Paul and Barnabas (15:12)

[12]**The whole assembly became silent as they listened to Barnabas and Paul telling about the miraculous signs and wonders God had done among the Gentiles through them.**

Peter's address brought silence to the crowd. Next on the agenda were reports by Paul and Barnabas of the powerful work of God in their missionary tour. At this point the reader may remember such detailed incidents as the healing of the crippled man in Lystra. Luke has provided enough information about the journey that when Paul and Barnabas reflected on the "miraculous signs and wonders" there can be little doubt what the missionaries described. Their testimony also made the point that God demonstrated his acceptance of Gentiles without benefit of circumcision.

6. The Summation by James (15:13-21)

[13]**When they finished, James spoke up: "Brothers, listen to me. [14]Simon[a] has described to us how God at first showed his concern by taking from the Gentiles a people for himself. [15]The words of the prophets are in agreement with this, as it is written: [16]"After this I will return and rebuild David's fallen tent. Its ruins I will**

---

[12]This positive sense of the term "yoke" was also used by Jesus when he invited disciples to come and take his yoke upon them (Matt 11:29). Also see E.P. Sanders, *Paul and Palestinian Judaism* (Philadelphia: Fortress, 1977).

rebuild, and I will restore it, [17]that the remnant of men may seek the Lord, and all the Gentiles who bear my name, says the Lord, who does these things'[b] [18]that have been known for ages.[c] [19]"It is my judgment, therefore, that we should not make it difficult for the Gentiles who are turning to God. [20]Instead we should write to them, telling them to abstain from food polluted by idols, from sexual immorality, from the meat of strangled animals and from blood. [21]For Moses has been preached in every city from the earliest times and is read in the synagogues on every Sabbath."

[a]*14* Greek *Simeon*, a variant of *Simon*; that is, Peter   [b]*17* Amos 9:11,12
[c]*17,18* Some manuscripts *things'—[18]known to the Lord for ages is his work*

The final address was delivered by James, the brother of the Lord.[13] Not one of the original apostles, James nevertheless had gained a prominent place as a church leader as is indicated in 12:17. He is also mentioned by Paul in his description of the Jerusalem conference (Gal 2:9).

In addressing the assembly, James refers to Peter as Simon, his original Jewish name, which would suit those of the Pharisaic group quite well. The contention of James was that God wanted to take "from the Gentiles a people (λαός, *laos*)," a word used throughout the Old Testament to describe God's chosen people. In other words, James was saying that God decided to find a "chosen people" from among the Gentiles.[14] His point seems to be that both Jewish and Gentile believers were now counted as God's people. James is referring to what God had done in the case of Cornelius.

To support this conclusion, James cited Amos 9:11-12. His quotation comes from the Septuagint, a fact which causes many scholars to doubt James could have said it.[15] How could a Jewish

---

[13]Jervell observes that "James appears at precisely those places where the church's Judaism no longer appears to be orthodox, and where the church's claim to be the restored Israel is endangered." He sees in the words (and reputation as a strict Jew) of James a position which would help Paul by reducing the suspicions about his mission to the Gentiles. See *People of God*, p. 188.

[14]Zech 2:11 also uses *laos* to describe how God will choose a people from the Gentiles.

[15]See Haenchen, p. 448.

Christian make his argument to Pharisaic elements in Jerusalem by quoting the Greek Old Testament rather than the Hebrew Old Testament?

But the point of the argument by James is found in both versions of the Old Testament. His major emphasis was that "David's fallen tent" would be rebuilt, a reference to the restoration of the kingdom over which David ruled to its former glory. He also focused on the phrase "the Gentiles who bear my name," a concept which could also have been drawn from the Hebrew text.

Whether James quoted the Septuagint version in the meeting to benefit Greek visitors, or Luke drew the Scripture James quoted from the Septuagint, therefore makes little difference. Either way, these verses reflect accurately the line of argument used by James.

Declaring his conclusion, James argues that there is no reason to "make it difficult" for Gentile converts by imposing the law of Moses, and circumcision in particular. But if Gentiles need not be circumcised, still remaining was the question of how Jewish Christians could share meals with Gentile converts without becoming defiled. James thus proposed a solution to this problem.

The solution listed four things which were important to Jews. Each of these items were commonly associated with the idolatrous Gentile world, and were thus considered to have universal application to Gentile converts. The items also were associated with pagan worship in a Gentile context.

First, Gentile converts were to "abstain from food polluted by idols," a clear reference to pagan sacrifices and the meals often eaten at the pagan temple. "Sexual immorality" (πορνεία, *porneia*) may refer to the sexual activities which defile a person as listed in Leviticus 18:6-18, or more likely the sexual immorality often associated with pagan religious festivals. The third item was abstaining from "meat of strangled animals,"[16] a reference to animals killed so

---

[16]Moore describes the Jewish legal restrictions regarding the eating of meat. Laws forbade eating animals which died of natural causes or were torn by wild animals, in addition to those that were killed by strangulation. See his *Judaism*, 2:74. Conzelmann (pp. 118-119) gives details on the stipulations given by the apostles. For a discussion of the text of the decrees, as well as their intent see John Hurd, *The Origin of I Corinthians* (London: SPCK, 1965), pp. 246-253.

that the blood remained in the meat. Because the Old Testament required that animal sacrifices were drained of their blood (Lev 17:10-14), Jews did not eat such meat because of the threat of being defiled. The last item belongs in the same category (Gen 9:4; Lev 3:17), though in some pagan practices blood was drunk apart from the meat.

These proposals by James may be traced to the Old Testament. As a matter of fact they were originally applied to aliens dwelling among the congregation of Israel, an application very appropriate in reference to Gentile converts.

To conclude, James stated that Moses "has been preached (κηρύσσοντας, kēryssontas) in every city" and "is read (ἀναγινωσκόμενος, anaginōskomenos) in the synagogues on every Sabbath."[17] His point was that all other points of the law were readily accessible to Gentile converts, including the moral principles of the law, which no one doubted were essential to the Christian faith.

7. The Apostolic Letter to Gentile Christians (15:22-29)

[22]**Then the apostles and elders, with the whole church, decided to choose some of their own men and send them to Antioch with Paul and Barnabas. They chose Judas (called Barsabbas) and Silas, two men who were leaders among the brothers.** [23]**With them they sent the following letter: The apostles and elders, your brothers, To the Gentile believers in Antioch, Syria and Cilicia: Greetings.** [24]**We have heard that some went out from us without our authorization and disturbed you, troubling your minds by what they said.** [25]**So we all agreed to choose some men and send them to you with our dear friends Barnabas and Paul—**[26]**men who have risked their lives for the name of our Lord Jesus Christ.** [27]**Therefore we are sending Judas and Silas to confirm by word of mouth what we are writing.** [28]**It seemed good to the Holy Spirit and to us not to burden you with anything beyond the following requirements:**

---

[17]Both the phrases "has been preached" and "is read" are present participles and carry the idea of continuous action.

²⁹You are to abstain from food sacrificed to idols, from blood, from the meat of strangled animals and from sexual immorality. You will do well to avoid these things. Farewell.

After approving the content of the proposals by James the decision was made to state in a letter to the churches the conclusions of the council. "Some of their own men" were chosen, including Judas (called Barsabbas, or "son of the Sabbath") and Silas who later became the companion of Paul in his mission work (15:40; 2 Cor 1:19; 1 Thess 1:1; 2 Thess 1:1). These men, with Paul and Barnabas, were sent "to Antioch," out of respect for the ministry of this church and the fact that the question had become urgent first in this church.

The letter was addressed to "the Gentile believers in Antioch, Syria and Cilicia," areas over which Antioch was the leading city. The style of the letter is very formal, especially in its opening "greetings" (χαίρειν, *chairein*) and its "farewell" (ἔρρωσθε, *errōsthe*). Another indication of formality is its long sentence structure running from 15:24-26.

Believers in Antioch were told in the letter that the teachers who came from Judea arrived without "authorization" from the apostles. The letter even apologized that these teachers "disturbed" the disciples, "troubling" (ἀνασκευάζω, *anaskeuazō*) them by what they said. The idea is that they were "plundering," or "tearing down" the disciples as an advancing army does.

Paul and Barnabas were described as "men who have risked (παραδίδομαι, *paradidomai*)[18] their lives" in service for Christ, a phrase which reflects on the dangers they experienced on their mission tour. Judas and Silas were present to "confirm by word of mouth" that the proceedings had occurred in such a manner that these conclusions came about. The role of "the Holy Spirit" was mentioned, demonstrating again the sense that all of the efforts to take the gospel to the Gentiles were directed by the hand of God's

---

[18]The verb may also mean "devoted." Paul and Barnabas were referred to in the letter as "dear friends," a phrase which corresponds to Paul's report that in the meeting the Jerusalem leaders extended to him "the right hand of fellowship" (Gal 2:9).

Spirit (see 10:44-47; 11:12,15-17; 13:1-4; 15:8).[19]

Finally the letter summarized the same four requirements as mentioned in v. 20, with a slight change in order. The phrase "food sacrificed to idols" (εἰδωλοθύτων, *eidōlothytōn*) replaced "food polluted by idols" in v. 20. One more time in Acts this list of demands will be mentioned (21:25) and the churches addressed in Revelation apparently knew of them, as well (Rev 2:14,20).

Frequently the question has been raised as to why Paul never mentions these decrees in his letters. Some critics have charged that he does not mention them because he did not know about them, thus impugning the credibility of Luke's account in Acts 15.[20] But this ignores the places in Paul's letters where he speaks to the issues given in the "apostolic decrees." In 1 Corinthians 5-10, for example, he first deals with the issue of immorality (5-7) and then with the issue of eating meat offered to idols (8-10). Also Romans 14-15 reflects on some of these principles.

8. The Reception of the Apostolic
Letter by the Church in Antioch (15:30-35)

[30]**The men were sent off and went down to Antioch, where they gathered the church together and delivered the letter.** [31]**The people read it and were glad for its encouraging message.** [32]**Judas and Silas, who themselves were prophets, said much to encourage and strengthen the brothers.** [33]**After spending some time there, they were sent off by the brothers with the blessing of peace to return to those who had sent them.**[a] [35]**But Paul and Barnabas remained in Antioch, where they and many others taught and preached the word of the Lord.**

[a]*33 Some manuscripts them, [34]but Silas decided to remain there*

The decrees from the council in Jerusalem were received with genuine happiness because of their "encouraging message." For the disciples at Antioch the decision of the council was a victory,

---

[19]One of the intentions of this account is to show how the Gentile mission was validated. See Wilson, *Gentile Mission*, p. 241.

[20]Haenchen, pp. 468-472.

confirming their policy toward Gentile converts who were not forced to be circumcised.[21] The four requirements were viewed as a measure to ease the fellowship of Jewish and Gentile believers.

The prophetic ministry of Judas and Silas also contributed to the encouragement of the believers in Antioch. New Testament prophets often used their gifts to challenge the church in matters of meeting the present needs of the congregation. After their ministry was completed "they were sent off by the brothers with the blessing of peace." The pronoun "they" refers to Silas and Barsabbas and their return to Jerusalem. The "blessing of peace" was the Jewish farewell "shalom," which can be translated "peace."

A textual problem exists with 15:34. One of the readings from the Western text includes the statement that Silas remained in Antioch. The verse lacks solid manuscript support, and may have been penned by a scribe who was trying to establish harmony with v. 40 where Silas is in Antioch when Paul chooses him for the journey. In so doing the scribe set up a conflict with v. 33, which says "they were sent off."

C. THE SECOND MISSIONARY JOURNEY (15:36–18:22)

1. The Proposal and the Debate about John Mark (15:36-39)

[36]Some time later Paul said to Barnabas, "Let us go back and visit the brothers in all the towns where we preached the word of the Lord and see how they are doing." [37]Barnabas wanted to take John, also called Mark, with them, [38]but Paul did not think it wise to take him, because he had deserted them in Pamphylia and had not continued with them in the work. [39]They had such a sharp disagreement that they parted company. Barnabas took Mark and sailed for Cyprus,

After spending some time in Antioch, Paul approached Barnabas regarding a return to the churches they had established.

---

[21]Jervell notes that the decrees are mentioned in Acts always in connection with the issue of Paul and his missionary activity (15:19-20; 16:3-4; 21:21,25). See his *People of God*, 192.

Paul's policy was not to abandon the churches he founded (see 1 Thess 2:17-20; 2 Cor 13:1). He looked forward to strengthening these congregations.

A major disagreement developed, however, when Barnabas wanted to take John Mark along. He was the mission helper who had abandoned the effort during the first journey (see 13:13). Barnabas was the cousin of John Mark and wanted to give him another chance, probably because he saw some potential in him. But Paul remembered too clearly how Mark had abandoned the work at a crucial moment. The difference of opinion became "a sharp disagreement." There was no reconciliation on the issue. Possibly the matter of the withdrawal by Barnabas from eating with Gentiles also entered into this conflict (Gal 2:11-13).

So "they parted company," but the result to the kingdom was two mission teams instead of one. Barnabas and Mark visited the churches on the island of Cyprus.

2. The Journey through Syria and Cilicia (15:40-41)

[40]but Paul chose Silas and left, commended by the brothers to the grace of the Lord. [41]He went through Syria and Cilicia, strengthening the churches.

While Barnabas and Mark were visiting Cyprus, Paul chose Silas to accompany him "through Syria and Cilicia." By now Paul had gained enough confidence in Silas to see in him a potential mission partner. They departed from Antioch, being "commended by the brothers to the grace of the Lord." This phrase does not imply that Barnabas and Mark were considered renegades by the church at Antioch, but simply serves Luke's purpose of keeping the focus on Paul throughout the remainder of Acts. Paul and Silas (called Silvanus in Paul's letters) would be traveling through the same cities as had been visited in the first journey.

ACTS 16

3. The Visit to Derbe and Lystra (16:1-4)

[1]He came to Derbe and then to Lystra, where a disciple named Timothy lived, whose mother was a Jewess and a believer, but whose father was a Greek. [2]The brothers at Lystra and Iconium spoke well of him. [3]Paul wanted to take him along on the journey, so he circumcised him because of the Jews who lived in that area, for they all knew that his father was a Greek. [4]As they traveled from town to town, they delivered the decisions reached by the apostles and elders in Jerusalem for the people to obey.

As on the first mission tour, Paul came to "Derbe and then to Lystra," though here the cities are in reverse order since Paul was now traveling east to west (see 14:6). At Lystra he met Timothy, a young man "whose mother was a Jewess and a believer." This description indicates that Timothy's mother had grown up in Judaism, but had become a Christian, possibly as a result of the preaching of Paul on the first tour. In 2 Timothy 1:5 her name is given as Eunice.

Timothy's father, however, "was a Greek." Though Judaism did not encourage marriage of Jews with Gentiles, it was not uncommon. In this situation the child would be considered by the Jews to be Jewish, taking his lineage through his mother. The language of the text implies that Timothy's father was dead.[1]

Timothy's reputation was such that "the brothers at Lystra and Iconium (some twenty miles to the west) spoke well of him." Paul recognized in him the potential for effective service as a missionary. Because of this mixture of Jewish and Gentile elements in young

---

[1]The imperfect tense of "was" (ὑπῆρχεν, *hypērchen*) is used.

Timothy's background, he had never been circumcised, and the Jews in that area knew the situation. So Paul had the young man circumcised.[2]

Such a move by Paul may seem surprising in light of the preceding chapter of Acts. After the Jerusalem conference, why would Paul insist on circumcision here? It must be remembered, however, that the Jerusalem conference dealt with circumcising Gentiles, not Jews. As Polhill notes, there "is absolutely no evidence that Paul ever asked Jews to abandon circumcision as their mark of membership in God's covenant people." As a matter of fact, Paul himself never lost his identity as a Jew (Rom 9:1-2; 10:1; Phil 3:5-6), though he had become one who knew Jesus as the Christ.

Paul's relationship to Timothy became very close. Timothy is mentioned throughout the letters as one of Paul's companions (2 Cor 1:1; Phil 1:1; Col 1:1; 1 Thess 1:1; 2 Thess 1:1; Phlm 1). Paul referred to him as a "dear son" (1 Cor 4:17; 1 Tim 1:2). Timothy must have been quite young when Paul met him in Lystra, since some fifteen years later Paul calls him a young man (1 Tim 4:12).

As Paul and Silas "traveled from town to town," they delivered "the decisions" (τὰ δόγματα, *ta dogmata*) which had come from the Jerusalem Conference. Though the decrees had been addressed to Syria and Cilicia (see (15:23), they may have decided to deliver them to churches outside of this province, as well. The Antioch church had, after all, sponsored the evangelism which built these churches.

4. The Growth of the Churches (16:5)

[5]So the churches were strengthened in the faith and grew daily in numbers.

---

[2]Ladd understands Paul's motivations for the circumcision of Timothy as due to the fact that Timothy was half Jewish (*Theology*, p. 355, n. 29). Compare this with 21:21. The silence of Luke regarding Titus continues to puzzle scholars. Though Timothy's circumcision is mentioned here, Acts does not relate the problem that Paul alludes to concerning his refusal to circumcise Titus (see Gal 2:3). For a discussion of the problem along with a suggestion that the name of Titus was still a sensitive problem when Luke wrote Acts, see William Walker, "The Timothy-Titus Problem Reconsidered," *ExpT* 92 (1981): 231-235.

Luke now adds a brief report on the church's progress before recording the pioneer efforts of Paul and Silas into new territories. The churches "were strengthened" and "grew daily," verbs that are both in the imperfect tense to emphasize the continuous progress of these congregations. This summary follows a long list of such summaries so far in Acts (2:41,47; 4:4; 5:14; 6:7; 9:31,42).

5. The Journey through Phrygia and Galatia (16:6-7)

[6]Paul and his companions traveled throughout the region of Phrygia and Galatia, having been kept by the Holy Spirit from preaching the word in the province of Asia. [7]When they came to the border of Mysia, they tried to enter Bithynia, but the Spirit of Jesus would not allow them to.

The missionaries' road led them beyond the cities in which they had previously started churches. Traveling "throughout the region of Phrygia and Galatia,"[3] they now moved strictly by the direction of the Holy Spirit. As always, Paul's work for Christ was a combination of his own careful planning and the leading of God.

Apparently the original plan was to leave Pisidian Antioch and journey westward to Ephesus. This plan would have the apostles moving through Phrygia, a district which had been divided between the Roman provinces of Asia and Galatia. Perhaps at this point Paul and his companions were "kept by the Holy Spirit" from going on toward Ephesus in the province of Asia. How this message was communicated is not stated.

If the missionaries could not go straight west, perhaps they could go in a direction leading northwest. Mysia was a district in the northern part of Asia, and presented a fruitful place for evangelism on the way to Bithynia, a district with such major cities as Nicomedia, Nicea, and Byzantium. But once again the Spirit (this time called "Spirit

---

[3]Bruce thinks this is a reference to the Phrygian territory of the province of Galatia (p. 306). Hemer provides a thorough discussion of the geographical problems associated with the mention of Galatia in Acts. See his *Book of Acts*, pp. 277-307.

of Jesus")[4] directed that they not travel into Bithynia. This latter divine message forced them to redirect their steps straight westward to Troas.

6. The Macedonian Vision in Troas (16:8-10)

[8]**So they passed by Mysia and went down to Troas.** [9]**During the night Paul had a vision of a man of Macedonia standing and begging him, "Come over to Macedonia and help us."** [10]**After Paul had seen the vision, we got ready at once to leave for Macedonia, concluding that God had called us to preach the gospel to them.**

As they "passed by Mysia," they probably wondered why so many promising locations for evangelism were being neglected. Troas itself would have been worth considering for establishing a church. The city was associated from ancient times with Troy, located some ten miles to the north. Because of its location, it was an important port city with connections to much of the shipping traffic between Asia and Macedonia. Since the time of Augustus the Romans saw it as a colony city. The sizable population of Troas favored church planting, and Paul may indeed have founded a church on this visit (see Acts 20:5-12; 2 Cor 2:12).

But the text seems to indicate that not much time was spent in Troas because "during the night Paul had a vision." This incident may answer one question relating to how the Spirit was directing the missionaries. A "vision" had been experienced once in Acts already (10:3). The Spirit now used a vision again to reveal his will for future travel, communicating to Paul the need for evangelism in Macedonia.[5]

---

[4]This text gives some idea of the flexibility of terminology in referring to God and the things of God. The Holy Spirit is also called "the Spirit of Christ" (Rom 8:9), "the Spirit of him who raised Jesus from the dead" (Rom 8:11), "the Spirit of truth" (John 14:17), the "Spirit of the Lord" (Act 8:39), just to name a few. Compare Dunn, *Jesus*, p. 180.

[5]Hubbard analyzes this "commissioning account" by comparing it to others found in Acts. See his "Commissioning Accounts," *Perspectives on Luke-Acts*, pp. 188-198. He also finds parallels in other ancient literature.

The province of Macedonia became a Roman province in 148
B.C., though it had been a dominant power in the Greek world
since the days of Philip II and Alexander the Great. Paul saw in his
vision a man from Macedonia (whose identity is unknown) inviting
him to come and help. Though some have assumed that the
Macedonian was Luke, the evidence is weak.[6]

Luke does seem to inject himself more directly into the journey
at this point, however, by using in v. 10 the pronoun "we." Paul saw
the vision, but Luke says "we" immediately prepared "to leave for
Macedonia." This way of speaking is best explained by suggesting
that at this point, Luke himself joined the missionary team and
began traveling with them. His descriptions thus become eyewitness
reports.[7]

7. The Visits to Samothrace and Neapolis (16:11)

[11]From Troas we put out to sea and sailed straight for Samothrace, and the next day on to Neapolis.

See his "Commissioning Stories in Luke-Acts: A Study of their Antecedents, Form and Content," *Semeia* 8 (1977): 103-123.

[6]Because 16:10 uses the pronoun "we," probably a reference to our author, some assume that our author, Luke, was also the Macedonian (see Ramsay, *Traveller*, pp. 200-205).

[7]Many who reject Lukan authorship deny this conclusion, explaining that the use of the first person is a literary device intended to bring the reader more personally into the narrative. See Haenchen, pp. 490-491. One problem with this suggestion is accounting for the change to first person here and in a limited few passages (see also 20:5-21:18; 27:1-28:16) rather than throughout Acts. Also, it is difficult to explain why, if Luke found the "we" passages in his source, he permitted only these to remain, while allegedly transforming all other parts of the narrative into the third person. Vernon Robbins has recently argued that the use of the first person was an ancient literary device especially used in descriptions of sea voyages. See his "By Land and by Sea: The We-Passages and Ancient Sea Voyages," *Perspectives on Luke-Acts*, ed. Talbert, pp. 215-242. The problem with this position is that the "we-passages" extend well beyond the sea voyages into other activities of the missionaries (e.g., 16:16-18). In addition to this observation is the fact that the first person is used in only three of the ten voyages in Acts (Polhill, p. 346, n. 17).

Boarding a vessel, the missionaries "sailed straight for Samothrace," a mountainous island which rose 5,500 feet above sea level. The wind was favorable and the journey from Troas took only one day. Later in Acts (20:6) a similar journey will require five days.[8]

The following day brought the mission group to Neapolis. This city served as the port for Philippi, which lay ten miles inland. At Neapolis the Egnatian Way, one of the oldest of the major Roman roads, began its way across Macedonia to the Adriatic Sea.

8. The Visit to Philippi (16:12-40)

The Faith of Lydia (16:12-15)

[12]**From there we traveled to Philippi, a Roman colony and the leading city of that district of Macedonia. And we stayed there several days. [13]On the Sabbath we went outside the city gate to the river, where we expected to find a place of prayer. We sat down and began to speak to the women who had gathered there. [14]One of those listening was a woman named Lydia, a dealer in purple cloth from the city of Thyatira, who was a worshiper of God. The Lord opened her heart to respond to Paul's message. [15]When she and the members of her household were baptized, she invited us to her home. "If you consider me a believer in the Lord," she said, "come and stay at my house." And she persuaded us.**

From Neapolis the missionaries walked on the Egnatian Way the ten miles to Philippi. This city was also "a Roman colony," and enjoyed a rich history. Named after the father of Alexander the Great, Philip II, the city had come under Roman control in 168 B.C. At that time Macedonia was divided into four administrative districts. Thessalonica was the capital of Macedonia, but Philippi was a "leading city" in the first of the four districts.[9] Because of its

---

[8]See Robert Jewett regarding the favorable wind in the journey from Troas (*Chronology*, p. 47).

[9]Actually, Amphipolis was larger, and was capital of the district before the provinces were organized. The adjective "first" (πρώτη, *prōtē*) can be a title

status as a colony, the city was populated with many retired Roman soldiers, but there were few Jews.

Rather than going to the synagogue as in past visits to a new city (14:1), Paul and his companions "went outside the city gate to the river." Here he met a group of women gathered for prayer. The presence of these women outside the city probably indicates that there was no Jewish synagogue in Philippi, and Paul had learned that they met instead outside of the city. Perhaps the women were required to meet here because their religion was considered suspect by the local authorities.[10] Thus they chose a place on the banks of the Gangites River about a mile south of the city.

The Jewish character of the meeting becomes obvious in Luke's description of Lydia. She was from Thyatira, a city in Roman Asia (in the Hellenistic kingdom of Lydda). By occupation she was "a dealer in purple cloth," a trade well known in Thyatira,[11] and a business which produced expensive material often used for royalty. She was thus a woman of some wealth, a trait also indicated by her possession of a home large enough to keep the missionaries (16:15). But by religion she is described as "a worshiper of God," a phrase used of Gentiles like Cornelius who were informally connected to Judaism.[12]

Macedonian women had a reputation for independence by the time Paul visited. Among their legal rights were the initiating of

---

of honor (Conzelmann, p. 130). Sherwin-White observes that Philippi was considered to be located in the *first* of the four districts of Macedonia. These districts were "genuine sub-provinces with a separate regional council or *sunedrion* for each district." He thinks that the phrase was garbled "at an early date" and made to refer to the city rather than to the province. See A.N. Sherwin-White, *Roman Society and Roman Law in the New Testament* (Oxford: Clarendon, 1963), p. 93.

[10]The Romans were usually officially tolerant of Judaism, though in a case where no synagogue was organized, such religious meetings may not have been welcome. Ten Jewish men were required to form a synagogue.

[11]The cloth was used for the official Roman toga. The guild of "purple dealers" from Thyatira honored some of their own at Thessalonica with a monument that has been excavated. See Haenchen, p. 494, n. 9. The method for dying cloth involved using a root known as the madder.

[12]C.K. Barrett provides Jewish reflections on the acceptance of proselytes into the faith. See his *The New Testament Background: Selected Documents* (New York: Harper & Row, 1961), pp. 164-166.

divorce, engaging in legal transactions, and even holding honorary public titles.

Paul and his friends "sat down" with these women, taking the position assumed by teachers in the synagogue. As they spoke about the gospel, Lydia listened and "the Lord opened her heart to respond to Paul's message." Just as the hearts of the disciples had been opened up by the Lord (Luke 24:45), so now God used the gospel to speak to her heart, and she responded in faith.

As is customary in Acts, faith is followed by baptism (see 2:38, 41; 8:13,36,38; 16:31,33; 18:8). She and "the members of her household" were baptized. As with Cornelius (10:47-48), several members of the family besides Lydia wanted to be baptized. Another "household baptism" occurs later in 16:33. There is no evidence in any of these that infants were involved.[13] In the case of Cornelius, for example, they were "praising God" (10:46), evidence that they were old enough to make a personal decision for baptism.

Lydia then insisted that the missionaries stay in her house as evidence of her sincerity in the faith. For them it would have been a considerable relief from what they were paying for rented quarters. She was truly contributing to the work of the gospel, even offering her house as a meeting place for the believers (see 16:40).

The Slave Girl with the Spirit of Divination (16:16-22)

[16]Once when we were going to the place of prayer, we were met by a slave girl who had a spirit by which she predicted the future. She earned a great deal of money for her owners by fortune-telling. [17]This girl followed Paul and the rest of us, shouting, "These men are servants of the Most High God, who are telling you the way to be saved." [18]She kept this up for many days. Finally Paul became so troubled that he turned around and said to the spirit, "In the name of Jesus Christ I command you to come out of her!" At that moment the spirit left her. [19]When the owners of the slave girl realized that their hope of making money was gone, they seized Paul and Silas and dragged them into the marketplace to face the authorities. [20]They brought them before the magistrates and said,

---

[13]See Conzelmann, p. 130; Jewett, *Baptism*, p. 49.

**"These men are Jews, and are throwing our city into an uproar [21]by advocating customs unlawful for us Romans to accept or practice."
[22]The crowd joined in the attack against Paul and Silas, and the magistrates ordered them to be stripped and beaten.**

During their ministry in Philippi they "were met by a slave girl who had a spirit by which she predicted the future." The term for this spirit is πνεῦμα πύθωνα (*pneuma pythōna*), and refers to a spirit which possessed people for the purpose of uttering inspired predictions for the future. The term comes from the "serpent that guarded the Delphic oracle" where Apollo was worshiped. The word came to denote a "spirit of divination, then also a ventriloquist, who was believed to have such a spirit dwelling in his belly."[14]

Because the Roman world was very much influenced by magic and divination, many people relied on consulting those who had power to discern the future. Even political and military leaders refused to make major decisions without consulting a diviner. The girl in Philippi was thus a valuable commodity to her owners. As Luke says, "she earned a great deal of money for her owners by fortune-telling."

After Paul met her he could not seem to rid himself of her. She kept following (κατακολουθοῦσα, *katakolouthousa*)[15] Paul "for many days." The spirit within her caused her to shout that Paul and his friends were "servants of the Most High God" (θεοῦ τοῦ ὑψίστου, *theou tou hypsistou*).[16] In a manner which reminds us of the evil spirits crying out in testimony to Christ (see Mark 5:7),[17] the girl's words spoke the truth, but in a manner not appreciated by Paul. What misunderstanding of the gospel might be generated by the persistent shouting of this "pythoness?"

Paul "became so troubled" that he commanded the spirit to come out of the girl. Polhill notes that Luke's language contains a

---

[14]Rienecker, p. 303.

[15]The participle in the present tense can indicate repeated action over a period of time.

[16]The title was common to Jews (Num 24:16; Isa 14:14; Dan 3:26), and inscriptions show it was also frequently used by Gentiles (Bruce, p. 313).

[17]Other examples in the Gospels are Mark 1:44; Matt 8:4; Luke 5:14. See Trites, *Witness*, pp. 177-178; Haenchen, p. 495.

bit of humor here.[18] The same verb (ἐξῆλθεν, *exēlthen*) is used for
the exit of the spirit and the exit of "their hope of making money."
Luke seems to say "out went the spirit and out went their profit."
The words "at that moment" describe the miraculous nature of this
incident.

No wonder the owners were furious! They "seized Paul and Silas
and dragged them into the marketplace to face the authorities." No
mention is made of what happened to Timothy and Luke. "Marketplace" (ἀγορά, *agora*) should be understood as more than a shop-
ping mall, since it was the location of the city forum. Here they
were placed before the "magistrates" (στρατηγός, *stratēgos*), the two
men responsible for trying civil cases and keeping the peace.
Serving under them were the "lictors," called ῥαβδοῦχοι (*rhabdou-
choi*) in vv. 35 and 38. The lictors administered the beatings to those
found guilty. They were pictured in the Roman world as men who
carried the bundle of rods with an axe in the middle of the bundle
and tied with a red band (called the *fasces*).

The charges the owners brought did not mention money. They
focused on arguments which would influence the case. Identifying
the men as Jews would prejudice the case immediately in the minds
of many Romans. That they were throwing the city "into an
uproar" would concern any Roman magistrate charged with keeping the peace. Their advocating of "customs unlawful" for Romans
may be a reference to attempts by Paul to win converts, since pros-
elyting among Roman citizens met with much disapproval in the
Roman world.[19]

Finally, Paul and Silas endured a severe Roman beating. The
crowd "joined in the attack," placing additional pressure on the

---

[18]Polhill, p. 351.

[19]Haenchen says it was illegal to do so (p. 496, n. 5), though the better
evidence makes this doubtful. See Sherwin-White, *Roman Society and Roman
Law*, pp. 78-82. The official Roman stance was one of toleration toward reli-
gions which had been sanctioned by the state. In practical terms, however,
the practice of a religion was not discouraged by the Romans unless it
involved some social or political crime. During the Julio-Claudian period
the enforcement of regulations in matters of religion was not strict, except
in a few cases. Actions were taken against the Druids, Magians, and
worshipers of Isis. In addition, Claudius expelled the Jews from Rome
because of disturbances about one "Chrestus." See notes on 18:1.

magistrates so that they ordered the men beaten on their bare backs. This incident is one which Paul remembers later when he writes to the Corinthians about his hardships for Christ (2 Cor 11:25).

The Imprisonment (16:23-26)

[23]**After they had been severely flogged, they were thrown into prison, and the jailer was commanded to guard them carefully. [24]Upon receiving such orders, he put them in the inner cell and fastened their feet in the stocks. [25]About midnight Paul and Silas were praying and singing hymns to God, and the other prisoners were listening to them. [26]Suddenly there was such a violent earthquake that the foundations of the prison were shaken. At once all the prison doors flew open, and everybody's chains came loose.**

Located in the same marketplace (*agora*) was the jail. Paul and Barnabas were placed "in the inner cell," a detail which emphasizes how securely they were being kept. The Roman stocks which held their feet had several holes which allowed the jailer to force their legs into a painful position, resulting in the stretching and cramping of muscles.

In spite of these hardships, Paul and Silas demonstrated the joy and hope of their faith. About midnight they were "praying and singing hymns," loudly enough that the other prisoners, even at that hour, "were listening to them."[20] After demonstrating their power over the "pythoness," these would have been impressive prisoners.

An earthquake heightened the drama, as if a Divine response to the courage of the prisoners. Though earthquakes are common in Macedonia, this one was so violent that "the foundations of the prison were shaken." Not surprisingly, perhaps, the prison doors which probably locked with bars across the door, were shaken so that they sprang open. What was more surprising was that "everybody's chains came loose." Though this might mean that the chains merely shook free of the prison wall, it seems more probable that a

---

[20]See Haenchen for citations from ancient literature of saintly prisoners singing and praising God in their cells (p. 497).

miracle is being described in which even the chains around arms and legs fell loose to the floor.

The Conversion of the Jailer (16:27-34)

[27]The jailer woke up, and when he saw the prison doors open, he drew his sword and was about to kill himself because he thought the prisoners had escaped. [28]But Paul shouted, "Don't harm yourself! We are all here!" [29]The jailer called for lights, rushed in and fell trembling before Paul and Silas. [30]He then brought them out and asked, "Sirs, what must I do to be saved?" [31]They replied, "Believe in the Lord Jesus, and you will be saved—you and your household." [32]Then they spoke the word of the Lord to him and to all the others in his house. [33]At that hour of the night the jailer took them and washed their wounds; then immediately he and all his family were baptized. [34]The jailer brought them into his house and set a meal before them; he was filled with joy because he had come to believe in God—he and his whole family.

The jailer assumed that the prisoners had escaped until he heard Paul's shout. Jailers and guards within the Roman system knew that they were held personally responsible for keeping prisoners secured (see 12:19). This jailer saw no reason to face his superiors, and was ready to commit suicide.

But Paul was able to see the jailer through the opened doors. He called to him to say that the other prisoners were still there. Perhaps they had found no opportunity to escape, or were so intimidated by these prisoners who had power over a *pythoness*, sang in their cell, and were answered with earthquakes, that they were too afraid to escape.

At any rate, the jailer got a torch, hurried in and "fell trembling before Paul and Silas." These events had struck fear into his heart. His response implied some acquaintance with their message. The issue of "salvation" in the context of gospel preaching involves reconciliation to God, a pardon from sin, and restoration to life. How the jailer knew of these things Luke does not say. Whether he heard reports of their preaching in Philippi, or heard about the incident with the pythoness, or drew information from the singing in the prison is not clear. Whatever the means of finding out, the jailer seemed to know enough to ask the correct question about becoming a disciple of Christ.[21]

The response of Paul and Silas differs from previous invitations to accept the gospel truth in that faith is mentioned without the command to repent or be baptized (see 2:38; 3:19; 14:15). This fact does not mean that inconsistencies exist between the commands. The response of faith includes repentance and baptism. Faith was presented as the means for salvation with Christ as the object of that faith. This language, of course, is very similar to Paul's language in his letters (see Rom 3:21-31; Eph 2:8-9; Phil 3:8-9).

Again the "household" was included (see 16:15). But the fact that they "spoke the word of the Lord to him and all the others in his house" implies that the jailer's household consisted of members old enough to hear and respond to the gospel.

The response of the jailer was sincere. He not only submitted to baptism, but demonstrated his sincerity by taking Paul and Silas to a pool of water in the courtyard where he washed their wounded backs. In addition he invited these prisoners into his own home and placed a meal before them.

As Luke consistently shows interest in the evidence of conversions, so he does here. In some cases it was speaking in tongues (10:44) or rejoicing (8:39). Now it is hospitality, as it was in v. 15 with Lydia. The jailer was "filled with joy" and ready to offer his home as a way of assisting the missionaries.

The Departure (16:35-40)

[35]When it was daylight, the magistrates sent their officers to the jailer with the order: "Release those men." [36]The jailer told Paul, "The magistrates have ordered that you and Silas be released. Now you can leave. Go in peace." [37]But Paul said to the officers: "They beat us publicly without a trial, even though we are Roman citi-

---

[21]No concept of "secular salvation" appears in the jailer's question as if he was asking about salvation from the penalty of losing his prisoners. He already knew that he had escaped that penalty.

259

**zens, and threw us into prison. And now do they want to get rid of us quietly? No! Let them come themselves and escort us out."
[38]The officers reported this to the magistrates, and when they heard that Paul and Silas were Roman citizens, they were alarmed. [39]They came to appease them and escorted them from the prison, requesting them to leave the city. [40]After Paul and Silas came out of the prison, they went to Lydia's house, where they met with the brothers and encouraged them. Then they left.**

Very early the next morning the magistrates (*stratēgoi*) sent the lictors (*rhabdouchous*) who had beaten Paul and Silas to the jail. Evidently the magistrates were convinced that the lesson had been learned by Paul and Silas. Though imprisonment for breaches of the civil law was not customary, Bruce sees in their action a case of "summary correction."[22] Satisfied that this goal had been met, they were ready to set the prisoners free.

At this point Paul revealed a fact that the authorities had not bothered to investigate the day before. He informed the lictors that he and Silas were "Roman citizens." Paul's point in bringing this to their attention was to demonstrate the unfairness in the sentence. They had committed no crime. Their ministry in the gospel deserved no stain against its reputation.

For this reason Paul wanted the record wiped clean. A public acknowledgment of the mistake by the authorities was needed. The magistrates became nervous. Taking such measures against Roman citizens, and without a trial, was a serious infraction of Roman policy. Philippi could have lost its status as a Roman colony. Roman citizenship was a rare privilege which guaranteed particular rights. Since the early second century B.C., Roman citizens had been exempted from humiliating forms of punishment. Although the protection of these rights often depended on the whim of the local magistrate, Rome frequently investigated officials accused of departing from accepted customs of law enforcement.

How a citizen managed to prove the fact of citizenship is unclear. In some cases wooden diptychs were carried by citizens as a record of citizenship, but this was not common.

---

[22]Bruce, p. 319.

At any rate, the officials came to Paul and urged him to depart from the city, apologizing and hoping for as little publicity as possible. For his part, Paul was ready to leave. But he first wanted to say good-by to Lydia. At her house he found a gathering of believers.[23] The church was already growing. Paul encouraged them and then left the city with Silas and Timothy.

The use of the first person pronoun ends here, implying that Luke may have remained in Philippi to help strengthen the church. Later the first person begins again where Paul arrives in Philippi (20:5-6). From what Paul says in Philippians 1:27-28 it is evident that the Philippian church had to deal with suffering for the faith. Perhaps the events surrounding Paul's imprisonment had brought resentment to such a pitch that persecution broke out long after Paul's visit. The same letter shows, however, that the church never stopped supporting Paul (see 1:24-25; 4:2-3,14-19).

---

[23]For other examples of women providing a house for a church, see the comments on 12:12.

ACTS 17

9. The Visits at Amphipolis and Apollonia (17:1a)

¹When they had passed through Amphipolis and Apollonia,

After leaving Philippi Paul's steps turned westward. Ultimately he was heading toward Thessalonica. But Luke mentions a couple of the cities the missionaries passed through on the way.

As the mission journey is described by Luke, a familiar pattern will develop. Each time Paul and his companions enter a new city, the preaching will gain early success, but then be faced with animosity. This was true in Philippi, and the pattern will be repeated in Thessalonica, Athens, and Corinth.[1] Luke is always careful to show in all of this that the gospel was triumphant over hardships.

Another pattern which becomes obvious is the trial scenes. In the Macedonian cities Luke usually describes how Paul and his co-workers were forced to stand before the authorities. Again this was true when Paul visited Philippi, but will also happen when he arrives at Thessalonica, Athens,[2] and Corinth.

The two cities Paul passed through on his way to Thessalonica do not appear to be places he stayed long. Amphipolis was linked with Philippi by the Egnatian Way,[3] one of the most traveled of the

---

[1]In cities previously visited by Paul, the same pattern had been obvious. It was true in Paphos (13:7-8), Pisidian Antioch (13:44-50), Iconium (14:4-6), and Lystra (14:8-20).

[2]This is true if we assume that the Areopagus consisted of a type of Athenian council. See comments below.

[3]The Egnatian Way, one of the most important of the Roman roads, was constructed about 130 B.C. It crossed all of Macedonia, running a total distance of nearly 500 miles. Thessalonica was the midpoint along this route. Roman road-building was well advanced and some roads continue in

Roman roads. Also on this route were Apollonia and Thessalonica. The cities were evenly spaced, each approximately thirty miles from the other.[4] If travel was done on horseback, the distance between cities could be traveled in a day. It is likely, though, that the missionaries could not use this more expensive means of travel. Walking between cities would probably require most of two days, with an overnight stop at a hostel (inn) along the road.

10. The Visit at Thessalonica (17:1b-9)

Paul's Preaching in the Synagogue (17:1b-4)

[T]hey came to Thessalonica, where there was a Jewish synagogue. [2]As his custom was, Paul went into the synagogue, and on three Sabbath days he reasoned with them from the Scriptures, [3]explaining and proving that the Christ[a] had to suffer and rise from the dead. "This Jesus I am proclaiming to you is the Christ," he said. [4]Some of the Jews were persuaded and joined Paul and Silas, as did a large number of God-fearing Greeks and not a few prominent women.

[a]3 Or *Messiah*

Finally the missionaries arrived at Thessalonica, about 100 miles from Philippi. Thessalonica was an old Macedonian city, established in 315 B.C., and named after the half-sister of Alexander the Great. It had become the second largest city in Greece with a population of about 200,000. When the Romans assumed dominance in 148 B.C., they realized the significance of this city and made it the center of Roman administration in Macedonia. Later, Thessalonica

---

use after 2,000 years. At the peak of the Roman Empire some 56,000 miles of roads were in use. Usually constructed with four distinct layers of materials, often the roadway was twenty-five feet wide and the roadbed was almost three feet deep. For a full discussion of Roman roads, see L.A. and J.A. Hamey, *The Roman Engineers* (Cambridge: Cambridge University Press, 1981); John McRay, *Archaeology and the New Testament* (Grand Rapids: Baker, 1991). Though these roads were the links which held the Empire together, Luke never mentions them by name.

[4]Thessalonica was the exception, though its distance was just thirty-eight miles from Apollonia.

was made a free city in 42 B.C. because of its loyalty to Octavian and Antony in the battle of Philippi. Such a city was a tempting location for Paul in his plans for establishing churches. The Jewish synagogue was Paul's first target "as his custom was" (see 14:1; "as usual"), and he spent "three Sabbath days" working there. This indication of time makes Paul's visit to Thessalonica quite short if it is taken absolutely.

Paul's letter to the Thessalonians some weeks after his stay in the city, however, seems to imply a longer stay than three weeks. In 1 Thessalonians 2:9, for example, Paul speaks of using his trade to support himself in Thessalonica. He also spent enough time there to have received a number of gifts from the church in Philippi (Phil 4:16). The "three Sabbaths" which Luke mentions may be intended only to identify the time Paul was able to spend in the synagogue itself.

While in the synagogue Paul "reasoned with them from the Scriptures." The verb διαλέγομαι (dialegomai) gives the sense that Paul's reasoning included teaching or discourse which may even have involved the method of question and answer. Perhaps the message of Paul made it impossible for the Jewish audience to keep silent. His doctrine in this setting turned attention to the Old Testament "Scriptures." His goal was that of "explaining and proving"[5] the fact that the Christ "had to suffer." This theme is common in passages from Luke and Acts, including Luke 9:22; 24:26,44,46; Acts 3:18, and 26:23. Paul's letters also refer to the suffering Messiah (1 Cor 15:3-4), along with those of Peter (1 Pet 1:11). This aspect of the gospel is what the Jews so frequently denounced as foolishness (1 Cor 1:18).[6] The direct connection Paul was making with these Old Testament passages centered on Jesus. He was demonstrating that "this Jesus" was the Christ spoken of in the Old Testament.

Among those who responded to Paul's message were "some of the Jews," as well as "a large number of God-fearing Greeks," a

---

[5]The Greek term for "proving" is παρατιθέμενος (paratithemenos), a participle in the present tense. It means "to present evidence" by "bringing forward in proof passages of Scriptures." See Rienecker, p. 306. Polhill notes that Luke chooses the terminology of formal rhetoric here in describing Paul's way of presenting the case for Christ (p. 360, n. 50).

[6]The Old Testament Scriptures used would probably have been the Servant Psalms of Isaiah (chapters 42-53).

group which included "not a few prominent women." Of these, the God-fearing Greeks again represented Gentiles associated with the synagogue, but not full converts.[7] The prominent women were those holding a high status in the Macedonian society, a feature of the Roman world that is attested in ancient literature.[8]

Paul's own description of results from his preaching in Thessalonica is given in 1 Thessalonians 1:9. He says that they "turned to God from idols to serve the living and true God."

The Backlash from the Jews (17:5-9)

[5]**But the Jews were jealous; so they rounded up some bad characters from the marketplace, formed a mob and started a riot in the city. They rushed to Jason's house in search of Paul and Silas in order to bring them out to the crowd.[a] [6]But when they did not find them, they dragged Jason and some other brothers before the city officials, shouting: "These men who have caused trouble all over the world have now come here, [7]and Jason has welcomed them into his house. They are all defying Caesar's decrees, saying that there is another king, one called Jesus." [8]When they heard this, the crowd and the city officials were thrown into turmoil. [9]Then they made Jason and the others post bond and let them go.**

[a]**5 Or** *the assembly of the people*

Once again, though, many Jews responded with jealousy. The specific nature of their jealousy is not mentioned by Luke, but the loss of so many God-fearers and prominent women would be a legitimate supposition. For the synagogue these people represented potential converts. Their association with Judaism on an informal

---

[7]Compare the description of Cornelius in 10:2.

[8]The position of Macedonian women had been elevated since the days following Alexander the Great. Stoicism was one factor which brought to married women a higher status. At times women took positions such as city magistrates, founders of clubs, and even philosophers. See W.W. Tarn and G.T. Griffith, *Hellenistic Civilization* (Cleveland: World Publishing, 1969), pp. 98-99.

basis implied that they had intentions of becoming more involved in the future. Synagogue leaders would have been furious with Paul for "stealing" these prospects by converting them to Christ.

Regarding the converts made in Thessalonica, few specifics are known. Jason[9] is mentioned in this text, but he is unknown anywhere else in the New Testament. Aristarchus and Secundus are described in 20:4 as Thessalonians, and were probably among those converted at this point. No other names from the Thessalonian converts are known.

Rather than facing the issue directly the Jewish leaders used "bad characters from the marketplace" to create troubles for Paul's ministry. They instigated a riot, and then began searching for the missionaries at the house of Jason, who may have given them employment. Perhaps after working with Paul and Silas, Jason heard enough of the gospel to be converted.

When the rioters could not locate Paul and Silas, they vented their rage on Jason, dragging him and some other believers before "the city officials" (πολιτάρχης, politarchēs). Luke employs the Greek term here (and in v. 8) which cannot be found anywhere else in Greek literature. In 1835, however, an archaeological discovery confirmed Luke's accuracy in using the term. An arch was found which spanned the Egnatian Way on the west side of Thessalonica and on the surface of the arch was an inscription speaking of city officials called "politarchs."[10] Luke's precision was confirmed again.

Standing before the "politarchs" in Thessalonica was just the first step in the legal process. These disciples were also forced to answer to "the crowd" (δῆμος, dēmos), which was a citizen body in Thessalonica, responsible for legislative and juridical functions.[11]

---

[9]His name was a variation of "Jesus" or "Joshua" meaning "savior."

[10]Though the arch was destroyed in 1867, the block containing the inscription may be viewed today in the British Museum. Since that time many other inscriptions have been discovered in the area of Macedonia with the term "politarch" in them. See Bruce, p. 324. Luke's accuracy here has been convincing evidence that Acts must have been written in the first century. See Gasque, *History of Criticism*, p. 277. See also G.H.R. Horsley, "The Inscriptions of Ephesos and the New Testament," *NovT* 34 (1992): 105-168.

[11]Bruce, p. 324, n. 7; see also NIV footnote for v. 5. In v. 8, however, the word is οχλος (ochlos), a crowd.

The charges brought against the believers were first that they were causing "trouble all over the world," and that Jason was guilty by association. Though this charge was highly exaggerated, it may be that it was based on news which came from Philippi.[12] Secondly, the charge was made that they were "defying Caesar's decrees," which included saying that there was "another king" (or "emperor")[13] named "Jesus." These decrees, it was implied, protected the claim of Caesar to the throne. Saying that there was another emperor than Caesar was one of the most dangerous crimes one could commit.

Readers of the four Gospels will recognize in this charge the same one which was leveled against Jesus (see Luke 23:2-4; John 19:12,15). To Romans the charge sounded like a violation of the oath of loyalty demanded of every resident in the Roman Empire.[14]

The turmoil caused by these charges forced Jason to be held responsible. The "politarchs" were more interested, however, in maintaining the peace than taking retribution. Therefore they required Jason to "post bond," paying a sum of money which would be forfeited if there was a recurrence of the trouble. Then they let them go. This relatively light response of the "politarchs" (especially in contrast with the officials in Philippi; 16:22) implied that they were not convinced that the evidence was strong against the believers.

11. The Visit of Paul and Silas in Berea (17:10-14)

[10]As soon as it was night, the brothers sent Paul and Silas away to Berea. On arriving there, they went to the Jewish synagogue. [11]Now the Bereans were of more noble character than the Thessalonians, for they received the message with great eagerness and examined the Scriptures every day to see if what Paul said was true. [12]Many of the Jews believed, as did also a number of prominent Greek women and many Greek men. [13]When the Jews in Thessalonica learned that Paul was preaching the word of God

---

[12]Marshall, p. 279. Sherwin-White notes how concerned the Romans were about preventing "disturbances of the world." See his *Roman Society and Roman Law*, pp. 51,103.

[13]Lake and Cadbury, p. 206.

[14]Polhill, p. 362.

at Berea, they went there too, agitating the crowds and stirring them up. [14]The brothers immediately sent Paul to the coast, but Silas and Timothy stayed at Berea.

Once again Paul and Silas were forced to leave a city in which they had preached. Christians in the city helped sneak them out of town. As the missionaries moved toward Berea, they left the Egnatian Way, which continued westward to Dyrrachium on the Adriatic Sea. From there a traveler heading west on this road could take a boat across the sea to Brundisium in southern Italy and then go north toward Rome. It is sometimes suggested that Paul may have thought about going on to Rome at this point, since he states in his letter to the Romans that he had wanted to go there with the gospel (Rom 1:13; 15:22). As Bruce points out, however, if he

> had tried to do so at this time, he might have found his plan frustrated: he would probably have met Jews from Rome traveling eastward along the Egnatian Way, telling how the Emperor Claudius had expelled them from the capital.[15]

Whatever the case with Paul's intentions for Rome, the missionaries made their way to Berea. Located about fifty miles from Thessalonica, this city at one time was the capital of one of the four divisions of Macedonia (from 167-148 B.C.). The journey to this populous city took about three days to walk, and the missionaries went immediately to the synagogue.

Luke gives only a brief summary of the ministry in Berea, but the report is far more positive than much of the tour. The Bereans were "of more noble character (εὐγενέστεροι, *eugenesteroi*; from εὐγενής) than the Thessalonians," a term which originally applied to people born of high or noble status. In this context, though, the meaning refers to an attitude of tolerance with regard to the ideas Paul shared. The Bereans did not reject the gospel on impulse, but exhibited a freedom from prejudice in their willingness to examine his message. They even "examined the Scriptures," not once, but "every day to see if what Paul said was true."

The daily examination of the Old Testament Scriptures allowed

---

[15]Bruce, p. 327.

them to look for the evidence Paul used to prove Jesus as Messiah.[16]
The Bereans were eager to see if his claims could be supported.
Their example of open-minded Scripture study has become a model
for Christians who sometimes even label themselves "Bereans."

Again the results included converts from among the ranks of the
Jews and prominent Greeks (see v. 4), and again resistance came
from Jews from another location (see 14:19), this time Thessalonica.
These Jews succeeded in agitating the crowds, probably by carrying
the same charges made in Thessalonica about the missionaries'
disloyalty to Caesar.

Once again the converts found themselves providing an escape
for the ones who converted them (see 9:25; 14:20; 17:10). They sent
Paul "to the coast," a destination which could mean he boarded a
ship headed to Athens. It could also mean simply that Paul went to
the coast to reach a road which continued to Athens. If so, the journey was about a twenty-mile walk.[17] At any rate, the believers who
helped him get away secretly made sure that he had company all the
way to Athens.

12. The Visit at Athens (17:15-34)

Paul's Preaching in Athens (17:15-17)

[15]The men who escorted Paul brought him to Athens and then
left with instructions for Silas and Timothy to join him as soon as
possible. [16]While Paul was waiting for them in Athens, he was greatly
distressed to see that the city was full of idols. [17]So he reasoned in
the synagogue with the Jews and the God-fearing Greeks, as well as
in the marketplace day by day with those who happened to be there.

---

[16]The Scriptures they examined were probably the passages from the
Psalms and Prophets so often used by the apostles to prove that Jesus was
sent as the Messiah (see 2:25-28,34; 4:25; 8:32-33; 13:33-35). The term for
"examined" (ἀνακρίνω, anakrinō) implies a "sifting of data up and down," a
"careful and exact research as in legal processes" (Rienecker, p. 307).

[17]The Byzantine text suggests that Paul and Silas went to the coast as a
kind of decoy so that their enemies would think they were going by sea
when they were actually intending to go by land.

The last word Paul had for his companions when they arrived in Athens was a message for Silas and Timothy to meet him in Athens as soon as possible. Silas and Timothy had "stayed at Berea." In 1 Thessalonians 3:1-2 Paul describes how he sent Timothy to Thessalonica. Some scholars point to this fact as evidence that Luke's report is inaccurate, but it is more likely that Luke is merely abbreviating what were very complicated movements of the various individuals between cities.[18] Paul may, for example, have arrived alone in Athens, but then was rejoined by Silas and Timothy, who were then sent off again to Thessalonica. Describing all of these movements did not fit into Luke's purpose for Acts.

According to his usual practice, on the Sabbath "he reasoned (*dialegomai* as in v. 2) in the synagogue with the Jews and the God-fearing Greeks." The content of his message was exactly what he had preached in Thessalonica (v. 3). But in Athens, Paul spent weekdays in "the marketplace," discussing the gospel with those who happened to be there. All the while he was waiting for Silas and Timothy.

The condition of the city "greatly distressed" him. Athens was "full of idols." The city by Paul's day was no longer the glorious political and cultural giant it had been 500 years earlier. Its population included only about 5,000 voting citizens and its political power was granted by the Romans for the purpose of maintaining its own institutions as a free city in the Roman Empire. Nevertheless, Athens remained a center of education and art.

Paul's reaction to the artistic symbols in the city did not come because of his lack of culturing. Paul realized that these pieces of art in many cases represented objects of worship. Statues and engravings in Athens were everywhere, depicting exploits of the gods. No matter where he looked there were herms (pillars on which the head of Hermes was mounted). Temples stood in tribute to deities with altars available to pagans for sacrificing what was really an offering to demons (see 1 Cor 10:20). Paul was "greatly distressed" (παροξύνω, *paroxynō*), a term with the sense of being "infuriated."[19]

---

[18]See Haenchen, pp. 512-513; Bruce, p. 328, n. 30.
[19]Polhill, p. 366.

Paul's Encounter with the Philosophers (17:18)

[18]A group of Epicurean and Stoic philosophers began to dispute with him. Some of them asked, "What is this babbler trying to say?" Others remarked, "He seems to be advocating foreign gods." They said this because Paul was preaching the good news about Jesus and the resurrection.

Paul's daily presence in the marketplace led him to discussions with a group which represented two classical philosophies of his day—Epicureanism and Stoicism. The Epicureans descended from Epicurus (340-270 B.C.), and believed that the universe and all beings consisted of atoms (tiny particles) which were active only temporarily. Thus they rejected any thought of life beyond this world. Though they did not deny the existence of the gods, they believed them to be uninvolved in this world. For them the greatest good was happiness, pleasure, and finding freedom from pain, disturbing passions, and superstitious fears about death.

The Stoics came from a school of philosophy founded by Zeno (c. 340-265 B.C.). His meeting place was the στοά ποικίλη (*stoa poikilē*) ("painted colonnade") in the marketplace of Athens, and from this meeting place the school took the name "Stoics." Their belief in the *logos* or Universal Reason as the divine force which held the universe together gave them a confidence that life could be lived in harmony with nature. They were pantheistic, believing that the spark of divinity was in all of the creation. They also taught that self-sufficiency and an acceptance of fate was essential. Stoics were characterized by a high standard of ethics, and their belief that everyone had the spark of divinity led them to a sense of universal brotherhood, even for slaves.

When the Epicureans and Stoics heard of Paul's message they disputed with him, referring to him as a "babbler." Paul was behaving like a bird picking up seeds of information here and there and carrying them around without using any critical thinking.[20] It was

---

[20]The question the philosophers asked might be paraphrased, "What would he wish to say, if he could say anything?" Another possible interpretation is, "What might he be trying to say?" The verb θέλοι (*theloi*) (want) is

not a flattering remark. Others interpreted his emphasis on "Jesus" and "the resurrection" (ἀνάστασις, *anastasis*) to be the names of new gods, and took Paul's discussion to be a promotion of a new god and goddess.[21] Thus they understood Paul to be another polytheist like themselves.

Paul's Address in the Areopagus (17:19-31)

[19]**Then they took him and brought him to a meeting of the Areopagus, where they said to him, "May we know what this new teaching is that you are presenting? [20]You are bringing some strange ideas to our ears, and we want to know what they mean." [21](All the Athenians and the foreigners who lived there spent their time doing nothing but talking about and listening to the latest ideas.) [22]Paul then stood up in the meeting of the Areopagus and said: "Men of Athens! I see that in every way you are very religious. [23]For as I walked around and looked carefully at your objects of worship, I even found an altar with this inscription: TO AN UNKNOWN GOD. Now what you worship as something unknown I am going to proclaim to you. [24]"The God who made the world and everything in it is the Lord of heaven and earth and does not live in temples built by hands. [25]And he is not served by human hands, as if he needed anything, because he himself gives all men life and breath and everything else. [26]From one man he made every nation of men, that they should inhabit the whole earth; and he determined the times set for them and the exact places where they should live. [27]God did this so that men would seek him and perhaps reach out for him and find him, though he is not far from each one of us. [28]'For in him we live and move and have our being.' As some of your own poets have said, 'We are his offspring.' [29]"Therefore since we are God's offspring, we should not think that the divine being is like gold or silver or stone—an**

---

used in the present optative, and is to be understood perhaps as a potential optative. See Dana and Mantey, p. 174. The term for "babbler" (σπερμο-λόγος, *spermologos*) carries this idea (Rienecker, p. 307).

[21]Polhill, p. 367.

image made by man's design and skill. ³⁰In the past God over-looked such ignorance, but now he commands all people every-where to repent. ³¹For he has set a day when he will judge the world with justice by the man he has appointed. He has given proof of this to all men by raising him from the dead."

Paul's daily discussions prompted a more formal meeting of the philosophers who were interested in his words. At this point Luke's language poses some difficulties for the modern reader. What is meant when the text says "they brought him to a meeting of the Areopagus" where they asked to know about his teaching? The question is whether Luke refers to a place of meeting or to the name of the council with whom Paul met.

The Areopagus was a hill located to the southwest of the market-place (ἀγορά, *agora*). Originally the site was the place at which civil and criminal cases were heard. The name means "hill of Ares," a reference to the god of war in the Greek pantheon.[22] But the Areopagus was also a respected council which exercised jurisdiction in religious and moral questions. By the time of Paul this council met in the Royal Portico (στοά βασιλείος, *stoa basileios*).

The question as to which of these meanings Luke uses here is best answered by considering several points argued by Polhill.[23] First, Luke seems to describe Paul's experience with terms that are parallel to the hearing experienced by Socrates 500 years before. Socrates had to stand before a council, a point which argues that Luke intends to portray Paul's experience as one before a council.

Second, one of Paul's converts came from the Areopagus, an item which argues that Luke's use of the term speaks of people rather than a place. Finally, Luke's tendency in Acts is to show how Paul had to stand trial before city councils of various types in many of the major cities he visited. This observation also argues for a council rather than a place. The NIV takes this position when it says that they took him "to a meeting of the Areopagus."

Bringing Paul into their council, they asked him to explain in

---

[22]The Roman name for this god was Mars, prompting the KJV to translate the phrase Mars' hill.

[23]Polhill, p. 368.

detail "this new teaching" he promoted. Their request of Paul demonstrated their perception that they were the guardians of new doctrines about gods and religion. Luke's parenthetical remark characterizes the Athenians in a way that was well understood in the first century. The orator Demosthenes had commented 400 years before that the Athenians were scurrying about asking the latest news at the very moment Philip of Macedon threatened their security.[24] The characterization was not complimentary.

The address delivered by Paul has attracted more attention from scholarship than any other passage in Acts. Multitudes of volumes and articles have raised issues concerning the background of Paul's ideas. Some argue that Paul's thinking appears to come from Greek philosophical thought.[25] On the other hand, some scholars insist that the roots of Paul's message come directly from the Old Testament or from Judaism.[26] Those who argue for the Greek background of Paul's words express doubts that Paul could have spoken these words. The argument is that the speech sounds unlike him.

This line of reasoning does not give enough attention to the similarities of the content of the Areopagus address with Paul's letters. These similarities will be considered below. At any rate, his Areopagus message aimed at a direct critique of pagan idolatry described in contrast to the relationship possible with the living God.

Paul's Acknowledgment of Their Idols (17:19-23). His beginning point was a description of their sense of the religious. He pointed out that in arriving in the city, he had observed an altar with the inscription "TO AN UNKNOWN GOD" (ΑΓΝΩΣΤΩ ΘΕΩ, *Agnōstō theō*). The

---

[24]Bruce, p. 332.

[25]Eduard Norden, *Agnostos Theos* (Stuttgart: Teubner, 1923); Martin Dibelius, "Paul on the Areopagus," *Studies in the Acts of the Apostles* (London: SCM, 1956); and Hans Conzelmann, "The Address of Paul on the Areopagus," *Studies in Luke-Acts*, ed. Leander Keck and J.L. Martyn (Nashville: Abingdon, 1966), pp. 217-230, are examples of this position in one form or another.

[26]Such scholars as Gärtner, *Areopagus Speech*; and F.G. Downing, "Common Ground with Paganism in Luke and in Josephus," *NTS* 28 (1982): 546-559, are examples. See also Edward Fudge, "Paul's Apostolic Self-Consciousness at Athens," *JETS* 14 (1971): 193-198; Gasque, *History of Criticism*, pp. 217-250. Vielhauer sees the theology of the speech as a combination of the two. See his "'Paulinism' of Acts," *Studies in Luke-Acts*, ed. Keck and Martyn, pp. 33-50.

Greek phrase may also be translated "TO THE UNKNOWN GOD,"
a point which raised the question as to whether such an inscription
has been discovered in the ruins of Athens. As early as the church
father Jerome, questions were being raised regarding whether such
an inscription was known in Athens.[27]

This difficulty disappears altogether, however, when we remember that the argument against Paul's citation is built on the silence
of the literary and archaeological record. Just because the inscription is not known to have existed (in its verbatim form) does not
mean that it did not exist.

Besides this point is the fact that inscriptions were often abbreviated phrases with no intention of grammatical correctness. The
difference between "the unknown God" and "an unknown God"[28] is
meaningless since inscriptions frequently contained this degree of
ambiguity.

While calling attention to the inscription, Paul made use of it to
offer a description of the Athenians as "very religious" (δεισιδαιμον-
εστέρος, *deisidaimonesteros*). The word is so ambiguous that it could
be understood either as a compliment or an insult, depending on
the context. It can carry the idea of "superstitious," or "overly
scrupulous," but it can also mean "highly devoted to religious
matters."[29] Paul's audience would perhaps not have known for sure
what he meant by the phrase, though it is likely he meant to compliment them as far as he could, given his abhorrence of their idols.

Next Paul made further use of the inscription by using the
theme of a deity unknown to declare a God who could be known.
His terminology even reflected their dilemma. Paul said "what" (ὅ,

---

[27]*Commentary on 2 Corinthians* 10:5. Bruce thinks Jerome was describing
an inscription which read "TO THE GODS OF ASIA, EUROPE AND
AFRICA, TO UNKNOWN AND FOREIGN GODS," and that Paul used
some license in his own reference to these words, making the plural "gods"
into a singular "god" (Bruce, p. 335).

[28]Ancient writers do attest to the presence of inscriptions reading "to
unknown gods." See Pausanias, *Description of Greece* 1:1:4, and Philostratus,
Life of Apollonius 6:3:5.

[29]Bruce gives several citations of ancient writers who described the highly
religious Athenians, including Sophocles, Josephus, Pausanius, Strabo, and
Livy.

ho, neuter pronoun) you worship, rather than "who" you worship. He also described their worship in terms of "something unknown" (ἀγνοοῦντες, *agnoountes*), using language which emphasized their lack of truth with regard to their gods.[30] Paul's point was to say that what the Athenians "did not know" about God, he himself would proclaim to them. He began by speaking about the first works of God.

God the Creator of Everything (17:24-26). Perhaps wishing to find some common ground with his hearers, Paul began by focusing on the creation. God, he said, "made the world" (κόσμος, *kosmos*). The Greek audience would have been unfamiliar, however, with the notion of a personal, transcendent Creator. Their concept of deity was one which was unavoidably connected with the universe, but never totally above the universe, controlling it and maintaining it. Paul's emphasis was on a God who not only created everything, but who "is the Lord (κύριος, *kyrios*) of heaven and earth."

This God, said Paul, "does not live in temples built by hands," a point made by Stephen in his address before the Sanhedrin (Acts 7:48-50; see also 1 Kgs 8:27). Paul elaborated on the point, adding "he is not served by human hands, as if he needed anything," a direct reference to the idols and temples he had seen in the city. Rather than needing material structures, insisted Paul, God himself "gives all men life and breath and everything else."

Paul's portrait of the Creator God who rules the universe may be seen throughout the Old Testament (see Job 38:4–39:30; Isa 40:10-31; 42:5; 66:1-2; Ps 2:4; 50:9-12). The Old Testament, as well as Judaism, seems very much Paul's reference point in his presentation of the God who can be known.

His emphasis on a personal God who created everything, and who rules over all things, was followed by another trait of the God revealed from Old Testament times. This God also involves himself in human history. Paul said that God "made every nation of men, that they should inhabit the whole earth." This point seems to refer to God's providential hand as it moves in history. He made every

---

[30]Paul's use of the present participle serves to emphasize the condition of ignorance of the Athenians. Gärtner takes the use of ἄγνοια (*agnoia*) as a condemnation of the Athenians. See his *Areopagus Speech*, p. 237.

nation "from one man," meaning Adam, and he "determined the times set for them and the exact places where they should live." This reference to "times" (καιρούς, *kairous*) describes periods in which nations rise or fall, as well as what territories they might occupy. From this point, Paul was able to move to his major theme— the living God is near enough to be known by the Athenians and everyone else.

God Who Is Near Enough to Touch (17:27-29). Having established that the Athenians were worshiping something unknown when the Creator of the universe can indeed be known, Paul now brought his address to its climax. Why had God appointed the territories and the times for the nations of the earth? Why had he shown himself to be the Creator of the universe? He did all this, said Paul, so that "men would seek him." Thus Paul delivered to the Athenians the message that God is so personal that he wants a relationship with people.

The seeking of God, however, is only part of the story. The rest of Paul's statement is that humans can "perhaps reach out for him and find him." In making this statement, Paul uses the strongest possible grammatical structure to indicate how uncertain it is to find God only through a respect for creation.[31] Yet his message argued that it was, nevertheless, possible to find God, especially in the present time.

God is "not far from each one of us," Paul declared. He is close enough to touch, for "in him we live and move and have our being." Then Paul added that some of the Greek poets had declared the truth, "we are his offspring." These words are indeed citations from the lines of poets whose works were often quoted in the ancient world. The first of the two quotations (indicated as a quote by the NIV), can be found in a quatrain of the poet Epimenides (c. 600 B.C.) in his *Cretica*. The second quotation seems to be taken from

---

[31]The verbs "reach out"(ψηλαφήσειαν, *psēlapheseian*) and "find"(εὕροιεν, *heuroien*) are both in the optative mood, a mood which denotes remote possibility. A.T. Robertson argues that this case is an example of indirect discourse in which the optative may be substituted for the subjunctive mood. See his *A Grammar of the Greek New Testament in the Light of Historical Research* (Nashville: Broadman, 1934), p. 1044.

the Cilician poet Aratus (c. 315-240) in his *Phaenomena*, although it is also found in another poet's work — Cleanthes (331-233) in his *Hymn to Zeus*.[32]

Paul's reason for calling attention to these quotes was to make the point that even Greek poets, often considered to be themselves inspired, attested to the fact that people are made like the gods. If this is so, there was no reason to construct objects of worship made of "gold or silver or stone." Thus he expressed in one statement the strong opposition of the Old Testament to pagan idolatry, but at the same time he offered to the Athenians an appropriate means of calling upon the living God.

God Who Judges and Demands Repentance (17:30-31). Paul brought his remarks to their conclusion with a customary offer of hope. The times of worshiping gods which could not be known have passed, including the practice of setting up idols and sacrificial altars to the gods. These times with their "ignorance" and worship of inanimate idols, said Paul, God patiently "overlooked." Paul had made a similar statement in his speech in Lystra (14:16), and it is a point which also surfaces in his letter to the Romans (3:25) where he describes how God's forbearance moved him to leave "the sins committed beforehand unpunished."

Paul did not mean that God never moved against idolatry in any form of punishment. This point would contradict the numerous occasions in the Old Testament where God acted against the idolatry of Israel. Paul's point leaves room for these cases, but emphasizes that the ultimate punishment by God has been withheld because of his grace (see Exod 32:31-35).

A new day has arrived, however, and Paul announced it with the words "but now," a phrase intended in the eschatological sense (as in Rom 3:21). The old age was marked by God's patiently forbearing while sins were left unpunished. The new age has come, and this age will be marked by God's command for "all people everywhere to repent."

Not only was a new age dawning in which God was calling all

---

[32]Paul uses other quotations from pagan poets, as well (see 1 Cor 15:33; Titus 1:12).

people everywhere to turn to him, but this new age will conclude
with a day appointed for the judgment of all the nations. At this
point in his sermon Paul's audience would have found his message
quite foreign to their own perceptions. Stoicism and Epicureanism
saw no reason for the doctrine of repentance, nor the idea of a
judgment day. But once again, Paul's thinking has plenty of Old
Testament precedents (see Obad 15; Jer 46:10; Ezek 30:3; Joel 2:31;
Amos 5:18). That the judgment would be presided over by "the man
he has appointed" was a theme that is presented in Daniel 7:13.
Paul's reference, of course, was to Jesus Christ (see Matt 25:31-46;
Acts 10:42) and God's decisive action in "raising him from the
dead."

The Reaction to Paul's Preaching (17:32-34)

[32]**When they heard about the resurrection of the dead, some of
them sneered, but others said, "We want to hear you again on this
subject."** [33]**At that, Paul left the Council.** [34]**A few men became
followers of Paul and believed. Among them was Dionysius, a
member of the Areopagus, also a woman named Damaris, and a
number of others.**

The doctrine of the resurrection was the point which separated
Paul from many in this audience in the Areopagus. The Epicureans
did not believe in immortality in any form, while the Stoics accepted
the concept of the soul enduring beyond the grave, but never in a
bodily existence. In Greek philosophical reasoning there was simply
no room for a resurrected body.[33] Nevertheless, some were curious
enough about Paul's doctrine to suggest that he come back to
discuss it again.

With this invitation, Luke brings Paul's ministry in Athens to a
close, summarizing his success there with the mention of "a few
men" who became followers. Included among them was Dionysius,
who was himself a "member of the Areopagus," that is, the council

---

[33]Bruce adds a quote attributed to the god Apollo: "Once a man dies and
the earth drinks up his blood, there is no resurrection." The Greek word in
this quote is ἀνάστασις (anastasis), the same word used by Paul (p. 343).

which had listened to Paul's message. Nothing else is known about him in the New Testament, though later tradition makes him a bishop of Athens.[34] Also included was a woman[35] named Damaris. The text does not necessarily imply that she was present during Paul's address, since Luke's intent is to summarize the results of Paul's total ministry in Athens.

---

[34]Eusebius, *Ecclesiastical History* 3:4:11; 4:23:3.

[35]Her name here means that Luke's phrase "a few men" uses the word "men" in the generic sense of the word.

ACTS 18

13. The Visit at Corinth (18:1-17)

Paul's Arrival and Ministry with Aquila and Priscilla (18:1-4)

¹After this, Paul left Athens and went to Corinth. ²There he met a Jew named Aquila, a native of Pontus, who had recently come from Italy with his wife Priscilla, because Claudius had ordered all the Jews to leave Rome. Paul went to see them, ³and because he was a tentmaker as they were, he stayed and worked with them. ⁴Every Sabbath he reasoned in the synagogue, trying to persuade Jews and Greeks.

Leaving Athens, Paul walked fifty miles due west to Corinth, a trip lasting about three days. Corinth was an impressive city in Paul's day, with a long history dating back to the early Bronze Age (3000 B.C.).

Located on a land bridge between Roman Macedonia and Achaia, Corinth commanded a powerful position among commercial giants of the time. The city had access to two seaports—one at Lechaeum on the west, which gave it access to the Adriatic Sea, and one at Cenchrea on the east, giving it access to the Aegean Sea as well. Commercial ships arriving at Corinth also enjoyed the advantage of the *diolkos*. During the reign of Nero the attempt was made to relieve sea-going vessels from the dangerous journey around the Peloponnesus (south of the city). By digging a canal across the three-and-a-half mile isthmus, the Emperor hoped to permit vessels to easily pass through to the sea. The attempt was unsuccessful, however, so the *diolkos* was used. It was a kind of "track" which allowed cargo or even small vessels to be pulled across on dry land.

Having been destroyed in 146 B.C. by the Roman General

Mummius, Corinth was by the time of Paul a very new city, with no major building older than 100 years. Julius Caesar had rebuilt the city in 44 B.C. and made it a Roman colony. So quickly had the city regained its power that in A.D. 27 it became the capital of Achaia and the seat of the Roman proconsul. Nevertheless, its reputation as a pagan city was reinforced by the presence of temples to Aphrodite, to Apollo, and to Asclepius.[1]

Paul had arrived to present the gospel of salvation through one, living God. His arrival came about the same time as the arrival of two people who would become his companions—"a Jew named Aquila" and "his wife Priscilla." Aquila was originally from the province of Pontus along the Black Sea, but had recently been forced to leave Rome "because Claudius had ordered" that Jews be expelled from the city.[2] This action by Claudius Caesar (A.D. 41-54) is described by Suetonius, the Roman historian who wrote biographies on the twelve caesars beginning with Julius Caesar. His *Life of Claudius* (25:4) speaks of riots in Rome that were instigated by "Chrestus." Most scholars take this name as a misspelled reference to Christ, indicating that Jewish and Christian tensions in Rome produced the action by Claudius.[3] Orosius, a church historian, later fixed the date for this edict between A.D. 49 and 50. These calculations are very valuable in determining the date of Paul's visit to Corinth.

---

[1]The temple to Aphrodite was located on top of the Acrocorinth, 1,900 feet above the city and may have been the home of hundreds of temple prostitutes. The byword "to act as a Corinthian" held meaning (especially of the Old Corinth) only because the city had gained a reputation for its sexual immorality (see 1 Cor 6:12-20). The Asclepius cult concerned itself with physical healing, and clay replicas of body parts, which probably were used as offerings to the god, have been discovered at the site of the temple. Also located in Corinth was at least one Jewish synagogue, a fact attested to by the discovery of a large stone lintel with an inscription that reads "synagogue of the Jews."

[2]The fact that their conversion is not mentioned implies that they were already Christians.

[3]Bruce, p. 347. See also C.K. Barrett, *The New Testament Background: Selected Documents* (New York: Harper & Row, 1961), pp. 13-15; Jewett, *Chronology*, pp. 36-38.

Aquila and Priscilla[4] had "recently come from Italy," so that Paul's ministry at Corinth may have begun as early as A.D. 49 or 50. He began his efforts by establishing a place for his trade as a "tent-maker"[5] because this was the occupation of Aquila and Priscilla,[6] and their combined efforts would increase the opportunity for gaining an income to meet their needs. Working with his hands is a point Paul will later have to defend when he writes to the Corinthians, since in most cases such traveling teachers expected to be supported financially by their followers.[7]

Because of Paul's labors in supporting himself, his mission work was limited somewhat, but still "every Sabbath he reasoned in the synagogue." True to his policy of reaching to the Jews, Paul used his opportunities to argue that Jesus was the Christ (see 13:14; 14:1; 17:1,10,17). In doing so he also came into contact with Greek "God-fearers."

Resistance from the Jews and Paul's Decision to Preach to the Gentiles (18:5-6)

⁵When Silas and Timothy came from Macedonia, Paul devoted himself exclusively to preaching, testifying to the Jews that Jesus

---

[4]Priscilla is generally named first when the two are mentioned (see 18:18,24; Rom 16:3; 2 Tim 4:19), a fact which says less about her social standing as a Roman than about her prominence in the church.

[5]The occupation is better thought of as a "leather worker," a job that would include making tents. See Rienecker, p. 309.

[6]Hellenistic women often possessed extensive rights in the economic sphere. See Swidler, *Biblical Affirmations*, pp. 16, 297.

[7]The Cynics, for example, made their living by moving from city to city and receiving offerings from their hearers. See Abraham Malherbe, "Gentle as a Nurse," *NovT* 12 (1970), 203-217. Paul's policy of working with his hands (1 Cor 4:12; 9:19; 2 Cor 11:7; Acts 20:34) was intended to separate him from the more mercenary style of other itinerant preachers (1 Thess 2:6-10). But some Corinthians took his habit of working for a living as evidence he was not a true apostle (2 Cor 11:7-11). For an illustration of the way houses may have been transformed into places for the church to gather, as well as some of the worship practices of the early church, see the entire issue of *Christian History* 12 (37, 1993).

was the Christ.ᵃ **⁶But when the Jews opposed Paul and became
abusive, he shook out his clothes in protest and said to them,
"Your blood be on your own heads! I am clear of my responsibility. From now on I will go to the Gentiles."**

ᵃ5 Or *Messiah*; also in verse 28

Relief for Paul came in the arrival of Silas and Timothy from
Macedonia. Now he "devoted himself exclusively to preaching"
because they brought with them a gift from the Philippian congregation (Phil 4:15-19).[8] Now he could discontinue his tentmaking and
concentrate on his contacts with potential converts in the city. His
message remained constant as he sought to persuade Jews and
Gentiles "that Jesus was the Christ" (see 9:22).

Once again Paul was met with opposition from the Jews and
once again he demonstrated his resolve when he "shook out his
clothes in protest" (see 13:51). Paul's action was accompanied with a
reference to the Old Testament warning of the prophet mentioned
in Ezekiel 33:1-7. If the watchman of the city warned the citizens
that the enemy was near, and the warning was heard by a person
who took no action to protect himself, then "his blood will be on his
own head." The words were never more appropriate than in Paul's
warning to the Jews that they were ignoring the only deliverance
offered by the Lord. But if the Jews were going to ignore God's
deliverance, Paul would go to the Gentiles with the message.

Encouragement in a Night Vision (18:7-10)

**⁷Then Paul left the synagogue and went next door to the house
of Titius Justus, a worshiper of God. ⁸Crispus, the synagogue ruler,
and his entire household believed in the Lord; and many of the
Corinthians who heard him believed and were baptized. ⁹One night
the Lord spoke to Paul in a vision: "Do not be afraid; keep on
speaking, do not be silent. ¹⁰For I am with you, and no one is going
to attack and harm you, because I have many people in this city."**

---

[8]It may be at this point that Timothy shared the good news about the
progress of the Thessalonian church, as well (1 Thess 3:6-10).

In order to focus on taking the message to the Gentiles, Paul moved into a house owned by Titius Justus who was a Gentile God-fearer. This may not mean that he took up residence in this house, since he was already living with Aquila and Priscilla (18:3).

The mention of this Titius Justus has caused some scholars to wonder if the Gaius spoken of in 1 Corinthians 1:14 as one of the few Corinthians baptized by Paul might be a man whose full name was Gaius Titius Justus.[9] Evidence for this position, however, is scarce. With "Crispus, the synagogue ruler," however, the story is different. The mention of his name in 1 Corinthians 1:14 seems an unmistakable reference to this Jewish synagogue ruler whose position brought him into contact with Paul's gospel and faith in Christ.

Paul's success was evident not only in the conversion of Crispus and his household, but in the fact that "many of the Corinthians" were receptive to the message. The nucleus of believers was large enough that a solid congregation was established in Corinth which lasted for years to come. Several years later, Paul still had contact with these Christians through visits and letters (including 1 Cor and 2 Cor). At the end of the first century, Clement of Rome addressed this church in Corinth as it struggled to meet challenges to its leaders.

As is quite customary, Luke summarizes the conversions of the Corinthians by mentioning faith and baptism (see 16:14-15; 31-33). It appears naturally and reminds us that when the apostles preached the gospel, faith and baptism were considered complementary to each other,[10] a state of things which continued in the church until centuries later.

At this point in Paul's ministry the Lord decided to encourage him. In view of the trials which were coming, "the Lord," a reference to Jesus Christ, spoke to him in a "vision," urging him not to be afraid.[11] After assuring Paul of his continued presence, he promised him that the mission would not be overwhelmed by opponents, perhaps in contrast to cities where Paul was forced to leave

---

[9]See E.J. Goodspeed, "Gaius Titius Justus," *JBL* 69 (1950): 382-383; Sherwin-White, *Roman Law and Roman Society*, pp. 158-159.

[10]See comments on 2:38.

[11]Other cases of divine encouragement of the apostles appear in 5:17-21; 9:10-18; 16:6-10.

quickly (see 16:39-40; 17:9,15). This fact was the reason the Lord mentioned the number of people he had in this city. His words counseled Paul to continue his ministry, confident that the Lord's foreknowledge of conversions to Christ would be a constant encouragement and support for his work.

Paul's Trial before Gallio (18:11-17)

[11]**So Paul stayed for a year and a half, teaching them the word of God.** [12]**While Gallio was proconsul of Achaia, the Jews made a united attack on Paul and brought him into court.** [13]**"This man,"** **they charged, "is persuading the people to worship God in ways contrary to the law."** [14]**Just as Paul was about to speak, Gallio said to the Jews, "If you Jews were making a complaint about some misdemeanor or serious crime, it would be reasonable for me to listen to you.** [15]**But since it involves questions about words and names and your own law—settle the matter yourselves. I will not be a judge of such things."** [16]**So he had them ejected from the court.** [17]**Then they all turned on Sosthenes the synagogue ruler and beat him in front of the court. But Gallio showed no concern whatever.**

The Lord kept his promise to Paul regarding his Corinthian ministry. Paul's work in Corinth may be the longest he stayed in any city since the day the Holy Spirit's voice had commissioned them to leave Antioch (13:1-3). For eighteen months Paul ministered in Corinth.

Trouble was not far away, however, because the Jews of Corinth "made a united attack" on Paul. When they found the appropriate opportunity they "brought him into court" (βῆμα, *bēma*). The *bēma* was located on the south side of the marketplace in Corinth. Modern archaeologists have discovered the raised platform made of blue marble which held the seat on which the judge sat for civil cases such as this one. This judgment seat must have been very impressive. Later when Paul writes to the Corinthians he will tell them "we must all appear before the judgment seat (*bēma*) of Christ" (2 Cor 5:10).

All of these things occurred "while Gallio was proconsul of

Achaia." For those concerned with the chronology of Paul's ministry, the incidental mention here of Gallio is most fortunate. Enough is known about Gallio through ancient literary references[12] and inscriptions that the date of this trial can be ascertained with some degree of precision.

Gallio was born in Spain and taken to Rome very early in his life. His younger brother was the philosopher Seneca who served as the tutor and adviser for Nero. During his career he served as a praetor, then a proconsul, and finally a consul. It was in this second stage that his path crossed with that of the Apostle Paul.

From an inscription discovered in Delphi at the close of the last century, new confidence has been established concerning the years he served in Corinth as proconsul. The inscription originally consisted of a letter written from Claudius Caesar to Gallio. What remains of the inscription is fragmentary, but enough of its content can be established to determine the year in which Claudius wrote to Gallio in Achaia. The years of his term can be determined to include A.D. 51-52.[13]

If the Jews forced the issue with Paul early in Gallio's proconsulship (perhaps likely because of the opportunity to influence a new political leader), then Paul's trial can be dated at A.D. 51. His eighteen-month ministry may have ended sometime in A.D. 52.

The charges made against Paul were that he was "persuading the people to worship God in ways contrary to the law." This very vague accusation leaves open a number of possibilities. Were they accusing Paul of challenging the Roman law (as in 16:21) or were they saying that his doctrine forced them to worship contrary to the Jewish law? Either one is possible, but Gallio evidently took the

---

[12]The sources are, for the most part, Seneca and Tacitus.

[13]The method for determining this date is based on the inscription's mention of the twenty-sixth acclamation of Claudius Caesar, an event which can be dated by other sources to the first seven months of A.D. 52. Since Gallio was already in place when the letter was written, it is assumed that he came to Corinth in the early summer of A.D. 51. Ancient sources also comment on Gallio's personality, describing him as a most amiable ruler. His life came to an end in A.D. 65 when Nero's suspicions against Gallio's family forced Gallio to commit suicide. See Barrett, *Background*, pp. 48-49; Jewett, *Chronology*, pp. 38-40.

latter to be the case. His conclusion was that their argument involved "questions about words and names and your own law," perhaps a reference to names like "Messiah," "suffering servant," and "resurrected Lord." Because Gallio saw nothing at stake as far as Roman law was concerned, he "ejected them from the court" (probably including Paul).[14]

Gallio's conclusion confirms the fact that in the middle of the first century Roman administrators did not distinguish between Jews and Christians. He understood the debate to be an internal struggle among adherents to Judaism. His refusal to condemn Paul's mission set a kind of precedent which may have served for years to protect the believers in Corinth against persecution. For Luke's record of Paul's work, this incident underscores again the conclusions of judicial bodies in the major cities Paul visited. The Christian cause was not a threat to the Roman government.

The next incident raises some puzzling problems. After being ejected from the court, "they" took action against Sosthenes. The problem is determining who is meant by the pronoun "they." Was it the Jews who beat Sosthenes or the Greeks? The name Sosthenes is mentioned by Paul in 1 Corinthians 1:1, a point which implies that this Sosthenes became a Christian. Were the Jews beating him here because of his sympathies toward the Christian missionaries? Or did his conversion result from the beating by Jews who suspected him of helping Paul?

The other possibility is that the Greeks used the opportunity to beat up a Jew. Perhaps the incident stirred up latent hostilities against the Jews in Corinth, and Gallio's indifference made the "synagogue ruler" Sosthenes an easy and safe target for this anger. At any rate, Paul's ministry was able to continue.

---

[14]The technical term for cases where a Roman judge saw no threat to Roman law was *cognitio extra ordinem*, and in such cases the judge had authority to handle the matter at his own discretion. See Sherwin-White, *Roman Society and Roman Law*, pp. 101-107.

14. The Visit at Cenchrea (18:18)

[18]**Paul stayed on in Corinth for some time. Then he left the brothers and sailed for Syria, accompanied by Priscilla and Aquila. Before he sailed, he had his hair cut off at Cenchrea because of a vow he had taken.**

With the opposition to Paul's ministry silent, his work went on "for some time." When it came time to leave, his destination was Syria. Priscilla and Aquila went with him.

At this point Luke mentions that Paul had taken a vow at Cenchrea, the eastern seaport of Corinth. The vow included the cutting of his hair, and thus shows some similarity with the Nazirite vow described in Numbers 6:1-21. Though the Nazirite vow in most cases required the believer to cut his hair at the end of the vow and then offer a sacrifice in the temple at Jerusalem, throwing his hair into the burnt offering, in some cases there were shorter vows (thirty days) available. This offering may be what Paul had in mind as he set his course for Roman Syria, which officially included Jerusalem.

Paul's participation in this vow demonstrated his continued sense of being Jewish. This perception is reflected in his letters, as well (see Phil 3:4-6; 1 Cor 9:20-21). Though saved by faith, he saw no contradiction in participating in some of the rituals of the law of Moses.

15. The Visit at Ephesus (18:19-21)

[19]**They arrived at Ephesus, where Paul left Priscilla and Aquila. He himself went into the synagogue and reasoned with the Jews. [20]When they asked him to spend more time with them, he declined. [21]But as he left, he promised, "I will come back if it is God's will." Then he set sail from Ephesus.**

Paul's journey to Syria included a brief visit to Ephesus. This stop may have resulted as much from the necessities of the Aegean sea lanes as anything else. Paul was leaving Priscilla and Aquila in the city to establish a base for the preaching of the gospel, while he himself took the opportunity to visit the synagogue where he "reasoned with the Jews" (see 18:4).

Paul's message was received with some interest, and "they asked him to spend more time with them." Because he was hurrying to move on to Syria, he declined the invitation, but promised to return if it was "God's will." In this way Luke prepares for his upcoming description of the ministry of Paul at Ephesus in Acts 19.[15] Meanwhile, Paul boarded a vessel bound for Caesarea.

16. The Journey to Caesarea, Jerusalem, and Antioch of Syria (18:22)

[22]**When he landed at Caesarea, he went up and greeted the church and then went down to Antioch.**

The ship on which Paul traveled landed in Caesarea, a city which had become the Mediterranean port city for Jerusalem. Bruce notes that the winds often made putting in at Caesarea easier than at Seleucia, farther to the north.[16]

Wasting no time after arriving, Paul immediately "went up and greeted the church." Though Jerusalem is not mentioned by name, this language of "going up" implies that Paul went to Jerusalem, since the traditional way of describing a trip to the Holy City included ascending the 2,500 feet to the elevation of Mt. Zion. It was natural that he would take time to visit the church at this time.[17] Then Paul "went down to Antioch," appropriate language if he was going from Jerusalem to Antioch (see 15:1).

---

[15]For details about the city of Ephesus see comments on 19:1.

[16]Bruce, p. 356.

[17]Polhill (p. 391, n. 130) observes that the common thread running through the itinerary of Paul's journeys was a trip which started in Antioch, ended in Jerusalem, and included a major speech (in Pisidian Antioch, then in Athens, then in Miletus).

D. THE THIRD MISSIONARY JOURNEY (18:23–21:16)

1. The Journey through Galatia and Phrygia (18:23)

[23]After spending some time in Antioch, Paul set out from there and traveled from place to place throughout the region of Galatia and Phrygia, strengthening all the disciples.

Without a doubt Paul was refreshed by "spending some time in Antioch" with believers who had appreciated his work, commissioned his journeys, and perhaps even supported him financially at times (see 13:1-3). But he was also eager to strengthen the new congregations already facing challenges from persecutions and hardships (see 14:21-22). Thus he departed for a third missionary journey which would take him to the congregations established earlier, as well as into brand new territories ripe for evangelism.

The third of Paul's journeys focuses especially on Ephesus (19:1). Paul's tour through "Galatia and Phrygia"[18] receives little in the way of details as Luke tells the story of Paul's efforts in pushing the gospel into newer frontiers. Paul's efforts in "strengthening all the disciples," however, were vital to the well-being of the church. For this reason, Paul passed up the opportunity to journey to Ephesus by sea, choosing instead to travel the more than 1,000 miles on foot.

His trip would have taken the Roman road north and then east to Tarsus, and from there through the Cilician Gates in the Taurus Mountains to Derbe, Lystra, Iconium, and Pisidian Antioch. Revisiting old friends and discovering what progress the churches had made would have been a welcome experience for Paul.

2. The Ministry of Apollos in Ephesus and Corinth (18:24-28)

[24]Meanwhile a Jew named Apollos, a native of Alexandria, came to Ephesus. He was a learned man, with a thorough knowledge of the Scriptures. [25]He had been instructed in the way of the Lord, and he spoke with great fervor[a] and taught about Jesus accurately,

---

[18]This territory is the same as that mentioned in 16:6 where the names appear in reverse order.

though he knew only the baptism of John. [26]He began to speak
boldly in the synagogue. When Priscilla and Aquila heard him,
they invited him to their home and explained to him the way of
God more adequately. [27]When Apollos wanted to go to Achaia, the
brothers encouraged him and wrote to the disciples there to
welcome him. On arriving, he was a great help to those who by
grace had believed. [28]For he vigorously refuted the Jews in public
debate, proving from the Scriptures that Jesus was the Christ.

[a]25 Or *with fervor in the Spirit*

Between the time Paul left Ephesus (18:21) and his return on the
third missionary journey a new leader entered the picture at
Ephesus. His name was Apollos. He was a Jew from Alexandria who
had come to Ephesus, perhaps in much the same way that Priscilla
and Aquila appeared in Corinth and then in Ephesus. Jews with
business connections were known to travel extensively in the Roman
world in pursuit of their commercial interests.

Although Luke does not mention the trade of Apollos, he does
describe him as "a learned man, with a thorough knowledge of the
Scriptures." This trait would involve a Jewish education in the Old
Testament. Whether the famous Alexandrian school of interpretation with its allegorical methods is intended is unclear.[19]

Apollos had some Christian teaching, since he was "instructed in
the way of the Lord" and he "taught about Jesus accurately," but
was limited in his understanding of the gospel, knowing "only the
baptism of John." These bits of information about Apollos present
to us a very unusual case in the New Testament, though twelve
more disciples with a similar background will appear in 19:1-7.
Determining what Apollos was accurately teaching about Jesus is
not easy if all he knew was the baptism of John. If his information
about Jesus was limited to the ideas proclaimed by John the Baptist
(as recorded in the Gospels), his teaching would have focused on
the coming of the Messiah. Perhaps he had even made the connection between particular Old Testament passages and the coming of

---

[19]This method of interpretation reached its peak with Christian scholars
such as Clement and Origin, but was also found in the writings of the
Jewish scholar Philo.

the Messiah, the same message frequently preached by the apostles (see v. 3). If so, Apollos could have been quite prolific in all matters except Christian baptism and the Holy Spirit.

The statement that Apollos "spoke with great fervor" (ζέων τῷ πνεύματι, zeōn tō pneumati) also creates some difficulties. The NIV takes the phrase to be a reference not to the Holy Spirit, but an eagerness of human spirit possessed by Apollos. Some commentators understand this phrase to mean that Apollos had already received the Holy Spirit, though he had not received Christian baptism and knew only the baptism of John.[20] But the phrase does not have to be interpreted this way, and the case of the twelve disciples in the next chapter of Acts leads us away from the idea that Apollos had received the Holy Spirit.

At any rate, Priscilla and Aquila came into contact with Apollos and "invited him to their home" (προσλαμβάνομαι, proslambanomai). The Greek term means "to take someone to oneself," and thus is interpreted by the NIV to mean a private meeting in the home (and justly so). Evidently the fact that Priscilla was a woman did not prohibit her from being involved in this instruction of Apollos.[21] The action of Priscilla and Aquila was private so as to protect the dignity of Apollos and it was effective in producing a Christian preacher who later accomplished enough at Corinth that Paul said of him, "I planted the seed, Apollos watered it, but God made it grow" (1 Cor 3:6).

When Apollos received an invitation to "go to Achaia," the Roman province in which Corinth was the capital city, he accepted. He proved to be quite effective in "refuting the Jews in public debate" with regard to scriptural evidence that "Jesus was the Christ."

---

[20]See, for example, Bruce, p. 359. The same phrase appears in Rom 12:11 where it might refer to having the Holy Spirit, although the same ambiguity persists there, as well. Dunn takes this language to mean Apollos had already received the Holy Spirit. See his *Baptism*, pp. 88-89.

[21]See Frank and Evelyn Stagg, *Woman in the World of Jesus* (Philadelphia: Westminster, 1978), pp. 230-231.

ACTS 19

3. The Twelve Disciples at Ephesus (19:1-7)

[1]While Apollos was at Corinth, Paul took the road through the interior and arrived at Ephesus. There he found some disciples [2]and asked them, "Did you receive the Holy Spirit when[a] you believed?" They answered, "No, we have not even heard that there is a Holy Spirit." [3]So Paul asked, "Then what baptism did you receive?" "John's baptism," they replied. [4]Paul said, "John's baptism was a baptism of repentance. He told the people to believe in the one coming after him, that is, in Jesus." [5]On hearing this, they were baptized into[b] the name of the Lord Jesus. [6]When Paul placed his hands on them, the Holy Spirit came on them, and they spoke in tongues[c] and prophesied. [7]There were about twelve men in all.

[a]2 Or *after*   [b]5 Or *in*   [c]6 Or *other languages*

Luke now turns attention away from Apollos in Corinth to describe Paul's journey to Ephesus (which begins in 18:23). Just as Priscilla and Aquila had found in Apollos a man who "knew only the baptism of John" (18:25), so Paul now came into contact with "some disciples" whose knowledge may be summarized in the same way. Also, in the same way that Priscilla and Aquila explained to Apollos "the way of God more adequately" (18:26), so Paul must now further instruct the disciples he found at Ephesus. Though Luke does not say explicitly, these men had probably been influenced by Apollos before the instruction by Priscilla and Aquila.

In his journey to Ephesus, Paul "took the road through the interior," a phrase describing the route through the higher ground as

297

contrasted with the more direct trade route that ran through the Lycus and Meander valleys. Traveling through Upper Phrygia, he thus approached Ephesus from a northern direction.[1]

Ephesus was the most important city of Roman Asia. A harbor was located next to the city which was connected to the Aegean Sea by the Cayster River. The religious life of this city was dominated by the worship of Artemis to whom a magnificent temple was dedicated.

Paul arrived at Ephesus at a time when Apollos was already in Corinth. Nevertheless, he met some "disciples" whose situation was quite similar to that of Apollos before he had gone to Corinth. Some commentators take the term "disciples" to mean that they were considered Christians,[2] but this would imply the possibility of calling people Christians who had not received the Holy Spirit. Not only in Acts, but in many other New Testament passages the connection between being counted a Christian and receiving the Holy Spirit is too strong for this conclusion to be justified (see 2:38; 11:16-18; John 3:5; Rom 8:9; 1 Cor 12:3,13; Gal 3:2; Heb 6:4).

Luke's use of the term "disciples" here reflects Paul's perception of these men when he arrived at Ephesus. Initially there was nothing about them which indicated an inadequate instruction in the faith. The deficiency did not become apparent until the conversation between them and Paul, which Luke now records.[3]

No information is given to explain why Paul asked these disciples (v. 7 says there were twelve) the question about whether they had received the Spirit. Possibly he became aware of an absence of the spiritual gifts which had marked other churches where the Spirit had been given. At any rate, the question about receiving the Spirit implies how significant the presence of the Spirit is in defining the identity of believers.[4]

The answer of the disciples presents some difficulty. How could they know about John's baptism, but not know about the Holy

[1]The route through the Lycus valley would have taken him into the region of such cities as Colosse, Hieropolis, and Laodicea.
[2]See Haenchen, pp. 552-553; Munck, p. 187; Bruce, p. 363.
[3]See Marshall, pp. 305-306.
[4]The Greek question in 19:2 uses the aorist verb "receive" (ἐλάβετε, *elabete*) with an aorist participle "believed" (πιστεύσαντες, *pisteusantes*) as a coincident aorist participle, as if to say "Did you receive the Spirit when (not after) you believed?" Rienecker, p. 312.

Spirit? John himself had predicted that the Coming One would baptize with the Holy Spirit (see John 1:26-34). Besides John's reference to the Spirit, the Old Testament teaching about the Spirit of God would have been readily available.

The response of these disciples, however, may be intended to say that they were unaware that the decisive moment of the Spirit's pouring out had come. With the gospel emanating from Jerusalem by word of mouth for twenty years since the Day of Pentecost it is not surprising that in some places believers would be found with only a partial understanding of the Spirit.

Paul's next question demonstrates the connection between baptism and the reception of the Spirit. He would have no other reason to ask about their baptism if not for the truth emphasized in Acts that with a believer's baptism comes the moment of receiving the Spirit.[5] Thus Paul's question came: "What baptism did you receive?" The word "what" is a prepositional phrase "into what" (εἰς τί, *eis ti*), and refers to "into what name" (or "to what end") they had been baptized.

Their response to Paul's question was "John's baptism." In other words these were men who believed in the teaching of John the Baptist. They were baptized to indicate their repentance and instructed to look for the coming Messiah who would one day baptize believers with the Holy Spirit.[6] Paul explained the significance of John's baptism to the men, giving a summary that blended the information of Luke 3:3-6 with John 1:26-27. The immediate response of the twelve disciples was to "be baptized into the name of the Lord Jesus," the exact same phrase used with the baptism of the Samaritans (8:15-17).

---

[5]Dunn comments on the close connection between baptism and reception of the Spirit in this passage. He says that the sequence of Paul's questions shows that "to believe" and "to be baptized" are "interchangeable ways of describing the act of faith: baptism was the necessary expression of commitment, without which they could not be said to have truly 'believed.'" See his *Baptism*, p. 96.

[6]The significant difference between John's baptism and baptism in the name of the Lord Jesus is shown here to be that of receiving the Holy Spirit. J.K. Parrat's conclusion that the only difference in the two baptisms is that John's looked forward while that of Jesus looked back is certainly inadequate. See his "The Rebaptism of the Ephesian Disciples," *ExpT* (1968): 182-183.

Paul then "placed his hands on them," and "the Holy Spirit came on them,[7] and they spoke in tongues." Again the parallels with the Samaritan believers are numerous. Those believers also received the laying on of hands by the apostles and then "received the Holy Spirit." The Samaritans also demonstrated the Spirit's presence in a visible way, leading Simon the sorcerer to seek to purchase the ability to pass on the power. In the same way, the disciples at Ephesus, after receiving the laying on of hands by Paul, also experienced the Spirit coming on them, so that "they spoke in tongues and prophesied."[8] Thus the laying on of hands seems particularly connected to the reception of the spiritual gifts.

4. Paul's Preaching in the Synagogue and the School of Tyrannus (19:8-10)

[8]Paul entered the synagogue and spoke boldly there for three months, arguing persuasively about the kingdom of God. [9]But some of them became obstinate; they refused to believe and publicly maligned the Way. So Paul left them. He took the disciples with him and had discussions daily in the lecture hall of Tyrannus. [10]This went on for two years, so that all the Jews and Greeks who lived in the province of Asia heard the word of the Lord.

Paul's ministry now moved to the synagogue where he was able to maintain an active witness for three months. This arrangement implies that he was again working his trade during the week and using Sabbath days for preaching, as was true in Thessalonica (except there his work in the synagogue lasted only three weeks; 17:2).

---

[7]Dunn presents a chart showing the various terminology used in Acts for the giving of the Spirit. See his *Baptism*, p. 70.

[8]Dupont uses this passage to compare the gifts of the Spirit with the outpouring of the Spirit at Pentecost, as well as the spiritual gifts described in 1 Corinthians 12,14. He concludes that "the charism the Spirit gave the apostles at Pentecost was of a different type, and that it more closely resembled the genre of prophecy, as exemplified by inspired canticles." See his *Salvation*, pp. 48-50.

The content of his message had not changed, and Luke summarizes the preaching as matters pertaining to "the kingdom of God" (see 1:3). Paul's proclamation divided the Jews, and once again those who refused to accept his message "became obstinate" and "publicly maligned the Way."[9] Thus Paul found himself relocating his ministry, this time in a place less dominated by antagonistic Jews. Those Jews who had become "disciples" he took with him to a new meeting place called "the lecture hall of Tyrannus." Whether the name of the site implies that the place was used by a philosopher or instructor named Tyrannus[10] or owned by a man named Tyrannus cannot be determined. The Western text adds to v. 9 the note that Paul conducted these discussions between the hours of 11 a.m. and 4 p.m., the hottest time of the day when most Romans refrained from working. If reliable, the implication is that Paul worked his trade until work hours were finished and then continued his labor in the lecture hall.

Paul continued this ministry for "two years." If this time is added to the three months of work in the synagogue, plus the "little longer" of v. 22, Paul's stay in Ephesus amounts to the better part of three years, the longest of Paul's ministries recorded in Acts. This length of time gave him the opportunity to expand his witness throughout the entire area, so that "all the Jews and Greeks who lived in the province of Asia" were reached. This language leaves room for the founding of churches in such nearby cities as Colosse, Laodicea, and Hieropolis. Besides these efforts in Asia, evidence indicates that during Paul's stay in Ephesus his contacts with churches in Macedonia and Achaia continued, including in some cases letters and visits.[11]

---

[9]See the note on 9:2.

[10]With a name like Tyrannus (meaning "tyrant") one wonders how many students he would have had!

[11]Lake and Cadbury list fifteen things that we know were accomplished by Paul during this three-year period. The list includes the four letters and three visits to Corinth, as well as his efforts in getting the churches ready for the collection. For a full discussion of these activities see Hurd, *Origin of 1 Corinthians* where his reconstruction of Paul's activities during these years is more appropriate than his explanation of the problems between Paul and the Corinthian church.

5. The Conflict with the Exorcists (19:11-19)

[11]God did extraordinary miracles through Paul, [12]so that even handkerchiefs and aprons that had touched him were taken to the sick, and their illnesses were cured and the evil spirits left them. [13]Some Jews who went around driving out evil spirits tried to invoke the name of the Lord Jesus over those who were demon-possessed. They would say, "In the name of Jesus, whom Paul preaches, I command you to come out." [14]Seven sons of Sceva, a Jewish chief priest, were doing this. [15][One day] the evil spirit answered them, "Jesus I know, and I know about Paul, but who are you?" [16]Then the man who had the evil spirit jumped on them and overpowered them all. He gave them such a beating that they ran out of the house naked and bleeding. [17]When this became known to the Jews and Greeks living in Ephesus, they were all seized with fear, and the name of the Lord Jesus was held in high honor. [18]Many of those who believed now came and openly confessed their evil deeds. [19]A number who had practiced sorcery brought their scrolls together and burned them publicly. When they calculated the value of the scrolls, the total came to fifty thousand drachmas.[a]

[a]*19* A drachma was a silver coin worth about a day's wages.

As Athens was known for its philosophers, Ephesus was known for its sorcerers. It is not surprising, then, that Paul came into conflict with these practitioners of magic arts. The contrast between the power that energized Paul's ministry and that which the sorcerers trusted now became evident.

Paul's ministry included powerful acts of healing, so that "even handkerchiefs and aprons" used by the Apostle became instruments of divine blessing. The "handkerchief" (σουδάρια, *soudaria*) was likely a kind of sweat rag, perhaps worn around the head to keep perspiration out of the eyes while working. An "apron" (σιμικίνθιον, *simikinthion*) was a cloth worn around the waist by workers.

Though the modern reader might be surprised that healing would be generated through such material items as these, this situation was not unlike the healing which took place when the woman reached to touch the hem of Jesus' garment (Mark 5:27-34) and when the shadow of Peter fell over the sick (Acts 5:15). These items were seen by the ancients as extensions of the person himself, and in the case of Jesus and the apostles, were viewed with special respect. The healings were, at any rate, accomplished through faith in the only One able to bring health and strength.

These mighty works of Paul included cases where "the evil spirits left" and people were thus delivered from the power of Satan. Such exorcisms immediately set up a showdown between Paul and some Ephesian Jews[12] who likewise "went around driving out evil spirits." In the same way that the Jewish Simon the sorcerer was captivated by the work of Philip in Samaria (8:13-19), some Jews watched Paul's powers over evil spirits and wanted to exercise the same authority.

The presence of Jewish sorcerers in Hellenistic cities was well known in the Roman world. Magical arts were common, and Bruce gives examples of the kind of magical spells which have been discovered by historians.[13] In many of these chants, Jewish elements are quite obvious. One spell, for example, reads, "I abjure thee by Jesus, the God of the Hebrews."[14]

Evidently, the Jewish exorcists in Ephesus also thought they could have a more powerful effectiveness if they used the same name by which Paul was healing and driving out evil spirits. But when they attempted to use the name of Jesus, the action backfired on them.[15] "Seven sons of Sceva" were among those who attempted this. The name "Sceva" is unknown to the rest of the New Testament, and his position as "chief priest" (ἀρχιερεύς, archiereus) is also

---

[12]Hengel cites this event as evidence of the presence of "Jewish syncretistic groups" in which Jewish communities were strongly influenced by paganism. In Asia Minor there are many examples of syncretism with such pagan deities as Sambatheion (at Thyatira) and Hypsistos. It seems that Jewish magical practices made Jews especially open to such influences. See Hengel, *Judaism and Hellenism*, 1:308. See also B.A. Mastin, "Scaeva the Chief Priest," *JTS* 27 (1976): 405-412.

[13]Bruce, p. 369. He notes that a number of ancient magical scrolls can be seen in collections in London, Paris and Leiden.

[14]Lake and Cadbury, p. 241.

[15]Dunn notes that the power belonged to God, and "the name of Jesus could be invoked only by those who already stood in a relation of discipleship to him." See his *Jesus*, p. 165.

a problem. Because Josephus informs us completely as to the names of all the high priests who served in the first century, scholars have no difficulty checking the historical record for the presence of the name "Sceva." The name cannot be found. Possibly this Jewish exorcist had assumed the title for himself or was related in some way to a high priestly family in Jerusalem.

At any rate, the evil spirits exerted themselves in such a way as to prove that the Jewish exorcists were powerless against them. When the exorcists tried to drive them out of people who were demon-possessed, the spirits turned on them. Polhill notes the language of these spirits: "Jesus I know (γινώσκω, ginōskō), and Paul I respect (ἐπίσταμαι, epistamai), but who are you?"[16] Thus the demons confessed the identity of Jesus and his servants much the same way as during Jesus' own ministry (see Mark 1:24; 5:9). The sons of Sceva were put to shame and then to flight so that they "ran out of the house naked and bleeding."

The news of this event spread through Ephesus and the citizens "were all seized with fear." As a result, the confidence of the Ephesians in their magical arts evaporated. They realized that the power in Jesus Christ was greater than their own spells and charms.

Many of the city's citizens responded to the gospel message, and a number of these "now came and openly confessed their evil deeds." In some cases, these converts had come from a background of practicing magical arts. As evidence of their conversion, these disciples now brought "their scrolls together and burned them publicly." Any scroll was expensive in the ancient world, but scrolls containing magical spells or secret formulae were considered quite valuable. Romans treasured any resource which gave them divine assistance with the puzzles of life. Magic seemed to meet this need.

When the value of the scrolls was calculated it came to 50,000 drachmas, a sum worth about 50,000 days of labor, since a silver drachma was worth one day's labors. The Ephesians had truly turned from their sin.

---

[16]Polhill, p. 404.

6. The Growth of Paul's Ministry (19:20)

20In this way the word of the Lord spread widely and grew in power.

To emphasize the effects of this event on the population of Ephesus, Luke includes another of his summaries (see 6:7; 9:31; 12:24; 16:5; 28:31). The verbs "spread" (ηὔξανεν, *ēuxanen*) and "grew" (ἴσχυεν, *ischyen*) are used to describe a progress continued on a daily basis.[17] This summary reports on the progress of Paul's ministry in Ephesus (see v. 10)[18] and appears just before Luke turns to a final event in this period of Paul's work, and also his decision to go to Jerusalem.

7. Paul's Plans to Visit Rome (19:21-22)

21After all this had happened, Paul decided to go to Jerusalem, passing through Macedonia and Achaia. "After I have been there," he said, "I must visit Rome also." 22He sent two of his helpers, Timothy and Erastus, to Macedonia, while he stayed in the province of Asia a little longer.

Near the end of his ministry in Ephesus a decision was reached by Paul. By now his work had established churches in provinces from Antioch to Troas and also in a ring around both sides of the Aegean Sea. Paul thus began looking for new territories to plant the gospel seed. His stated policy was that he would not build on "someone else's foundation" (Rom 15:20), intending instead to be the one planting in fresh areas, while others followed him for the purpose of adding strength (see 1 Cor 3:6).

He now concluded that he would press his mission westward to Rome. Paul reflects on this decision in Romans 15:23-33. Before

---

[17]Both verbs are in the imperfect tense.

[18]G.S. Duncan thinks that Paul was imprisoned at some point during this period of time. See his "Paul's Ministry in Asia—The Last Phase," *NTS* 3 (1957): 211-218.

doing this, however, he determined to return to Jerusalem, after going first to visit the churches in Macedonia and Achaia. His visit to Jerusalem included his efforts in organizing the collection for the famine-plagued believers in Judea, a project about which Acts is silent.

Paul's decision to go to Jerusalem has parallels with the decision of Jesus to go to Jerusalem during his ministry (Luke 9:51).[19] He knew of opponents who would be waiting for him (see Rom 15:31-32) and sensed that he was walking into a volatile situation.

He now sent two of his companions, Timothy and Erastus, ahead of him to Macedonia, probably to prepare the churches for the offering. Timothy, who was with Paul continuously since joining the missionaries in Lystra (16:3), was familiar with the believers in the churches of Macedonia, and would be quite effective working with them on this delicate issue of the collection. Erastus was a resident of Corinth and also served as a companion of Paul (see Rom 16:23).[20]

8. The Riot of Demetrius and the Silversmiths (19:23-41)

The Anger of the Silversmiths (19:23-28)

[23]About that time there arose a great disturbance about the Way. [24]A silversmith named Demetrius, who made silver shrines of Artemis, brought in no little business for the craftsmen. [25]He called them together, along with the workmen in related trades, and said: "Men, you know we receive a good income from this business. [26]And you see and hear how this fellow Paul has convinced

---

[19]Beginning in Acts 20 the rest of Acts is dominated by Paul's trip to Jerusalem and its consequences, a theme mirrored in Luke's Gospel where Christ's journey to Jerusalem occupies the last half of the story. In the same way that Paul hears warnings along the way about the consequences of going to Jerusalem (see 20:10-11), Jesus had traveled to the Jerusalem which "kills the prophets" (Luke 13:33).

[20]Whether this Erastus is the same person mentioned in the inscription discovered at Corinth on a paving stone is unclear. See H.J. Cadbury, "Erastus of Corinth," *JBL* 50 (1930): 42-58.

and led astray large numbers of people here in Ephesus and in practically the whole province of Asia. He says that man-made gods are no gods at all. [27]There is danger not only that our trade will lose its good name, but also that the temple of the great goddess Artemis will be discredited, and the goddess herself, who is worshiped throughout the province of Asia and the world, will be robbed of her divine majesty." [28]When they heard this, they were furious and began shouting: "Great is Artemis of the Ephesians!"

Toward the conclusion of Paul's ministry at Ephesus "a great disturbance about the Way" arose. Luke's description of the believers in his report of the Ephesian ministry is to call them "the Way" (see also 18:26; 19:9). The disturbance was the direct result of Paul's preaching about idols.

Demetrius was "a silversmith," whose occupation depended on the worship of Artemis. In Ephesus the worship of the goddess Artemis (or Diana) had dominated the religious scene for centuries. The temple of Artemis, which replaced an earlier temple that burned down in 356 B.C., was considered one of the seven wonders of the ancient world. The structure was massive, extending some 165 feet by 345 feet in dimension, and situated on a platform which was 240 by 420 feet. Its beautiful decorations included brilliant colors and trappings in gold. One hundred twenty-seven white marble pillars, each of them sixty feet high, supported the structure.[21] The temple was magnificent and gave testimony to a religion with a long history. When Paul began preaching in Ephesus he was taking on an entrenched and powerful religious tradition.

The goddess herself carried the name "Artemis" for Greeks, but for Romans the name was "Diana." The Ephesian goddess had developed characteristics similar to Cybele, the Asian Mother Goddess of fertility. Her image included a torso covered with many breasts[22] in order to emphasize her role as fertile mother.

---

[21]The site of this temple was lost to the modern age until 1869 when it was discovered by J.T. Wood. The huge altar (an area that was twenty feet square) was also discovered in 1965. Of the 127 pillars only one stands today. See G.H.R. Horsley, "The Inscriptions of Ephesos and the New Testament," *NovT* 34 (1992): 105-168.

[22]It has also been suggested that the protrusions were dates. See C.S.C.

The business of Demetrius was one of producing "silver shrines of Artemis," which appeared as replicas of the temple used by worshipers as votive offerings when they came to the temple. An abundance of these replicas have been unearthed by archaeologists, but they are made of *terra cotta* rather than silver. No silver replicas have been found, probably because of their value to anyone who happened to find them over the centuries.[23]

Paul's message about idols smashed head-on into the purpose of these miniature shrines. Demetrius was not interested in making the kind of personal sacrifices exemplified by those who had brought their magical scrolls (16:19). He brought together his fellow craftsmen, acting perhaps as president of the trade guild, and challenged them to consider how much profit was at stake. His words about Paul were close to the truth. Paul's preaching had attacked the value of idols in the worship of the true God, as his address on the Areopagus demonstrates (see 17:29; also 1 Cor 8:5-6).

Besides this, the radical acts of repentance, as seen in the burning of the scrolls, may have been imitated by those who had formerly used the silver replicas. If Paul's preaching caused Ephesian citizens to cease purchasing the shrines, then Demetrius and his craftsmen would suffer severe economic loss.

Demetrius, however, did not limit his argument to the issue of economics. Paul's preaching would cause the "temple of the great goddess Artemis" to be "discredited," and even the goddess herself would lose prestige. He now was turning the issue to more religious sentiments. Since Ephesus was the center of the cult of Artemis, the damage to her worship would be felt all over the region.[24] Paul's ministry, said Demetrius, was thus a personal slap at the venerated goddess, herself.

The craftsmen responded to the challenge of Demetrius with loud acclamations of their devotion to Artemis. Before long, the scene would get ugly.

Williams, *A Commentary on the Acts of the Apostles* (Peabody, MA: Hendrickson, 1988), p. 223.

[23]Sherwin-White, *Roman Society and Roman Law*, pp. 90-91.

[24]Polhill observes that the temple of Artemis was so wealthy that it conducted business much like a bank, even receiving deposits and extending loans (p. 409).

The Demonstration in the Theater (19:29-34)

²⁹**Soon the whole city was in an uproar. The people seized Gaius and Aristarchus, Paul's traveling companions from Macedonia, and rushed as one man into the theater. ³⁰Paul wanted to appear before the crowd, but the disciples would not let him. ³¹Even some of the officials of the province, friends of Paul, sent him a message begging him not to venture into the theater. ³²The assembly was in confusion: Some were shouting one thing, some another. Most of the people did not even know why they were there. ³³The Jews pushed Alexander to the front, and some of the crowd shouted instructions to him. He motioned for silence in order to make a defense before the people. ³⁴But when they realized he was a Jew, they all shouted in unison for about two hours: "Great is Artemis of the Ephesians!"**

The loud demonstration of the silversmiths infected the whole city. The people rushed to the largest facility in Ephesus—the open-air theater. Cut into the western slope of Mt. Pion, the theater had a seating capacity of 24,500 and served as the regular meeting place for the city meeting (δῆμος, *dēmos*) three times a month.²⁵ This time the assembly was not an organized one.

The unruly mob had seized two of Paul's "traveling companions from Macedonia," Gaius and Aristarchus, whom they evidently intended to make the objects of their anger. Perhaps they seized these two because they could not find Paul. Meanwhile, when Paul found out what was going on, he was eager to get to the theater and present a defense. Some of the disciples convinced him it would be disaster, and even "the officials of the province" ('Ασιαρχῶν, *Asiarchōn*), with whom Paul had become friends, insisted that Paul not enter the theater.

"Asiarchs" were leading citizens from towns in Roman Asia, which were bound together in a league to promote the cult of the ruling Caesar. Their term lasted one year and from among all of the Asiarchs one leader would be elected to serve a position supervising all of the towns of the league. In Paul's time there would have been

²⁵Bruce, p. 376.

three or four Asiarchs in office.[26]

At the theater the "assembly was in confusion." Shouts and chanting of slogans filled the air, mixed with expressions of anger against those who were dishonoring their deity. Luke notes with some humor that most of the citizens "did not even know why they were there."

Some of the Jews, fearful that the people of Ephesus would blame them for Paul's disrespect for Artemis, "pushed Alexander to the front," hoping that he would be able to explain that Paul's ministry had no connection with them. The identity of this Alexander is uncertain[27] and his efforts were useless. The Ephesians gathered in the theater began to chant in unison for two hours, "Great is Artemis of the Ephesians."

The Calming Words of the Town Clerk (19:35-41)

[35]The city clerk quieted the crowd and said: "Men of Ephesus, doesn't all the world know that the city of Ephesus is the guardian of the temple of the great Artemis and of her image, which fell from heaven? [36]Therefore, since these facts are undeniable, you ought to be quiet and not do anything rash. [37]You have brought these men here, though they have neither robbed temples nor blasphemed our goddess. [38]If, then, Demetrius and his fellow craftsmen have a grievance against anybody, the courts are open and there are proconsuls. They can press charges. [39]If there is anything further you want to bring up, it must be settled in a legal assembly. [40]As it is, we are in danger of being charged with rioting because of today's events. In that case we would not be able to account for this commotion, since there is no reason for it." [41]After he had said this, he dismissed the assembly.

---

[26]Haenchen, p. 574, n. 1.

[27]It is doubtful that he is the same Alexander mentioned in 1 Tim 1:20; 2 Tim 4:14. Another purpose for this maneuver has been suggested by R.F. Stoops, Jr., "Riot and Assembly: The Social Context of Acts 19:23-41," *JBL* 108 (1989): 73-91. He says that disturbances could mean confirmation of Jewish civil rights when the disturbance was caused by their opponents.

Just when the situation in the Ephesian theater seemed to be completely lost, the "city clerk" (γραμματεύς, *grammateus*) stepped forward to address the crowd. His position commanded respect, since he was the executive officer over both the city magistrates and the civic assembly. His job included the duty of publishing the decisions of the civic assembly. This role made him the liaison between the Roman administration and the city's citizens.

His message was two-sided. First, there was no reason to fear for the well-being of Artemis, since she was revered in "all the world" and the city of Ephesus was considered "the guardian of the temple."[28] Such a distinction was deserved, argued the clerk, because of her image, "which fell from heaven"(διοπετοῦς, *diopetous*), a reference to the belief that Artemis was not the work of human hands, but an image which had come directly out of the sky.[29]

The clerk's second point was that assemblies in Ephesus were required to be handled according to legal procedures. Gaius and Aristarchus had not "robbed temples" (of their reputation) "nor blasphemed" the goddess in any way that could be considered serious. If the Ephesians wanted to pursue the matter further, there were legal means through orderly steps which could be followed. The "courts" (ἀγοραῖοι, *agoraioi*) and the "proconsuls" were available in such cases, not to mention the "legal assembly" (τῇ ἐννόμῳ ἐκκλησίᾳ, *tē ennomō ekklēsia*). These features of Roman administration allowed for citizens to "press charges" where they felt the need.[30]

As things stood, warned the clerk, the city was "in danger" (κινδυνέω, *kindyneō*) of angering the Roman authorities because of the commotion. If this happened, the city could be punished by the loss of rights and privileges.

---

[28]Inscriptional evidence shows that Ephesus bore the designation "temple warden of Artemis." See Sherwin-White, *Roman Society and Roman Law*, pp. 88-89.

[29]This Greek word initially had the idea of "meteorite," and then became a reference to sacred objects in general. Meteorites were associated with the worship of the Mother Goddess.

[30]The reference to "civic assemblies" appears to reflect on the remnants of the old pattern of city-state government which was passing out of practice. See Sherwin-White, *Roman Society and Roman Law*, pp. 83-92. For epigraphic evidence from Ephesus bearing on the role of civic assemblies and of the Asiarchs, see Horsley, "Inscriptions," 136-138.

Thus Luke closes the episode in Ephesus with the clear message that the charges brought against Paul and his companions could not stand the test of due process. The theme of the gospel as powerful in spiritual terms, but harmless to the political requirements of Rome, continues here, and will grow even stronger as the rest of Acts unfolds.

ACTS 20

9. The Journey through Macedonia and Greece (20:1-6)

[1]When the uproar had ended, Paul sent for the disciples and, after encouraging them, said good-by and set out for Macedonia. [2]He traveled through that area, speaking many words of encouragement to the people, and finally arrived in Greece, [3]where he stayed three months. Because the Jews made a plot against him just as he was about to sail for Syria, he decided to go back through Macedonia. [4]He was accompanied by Sopater son of Pyrrhus from Berea, Aristarchus and Secundus from Thessalonica, Gaius from Derbe, Timothy also, and Tychicus and Trophimus from the province of Asia. [5]These men went on ahead and waited for us at Troas. [6]But we sailed from Philippi after the Feast of Unleavened Bread, and five days later joined the others at Troas, where we stayed seven days.

The riot at Ephesus brought Paul's stay in the city to a close. He gathered together "the disciples" and said good-by. His plans included journeying to Macedonia,[1] but on the way he wanted to take care of several other matters which are not mentioned in Acts.

---

[1]Donald Miesner thinks that a distinct pattern emerges in Luke's description of the last part of Paul's journey. See his "The Missionary Journeys Narrative: Patterns and Implications," *Perspectives on Luke-Acts*, ed. Charles Talbert (Edinburgh: T & T Clark, 1978), pp. 199-214. Floyd Filson says that "it would capture the essential geographical outlook of Luke to entitle the Gospel of Luke 'From Galilee to Jerusalem', and the Book of the Acts 'From Jerusalem to Rome'." See his "The Journey Motif in Luke-Acts," *Apostolic History and the Gospel*, ed. W.W. Gasque, Ralph Martin (Grand Rapids: Eerdmans, 1970), pp. 68-77.

This information is supplied by his letters to the churches at Corinth, at Rome, and in Galatia.

One concern on Paul's mind was the church at Corinth. In 2 Corinthians 1–7 he gives details about his relationship with this congregation. Apparently Paul had already written a letter to the church which he describes as a "painful" letter, written with "many tears" (2 Cor 2:3-4).[2] In addition, Paul had made a hasty, but disastrous, visit to Corinth during the period of his Ephesian ministry (2 Cor 2:1; 13:1). Now he was leaving Ephesus in order to make a third visit to the church in order to restore a more respectful relationship with them.[3] He had sent Titus to Corinth to deliver his "painful" letter, and waited as patiently as he could for Titus to return with news about the situation in Corinth.

Another objective of Paul as he was leaving Ephesus was to preach in Troas. In 2 Corinthians 2:12 Paul says that he went to Troas "to preach the gospel of Christ and found that the Lord had opened a door for me." His attentions were divided, however, as he waited for Titus to return from Corinth with news about how the church at Corinth had reacted to his letter (2 Cor 2:13). When Titus was delayed, Paul said good-by to the Christians at Troas and headed for Macedonia.

Traveling "through that area," he revisited churches he had established in Philippi, Thessalonica, and Berea, "speaking many words of encouragement." Perhaps at Philippi, he finally met Titus who brought good news from Corinth, permitting Paul the first relief and peace of mind he had experienced for days (2 Cor 1-2). It was at this time, in A.D. 55, that he wrote 2 Corinthians.

Bruce suggests that Paul's stay in Macedonia was a long one, and may have given him time to carry the gospel as far as Illyricum (Rom 15:19). If so, he may have traveled westward on the Ignatian

---

[2]This letter was evidently the third letter Paul had written to the church at Corinth. His first letter, now lost, was a letter warning them about immorality (see 1 Cor 5:9). The second letter was our 1 Corinthians, and the third letter was this "painful letter."

[3]Paul's visits to Corinth mentioned or implied in the New Testament amount to three. The first was when he founded the church (Acts 18:1-18), followed a few years later by the disastrous visit and then, thirdly, the visit to restore his relationship with the church.

Way as far as the Adriatic Sea, and then turned north.[4]

At the conclusion of his travels in Macedonia Paul came to Greece (or Achaia), where "he stayed three months," implying that his relationship with the church at Corinth had healed. His stay here may have been determined by the fact that the winter months had come, and shipping was infrequent. At this point Paul probably wrote the letter to the Romans (A.D. 57).

When spring came and with it the opportunity for boarding a ship for Jerusalem (see 20:16),[5] Paul was ready to move again. At the last minute it was discovered that the Jews had made "a plot" against Paul, possibly a plan to murder him during the voyage of Jewish pilgrims going to Jerusalem for Pentecost. To foil their plan Paul decided to travel by foot "back through Macedonia" where he could sail from Neapolis to Troas. In addition to these matters, one more issue weighed heavily on Paul's mind during this phase of his ministry. He was taking up a collection for the saints in Judea. Accompanying him during his departure from Corinth were several believers listed here by Luke. By comparing Luke's narrative with what Paul says in his letters about the collection, it is clear that these men represented churches which were contributing to the collection.[6] As delegates from the churches they would be in a position to verify Paul's use of the funds, as well as provide some protection in light of the fact that so much coinage was being carried in an age before paper money and bank drafts.

The list includes a delegate from Berea, Sopater (likely the same man mentioned in Rom 16:21 as Sosipater, which would imply he represented Corinth). From Thessalonica was Aristarchus (see Acts 19:29; 27:2; Col 4:10) and Secundus. Delegates from Roman Galatia included Gaius (not the same Gaius as in 19:29) and Timothy (see 16:1), and from the province of Asia came Tychicus (see Eph 6:21-22; Col 4:7-8; 2 Tim 4:12; Titus 3:12) and Trophimus (see Acts 21:29; 2 Tim 4:20).

In addition to these delegates another companion joined Paul at

---

[4]Bruce, p. 381.

[5]The Romans considered Jerusalem to be a city in the province of Syria.

[6]See Gal 2:10; 1 Cor 16:1-4; 2 Cor 8-9; Rom 15:25-32. See also Munck, *Paul*, pp. 293-294.

this time. The evidence is found in the "we" of these verses. As suggested above,[7] the narrator appears to be Luke, a companion who remained behind in Philippi when Paul departed for Thessalonica. Now he was joining Paul again for the journey to Jerusalem.

One of the biggest mysteries in Acts has to do with this collection. Though it is obvious from Paul's letters that he considered the collection a major priority of this period in his ministry, Luke is completely silent about it. Even the list he presents here does not explicitly mention the collection.[8]

Paul sent the delegates on to Troas by ship where they would wait for him,[9] and he (along with Luke, at least) walked to Philippi, a journey of several days. Here they waited until after "the Feast of Unleavened Bread" (or Passover)[10] was over, a period of one week. Then from Philippi (or, more specifically, Philippi's port city, Neapolis) they sailed to Troas, a voyage that took five days, twice as long as the previous sea voyage which brought the missionaries to Macedonia initially (see 16:11). At Troas they remained for seven days.

10. The Visit at Troas (20:7-12)

[7]On the first day of the week we came together to break bread. Paul spoke to the people and, because he intended to leave the next day, kept on talking until midnight. [8]There were many lamps in the upstairs room where we were meeting. [9]Seated in a window

---

[7]See comments on 16:40, as well as the Introduction. See also Gasque, *History of Criticism*, p. 68. For the view that the use of "we" is a literary device linked with ancient sea voyages see Robbins, "By Land and by Sea," *Perspectives on Luke-Acts*, pp. 213-242.

[8]Polhill (p. 417) lists some of the possible solutions to the problem, including the one presented by K.F. Nickle, *The Collection* (London: SCM, 1966), 148-151, in which he suggests that the money may have been confiscated by the Roman authorities who considered it illegal.

[9]The text (pronoun "they") is ambiguous as to whether all of the delegates went to Troas, or just Tychicus and Trophimus.

[10]Lake and Cadbury see in this note some evidence that Christians did not yet observe Easter as distinct from the Jewish Day of Passover (p. 254), but Luke's mention of this feast may serve only the purpose of reckoning time. For issues of chronology see Jewett, *Chronology*, pp. 49-50.

**was a young man named Eutychus, who was sinking into a deep
sleep as Paul talked on and on. When he was sound asleep, he fell
to the ground from the third story and was picked up dead. [10]Paul
went down, threw himself on the young man and put his arms
around him. "Don't be alarmed," he said. "He's alive!" [11]Then he
went upstairs again and broke bread and ate. After talking until
daylight, he left. [12]The people took the young man home alive and
were greatly comforted.**

Paul's delay in Troas, perhaps because of the need to wait for a
ship bound for Syria,[11] gave him the opportunity to meet with the
believers for worship. "On the first day of the week" was the time
for their meeting, a reference which represents the earliest evidence
that Sunday had become the day for worship among Christians.[12]
Their gathering "to break bread" (κλάσαι ἄρτον, *klasai arton*)[13]
implies that the Lord's Supper would be observed, though the
phrase "he ate" (20:11) indicates that a full meal may have been
included, as well. The phrase suggests that meeting to observe the
Lord's Supper on the first day of the week was a habitual practice.

Because Paul's departure was at hand, he spoke (διελέγετο,
dielegeto) to the believers and "kept on talking (παρέτεινεν,
pareteinen) until midnight."[14] Perhaps with a hint of humor Luke
describes the scene as the "young man" (νεανίας, *neanias*)[15] was
sitting in the "upstairs room," listening to the long discourse of

---

[11]Also possible is that Paul was waiting to gather with the believers for
worship. See DeWelt, pp. 270-271.

[12]The suggestion that the day was Saturday rather than Sunday assumes
that Luke is using Jewish reckoning to determine "the first day of the week"
when he mentions the preaching that went into the evening. The Jewish day
began at sunset and thus this time of meeting would actually be the day
before Sunday, that is Saturday, the Sabbath. But Roman reckoning, which
began the day at midnight, would make the day Sunday and would mean
that Paul's preaching extended into Sunday night.

[13]See Luke 22:19; Acts 2:42.

[14]Both verbs are in the imperfect tense indicating the ongoing nature of
Paul's preaching.

[15]Though νεανίας may give the impression of a young man, the term
παῖς (*pais*) in 20:12 indicates he was more like a youngster, between nine
and fourteen years of age.

Paul. "Many lamps" lighting the room were contributing to a warm and heavy atmosphere, and the youngster tumbled out of "the third story," a fall that evidently killed him. Now Paul's speaking came abruptly to a halt as he sprang into action in this dreadful moment.

When they reached the boy he was "picked up dead." But Paul took action, throwing himself on him and putting his arms around him. "He's alive," Paul exclaimed, indicating that he had restored life to the boy's body. The event was a resurrection, similar to examples from the ministry of Jesus and of Peter.[16] Paul's treatment of the boy even recalled actions of Elijah (1 Kgs 17:21) and Elisha (2 Kgs 4:34).

The excitement over, Paul went back upstairs and resumed the meeting by observing the Lord's Supper and enjoying the fellowship meal. His conversation with the believers did not end until after daybreak. The people took their son home alive and the memory of the incident provided comfort to the church.

11. The Visits at Assos, Mitylene, Kios (Chios), Samos, and Miletus (20:13-15)

[13]**We went on ahead to the ship and sailed for Assos, where we were going to take Paul aboard. He had made this arrangement because he was going there on foot. [14]When he met us at Assos, we took him aboard and went on to Mitylene. [15]The next day we set sail from there and arrived off Kios. The day after that we crossed over to Samos, and on the following day arrived at Miletus.**

Though Luke does not say why, Paul sent his companions (Luke included) down to the dock at Troas to board the ship while he himself determined to travel on foot to Assos. The journey on foot in this case would not take any more time than going by ship, both occupying a day's travel. Perhaps Paul did not wish to travel the difficult voyage around the cape, or maybe he felt the need for

---

[16]Jesus raised the widow's son at Nain (Luke 7:11-15), the daughter of Jairus (Luke 8:49-50), and Lazarus (John 11:38-44). Peter brought life back to Dorcas (Acts 9:36-41).

some solitude along the way.

At any rate, Paul had made plans to join his companions in Assos, a city which sat on a volcanic cone about 750 feet up. He reached them and boarded the ship in time to sail for Mitylene where the chief city was Lesbos, another one-day journey. The next day the ship sailed for Kios, an island which lay just off the coast of Asia Minor. "Crossing over" the bay which led to Ephesus, they arrived the next day at Samos where they stayed the night. The fifth day out was spent sailing to Miletus, a major Asian city on the coast of the Aegean, which had a history dating back to Hittite and Mycenaean times. Here the ship would put in for several days.

12. The Meeting with the Ephesian Elders (20:16-38)

Paul's Summons of the Ephesian Elders (20:16-17)

¹⁶Paul had decided to sail past Ephesus to avoid spending time in the province of Asia, for he was in a hurry to reach Jerusalem, if possible, by the day of Pentecost. ¹⁷From Miletus, Paul sent to Ephesus for the elders of the church.

The puzzle of this passage is Paul's desire to "sail past Ephesus to avoid spending time in the province of Asia," calling instead for the Ephesian elders to meet him in Miletus. The distance between Miletus and Ephesus was about thirty miles, and would mean a walk of about a day and a half. By the time the messenger made the return trip with the elders the better part of five days would have been used.

It is possible, however, that the disturbance in Ephesus would have meant delays if trouble should arise. Paul may have felt that his time was growing too short to risk it. He wanted to be in Jerusalem "by the day of Pentecost," just fifty days after the Passover. Five days were used on the voyage to Troas, a week in Troas, and then five more days on the journey to Miletus. The need for haste was pressing down on him.

From Ephesus the elders (πρεσβύτεροι, *presbyteroi*) of the church came to meet Paul. It is noteworthy that the Ephesian church had a

319

plurality of elders, and that the term "elder" (*presbyteros*) and "bishop" (ἐπίσκοπος, *episkopos*) were synonymous terms for the same office (see also Titus 1:5,7). The leaders of the local congregation might be called "elders" or "bishops" interchangeably.[17]

Nevertheless, Paul's reason for summoning them was to present his farewell address.[18] Commentators often note the similarities between this address and the letters of Paul. No other Pauline speech in Acts sounds so much like his letters. The simple reason for this is that in Acts the speeches of Paul thus far have been to non-Christian audiences. The speech in Antioch of Pisidia (13:16-41) was before a Jewish crowd in the synagogue. The speech at the Areopagus (17:22-31) was before a pagan audience. Only now do we find a speech by Paul which is addressed to fellow believers.

Paul's Reflections on His Ephesian Ministry (20:18-21)

[18]**When they arrived, he said to them: "You know how I lived the whole time I was with you, from the first day I came into the province of Asia** [19]**I served the Lord with great humility and with tears, although I was severely tested by the plots of the Jews.** [20]**You know that I have not hesitated to preach anything that would be helpful to you but have taught you publicly and from house to house.** [21]**I have declared to both Jews and Greeks that they must turn to God in repentance and have faith in our Lord Jesus.**

Paul's address to the Ephesian elders in many ways is a summary of his ministry not only at Ephesus, but in its entirety. He uses the opportunity not only to summarize his own preaching and style of ministry, but to warn these elders of future challenges to the church, and his confidence that they would be kept in the care of God.

His address to the elders took the form of an exhortation. He

---

[17]See Ladd, *Theology*, pp. 352-353, 532-533.

[18]William Kurz characterizes Paul's speech as a "testament." See his "Luke-Acts and Historiography in the Greek Bible," *SBL Seminar Papers 1980*, ed. P.J. Achtemeier (Chico, CA: Scholars Press, 1980), pp. 283-300.

began by reminding them of his character and the style of his ministry. Such a plea to the memory of those among whom Paul ministered was not uncommon in his letters (see Gal 4:13; Phil 4:15; 1 Thess 2:1-2,5,10-11; 3:3-4; 4:2). He calls their attention to the humility that characterized his work, serving the Lord even "with tears." Paul often referred to himself as a "servant" of the Lord (Rom 1:1; Gal 1:10; Phil 1:1).

He had served in spite of the fact that he was often opposed, especially by the Jews. Interestingly enough, persecutions from the Jews seemed to be less a factor in Ephesus than in other cities as far as the record in Acts is concerned. Nevertheless, it was because of Jewish resistance that he moved out of the synagogue and into the lecture hall of Tyrannus (See 19:9-10). His latest escape from a plot by the Jews had been in Corinth (20:3).

In spite of this resistance, Paul reminded them that he had proclaimed all of the gospel. He noted that he had done this "publicly," a claim that reflected on his preaching in the Ephesian synagogue, as well as the lecture hall of Tyrannus (see 19:8-10). He had also taught them "from house to house," a phrase that may refer to private instruction he had given to families or to his teaching in homes where the church met for worship.

In carrying out this preaching, however, Paul insisted that he never excluded anyone, whether Jew or Gentile. Perhaps at this point he was reflecting on the content of his own letter to the Romans, especially Romans 9–11. Without partiality he had proclaimed the need to "turn to God in repentance and have faith in our Lord Jesus." Though Paul's letters emphasize faith more often than repentance, C.F.D. Moule notes,

> Justification by faith involves such a response to that finished work (of Christ) as identifies the believer most intimately with the costly work of Christ, involving him inescapably in the *cost* and *pain* of *repentance*" [emphasis his].[19]

---

[19]C.F.D. Moule, "Obligation in the Ethic of Paul," *Essays in New Testament Interpretation* (Cambridge: Cambridge University Press, 1982), pp. 272-273.

Paul's Expectations for the Future (20:22-24)

[22]"And now, compelled by the Spirit, I am going to Jerusalem, not knowing what will happen to me there. [23]I only know that in every city the Holy Spirit warns me that prison and hardships are facing me. [24]However, I consider my life worth nothing to me, if only I may finish the race and complete the task the Lord Jesus has given me—the task of testifying to the gospel of God's grace.

At this point Paul makes clear that it is not his own will that was pushing him toward Jerusalem, but the Holy Spirit. He had to face the risks of going to Jerusalem in order to be obedient to God.

His efforts in organizing the collection was a major cause of his journey to the Holy City. Nevertheless, when he writes to the Romans he expresses particular concern about the opposition he will face when he arrives (Rom 15:31).

He was certain, however, that he would be making personal sacrifices. This reality had been brought home to him "in every city" along the way, probably by prophets in the churches who had fore-told the trouble he would face in Jerusalem. Even these hardships did not deter him, he said, because he considered his life "worth nothing" to him (see 2 Cor 4:7-12; 6:4-10; 12:9-10; Phil 1:20-21; 2:17; 3:8; Col 1:24), since his greatest goal in life was to finish the "race" (δρόμος, dromos). Paul uses such athletic terminology in several of his letters (1 Cor 9:24-27; Gal 2:2; Phil 2:16; 3:13-14).

All of this sacrifice, Paul said, he would make for the gospel "of God's grace." Though Paul's letters do not use this phrase to describe his gospel, the language seems quite appropriate to the content of his proclamation (see Eph 2:8-9).

Paul's Charge to the Ephesian Elders (20:25-31)

[25]"Now I know that none of you among whom I have gone about preaching the kingdom will ever see me again. [26]Therefore, I declare to you today that I am innocent of the blood of all men. [27]For I have not hesitated to proclaim to you the whole will of God. [28]Keep watch over yourselves and all the flock of which the

Holy Spirit has made you overseers.ᵃ Be shepherds of the church of God,ᵇ which he bought with his own blood. ²⁹I know that after I leave, savage wolves will come in among you and will not spare the flock. ³⁰Even from your own number men will arise and distort the truth in order to draw away disciples after them. ³¹So be on your guard! Remember that for three years I never stopped warning each of you night and day with tears.

ᵃ28 Traditionally *bishops*   ᵇ28 Many manuscripts *of the Lord*

Looking to the future, Paul considered it necessary to warn the Ephesian elders about the challenges ahead. This point was especially true in view of the fact that in this region where he had "gone about preaching the kingdom" he was convinced they would never see him again.[20] Such a conclusion resulted not from a specific word from the Lord regarding his death, but from the persistent prophetic warnings of trouble ahead in Jerusalem (see 21:11).

He thus reminded them that he had fulfilled his role as "watchman" for Christ. Just as Ezekiel described the responsibility of the city watchman to warn the citizens of the coming threat (33:1-6), Paul had presented the warning and was now "innocent of the blood of all men." He could make this declaration because he had been unswerving in his commitment to proclaim the "whole will of God" (πᾶσαν τὴν βουλὴν τοῦ θεοῦ, *pasan tēn boulēn tou theou*).

Now he warned the Ephesian elders first to "keep watch" over themselves. His style of ministry had serious implications for church leaders for whom his labors had provided an example. They must be careful to minister, as Paul had, with the good of "the flock"[21] in

---

[20]Some have used this prediction as evidence about the authorship of the Pastoral Epistles which seem to depend on Paul's release from his Roman imprisonment to travel again to Ephesus (see 1 Tim 1:3). The position has been taken that Luke would not have recorded Paul's prediction that the Ephesians would not see him again if, in fact, he later returned to Ephesus (see Haenchen, p. 592, n. 2). Such a prediction would, then, amount to false prophecy. This line of reasoning assumes that Paul's every anticipation was treated as a revelation from the Lord. His travel plans frequently did not turn out as he expected (see 20:3; Rom 1:13; 1 Cor 16:8-9; 2 Cor 1:15-2:13).

[21]The Old Testament often portrays the people of God as his flock (see Ezek 34:12-16; Jer 23:2; Zech 10:3; 11:4-17), as does the New Testament (see

mind. Paul's reference to the Ephesian elders took up the metaphor of the shepherd and the flock. Thus he commanded them to "be shepherds" (ποιμαίνειν, *poimainein*) of the church, a charge that would be especially appropriate in the face of the "savage wolves" which would come after his departure. His reference was to false teachers, a threat which soon became reality in the churches of Asia Minor (see Eph 5:6-14; Col 2:8; Rev 2:2; 1 Tim 1:19-20; 4:1-3; 2 Tim 1:15; 2:17-18; 3:1-9). In many cases these false doctrines arose from believers within the church.

Their duty was to care for "the church of God which he bought with his own blood." This phrase is open to two interpretations. The NIV text presents one possibility, that the phrase "his own blood" follows from the antecedent "God." The problem with this interpretation is that no other reference in the New Testament refers to "the blood of God," though the blood of Jesus is surely intended. But the Greek phrase διὰ τοῦ αἵματος τοῦ ἰδίου (*dia tou haimatos tou idiou*) can also be translated "with the blood of his own," that is "the blood of his own [son]." The latter interpretation would emphasize the relationship of Christ to God.

Thus Paul called attention to his own diligent labors extending at Ephesus for the better part of "three years" (see 19:10), a ministry which gave them the opportunity to witness how faithful he was in his warnings to them. His own "tears" were the brand of his sincerity.

Paul's Final Admonition (20:32-35)

[32]"Now I commit you to God and to the word of his grace, which can build you up and give you an inheritance among all those who are sanctified. [33]I have not coveted anyone's silver or gold or clothing. [34]You yourselves know that these hands of mine have supplied my own needs and the needs of my companions. [35]In everything I did, I showed you that by this kind of hard work

---

John 10:1-18; 21:15-17; 1 Pet 2:25; 5:2). Paul's comments here lead Kurz to the conclusion that Luke was writing after Paul's death when some of these woes had come upon the church. See his "Luke-Acts and Historiography," ibid., 283-300. Also see Wilson, *Gentile Mission*, p. 233.

we must help the weak, remembering the words the Lord Jesus himself said: 'It is more blessed to give than to receive.' "

Paul concluded his charge to the Ephesian elders with some final warnings. He began by entrusting them into the hands of God and "to the word of his grace," a reference to the truth of the gospel. He reminded them that only in this truth could they expect to grow spiritually and to receive "an inheritance (κληρονομίαν, *klēronomian*) among all those who are sanctified (ἡγιασμένοις, *hēgiasmenois*)." To refer to believers as "sanctified" is nothing unusual for Paul, who often describes Christians as "sanctified ones," or "saints" in his letters (see Rom 8:17; Col 1:12; Eph 1:14,18; 5:5).[22]

In bringing his remarks to a close Paul hit on one temptation which could not be neglected. As they were to follow in his footsteps in matters of compassion and doctrine, so they were to emulate his sacrificial style of ministry. He had never sought the trappings of wealth—"silver or gold or clothing." Instead he had followed a policy of working with his own hands to supply his needs, a practice he reflects on in his letters (1 Cor 4:12; 9:12,15; 2 Cor 11:7; 12:13; 1 Thess 2:9; 2 Thess 3:7-8). In many cases he had even provided for the needs of his companions.

Compassion ruled in the ministry of Paul. Whether in his preaching or in his efforts to receive the collection for the saints in Judea, Paul remembered the lesson that "we must help the weak." His ultimate inspiration was the Lord Jesus himself. Christ had said, "It is more blessed to give than to receive." This statement of Christ is not recorded in the gospels, and may be a quotation which Paul drew from the oral tradition of the ministry and teachings of Jesus.[23]

Thus he urged the Ephesian elders to avoid a ministry characterized by greed or materialism. With this quotation Paul closed his remarks.

---

[22]The basic idea of sanctified as "separate for God," both spiritually and ethically is very much in view in these passages.

[23]Bruce (p. 395, n. 80) notes that the substance of this quote may be found in some of the sayings of Jesus found in the Gospels (see Luke 6:38; 11:9-13; John 13:34).

The Emotional Parting (20:36-38)

36When he had said this, he knelt down with all of them and prayed. 37They all wept as they embraced him and kissed him. 38What grieved them most was his statement that they would never see his face again. Then they accompanied him to the ship.

Having heard Paul's farewell address, the elders knelt with him and prayed, doubtless seeking God's blessing on one another in their separate ministries. The parting was emotional and sincere. The probability that they would not see him again was the most painful part of his words. Nevertheless, "they accompanied him to the ship," a phrase which includes not only escorting Paul to the vessel, but also providing him with food and other necessities.

ACTS 21

13. The Stops at Cos, Rhodes, and Patara (21:1-2)

¹**After we had torn ourselves away from them, we put out to sea and sailed straight to Cos. The next day we went to Rhodes and from there to Patara. ²We found a ship crossing over to Phoenicia, went on board and set sail.**

Paul's journey toward Jerusalem was now well underway.[1] The similarities with Jesus' last journey to Jerusalem (see Luke 9:51) now become more and more evident, including the sense of doom about what will happen there (see Luke 13:33-35; 18:31-32) and the expressions of determination not to turn back.[2] Paul will also hear warnings from many of his Christian friends not to go on into Jerusalem because of the danger there.

Luke continues the description of the journey by noting each stop made on the sea voyage toward Jerusalem. After they[3] "had torn [themselves] away" (ἀποσπάω, *apospaō*) from the elders at Miletus, they boarded a vessel and "put out to sea." Favorable northeasterly winds assisted them, and they "sailed straight to Cos," an island where the capital city was also named Cos.[4] The following day the ship sailed on to Rhodes, another island where the main city

---

[1]Miesner sees in Luke's arrangement of Paul's return to Jerusalem a chiastic structure. See his "Missionary Journeys Narrative," in *Perspectives on Luke-Acts*, ed. Talbert, pp. 199-214.

[2]Luke 9:51 describes this determination in Jesus when it says, "Jesus resolutely set out for Jerusalem."

[3]This chapter continues the "we" narrative (see 20:6).

[4]Cos was famous as the home of the medical school which Hippocrates founded in the fifth century B.C.

was named Rhodes.[5] From Rhodes the vessel sailed on the next day to the coastal city of Patara located in Lycia.

To this point Paul was traveling on a coasting vessel, a smaller ship which of necessity stayed close to the coastline. At Patara they changed ships because they found one which was "crossing over to Phoenicia," that is, sailing a straight course farther out in the Mediterranean Sea.[6] The journey from Patara to Tyre was about 400 miles and usually took about five days.

14. The Arrival at Tyre (21:3-6)

³After sighting Cyprus and passing to the south of it, we sailed on to Syria. We landed at Tyre, where our ship was to unload its cargo. ⁴Finding the disciples there, we stayed with them seven days. Through the Spirit they urged Paul not to go on to Jerusalem. ⁵But when our time was up, we left and continued on our way. All the disciples and their wives and children accompanied us out of the city, and there on the beach we knelt to pray. ⁶After saying good-by to each other, we went aboard the ship, and they returned home.

Because Paul had boarded a larger vessel, he made very good time on the way toward Tyre. Luke notes (as a true eyewitness) that Cyprus was sighted to their north, a moment that gave the passengers their only glimpse of land before reaching their destination.[7] Finally they reached the Roman province of Syria, putting in at the

---

[5]Rhodes was once known for its harbor colossus which was one of the seven wonders of the ancient world. It had been demolished 200 years before Paul arrived.

[6]Among the reasons given by Lake and Cadbury for the necessity of such a change in vessels is that "local sailors would have a limited range of knowledge" about the waters once the ship moved farther away from his home. Also is the fact that the ship Paul found may have been a larger vessel which would help guarantee a quicker course in the open sea (p. 265).

[7]Paul had traveled through Cyprus, preaching in Salamis and Paphos (see Acts 13:4-12).

city of Tyre. This commercial city was known for its purple dye products. Its harbor had been formed by silt which gathered around the causeway laid down by Alexander the Great when he laid siege to the city.

Since the ship was now being unloaded, the missionaries felt they had some time to spend,[8] and they used it by "finding the disciples there." The verb ἀνευρίσκω (aneuriskō) implies that the missionaries did some searching to find them, a point which suggests that Paul was meeting them for the first time. The church at Tyre may have been established more than twenty years earlier by those Hellenists who were scattered after Stephen's death (see 11:19).

While they spent time in fellowship with these Christians, some of the prophets in the church were moved by the Holy Spirit to speak to Paul about his journey to Jerusalem. Speaking to him "through the Spirit" (διὰ τοῦ πνεύματος, dia tou pneumatos), they warned him not to go there.

This language presents a puzzle for those who remember that in 20:22 Paul said to the Ephesian elders that he was "compelled by the Spirit" to go to Jerusalem. Then in the next verse he said "in every city the Holy Spirit warns me that prison and hardships are facing me." Does this mean the Holy Spirit was contradicting himself?[9]

It seems best to explain the warnings which came from believers along the way as accurate forecasts of coming hardships meant to test Paul's resolve.[10] His primary message from the Spirit was that he should go on to Jerusalem. But the Spirit moved prophets in the churches to describe for him the trials he would face—messages which they took seriously—and out of personal concern for Paul tried to convince him not to go.

After spending seven days with these disciples the time came for

---

[8]Paul's rather lengthy stay in Tyre (seven days) implies that he had reached Syria in plenty of time to meet his goal of being in Jerusalem by Pentecost (20:16). Possibly the ship sailing to Syria had made exceptionally good time.

[9]Dunn seems to leave this possibility open (Jesus, pp. 175-176).

[10]Paul's letters reflect his conviction that hardships should not prevent his carrying out his ministry (see Rom 8:17; 2 Cor 4:7-12; 6:4-10; 11:23-29; 12:10; Col 1:24-25).

departing. Another very emotional scene occurred (similar to the one at Miletus in 20:36-37) once again down on the shore where "all the disciples and their wives and children" had come to say good-by. They all knelt to pray "on the beach" (αἰγιαλός, *aigialos*), a term which accurately describes the sandy shoreline at Tyre. The missionaries then boarded the ship.

15. The Arrival at Ptolemais and Caesarea (21:7-14)

The Entrance into the Home of Philip (21:7-9)

⁷We continued our voyage from Tyre and landed at Ptolemais, where we greeted the brothers and stayed with them for a day. ⁸Leaving the next day, we reached Caesarea and stayed at the house of Philip the evangelist, one of the Seven. ⁹He had four unmarried daughters who prophesied.

From Tyre the ship sailed to Ptolemais twenty-five miles south on the Phoenician coast.[11] Located just across the bay from Mount Carmel, the city had been declared a Roman colony by Paul's time. It was evangelized probably at the same time as Tyre (see 11:19). Paul was able to spend one day with the believers, a length of time which may have been determined by the ship's schedule.

The next day the missionaries set out for Caesarea,[12] some thirty-five miles south. Whether they traveled by ship or on foot is not clear. When they arrived they were welcomed into the home of "Philip the evangelist," one of the seven deacons chosen by the congregation in Jerusalem (6:3-6). His title "evangelist" came from his preaching efforts in Samaria and western Judea (see 8:4-40) and this distinguished him from Philip the apostle of Christ.[13] Philip had "four unmarried daughters who prophesied." Luke adds

---

[11]Ptolemais is mentioned in the Old Testament as the city of Acco (Judg 1:31). The name Ptolemais came from the ruler Ptolemais II Philadelphus (285-246 B.C.).

[12]For details about the city of Caesarea see comments on 10:1.

[13]The term "evangelist" is also mentioned in Eph 4:11 and 2 Tim 4:5.

this note even though nothing they prophesied is contained in his record. That the gift of prophecy would be given to women was implied in the quotation of Peter on the day the Spirit was poured out. He quoted Joel's words that "even on my servants, both men and women, I will pour out my Spirit in those days." It was a gift that women in the Corinthian church were permitted to exercise when their heads were covered (1 Cor 11:5-6) and when they abided by the limitations laid down by Paul (see 1 Cor 14:26-40; also 1 Tim 2:11-12).[14]

The Warning of Agabus and Paul's Response (21:10-14)

[10]After we had been there a number of days, a prophet named Agabus came down from Judea. [11]Coming over to us, he took Paul's belt, tied his own hands and feet with it and said, "The Holy Spirit says, 'In this way the Jews of Jerusalem will bind the owner of this belt and will hand him over to the Gentiles.'" [12]When we heard this, we and the people there pleaded with Paul not to go up to Jerusalem. [13]Then Paul answered, "Why are you weeping and breaking my heart? I am ready not only to be bound, but also to die in Jerusalem for the name of the Lord Jesus." [14]When he would not be dissuaded, we gave up and said, "The Lord's will be done."

Paul enjoyed his stay with Philip "a number of days," implying that the company had reached Syria in plenty of time to be in Jerusalem by Pentecost (see 20:16). While they were there the prophet Agabus arrived from Judea. He was the prophet who earlier had predicted the famine in Judea (see 11:27-29) Now he took the long cloth belt which was wound around Paul's waist several times in order to hold the garment in place and he wound it

---

[14]The gift of prophecy was one of the spiritual gifts discussed by Paul in 1 Cor 12:8-10. Luke had already described the role of the prophetess Anna in the presentation of Jesus at the temple (Luke 2:36-38). Swidler notes that the burial places of these Spirit-filled women were remembered in the time of Eusebius. See his *Biblical Affirmations*, pp. 301-302.

around his hands and feet. He then delivered a message from the Holy Spirit. The use of such actions by prophets was known in the Old Testament with such personalities as Ahijah (1 Kgs 11:29-31), Isaiah (8:1-4; 20:1-4), Jeremiah (13:1-11), and Hosea (1:2).[15]

He predicted that Paul himself would be bound in Jerusalem by the Jews and handed over to the Gentiles. What Agabus described as Paul's destiny was exactly what happened to Jesus after his journey to Jerusalem was complete (see Matt 20:18-19; Luke 18:32). Paul was going to suffer the same indignity. Though it would not be the Jews who bound him in Jerusalem, it would certainly be at their instigation that he would remain in the custody of the Roman authorities.[16]

The immediate reaction of the believers and even of Paul's companions (including Luke, who writes "we") was to plead with Paul not to go to Jerusalem. This scene serves to illustrate the kind of warnings from the Holy Spirit, which Paul had experienced along the way (see 20:23; 21:4).

Paul's response to this pleading was to ask, "Why are you weeping and breaking (συνθρύπτω, *synthryptō*) my heart?" The word for "breaking" means "to break up" or "to pound," and was often used of the practice of washing clothes by pounding them with stones. Paul sincerely felt the pain of his friends, but was determined that the Spirit wanted him to continue the journey to Jerusalem. Once again he stated his determination to press on, declaring that he was prepared "not only to be bound but also to die" for "the name" of Christ (see 9:16).

After making their case to Paul for a sufficient length of time, they saw that his mind could not be changed, and they resigned themselves to allowing the matter to rest in the hands of God. Their conclusion was that "the Lord's will be done," the same conclusion which Jesus had reached in the Garden of Gethsemane when he prayed to the Father, "not my will, but yours be done" (Luke 22:42).

---

[15]As a matter of fact, E.E. Ellis considers this text as evidence that the church viewed its prophets as true counterparts of their Old Testament antecedents. See his *Paul's Use of the Old Testament* (Grand Rapids: Baker, 1985), pp. 109-110.

[16]It is certainly pressing the language of Agabus too far to insist that the prophet falsely prophesied Paul's arrest because he described Paul's feet as being bound and v. 33 does not mention this (see Marshall, p. 349).

16. The Arrival at Jerusalem (21:15-16)

[15]After this, we got ready and went up to Jerusalem. [16]Some of
the disciples from Caesarea accompanied us and brought us to the
home of Mnason, where we were to stay. He was a man from
Cyprus and one of the early disciples.

After spending several days at Caesarea it was time for the sixty-
four mile journey up to Jerusalem. Paul and his companions "got
ready" (ἐπισκευάζομαι, *episkeuazomai*), a word which may imply that
they used pack animals for the trip to Jerusalem. Such a method of
travel would have been quite helpful in view of the fact that Paul's
company was carrying the collection for the Judean believers.

Some believers from Caesarea brought the missionaries to the
home of Mnason where they would reside. Bruce suggests that
Christians from Caesarea had possibly traveled to Mnason's house
in advance of the party in order to secure these arrangements.[17] He
also points out the great service of a believer in Jerusalem who
would be willing to give lodging to this missionary band with
Gentiles included.[18]

Mnason was "from Cyprus," also the home of Barnabas (see
4:36), and was probably one of the Greek-speaking Hellenists in
Jerusalem (see 11:20). He must have been a rather wealthy Christian
to have a house large enough to accommodate Paul's party of about
nine. His record of service was already a long one.

With v. 16 the third missionary journey of Paul comes to an end.
His ministry as apostle to the Gentiles now begins a brand new
phase. No longer will he travel among the churches as a free man.
His apostolic climax, however, is still before him, since the Lord had
determined he will preach the gospel in Rome.

---

[17]Bruce, p. 402, n. 17.

[18]Luke has shown throughout Acts an interest in the believers who give
lodging to servants of Christ (see 9:11,43; 16:15; 17:5; 18:3,7; 21:8).

E. PAUL'S VISIT TO THE
TEMPLE AND HIS ARREST (21:17–23:30)

1. Paul's Reception by the Church (21:17-26)

Paul's Report of the Gentile Response to the Gospel (21:17-19)

[17]**When we arrived at Jerusalem, the brothers received us warmly.** [18]**The next day Paul and the rest of us went to see James, and all the elders were present.** [19]**Paul greeted them and reported in detail what God had done among the Gentiles through his ministry.**

Paul's arrival in Jerusalem was met with a warm greeting.[19] The believers received them and provided lodging for them. Though it is tempting to associate the warm greeting[20] with the reception of Paul's offering from the Gentile churches, this does not seem to be Luke's intention, since he does not even mention the offering in Acts.

The next day they went to see "James and all the elders." The fact that the apostles are not mentioned here implies that they were no longer in Jerusalem and that leadership of the church had passed to James (the brother of the Lord) and the elders of the church.[21]

Paul related to them "in detail what God had done among the Gentiles through his ministry." This information would have included anything that had occurred on Paul's journeys that they had not heard about.

---

[19]Davies finds two interests at work in Luke's account of Paul's journeys to Jerusalem in Acts. The first is the issue of the Gentile mission and required the abandoning of the Jewish Law. The second is the association of the "young Christian movement" with Judaism for the purpose of its legal recognition by the Roman government. Davies, *Land*, pp. 277-278.

[20]Shepard's sense of a coolness in the greeting received by Paul does not seem warranted (*Life*, pp. 460-461).

[21]This James is the same leader who presided at the Jerusalem conference (15:13-21; see also Gal 1:19; 2:9).

The Proposal of James and the Elders (21:20-26)

[20]When they heard this, they praised God. Then they said to Paul: "You see, brother, how many thousands of Jews have believed, and all of them are zealous for the law. [21]They have been informed that you teach all the Jews who live among the Gentiles to turn away from Moses, telling them not to circumcise their children or live according to our customs. [22]What shall we do? They will certainly hear that you have come, [23]so do what we tell you. There are four men with us who have made a vow. [24]Take these men, join in their purification rites and pay their expenses, so that they can have their heads shaved. Then everybody will know there is no truth in these reports about you, but that you yourself are living in obedience to the law. [25]As for the Gentile believers, we have written to them our decision that they should abstain from food sacrificed to idols, from blood, from the meat of strangled animals and from sexual immorality." [26]The next day Paul took the men and purified himself along with them. Then he went to the temple to give notice of the date when the days of purification would end and the offering would be made for each of them.

James and the elders responded to Paul's account with great happiness, praising God. They not only rejoiced at the victories on the mission field, but were perhaps also pleased to know that Paul was not guilty of preaching anything like what his critics were saying.

Nevertheless, they informed Paul that some problems had surfaced in connection with his ministry. "Thousands of Jews" had become Christians in the twenty-five years since the gospel was preached by the apostles and the disciples.[22] Their tendency was to be "zealous for the law," since their background was so firmly rooted in Judaism.

The problem, however, was that these new Jewish Christians[23]

---

[22]Joachim Jeremias estimates that the population of Jerusalem at this time was between 25,000 and 55,000. See his *Jerusalem*, pp. 77-84.

[23]Munck construes the text to mean not Jewish Christians, but Judean Jews (*Paul*, pp. 238-241).

had been influenced to believe that Paul was teaching "all the Jews who live among the Gentiles to turn away from Moses." The source of this slander against Paul seems to have been located in the Diaspora Jews who were aware of Paul's ministry among the Gentile congregations.

An examination of Paul's letters demonstrates that he did emphasize salvation apart from the law of Moses (see Rom 3:21; Gal 2:15; Phil 3:9). But nowhere does he instruct Jewish Christians to cease their practice of the institutions of the law. As a matter of fact, Paul often speaks highly of the law (see Rom 7:12; Gal 3:21; 1 Tim 1:8). He also characterizes his own ministry as being free from the law, but nevertheless becoming a Jew to the Jews and as one under the law when ministering to those under the law (1 Cor 9:19-21). The idea that he would encourage Jews "not to circumcise their children" or follow Jewish customs was ridiculous. Such charges would strike at the very core of Jerusalem Jews who felt their identity so closely tied to the law and circumcision.

These critics of Paul were misrepresenting his teaching, but unfortunately they were doing so with some success. James and the believers hoped that Paul might demonstrate that his ministry to the Gentiles did not mean a rejection of the institutions of the Old Testament. Since participation in the ceremonies of the temple was no problem to Paul's faith, he readily agreed.

At this point, however, a problem arises for the modern reader. The problem is deciding exactly what kind of temple ceremony it was in which Paul participated. He could not have entered into a Nazirite vow, since these vows required thirty days.[24] He could, however, join other worshipers who were concluding a Nazirite vow. To conclude the vow "the four men" mentioned by James would need to go to the temple carrying the hair they had cut from their heads, and offer up several expensive sacrifices required by the law, including a male and female lamb, a ram and cereal and drink offerings (Num 6:14-15).

Paul could join these worshipers by going with them to the temple and helping them pay for their offerings, a practice which

---

[24]For a complete note on this question and three major interpretations of Paul's participation in this ceremony see Marshall, p. 345, n. 1.

was seen as both pious and gracious.[25] Paul's participation with the
four men would let everybody in Jerusalem know that there was no
truth to these reports about Paul's promoting a rejection of the law.
Indeed, he would put his critics on notice that he himself was "living
in obedience to the law."[26]

In addition to the ceremonial requirements for the four men,
Paul evidently had to participate in a purification rite for himself.
He not only went with them to the temple, but he "purified himself
along with them." In the case of Paul it seems that another requirement applied. Because he had just returned from a lengthy time of
residence among Gentiles, he went to the temple to participate in a
rite that involved sprinkling with water on the third and seventh
days. Paul now arranged for this seven-day purification to coincide
with the completion of the Nazirite vow taken by the four men. All
of this could be accomplished in seven days (see 21:27).[27] He would,
however, need "to give notice" at the temple of these arrangements
so that the priests could be prepared to offer the sacrifices.

If Paul would provide this example of his respect for the Jewish
law, James argued, nothing more would be needed. No further
action was needed regarding the Gentile believers, since the
Jerusalem conference had already issued the decrees (see 15:19-
31).[28] The issue of eating with Gentile believers and the role of
circumcision in the case of Gentile converts had already been
decided.

---

[25]Josephus suggests that Herod Agrippa I demonstrated his magnanimity
by directing Nazirites to shave their heads when he came to Jerusalem as
king (*Antiquities*, 19.294).

[26]Wilson observes that from this point on the law becomes the central
controversy with regard to charges made against Paul by angry Jews (21:28;
23:29; 24:5-6; 25:7). The charges will fall into three categories: "that he has
abandoned the laws and customs, profaned the temple, and generally
stirred up trouble." See his "Law and Judaism in Acts," *SBL Seminar Papers
1980*, ed. P.J. Achtemeier (Chico, CA: Scholars Press, 1980), pp. 251-265.

[27]See Haenchen, pp. 611-612.

[28]The meaning of the decrees is discussed completely in the comments on
15:19-20. For a summary of the decrees see Hurd, *Origin*, pp. 246-253.

2. The Riot in the Temple (21:27-30)

²⁷When the seven days were nearly over, some Jews from the province of Asia saw Paul at the temple. They stirred up the whole crowd and seized him, ²⁸shouting, "Men of Israel, help us! This is the man who teaches all men everywhere against our people and our law and this place. And besides, he has brought Greeks into the temple area and defiled this holy place." ²⁹(They had previously seen Trophimus the Ephesian in the city with Paul and assumed that Paul had brought him into the temple area.) ³⁰The whole city was aroused, and the people came running from all directions. Seizing Paul, they dragged him from the temple, and immediately the gates were shut.

The "seven days" for the purification were "nearly over" when Paul's troubles began. Paul's purification required a cleansing on the third and the seventh days of this period (Num 19:2), and his presence in the temple at this point was for the purpose of finishing his obligations with regard to the ceremony.

At this point "some Jews from the province of Asia" saw him at the temple. They recognized him because he had ministered in Asia for three years, some of it in the Jewish synagogue in Ephesus (see 19:8). Perhaps it was these same Jews who had stirred up trouble for him then (see 19:9; 20:19). They now saw another opportunity—one that was even better than any they had seen in Ephesus. Angry charges were shouted against Paul. They shouted out their accusations that Paul was teaching people wherever he went a doctrine that was opposed to the Jewish people, the Jewish law, and the Jewish temple ("this place"). To cap it off, they bellowed out the charge that Paul had "brought Greeks into the temple area" and "defiled it."

This last accusation was enough all by itself to start a riot in the temple. Luke notes in his parenthetical remark that the reason for their accusation about bringing Greeks into the temple was that they had previously seen Trophimus of Ephesus in the city (not the temple) with Paul and they assumed the Gentile had also gone into the temple court with Paul. They recognized Trophimus (see 20:4) as a Gentile because he was from their homeland and had probably worked with Paul before. Bringing a Gentile into the temple precinct was strictly forbidden.

The temple consisted not only of the sanctuary itself, but also of a series of courtyards spreading out around the sanctuary, each one more restrictive the nearer they were to the temple. The courtyard farthest out was the court of the Gentiles, into which anyone could enter. When worshipers passed through the gate to the next courtyard, Gentiles would have to stop, while all Jews could proceed into the court of the women. At the next gate Jewish women would have to stop while only the Jewish men proceeded into the next courtyard, the court of Israel. Finally the courtyard immediately next to the temple was reserved for members of the Israelite priesthood.

At the gate which led from the court of the Gentiles to the court of the women was located a stone wall[29] to prevent Gentiles from entering. On the wall was posted a sign which read: "No Gentile to defile our temple on pain of death." Two of these signs have been discovered by archaeologists.[30]

For Paul to have brought Trophimus, a Gentile, into the court of Israel when he went to accomplish his purification would have been disastrous. The charges of the Asian Jews were ridiculous. Why would Paul risk violating the customs of the temple on the very day that he was participating in a ceremony to show his respect for Jewish religious customs?

Nevertheless, the accusations so enraged the crowd at the temple that they seized Paul and "dragged him from the temple." News of the uproar drew people from all over the city. To the temple guards the scene looked like a full-scale riot. Their reaction was to protect the temple. As the violence escalated in the court of the Gentiles, the guards slammed shut the temple gates.

Thus the last words in Acts about the temple have the gates slamming shut on the apostle and his message of salvation for the Gentiles. It may be that Luke intends to let this event express the reality that from here on God's message was shut out of the temple

---

[29]Paul alludes to this "dividing wall" in Eph 2:14.

[30]The first to be found was in 1871 by C. Clermont-Ganneau, a piece that can be viewed today in the Museum of Ancient Orient in Istanbul. The second was found in 1935 and is displayed at the Palestine Archaeological Museum. See Barrett, *Background*, p. 50.

operation and the institution was ripe for God's judgment predicted by Jesus more than twenty-seven years before.

3. Paul's Rescue by the Romans (21:31-36)

[31]**While they were trying to kill him, news reached the commander of the Roman troops that the whole city of Jerusalem was in an uproar.** [32]**He at once took some officers and soldiers and ran down to the crowd. When the rioters saw the commander and his soldiers, they stopped beating Paul.** [33]**The commander came up and arrested him and ordered him to be bound with two chains. Then he asked who he was and what he had done.** [34]**Some in the crowd shouted one thing and some another, and since the commander could not get at the truth because of the uproar, he ordered that Paul be taken into the barracks.** [35]**When Paul reached the steps, the violence of the mob was so great he had to be carried by the soldiers.** [36]**The crowd that followed kept shouting, "Away with him!"**

The frenzied crowd pounded Paul to the point it was clear they wanted him dead. News of the commotion soon came to the attention of the "commander (χιλίαρχος, *chiliarchos*) of the Roman troops." A *chiliarchos* (or tribune) served as commander over 1000 troops, 760 of whom were infantry and a cavalry of 240. They were garrisoned at the Fortress of Antonia on the northwest corner of the temple complex, a vantage point from which the Romans kept a close eye on any disturbances in the Jewish temple. Since the Fortress had several high towers (perhaps 100 feet high) and was connected to the temple area by only two flights of steps, Roman soldiers could be at the site of trouble quickly.

In this case the tribune was Claudius Lysias (see 23:26). Since the procurator had headquarters in Caesarea and made infrequent visits to Jerusalem, Claudius was responsible for the peacefulness of the city. He summoned "some officers" (ἑκατοντάρχης, *hekatontarchēs*), or "centurions," as well as some soldiers and hurried down to the crowd. The fact that he called on more than one centurion means that the number of soldiers was at least 200, a force that immediately caught the attention of the rioters and they "stopped beating Paul."

Assuming that Paul was the perpetrator of the turmoil, the tribune arrested Paul and had him "bound with two chains," which indicates that he had one on each hand and then connected to a soldier on either side. Seeking to get information about Paul proved to be hopeless. The tribune could find out nothing by listening to the confusion of the rioters, since some shouted one thing and some another. Thus he decided to remove Paul to the barracks, but to separate Paul from the crowd it was necessary that he be "carried by the soldiers." Meanwhile the crowd was shouting, "Away with him!" These were the words that Jesus had listened to on this very spot more than twenty-seven years before (see Luke 23:18; John 19:15).

4. Paul's Request for Permission to Address the Mob (21:37-40)

[37]As the soldiers were about to take Paul into the barracks, he asked the commander, "May I say something to you?" "Do you speak Greek?" he replied. [38]"Aren't you the Egyptian who started a revolt and led four thousand terrorists out into the desert some time ago?" [39]Paul answered, "I am a Jew, from Tarsus in Cilicia, a citizen of no ordinary city. Please let me speak to the people." [40]Having received the commander's permission, Paul stood on the steps and motioned to the crowd. When they were all silent, he said to them in Aramaic[a]:

[a]40 Or possibly *Hebrew*; also in 22:2

Though torn and tattered, Paul was more interested in addressing the crowd than in being carried safely away from it. His request to the tribune was in a polite, polished Greek: "May I say (εἰ ἔξεστίν μοι, *ei exestin moi*) something to you?" Surprised that Paul would know how to speak Greek rather than Aramaic (the preferred language of Palestinian Jews), he immediately wanted to know if Paul was "the Egyptian who started a revolt."

His reference was to an incident also reported by Josephus. Three years earlier an Egyptian had arrived in Jerusalem promising the Jews that the walls of Jerusalem would tumble down if they joined him on the Mount of Olives. He then claimed that God would lead the Jews to victory over the Romans. Josephus says that 30,000 people followed him. Felix the procurator put an end to the adventure, however, sending troops who killed 400 of the rebels, took another 200 prisoners, and the rest fled. The Egyptian managed to disappear.[31]

Perhaps the commander suspected that Paul was the Egyptian who had returned to the temple and was recognized by Jews eager to get even with him. Paul may have surprised him when he replied that he was a Jew "from Tarsus in Cilicia,[32] a citizen of no ordinary city." Paul's comment here spoke of his citizenship in his hometown, not of his Roman citizenship.

Standing on the steps above the crowd, Paul received permission to speak. With a gesture of his hand the crowd quieted, and Paul addressed the crowd in Aramaic. Not only would Aramaic capture the interest of a Palestinian Jewish audience, it would also be appropriate for Jews outside of Palestine. It was the common language of all non-Greek speakers as far west as Western Asia and as far east as the Parthian Empire.

---

[31]Polhill attributes the discrepancy between Luke's 4,000 rebels and the 30,000 found in Josephus as an example of the tendency to exaggerate numbers which is seen in Josephus (p. 455). For a discussion of the chronology of this historical reference see Jewett, *Chronology*, p. 40.

[32]See comments below on 22:3.

ACTS 22

5. Paul's Defense to the Jews (22:1-21)

Paul's Early Days (22:1-5)

[1]"Brothers and fathers, listen now to my defense." [2]When they heard him speak to them in Aramaic, they became very quiet. Then Paul said: [3]"I am a Jew, born in Tarsus of Cilicia, but brought up in this city. Under Gamaliel I was thoroughly trained in the law of our fathers and was just as zealous for God as any of you are today. [4]I persecuted the followers of this Way to their death, arresting both men and women and throwing them into prison, [5]as also the high priest and all the Council can testify. I even obtained letters from them to their brothers in Damascus, and went there to bring these people as prisoners to Jerusalem to be punished.

Paul's address to the Jewish crowd did not, as might be expected, take the form of a defense of himself.[1] He did not refer to the charges made against him by the Asian Jews (see 21:28). Instead,

---

[1]Fred Veltman examines the defense speeches of Paul through the rest of Acts, especially as they compare to defense speeches in ancient literature from such writers as Thucydides, Livy, Rufus, Tacitus, and Josephus. He notes a common structure for these speeches and applies the model to the speeches of Paul in Acts 22–28. See his "The Defense Speeches of Paul in Acts," in *Perspectives on Luke-Acts*, ed. Charles Talbert (Edinburgh: T & T Clark, 1978), pp. 243-256. Trites discusses the legal terminology found in this section of Acts (especially in cases where speeches are presented). He thinks that Luke is motivated by the desire "to show that Christianity cannot be construed as a *religio illicita*" (illegal religion), and that the "claims of Christ are being debated" in the issues surrounding Paul's custody hearings. See his "The Importance of Legal Scenes and Language in the Book of Acts," *NovT* 16 (1974): 278-284.

Paul directed his remarks toward the larger issue of his relationship to Judaism. He demonstrated that he had been raised in orthodox Judaism and that his conversion came only as the result of an experience beyond his control and given by God. In reviewing this experience, the events on the Damascus Road are related for the second time in Acts (see also 9:1-22; 26:9-18).

Paul began his address with a formal introduction similar to the one Stephen used before the Sanhedrin (see 7:2). With his mention of "brothers and fathers" he used an introduction which would show respect toward any elders or temple authorities in the crowd. His request was that they hear his "defense" (ἀπολογία, apologia).

His use of Aramaic caught the attention of his audience because of its importance for Palestinian Judaism. Even Paul's language showed he was an orthodox Jew. They quieted in order to listen.

Paul's first point was his Jewish roots. He explained his birth, his upbringing, and his education,[2] and all of it in terms of his Judaism. He was born in Tarsus, but brought up in Jerusalem, and thus should not be characterized as some rebel from the Diaspora. The influence of Tarsus on his life was negligible. Not only his education, but also his rearing was in Jerusalem.

Tarsus was located in Cilicia, some ten miles from the coast on the Cyndus River. Thirty miles north stood the Taurus Mountains with its series of deep, narrow gorges called the Cilician Gates which permitted travelers access to the west. Tarsus had become an important educational and commercial center.

In addition to his birth and rearing, Paul said that he was educated "under Gamaliel," perhaps the most respected rabbi of the first century.[3] Modern scholars have established the link between Paul's letters and rabbinic patterns of thought.[4] Paul

---

[2]This triad, "born, reared, educated," was a set formula in ancient literature. See W.C. Van Unnik, "Tarsus or Jerusalem: The City of Paul's Youth," trans. G. Ogg, *Sparsa Collecta*, Part 1 (Leiden: E.J. Brill, 1973), pp. 259-320.

[3]See comments on Gamaliel at 5:34. For a summary of scholarly objections regarding Paul's claim to an education in Jerusalem under Gamaliel see Richard Longenecker, *Paul, Apostle of Liberty* (Grand Rapids: Baker, 1977), pp. 23-25; Seyoon Kim, *The Origin of Paul's Gospel* (Tübingen: J.C.B. Mohr, 1981), pp. 32-37.

[4]See, for example, W.D. Davies, *Paul and Rabbinic Judaism* (London: SPCK, 1958).

mentions the fact here in order to demonstrate how orthodox was his training in the Old Testament faith ("the law of our fathers").

Paul even described his zealous spirit in terms of the audience before him. He had been as "zealous for God" as any in the crowd who had attacked him in the temple, going so far as to attack Christians wherever he could find them (see 8:3; 9:1-4; 26:9-11; 1 Cor 15:9; 1 Tim 1:13). He referred to these Christians as "the Way," a descriptive term also used when Paul set out for Damascus (see 9:2).

Paul observed at this point in his address that "the high priest and all the Council" (Sanhedrin) had direct information on these matters, since at the time he had worked closely with them in this effort against the Christians. In addition some members of the Sanhedrin at the time Paul set out for Damascus were perhaps still active members, though by this time the high priesthood had changed hands. Caiaphas was dead by this time, but the new high priest, Ananias, would have records to corroborate Paul's account.

The Episode on the Damascus Road (22:6-11)

6"About noon as I came near Damascus, suddenly a bright light from heaven flashed around me. 7I fell to the ground and heard a voice say to me, 'Saul! Saul! Why do you persecute me?' 8"Who are you, Lord?' I asked. 'I am Jesus of Nazareth, whom you are persecuting,' he replied. 9My companions saw the light, but they did not understand the voice of him who was speaking to me. 10"What shall I do, Lord?' I asked. 'Get up,' the Lord said, 'and go into Damascus. There you will be told all that you have been assigned to do.' 11My companions led me by the hand into Damascus, because the brilliance of the light had blinded me.

Paul's description of the event on the road to Damascus differs only slightly from the previous account of the incident in 9:1-22.[5] Here, unlike in 9:1-22, Paul specified that the hour in which the event occurred was "about noon." The reason for this may have

---

[5]For a detailed comparison of the three accounts in Acts and the one in Galatians see Munck, *Paul*, pp. 13-35.

been to emphasize how bright the light was, even in comparison to the sun at its highest point. Indeed, Paul's account of his experience on the Damascus road places heavy emphasis on the light which "flashed around" (περιαστράπτω, *periastraptō*) him, which his companions saw (22:9), and which blinded Paul (22:11).

Also in this passage Paul quotes Jesus who identifies himself as "Jesus of Nazareth," unlike 9:1-22 and 26:9-18. This addition was also appropriate before Paul's Jewish audience.

Perhaps the biggest difference between the accounts is the detail in 22:9. Paul said his companions saw the light, but did not understand the voice. In 9:7 his companions had heard the sound, but not seen anything. This is hardly a contradiction. Quite possibly Paul intended here to imply that some sound was heard, but it was impossible for the companions to perceive what the voice said. At any rate, Polhill's observation is appropriate here. Paul intended to make it clear that the experience was his alone, and his companions stood very much on the outside of it. They saw light, but did not see Jesus the Lord; they heard a sound, but did not understand his words. His companions were thus corroborating witnesses, but the experience belonged to Paul.[6]

The Visit from Ananias of Damascus (22:12-16)

[12]"A man named Ananias came to see me. He was a devout observer of the law and highly respected by all the Jews living there. [13]He stood beside me and said, 'Brother Saul, receive your sight!' And at that very moment I was able to see him. [14]"Then he said: 'The God of our fathers has chosen you to know his will and to see the Righteous One and to hear words from his mouth. [15]You will be his witness to all men of what you have seen and heard. [16]And now what are you waiting for? Get up, be baptized and wash your sins away, calling on his name.'

Paul next related his journey into Damascus in a blinded condition and the visit from Ananias. Again the details are paralleled in 9:1-22 with no contradictions whatsoever.

---

[6]Polhill, pp. 459-460.

Paul did, however, shift the emphasis a bit with regard to Ananias. In 9:10 Ananias was described as "a disciple," with no mention of his Jewish heritage. With the temple crowd in front of him now, Paul characterized Ananias as "a devout observer of the law and highly respected by all the Jews living there." This additional information about Ananias served to highlight Paul's association with orthodox Judaism, as well as to point out the close connection between Christians and Jews. How could such a respected Jew as Ananias come to accept Jesus as Messiah and be sent to baptize another Jew into Christ? The next time in Acts when Paul will review this event (26:9-18) he will not even mention Ananias. Lacking from Paul's review of the event here is any of the conversation between the Lord and Ananias recorded in 9:10-16. This information was simply not important to Paul's objectives.

Paul's account of his baptism contains words not mentioned in the earlier account. His reference to the Lord as "the God of our fathers" and his allusion to Jesus as "the Righteous One" are not found in 9:1-22, but contribute a strongly Jewish flavor to the words of Ananias. Also important are the words "wash your sins away, calling on his name." These words communicate a strong sense of personal sin and the need for cleansing from the Lord.

Paul's words also point out his clear sense of the connection between baptism and the forgiveness of sins.[7] As has already been shown in Acts (see 2:38), the apostles found nothing contradictory about preaching salvation by faith and at the same time the necessity of baptism for the forgiveness of sins. They did not advocate a "baptismal regeneration" which eliminated faith from the moment of forgiveness, but neither did they shrink from making baptism a part of the expression of this faith. Thus the New Testament as a whole maintains a consistent role for baptism in the forgiveness of sins and the uniting with Christ at conversion (see Titus 3:5; 1 Pet 3:21; Gal 3:27; Rom 6:4).[8]

---

[7]The fact that Ananias calls Paul "brother" does not imply a forgiven state (see comments on 9:17).

[8]As Dunn correctly observes, "Paul's conversion was only completed when he called on Jesus as Lord, was filled with the Spirit and had his sins washed away; then, and only then, can he be called a Christian." See his *Baptism*, p. 78; also pp. 96-98. As in 2:38 the strong connection between baptism and

The Vision in the Temple (22:17-21)

[17]"When I returned to Jerusalem and was praying at the temple, I fell into a trance [18]and saw the Lord speaking. 'Quick!' he said to me. 'Leave Jerusalem immediately, because they will not accept your testimony about me.' [19]"'Lord,' I replied, 'these men know that I went from one synagogue to another to imprison and beat those who believe in you. [20]And when the blood of your martyr[a] Stephen was shed, I stood there giving my approval and guarding the clothes of those who were killing him.' [21]"Then the Lord said to me, 'Go; I will send you far away to the Gentiles.'"

[a]20 Or *witness*

Paul then recalled an experience which we read about for the first time in Acts. In 9:26-30 Luke reported Paul's visit to Jerusalem after his conversion. Apparently during this visit Paul was at the temple praying when he "fell into a trance" (ἔκστασις, *ekstasis*). Acts has already given the example of Peter's falling into a trance with respect to the conversion of Cornelius (10:10; 11:5).

Paul's vision at the temple recalls that of Isaiah when he was commissioned by the Lord to remain in Jerusalem despite the opposition and deliver the word of the Lord (Isa 6:1-13). In Paul's case, however, the Lord warned Paul that the resistance was coming and he should leave Jerusalem. By telling them about his vision in the temple, Paul was showing the crowd that his visits to the temple were prayerful and respectful, not for defiling the temple, as his critics charged.

When Paul protested[9] to the Lord in his vision that the Jews should be ready to hear one who had been so zealous in persecuting Christians, he gave details of his efforts. These details are valuable to the modern reader who wonders about the details of Paul's activities in opposing the church (see 7:58; 8:1,3; 9:1-3). Here he listed such things as imprisonment, beatings (δέρων, *derōn*), and even giving approval in the stoning of Stephen.[10]

forgiveness of sins is made again here. See Jack Cottrell, *Baptism: a Biblical Study* (Joplin, MO: College Press, 1989), pp. 67-77.

[9]Paul's zeal in evangelizing the Jews is evident in Rom 10:1.

[10]This item does not necessarily mean that Paul was a member of the Sanhedrin. See *NIV Study Bible*, notes on 22:20 and 26:10.

At this point Paul's words were taking him on a track completely at odds with his listeners. He had demonstrated his orthodoxy as a Jew, even in the persecution of Christians. By mentioning that Stephen was a martyr for the Lord ("your martyr"), he was parting company with his audience. Stephen's sentence had been passed by the Sanhedrin with plenty of sympathy from the Jewish populace (see 6:9-15).

The turning point in his argument was approaching. Paul's point in all of this was to argue that it could only have been an act of God which turned his course so completely around. For this reason he recalled that the Lord responded to his protest by telling him his mission would be among the Gentiles. At this point, he lost the crowd completely, and their respectful silence turned to an ugly frenzy.

6. The Reaction of the Mob and Paul's Imprisonment (22:22-29)

[22]The crowd listened to Paul until he said this. Then they raised their voices and shouted, "Rid the earth of him! He's not fit to live!" [23]As they were shouting and throwing off their cloaks and flinging dust into the air, [24]the commander ordered Paul to be taken into the barracks. He directed that he be flogged and questioned in order to find out why the people were shouting at him like this. [25]As they stretched him out to flog him, Paul said to the centurion standing there, "Is it legal for you to flog a Roman citizen who hasn't even been found guilty?" [26]When the centurion heard this, he went to the commander and reported it. "What are you going to do?" he asked. "This man is a Roman citizen." [27]The commander went to Paul and asked, "Tell me, are you a Roman citizen?" "Yes, I am," he answered. [28]Then the commander said, "I had to pay a big price for my citizenship." "But I was born a citizen," Paul replied. [29]Those who were about to question him withdrew immediately. The commander himself was alarmed when he realized that he had put Paul, a Roman citizen, in chains.

At Paul's mention of Gentiles the crowd burst forth with rage. Their cries filled the air. They wanted him dead. To demonstrate their hostility they were "throwing off their cloaks," a gesture that could mean several things. Polhill lists four possible ways to understand this action. It could be that they were tearing their clothes in horror (see 14:14) or that they were removing their clothes as if to cast stones at Paul (see 7:58). Other possibilities are that they were removing their clothes to shake them as if ridding themselves of the contamination represented by Paul. Finally, it may be that they took off outer garments to twirl in the air as a sign of outrage.[11]

The same problem arises with the other gesture of "flinging dust into the air." Does this mean that they were throwing dust upward into the air as a sign of their anger or were they throwing dust at Paul?[12]

The commander knew nothing more about the charges against Paul than he did when the riot first erupted. Paul's address, spoken in Aramaic, had not given him the information he needed. His next step was to use the method of questioning his prisoner under torture. He thus ordered that Paul "be flogged," a cruel beating with a whip (μάστιξ, *mastix*) that was made of leather thongs weighted on the ends with bits of bone and metal. Since the flogging was applied to the bare back of the victim, the physical damage done was enormous, often resulting in lifelong injury or even death. Paul's previous beatings with the rod (16:22-24) or with the lash of the Jews (2 Cor 11:24) were mild compared to what this one would have been.

While they were stretching him out (προτείνω, *proteinō*), an action which left the victim of flogging with hands bound around a post, perhaps even suspended slightly in the air, Paul spoke up in his own defense. Directing his question to the centurion who had been appointed by the commander over the flogging, Paul asked about the legality of beating a Roman citizen. The question was certainly relevant. A wealth of information indicates that Roman citizens had legal rights which prevented them from such punishment.[13]

When the centurion reported Paul's question to the tribune, the

---

[11]Polhill, p. 464.

[12]Bruce quotes (incorrectly) a caustic remark of Lake and Cadbury: "In England mud is more frequently available" (p. 420).

[13]The Valerian and Porcian Laws exempted a citizen from cruel forms of punishment, and especially from interrogation by torture, unless they were

tribune himself came to see Paul, still bound at the post. After asking directly if Paul was a Roman citizen and hearing Paul's confirmation, the tribune commented sarcastically, "I had to pay a big price for my citizenship." The intent of his comment was probably that if this tattered and undignified looking man had obtained citizenship, the privilege was becoming too easy in comparison to his own investment.

Roman citizenship was a rare privilege. The tribune's remark about what it cost him probably indicates that he had paid off as many officials as necessary to get his name placed high on the list when the candidates for citizenship were considered.[14] He was shocked when Paul replied, "I was born a citizen."

Speculation abounds about how Paul became a Roman citizen. The fact that he was born a Roman citizen means that his father or grandfather before him was a Roman citizen. Often citizenship was awarded because of some notable deed performed for the state. Also slaves received citizenship when freed by their citizen-owners. Besides this, residents of cities were sometimes declared citizens if the city was made a Roman colony.[15]

Because nothing is known of Paul's family, his road to citizenship is unclear. It is also unclear how Paul would have proved his claim to Roman citizenship.[16]

7. The Trial before the Sanhedrin (22:30-23:10)

The Confrontation with the High Priest (22:30-23:5)

[30]The next day, since the commander wanted to find out exactly why Paul was being accused by the Jews, he released him

convicted of some crime. See Bruce, p. 421; Sherwin-White, *Roman Society and Roman Law*, pp. 72-76.

[14]As Bruce points out, this opportunity was especially available during the reign of Claudius due to political considerations with regard to his wife Messalina. See Bruce, p. 421. Also see Sherwin-White, *Roman Society and Roman Law*, pp. 154-155.

[15]Bruce suggests that Paul's father may have performed some valuable service to either Pompey in 66-64 B.C. or Marc Antony (pp. 421-422).

[16]See comments on 16:38.

and ordered the chief priests and all the Sanhedrin to assemble. Then he brought Paul and had him stand before them.

So Paul spent the night in prison at the Fortress of Antonia. The next day the commander summoned together the Sanhedrin. As commander he apparently had the authority to call such a session, since his responsibilities included the application of Roman authority in the absence of the procurator, who was in Caesarea.[17] Present to provide information against Paul were "the chief priests and all the Sanhedrin." This body consisted of all those in the family of priests, including a large number of Sadducees and some Pharisees.

Paul was unchained for this session and now may well have been at the point of being released, depending on the outcome of the session with the Sanhedrin. The commander hoped to get information which would bring the matter to a close.

---

[17]Bruce, p. 423. Polhill takes the position that the commander had no such authority but summoned the Sanhedrin for an informal session (p. 467).

ACTS 23

7. The Trial before the Sanhedrin (22:30–23:10) (continued)

The Confrontation with the High Priest (23:1-5) (continued)

¹Paul looked straight at the Sanhedrin and said, "My brothers, I have fulfilled my duty to God in all good conscience to this day." ²At this the high priest Ananias ordered those standing near Paul to strike him on the mouth. ³Then Paul said to him, "God will strike you, you whitewashed wall! You sit there to judge me according to the law, yet you yourself violate the law by commanding that I be struck!" ⁴Those who were standing near Paul said, "You dare to insult God's high priest?" ⁵Paul replied, "Brothers, I did not realize that he was the high priest; for it is written: 'Do not speak evil about the ruler of your people.'ᵃ"

ᵃ5 Exodus 22:28

In an attempt to get the accurate information on the charges against Paul, the tribune, Claudius Lysias, brought him before the Sanhedrin. Paul seemed undaunted as he "looked straight at the Sanhedrin" and began his address.

His words also were confident. He said that he had fulfilled his "duty to God in all good conscience." Paul's word for the phrase "fulfilled my duty" was πεπολίτευμαι (*pepoliteumai*), a word which underscored his desire to "live as a good citizen." Appropriately enough, the issue of Paul's citizenship is a prominent theme in these last chapters of Acts (see 21:39; 22:28).

Some scholars have focused on this matter of Paul's conscience. It is probably true that the modern reader should not attach to the word "conscience" here the sense of a "moral faculty which is a guide for conduct." For Paul the thought is that his "conscious

record of his past acts" was that he had faithfully served the Lord.[1]
Nevertheless, Paul's memory of his past surprises those who remember his persecution of the church (see 7:58; 8:1,3; 9:1-2). How could he say that he served God "in all good conscience?"[2] In this context Paul was emphasizing his Jewish heritage (see 23:6). His service had been zealously rendered to God even when he persecuted the Christians.[3] Now he was still zealously serving God, though he had left behind his rage against Christians. In this way he could say that before the law he stood blameless (Phil 3:6).

Ananias became high priest in A.D. 47 and held the office for eleven or twelve years. His reputation for corruption is reported by Josephus,[4] a description which makes his careless disregard of the law in Paul's case very credible. When Ananias heard Paul's declaration of innocence, he ordered that Paul be struck on the mouth. Paul saw this move as so hypocritical that he could not remain silent. As a judge, Ananias was charged with maintaining fair treatment of those who were being heard. Now he himself was breaking the law by calling for the punishment of a defendant who had not been convicted of any offense. This was surely a violation of Jewish law.[5] Jesus had suffered the same injustice when he stood trial before the same body in Jerusalem (see John 18:22).

For this reason Paul spoke sharply to the high priest, calling him a "whitewashed wall." The metaphor speaks of a wall that has its

[1]Lake and Cadbury, p. 286.
[2]For the classic discussion on the conscience of Paul see Stendahl, "Paul and the Introspective Conscience," in *Paul among Jews and Gentiles*, pp. 78-96.
[3]This point is also made in 1 Tim 1:12-16 where Paul's committing of this violence against the Christians was done "in ignorance and unbelief."
[4]Ananias was the son of Nedebaeus and was appointed high priest by Herod of Chalcis (younger brother of Herod Agrippa I). He was guilty of such crimes as bribery and stealing tithes intended for the common priests (Josephus, *Antiquities* 20.103). Five years earlier he had to answer to Rome for his involvement in an ambush of some Samaritan pilgrims, but was cleared of the crime and restored to his position by Claudius. His wealth and power were often used to commit violence and assassination (*Antiquities* 20.131). For a discussion of the chronology of the office of Ananias see Jewett, *Chronology*, p. 44.
[5]Many commentators point to Leviticus 19:15 as Paul's reference here.

ugliness covered by whitewash so as to appear acceptable on the exterior. The word for "whitewash" (κονιάω, *koniaō*) is the same word used by Jesus when he spoke of Pharisees who were white-washed tombs (Matt 23:27). What Jesus had in mind was the Jewish practice of painting tombs white so that law-keeping Jews would not accidentally touch one and become ritually unclean. Paul was like-wise accusing Ananias of hypocrisy. Paul's prediction that God would strike Ananias may have found its fulfillment less than ten years later. When the Jewish revolt of A.D. 66 began, Ananias was dragged from an aqueduct where he was hiding and was murdered along with his brother Hezekiah.

When Paul uttered these words the officers of the Sanhedrin were shocked. They could not believe that he dared "to insult God's high priest." Paul's response is somewhat puzzling. How could Paul not know that Ananias was the high priest? Even if Paul were personally unfamiliar with him, the high priest could always be distinguished during hearings such as this by his white robes and prominent seat. In addition, no evidence exists to suggest that Paul was unable to see clearly who gave the command to strike him. Perhaps the best way to understand Paul's comment is to suggest that he spoke the words with some irony; as if to say that the behav-ior of Ananias made it difficult to recognize him as the high priest. After all, high priests were to be leaders who honored the laws they were charged with enforcing.[6]

The Division of the Pharisees and the Sadducees over the Resurrection Hope (23:6-10)

⁶Then Paul, knowing that some of them were Sadducees and the others Pharisees, called out in the Sanhedrin, "My brothers, I am a Pharisee, the son of a Pharisee. I stand on trial because of

---

[6]It has also been suggested that Paul's words could be understood to say, "I spoke without taking note of the fact that he is high priest." This inter-pretation would have Paul admitting that he had spoken words without thinking to whom he was addressing them. See Frank Stagg, *The Book of Acts: The Early Struggle for an Unhindered Gospel* (Nashville: Broadman, 1955), p. 232.

my hope in the resurrection of the dead." ⁷When he said this, a
dispute broke out between the Pharisees and the Sadducees, and
the assembly was divided. ⁸(The Sadducees say that there is no
resurrection, and that there are neither angels nor spirits, but the
Pharisees acknowledge them all.) ⁹There was a great uproar, and
some of the teachers of the law who were Pharisees stood up and
argued vigorously. "We find nothing wrong with this man," they
said. "What if a spirit or an angel has spoken to him?" ¹⁰The
dispute became so violent that the commander was afraid Paul
would be torn to pieces by them. He ordered the troops to go
down and take him away from them by force and bring him into
the barracks.

Having been interrupted when he began his defense, Paul now
continued by declaring his connection with Pharisaism. Far from
being dishonest in this situation, Paul merely accented a point in his
favor which he had emphasized many times before. He had called
himself a Pharisee even during his missionary travels (see Phil 3:5).
Especially when he stood before Jewish audiences he forcefully
insisted that his background and training was Pharisaic (see 22:3-5).
It was not unnatural for him to highlight this point before the
Sanhedrin.

Knowing that the Sanhedrin consisted of both Pharisees and
Sadducees, Paul raised a point which between them was controversial. Most of the time the Sanhedrin was composed of a large majority of Sadducees with a minority of Pharisees. As a Pharisee, Paul
held to the doctrine of the general resurrection at the end of time, a
belief that was not uncommon among Jews (see John 5:28-29; 11:24;
Dan 12:2). Paul himself insists on the importance of the concept of
resurrection in 1 Corinthians 15.

The Sadducees, on the other hand, rejected the notion of the
resurrection. Thus Paul summed up his ministry not only by calling
himself "a Pharisee, the son of a Pharisee," but also noting that he was
standing trial because of his "hope in the resurrection of the dead."⁷

---

⁷Robert Kepple discusses this point of Paul's message and its relation to
the theme of "the hope of Israel" (see 24:20-21; 26:6-8) as an issue of
contention in the trials of Paul through the rest of Acts. See his "The Hope

Again, Paul's contention was not fabricated. His proclamation of Jesus as the resurrected Christ was a major source of resistance against him (see 13:26-47).[8] The matter of Jesus as the Messiah raised from the dead stood very much in the way of Paul's acceptance by both the Pharisees and Sadducees. Of the two Jewish sects, however, the Pharisees had more sympathy with the gospel of the resurrected Jesus. Since they believed in the concept of the resurrection, they were just one step away from Paul. If only they could accept the fact that Jesus was raised from the dead, Paul would be able to feel a close kinship with them.

For the Sadducees, however, the story was different. The dispute that resulted from Paul's statement demonstrated how far apart the two groups were on the matter of the resurrection. Luke offers a parenthetical explanation for his non-Jewish readers who might not understand the difference between these Jewish sects. The Sadducees were characterized by denying that there is a resurrection "and that there are neither angels nor spirits." Though plenty of testimony can be found regarding the rejection of the resurrection by the Sadducees, no other verse or extra-biblical reference mentions their rejection of angels or spirits. What makes their denial of angels especially surprising is that the Sadducees were staunch believers in the Pentateuch, a part of the Old Testament which features angels in several passages (see Gen 18-19; 28:10-15; 32:22-30).

For this reason it is probably better to understand Luke's comment to mean that the Sadducees rejected "the belief in a spirit world of angels and demons" which included a hierarchy of spirit beings.[9] One other possibility is that they rejected the concept of an afterlife which involved an angelic or spiritual state of being.[10] Both of these concepts were part of Pharisaism (see Matt 22:30).

At any rate, the discussion now focused on the theological

---

of Israel, The Resurrection of the Dead, and Jesus: A Study of Their Relationship in Acts with Particular Regard to the Understanding of Paul's Trial Defense," *JETS* 20 (1977): 231-241.

[8]See Trites, "Legal Scenes," 280; note on 22:1.

[9]Bruce, p. 429, n. 22. T.W. Manson, *The Servant-Messiah* (Cambridge: Cambridge University Press, 1953), p. 17, n. 3. Bernard Bamberger understands the reference to mean that the Sadducees denied the possibility of

distinctions between the Pharisees and Sadducees on the matter of the resurrection.[11] The controversy was so heated that the meeting degenerated into chaos. Some of the Pharisees even found reasons to support Paul. His contention that an angel had spoken to him did not seem so far-fetched to them. Lysias soon realized that Paul was becoming the object of the wrath of the largest share of the council and he had him pulled away to safety within the Fortress of Antonia.

8. The Word of Encouragement from God (23:11)

[11]The following night the Lord stood near Paul and said, "Take courage! As you have testified about me in Jerusalem, so you must also testify in Rome."

After two days of attacks on Paul, he may have felt very much alone. He had been beaten in the temple, shouted down by a mob, tied to a post for a Roman flogging, and rejected by the Sanhedrin. Had Paul been brought to Jerusalem to accomplish anything? Would he ever see some good come from his suffering?

At this moment in Paul's life the Lord moved to lift him up. "Take courage" were the words spoken by the Lord Jesus[12] as he revealed that Paul would indeed "testify in Rome." Paul's endurance would pay off. He would not die before the angry mobs in Jerusalem. He was going to Rome.

---

communications from spirits or angels (in connection with v. 9). See his "The Sadducees and the Belief in Angels," *JBL* 82 (1963): 433-435.

[10]Marshall, p. 365; Polhill, p. 470. David Daube thinks the verse speaks of the rejection by the Sadducees of an interim state in the resurrection which held that people become "quasi angels." See his "On Acts 23: Sadducees and Angels," *JBL* 109 (1990): 493-497. Also see Benedict Viviano and Justin Taylor, "Sadducees, Angels, and Resurrection (Acts 23:8-9)," *JBL* 111 (1992): 496-498.

[11]Rivkin takes this incident as a reflection of the ongoing controversy between the Pharisees and Sadducees over the doctrine of the resurrection. See his *Hidden Revolution*, pp. 95-98.

[12]The words "take courage" are spoken only by Jesus in the New Testament (see Matt 9:2,22; 14:27; Mark 6:50; 10:49; John 16:33; Acts 23:11).

9. The Conspiracy against Paul's Life (23:12-15)

[12]The next morning the Jews formed a conspiracy and bound themselves with an oath not to eat or drink until they had killed Paul. [13]More than forty men were involved in this plot. [14]They went to the chief priests and elders and said, "We have taken a solemn oath not to eat anything until we have killed Paul. [15]Now then, you and the Sanhedrin petition the commander to bring him before you on the pretext of wanting more accurate information about his case. We are ready to kill him before he gets here."

Encouragement was just what Paul was going to need. Still another danger awaited. A conspiracy was agreed upon the next day by an impressive segment of the Jewish population. A group of forty men, especially if armed with small weapons, would represent a significant threat. When they obtained the cooperation of the "chief priests and elders" (all from the Sadducees), they placed themselves in a powerful position to accomplish their goal. Their determination was obvious in their vow "not to eat or drink until they had killed Paul."[13]

10. The Discovery of the Conspiracy (23:16-22)

[16]But when the son of Paul's sister heard of this plot, he went into the barracks and told Paul. [17]Then Paul called one of the centurions and said, "Take this young man to the commander; he has something to tell him." [18]So he took him to the commander. The centurion said, "Paul, the prisoner, sent for me and asked me to bring this young man to you because he has something to tell you." [19]The commander took the young man by the hand, drew him aside and asked, "What is it you want to tell me?" [20]He said: "The Jews have agreed to ask you to bring Paul before the Sanhedrin tomorrow on the pretext of wanting more accurate

---

[13]Commentators routinely observe that the means for escaping such a vow were provided in the Jewish laws (see for example Lake and Cadbury, p. 290; Bruce, p. 431).

information about him. [21]Don't give in to them, because more
than forty of them are waiting in ambush for him. They have
taken an oath not to eat or drink until they have killed him. They
are ready now, waiting for your consent to their request." [22]The
commander dismissed the young man and cautioned him, "Don't
tell anyone that you have reported this to me."

The plan was thwarted when the son of Paul's sister heard
rumors about the plot and went straight to the Fortress of Antonia
to reveal it. Nothing else is known regarding Paul's family, but his
sister's presence in Jerusalem with her son became Paul's salvation
now. His access to Paul is not surprising given the Roman customs
regarding prisoners of high rank (especially Roman citizens). Family
and friends could frequently visit. Paul's ability to receive attention
from a centurion also fits this model. The centurion took the
"young man" (νεανίας, neanias), who may have been as young as
twenty, to the tribune who listened seriously to the report. Luke
records the details of the plot again in this conversation between
Paul's nephew and the tribune. In doing so the drama of the situation rises to a peak. Will the tribune take action to avoid the trap?
The tribune dismissed the young man with the warning that he
should not reveal his visit to the Fortress.

11. The Decision to Transfer Paul to Caesarea (23:23-24)

[23]Then he called two of his centurions and ordered them, "Get
ready a detachment of two hundred soldiers, seventy horsemen
and two hundred spearmen[a] to go to Caesarea at nine tonight.
[24]Provide mounts for Paul so that he may be taken safely to
Governor Felix."

[a]23 The meaning of the Greek for this word is uncertain.

The tribune, Lysias, called two of his centurions to prepare a
detachment of soldiers to escort Paul away from the trouble. His
urgency was motivated by the fact that he did not want the assassination of a Roman citizen within his jurisdiction and he wanted
Paul safely out of reach of the danger. Besides this, the tribune

would have eventually transferred Paul to Caesarea anyway, since the Jews were accusing Paul of a capital offense.

Paul's protection required a total of 470 men—200 soldiers, seventy cavalry, and 200 "spearmen" (δεξιολάβους, *dexiolabous*).[14] Though Haenchen scoffs at so large a number of soldiers to protect one prisoner,[15] it should be remembered that the tribune had no way of knowing how large the rebel plot might be (perhaps beyond the forty men reported by Paul's nephew) against Paul. The detachment of such a large force would still leave 500 troops in Jerusalem, since the Fortress of Antonia held an auxiliary cohort of 1,000 men.

Given the urgency of the situation, the tribune ordered the force to leave immediately, even though it was long past nightfall. Paul was provided with "mounts" (κτήνη, *ktēnē*) which included horses or mules. The march would be a difficult one.

12. The Letter from the Tribune to Felix (23:25-30)

[25]He wrote a letter as follows: [26]Claudius Lysias, To His Excellency, Governor Felix: Greetings. [27]This man was seized by the Jews and they were about to kill him, but I came with my troops and rescued him, for I had learned that he is a Roman citizen. [28]I wanted to know why they were accusing him, so I brought him to their Sanhedrin. [29]I found that the accusation had to do with questions about their law, but there was no charge against him that deserved death or imprisonment. [30]When I was informed of a plot to be carried out against the man, I sent him to you at once. I also ordered his accusers to present to you their case against him.

As he sent his forces on their way toward Caesarea, the tribune also ordered them to carry a letter addressed to the procurator in

---

[14]The meaning of this term is quite uncertain. It appears only here in the New Testament and then not again until literature which dates from the sixth century. The etymology of the term suggests soldiers carrying something in their right hand. For the suggestion that the δεξιολάβοι were members of a local militia and therefore not a drain on the forces in the cohort at the Fortress of Antonia see G.D. Kilpatrick, "Acts XXIII.23 *DEXIOLABOI*," *NTS* 14 (1963): 393-394.

[15]Haenchen, p. 650.

Caesarea. The letter is given here, the only time in the New Testament that a secular letter is recorded. The phrase "as follows" (ἔχουσαν τὸν τύπον τοῦτον, *echousan ton typon touton*) suggests that Luke's report of this letter reflects not only the actual content, but also the form of this official governmental communication.[16] How Luke gained access to official documents is unclear.

The terminology and form of the letter are quite true to available samples of such correspondence in the first century. The commander began by identifying himself as Claudius Lysias, then naming the recipient, and finally giving the usual greeting (χαίρειν, *chairein*).[17] The name Claudius Lysias implies that the commander was a Greek, since Lysias was the name he would have taken when he became a Roman citizen. The name Claudius suggests that he became a citizen during the reign of the emperor Claudius.[18]

He addressed the letter to Governor (ἡγεμόνι, *hēgemoni*) Felix, an appropriate title for the position of Felix as procurator. Added to this address was the title "Excellency," a description that communicated respect for the position.[19] All of these elements gave the letter the official tone considered necessary for such a communication.

Claudius Lysias now summarized the events surrounding Paul's situation. As true with any story where politics is involved, Lysias described the incident in the way which most flattered himself. He mentioned the trouble in the temple courts, but carefully worded his report to make it look as if he had found out about Paul's Roman citizenship before the mob scene ever took place. Thus he portrayed himself as the vigilant ruler always prepared to come to the defense of a Roman citizen. Of course, the reader of Acts knows better!

---

[16]Polhill, p. 474, n. 89.

[17]The use of χαίρειν as a greeting in a letter is rare in the New Testament (found only here and in Acts 15:23 and Jas 1:1). The usual Pauline greeting is χάρις (*charis*) ("grace"). See Barrett for sample letters from the papyri which employ this greeting for letters (*Background*, pp. 27-29).

[18]See Bruce, p. 434.

[19]The title was originally applied to individuals of the equestrian class, one of the highest social positions in the Roman world. Though Felix was not from this social class, he was addressed with this term because of his position as governor.

One thing which Lysias had discovered for certain was that Paul was innocent of any crime "that deserved death or imprisonment." The commander had gathered enough facts to know the charges were motivated by "questions about their law." This means that Lysias had eliminated at least one charge which could have been serious — that Paul had taken a Gentile into the temple (see 21:28), a crime punishable by death.

Lysias concluded his letter by observing that he had advised (or would by the time the letter arrived) the Jewish accusers that they would need to prepare a case against Paul. Felix would soon have the opportunity to hear this case.

F. THE IMPRISONMENT AT CAESAREA (23:31–26:32)

1. Paul's Transfer to Caesarea (23:31-35)

[31]So the soldiers, carrying out their orders, took Paul with them during the night and brought him as far as Antipatris. [32]The next day they let the cavalry go on with him, while they returned to the barracks. [33]When the cavalry arrived in Caesarea, they delivered the letter to the governor and handed Paul over to him. [34]The governor read the letter and asked what province he was from. Learning that he was from Cilicia, [35]he said, "I will hear your case when your accusers get here." Then he ordered that Paul be kept under guard in Herod's palace.

With the letter in hand and the prisoner on a pack animal, the troops began their journey toward Caesarea three hours after sunset. Normally this kind of travel would be out of the question. In this highly-charged atmosphere, a sense of urgency surrounded the mission. They marched to Antipatris, a military station which had been fortified by Herod the Great and named for his father Antipater. From Jerusalem the force would travel some thirty-five miles. Such a distance could not be covered in one day unless the troops moved in a forced march.

The issue of the distance covered in this march has raised

eyebrows among commentators.[20] Looming above the whole discussion is some uncertainty of the location of Antipatris, but few doubt that the distance could be less than thirty-five miles. Usually troops moved a maximum distance of twenty to twenty-five miles in a day.

Marshall suggests that the problem is solved if one assumes that the infantry marched out of Jerusalem only as far as was necessary for Paul's safety, and then turned back to Jerusalem. At that point the cavalry could move on toward Antipatris, a distance which could be covered by horses in a day.[21]

The problem with this suggestion (and Marshall is aware of it) is that the text states that they reached Antipatris before the infantry turned back. The only solution that can be offered is to say that the sense of urgency made this a forced march that lasted through the night, the morning hours, and well into the afternoon hours. The march was possible, but unusual, and implies that the tribune Lysias was quite concerned about this mission.[22] At that point the infantry turned back to Jerusalem, and the cavalry prepared to go on to Caesarea.

The prisoner was finally brought to Caesarea, some twenty-eight miles from Antipatris. Caesarea was the seat of Roman administration for Judea. The governor Felix resided there and before him Paul now was going to stand. As far as the reputation of Felix is concerned, nothing good may be said. His full name was Claudius Felix,[23] a freedman who owed his rise to power to his brother Pallas, whose position in the court of Claudius meant plenty of political power. For a former slave, Felix had reached a position unheard of.

---

[20]Haenchen (p. 650) exclaims, "many commentators consider this a realistic description!" He argues that Luke did not know the distance between Jerusalem and Antipatris, so he erred in assuming it could be covered in a day.

[21]Marshall, p. 372.

[22]The fact that the march was downhill from Jerusalem to Antipatris may also account for their ability to travel such a long distance. In addition, it should be remembered that they were traveling in the cool of the day and in the spring of the year.

[23]Some uncertainty exists regarding the full name of Felix. See Polhill, p. 476.

...

The comment of Tacitus was that Felix "held the power of a tyrant with the disposition of a slave."[24]

During his reign as procurator (A.D. 52-59) the Jewish state was becoming more and more dangerous. Nationalism was on the rise, and the cruel manner in which Felix handled the Jewish problems alienated some of the more moderate Jews.

In addition to these problems, Felix made a mockery of the institution of marriage, pursuing and marrying in succession three different wives of royal birth. The first of these was a granddaughter of Antony and Cleopatra. The third of his wives was Drusilla, the daughter of Herod Agrippa I (the Herod of Acts 12), and sister of Herod Agrippa II, who appears in an upcoming trial scene in Acts (see 24:24).[25]

When Felix read the letter he immediately wanted to know from what Roman province Paul came. If Felix found that Paul was from one of the client kingdoms in the region, he may have initiated contacts with the client king before proceeding. As it stood, Paul was from the Roman province Cilicia, which was connected to Syria, and thus Felix prepared to hear the case. The hearing would take place when the accusers arrived, and until then Paul would be held prisoner in "Herod's palace," a residence constructed by Herod the Great. Now the structure served as the "praetorium," or procurator's headquarters.

[24]Tacitus, *History* 5.9. See *NIV Study Bible* on this verse; Conzelmann, pp. 194-195.

[25]Some of this information comes from Suetonius, *Life of Claudius* 28 and Tacitus, *History*.

ACTS 24

2. Paul's Trial before Felix (24:1-21)

The Accusations against Paul (24:1-9)

[1]Five days later the high priest Ananias went down to Caesarea with some of the elders and a lawyer named Tertullus, and they brought their charges against Paul before the governor. [2]When Paul was called in, Tertullus presented his case before Felix: "We have enjoyed a long period of peace under you, and your foresight has brought about reforms in this nation. [3]Everywhere and in every way, most excellent Felix, we acknowledge this with profound gratitude. [4]But in order not to weary you further, I would request that you be kind enough to hear us briefly. [5]We have found this man to be a troublemaker, stirring up riots among the Jews all over the world. He is a ringleader of the Nazarene sect [6]and even tried to desecrate the temple; so we seized him. [8]By[a] examining him yourself you will be able to learn the truth about all these charges we are bringing against him." [9]The Jews joined in the accusation, asserting that these things were true.

[a]*6-8 Some manuscripts him and wanted to judge him according to our law. [7]But the commander, Lysias, came and with the use of much force snatched him from our hands [8]and ordered his accusers to come before you. By*

Paul now gained another hearing, this time before Felix, the procurator. It had been "five days" since he arrived in Caesarea. From Jerusalem "the high priest Ananias"[1] came down, along with some of "the elders and a lawyer named Tertullus." Their objective was to bring formal charges against Paul.

---

[1]Ananias was high priest until A.D. 59 and this trial should be dated about A.D. 57. See Jewett, *Chronology*, pp. 40-44.

Tertullus came as the "lawyer" (ῥήτωρ, *rhētōr*), a term which applied to one skilled in legal speech and practice. His name was a common one; a variant of Tertius. It was not unusual for lawyers to be used in matters which required legal expertise, especially in Roman law. Tertullus was probably employed by the Sanhedrin for this purpose. Whether he was Jewish is not clear. He did use the pronoun "we" at some points in his address (see vv. 3,5,6), but in v. 9 he seemed to separate himself from the Jews.

Tertullus began his presentation with the conventional rhetoric which praised the achievements of the procurator. Such eulogies were filled with flattering comments that touched on all the appropriate points of pride with a Roman politician. The purpose was to gain the favor of the one rendering judgment in the case.

Thus Tertullus described the "long period of peace" enjoyed under Felix, a note that did not exactly correspond to reality, since political conditions under Felix were marked by increasing violence and rebellion. The truth was also stretched a bit when the rule of Felix was described as "long," since he probably began his rule only five years before.

In addition Tertullus complimented Felix on his "foresight" (πρόνοια, *pronoia*) which had produced many "reforms," or improvements. Again the skilled lawyer flattered Felix at a sensitive point, since Roman rulers loved to be characterized as generous to their subjects.[2]

Even the title Tertullus used to describe Felix was stretching the truth. In customary fashion for addressing a governor, Tertullus called him "most excellent" (κράτιστος, *kratistos*), a term which was normally reserved for members of the equestrian order (a social class just beneath the rank of senators). Felix, however, had not come to his position from the equestrian order, but rather from the status of freedman.

After this eloquent opening which occupied half of his entire presentation, Tertullus delivered three accusations. He charged Paul with being "a troublemaker"[3] in a very general sense, "stirring up riots among Jews all over the world." The charge was general

---

[2]Examples abound in which Roman coins bear political slogans which proclaim the generosity of the emperors.

[3]The word for "troublemaker" is λοιμός, (*loimos*), a term which means "a pest, plague, pestilence." See Rienecker, p. 329.

enough to include any type of disturbance from purely theological disagreements to political tumult. Of course, Felix would be much more concerned with the latter. Probably the reference of Tertullus is to the many times Paul's mission efforts had resulted in his expulsion from cities of the Roman empire. In Pisidian Antioch, in Iconium, in Lystra, in Philippi, in Thessalonica, in Berea, in Corinth, and in Ephesus the story had been the same.[4] Trouble had followed him all over the Roman world, but his message never attacked the political establishment.

The second accusation was that Paul was a "ringleader (πρωτο-στάτης, *prōtostatēs*) of the Nazarene sect (αἵρεσις, *hairesis*)." In other words, Paul was guilty of being a leader of the Christians. The term *hairesis* (from which we get the word "heresy") does not necessarily take on a negative connotation here.[5] The term Nazarene is used here of Christians, the only time in the New Testament where this is so. The name reflects on the hometown of Jesus of Nazareth (see 2:22; John 1:46). On this point Tertullus was correct—Paul was indeed a leader within the fellowship of the followers of Jesus.

Finally, Tertullus said that Paul "tried to desecrate (βεβηλόω, *bebēloō*)[6] the temple." This statement revived the accusation that Paul had taken the Gentile, Trophimus, into the temple area (see 21:28). Here Tertullus hedged a little by stating that Paul "tried" to desecrate the temple, as if he had not succeeded in bringing the Gentile in. Instead, Tertullus implied that the Jews intercepted Paul, probably for the purpose of putting him on trial for this crime.[7] Further details, concluded Tertullus, could be gained by "examining" (ἀνακρίνω, *anakrinō*)[8] Paul, an action he encouraged Felix to take.

---

[4]See 13:45,50; 14:2-5,19; 16:22,36-40; 17:5-9; 18:6,12-17; 19:9; 20:19.

[5]The Sadducees are called a sect (or "party") of the Jews (5:17) and the Pharisees likewise (15:5), with no negative perceptions intended.

[6]Tertullus used a different term for "desecrate" than was used in 21:28 where κοινόω (*koinoō*) is used to describe Paul's crime against the temple. The reason for the change is that here a Gentile audience is being addressed and there the audience was Jewish. See Lake and Cadbury, p. 299.

[7]A variant reading has Tertullus stating that the reason the trial did not proceed at the temple was because Claudius Lysias intervened with "much force," taking Paul away from the Jews. The NIV places this statement (which consists of vv. 6b-8a) in a footnote, since the textual evidence does not favor it.

Hearty "amens" came from all the Jews gathered before Felix. They concurred in everything their lawyer had stated concerning Paul. Modern readers should not forget that the complete discussion by the Jews, or even by Tertullus, is not recorded. Luke has given but a brief summary of the proceedings before Felix. Other statements were probably made by members of the Sanhedrin or even by Jews present in the temple on the day of the riot. It is also likely that the speech of Tertullus was many times longer and more detailed than the summary given here by Luke.

The Defense by Paul (24:10-21)

[10]When the governor motioned for him to speak, Paul replied: "I know that for a number of years you have been a judge over this nation; so I gladly make my defense. [11]You can easily verify that no more than twelve days ago I went up to Jerusalem to worship. [12]My accusers did not find me arguing with anyone at the temple, or stirring up a crowd in the synagogues or anywhere else in the city. [13]And they cannot prove to you the charges they are now making against me. [14]However, I admit that I worship the God of our fathers as a follower of the Way, which they call a sect. I believe everything that agrees with the Law and that is written in the Prophets, [15]and I have the same hope in God as these men, that there will be a resurrection of both the righteous and the wicked. [16]So I strive always to keep my conscience clear before God and man. [17]After an absence of several years, I came to Jerusalem to bring my people gifts for the poor and to present offerings. [18]I was ceremonially clean when they found me in the temple courts doing this. There was no crowd with me, nor was I involved in any disturbance. [19]But there are some Jews from the province of Asia, who ought to be here before you and bring charges if they have anything against me. [20]Or these who are here should state what crime they found in me when I stood before the

---

[8]The Greek word ἀνακρίνω was often used to speak of interrogating a prisoner, and thus has reference to the governor's questioning of Paul, not Claudius Lysias (though "him" is ambiguous here).

Sanhedrin–[21]unless it was this one thing I shouted as I stood in their presence: 'It is concerning the resurrection of the dead that I am on trial before you today.' "

With a royal gesture Felix gave Paul permission to defend himself.[9] As Tertullus had opened his address with the conventional flattery of the governor, so did Paul, only in Paul's case the truth was not stretched and the compliments were not so hollow. Paul cited the experience of Felix as "a judge over this nation," a reference to his "number of years" both as procurator and as a subordinate in Samaria in the court of Cumanus.[10] The governor's experience gave Paul the confidence that Felix would understand some of the complexities of Jewish law and customs.

Thus the Apostle began his "defense" (ἀπολογέω, apologeō) by denying that he could possibly be guilty of stirring up trouble at the temple. How could he create such a disturbance in only twelve days?

Paul's mention of twelve days creates some problems for commentators. Does he mean that it was twelve days from his arrival in Jerusalem to his address before Felix? This figure might result from simply adding the seven days of Paul's purification (21:27) and the five days spent in Caesarea (v. 1). But there are more days than this involved. A better solution is to see Paul's count as including the days from the time of his arrival in Jerusalem to his imprisonment. The Greek grammar allows this interpretation. This approach would make the first day the day of Paul's arrival in Jerusalem (21:17). The second day was Paul's visit with James (21:18). The third through the ninth days would be the days of purification (21:27) with the ninth day including the attack on Paul in the temple court (21:27-22:29). The tenth day saw Paul before the Sanhedrin (22:30-23:10) and on the eleventh day the plot against Paul was discovered (23:12-30). Finally, the twelfth day was the day Paul was transferred to Caesarea (23:31-33).[11]

Paul's point is to argue that his presence in Jerusalem was too short to stir up serious trouble. Twelve days was simply not long

---

[9]For a discussion on the structure of this speech see Veltman, "Defense Speeches," *Perspectives on Luke-Acts*, ed. Talbert, pp. 243-256.

[10]See Hemer, *Book of Acts*, p. 129.

[11]Bruce, p. 443, n. 22.

enough for him to create a significant following. How could he be guilty of being the cause of the riot in Jerusalem?

In addition Paul noted that his purpose in going to Jerusalem was "to worship" (προσκυνήσων, *proskynēsōn*).[12] His focus was a spiritual one. How could he be guilty of instigating trouble when his objective was one of worship at the temple? It was not as if they had found him "arguing with anyone at the temple, or stirring up a crowd in the synagogues or anywhere else in the city."

The true point of controversy, argued Paul, was doctrinal. Even here the difference was not radical, since he stood on common ground with much of Judaism. He could "worship the God of our fathers," just as any sincere Jew might do when going to the temple. He believed in the same Scriptures as did most of the Jews, accepting "everything that agrees with the Law," as well as "the Prophets."[13] He also had "the same hope in God" and the same belief that "there will be a resurrection of both the righteous and the wicked." But Paul did so "as a follower of the Way."[14] In this respect Paul was different from his Jewish brothers and sisters. Paul saw Christ as the ultimate fulfillment of Judaism.

His contention about the resurrection is unique for Paul. Frequently Paul stresses the centrality of the resurrection (see 1 Cor 15; Phil 3:20-21; 1 Thess 4:13-18). But Paul's perspective in his letters is usually that of the believer. Nowhere else does he clearly reflect on the resurrection of both the righteous and the wicked, though other New Testament references make this doctrine quite clear (see John 5:28-29; Rev 20:12-15; see also Dan 12:2).[15]

---

[12]The future participle of προσκυνέω expresses purpose here. The term was often used in the sense of making a pilgrimage (Polhill, p. 482, n. 109). These words correspond to Paul's words in Rom 15:31 where he speaks of this trip as a service to God. Longenecker comments about these words that "of all the practices of Paul in the Book of Acts, the claims made in defense are probably the most susceptible of being interpreted as a false representation by a later author or a compromise by the Apostle himself of his own high ethical teaching." But, on the contrary, "even here, we need not posit any real contradiction between the teaching and the practice of the Apostle Paul." See his *Paul*, p. 263.

[13]The Sadducees did not accept the Prophets, but the Pharisees did.

[14]See comments on 9:2.

Paul saw the resurrection as the battleline with other Jews only because they failed to apply their doctrine to the one example he could no longer deny — Jesus of Nazareth. The conviction that Jesus had been raised from death was the driving force of his ministry and thus the reason he was being persecuted by the Jews. It was no wonder he could exclaim before the Sanhedrin that he was on trial because of his "hope in the resurrection of the dead" (23:6).

It was also not surprising that he should "strive always" to keep his "conscience clear before God and man." If there would be a resurrection of both the righteous and the wicked, then there would also be a judgment of both the righteous and the wicked.

Thus Paul climaxed his address by reflecting on his journey to Jerusalem. He had not come to agitate. He had certainly not come to desecrate the temple. His purpose was to come back to Jerusalem "after an absence of several years" for two purposes — that of bringing to his people "gifts for the poor" and "to present offerings." His absence for these years should demonstrate that stirring up trouble at the temple was not a part of his life's mission. His last visit to Jerusalem had taken place at the end of his second missionary journey some three or four years earlier and is barely mentioned by Luke (see 18:22).

Most commentators find in his reference to "gifts for the poor" the only mention in Acts of the collection that was so important to Paul.[16] It may be that Paul's words described the gift meant for Jewish Christians in Palestine (see Rom 15:26; 2 Cor 8:1-9:15). If so, it must also be conceded that the reference is certainly a vague one. Gifts for the poor and offerings could be carried by almost any pilgrim to the Jerusalem temple. Paul's note that the gifts were for his "people" does not help solve our problem, since this phrase could apply either to Jews or to Jewish Christians. Perhaps we can see in Paul's words the possible allusion to the collection from the

---

[15]The Jews were not all agreed on the subject of the resurrection. The Sadducees denied the idea totally, while other Jews puzzled over whether the resurrection would involve only the righteous, or perhaps the wicked, as well.

[16]See Lake and Cadbury, p. 303; Marshall, pp. 378-379; Reese, p. 846; Bruce, p. 445.

Gentiles, but we must also admit that the problem persists as to why Acts is so silent about this major project of the Apostle Paul.[17]

At any rate, Paul told Felix that his presence in the temple had nothing to do with instigating trouble. He had even taken seriously the requirements for ceremonial purity (see 21:26). Why would he be involved in creating a disturbance? Beyond this, the "Jews from the province of Asia" were the ones who had made the accusation that he brought a Gentile into the temple (see 21:27-29). But where were they now? Without a doubt Paul now turned to gesture with his hand as if to say that the accusers could not be found. Their absence was mute testimony to the fact they had no case against him.

If the Asian Jews were absent, Paul declared, then let the members of the Sanhedrin speak out. They were well aware that no charge had been established against him. In that hearing their only point of contention with him was the doctrine of the resurrection, and that disagreement was as much with one another as with Paul. But the Sanhedrin knew all too well that Felix would not be interested in Jewish disagreements about the resurrection.

3. The Postponement of a Verdict by Felix (24:22-23)

[22]Then Felix, who was well acquainted with the Way, adjourned the proceedings. "When Lysias the commander comes," he said, "I will decide your case." [23]He ordered the centurion to keep Paul under guard but to give him some freedom and permit his friends to take care of his needs.

Paul's address was finished and the decision now belonged to Felix. Luke notes that Felix was "well acquainted with the Way,"[18] a fact which implied that the procurator could perceive the theological nature of the charges against Paul. For this reason he "adjourned (ἀναβάλλομαι, *anaballomai*) the proceedings." His hope

---

[17]Among those who deny that these words refer to the collection are Haenchen (p. 655) and Polhill (p. 485, n. 117).

[18]Believers are frequently referred to as "the Way" in Acts. See comments on 9:2.

was to get confirmation of his suspicions by interviewing Claudius Lysias when he came to Caesarea. Whether this interview ever happened is not stated.

Meanwhile, Paul remained in custody at Caesarea. His situation was not intolerable, however, because the centurion was ordered "to keep Paul under guard, but to give him some freedom," a kind of "free custody" which included the relaxing of the more severe forms of punishment. This arrangement resulted largely from Paul's status as a Roman citizen. It meant that permission was granted to "his friends to take care of his needs." Perhaps Paul's friends from the church in Caesarea were among those who contributed to his needs, including believers from the family of Cornelius (see 10:1-48). Because the Roman system did not supply the necessities of prisoners, Paul would have depended on such items as food and clothing from caring believers.

4. Paul's Interviews with Felix (24:24-26)

[24]**Several days later Felix came with his wife Drusilla, who was a Jewess. He sent for Paul and listened to him as he spoke about faith in Christ Jesus.** [25]**As Paul discoursed on righteousness, self-control and the judgment to come, Felix was afraid and said, "That's enough for now! You may leave. When I find it convenient, I will send for you."** [26]**At the same time he was hoping that Paul would offer him a bribe, so he sent for him frequently and talked with him.**

Luke now gives a peek into Paul's opportunities to present the gospel to one of the kings of the Gentiles (see 9:15). While Paul was in Caesarean imprisonment Felix and Drusilla came to visit him. Luke notes that Drusilla was a Jewess, a detail given perhaps to indicate why the procurator was interested in seeing Paul.

Drusilla's story would make entertainment headlines today. The youngest daughter of Agrippa I (the Herod of Acts 12), she was married at age fourteen to Azizus, king of Emesa, a Syrian petty state. When Felix saw the beautiful young woman he wanted her for his wife. Employing the services of a magician named Atomos, he convinced her to leave her husband when she was sixteen. He promised her that he could give her true happiness ("felicity," a word play on his own name). When she married Felix she was his third wife. Eventually she bore him a son named Agrippa who later died in the eruption of Mt. Vesuvius (A.D. 79).

Summoning Paul to their presence, they permitted him to discuss his message in some detail. He evidently pursued the same theme he had introduced in the hearing — the resurrection and judgment (see 23:6; 24:21). His emphasis on "the judgment to come" gave him the chance to focus on the kind of life demanded by the eternal Judge. His words about "self-control" (ἐγκράτεια, enkrateia) took on an ethical tone which may well have struck at the core of Felix and Drusilla. "Righteousness" (δικαιοσύνη, dikaiosynē) emphasized God's standards for a holy life. The effects of Paul's preaching brought a sense of fear to Felix. On the point of conviction, Felix could not tolerate any more of the truth served up by Paul. He called an end to the audience with this preacher, explaining that he would speak to him later when he found it "convenient."

Meanwhile, Felix kept Paul in prison. Justice was on hold. Luke explains that part of his motive was his hoping for "a bribe." Though the acceptance of a bribe by Roman officials was illegal, it happened frequently.[19] Though the note about Felix might be taken as evidence that Paul still had funds from the collection for the Jewish Christians, this conclusion is quite speculative. Paul had mentioned money, however, in his address before Felix when he spoke of his coming to Jerusalem bringing "gifts for the poor" (v. 17). Perhaps this comment was enough for Felix to hope for a bribe. Beyond the bribe Felix also wished to avoid stirring up unnecessary trouble with the Jews. It was easier for him to keep Paul's case on hold than to release the Apostle even if he was innocent of the charges against him.

---

[19]Polhill cites the Lex Iulia derepetundis as the prohibition which applied to bribery among officials (p. 487, n. 123).

5. The Ascension of Festus: Paul's Continued Custody (24:27)

²⁷When two years had passed, Felix was succeeded by Porcius Festus, but because Felix wanted to grant a favor to the Jews, he left Paul in prison.

For two years Paul remained a prisoner at Caesarea. At the end of this period the term of Felix came to an end. The occasion was a disturbance in Caesarea between Jewish and Gentile elements of the population. The actions taken by Felix were so anti-Jewish that the Jews sent a delegation to Rome in order to complain. Rome responded by removing Felix from office. Paul's case would now be taken up by a new procurator — Porcius Festus.

ACTS 25

6. The Visit of Festus to Jerusalem (25:1-5)

[1]Three days after arriving in the province, Festus went up from Caesarea to Jerusalem, [2]where the chief priests and Jewish leaders appeared before him and presented the charges against Paul. [3]They urgently requested Festus, as a favor to them, to have Paul transferred to Jerusalem, for they were preparing an ambush to kill him along the way. [4]Festus answered, "Paul is being held at Caesarea, and I myself am going there soon. [5]Let some of your leaders come with me and press charges against the man there, if he has done anything wrong."

Porcius Festus entered Judea with a burst of energy. Only three days after his arrival, he took the journey from Caesarea to Jerusalem. Such a visit was natural for a new procurator who wanted to begin his term with the best of relations. Since Jerusalem was the religious and cultural center of his province, Festus lost little time in traveling there.

Little information survives regarding the personal side of this procurator. Besides the details given in Acts, Josephus briefly mentions him but twice.[1] As far as we know, his term began about A.D. 59 and ended with his death in A.D. 62. Though his term was too short to know what he might have accomplished, the indications are that he was a competent procurator. At the very least, he apparently brought a more peaceful atmosphere to the region than was the case under Felix.

Greeting the new procurator in Jerusalem were "the chief priests

---

[1]Josephus, *War* 2. 272; *Antiquities*, 20.182-88. For a discussion of the dating of this incident see Jewett, *Chronology*, pp. 40-44.

and Jewish leaders." These were the members of the priestly circle in Jerusalem (the Sanhedrin) and their interest was not only in greeting the newcomer to Judea, but also to present "the charges against Paul." In so doing, they also "urgently requested" that he grant them "a favor" (χάριν, *charin*), which translated into a decision from Festus in accordance with their wishes (see vv. 11,16; 24:27). They wanted Paul to be "transferred to Jerusalem" because another plot had been conceived to ambush and "kill him along the way" from Caesarea to Jerusalem. Some of these conspirators may have been the same as those who, two years earlier, had sworn the oath to murder Paul (see 23:21).

Approaching a procurator while he was new in his office was good strategy on the part of the Jews. If they could catch him before he was acquainted with all of the details of his office or of the case, they might be able to influence Festus to accommodate their wishes.

Festus was not ready to go along with them on this matter. Whether out of his sense of judicial correctness or because he sensed something amiss in their request, Festus made it clear that Paul was his own responsibility.[2] He would be "held in Caesarea," not moved to Jerusalem, and Festus would be returning there where he himself would be dealing with the case.

He did, however, invite the Jewish leaders to send a delegation to Caesarea in order to present their case. This suggestion they would gladly accept.

7. Paul's Appeal to Caesar (25:6-12)

[6]After spending eight or ten days with them, he went down to Caesarea, and the next day he convened the court and ordered that Paul be brought before him. [7]When Paul appeared, the Jews who had come down from Jerusalem stood around him, bringing many serious charges against him, which they could not prove. [8]Then Paul made his defense: "I have done nothing wrong against the law of the Jews or against the temple or against Caesar."

---

[2]Polhill thinks that the decision was purely a pragmatic matter in which Festus regarded it more convenient for him to deal with Paul in Caesarea rather than in Jerusalem (p. 489).

[9]Festus, wishing to do the Jews a favor, said to Paul, "Are you willing to go up to Jerusalem and stand trial before me there on these charges?" [10]Paul answered: "I am now standing before Caesar's court, where I ought to be tried. I have not done any wrong to the Jews, as you yourself know very well. [11]If, however, I am guilty of doing anything deserving death, I do not refuse to die. But if the charges brought against me by these Jews are not true, no one has the right to hand me over to them. I appeal to Caesar!" [12]After Festus had conferred with his council, he declared: "You have appealed to Caesar. To Caesar you will go!"

Festus stayed in Jerusalem for "eight to ten days." This time allowed the Jewish leaders to formulate their strategy and gather their witnesses for the hearing. When the time came for Festus to return to Caesarea, the Jewish leaders traveled along. Since their means of travel would have made use of horses, it is likely that the journey was only two days.

When the large party arrived at Caesarea, Festus made the arrangements for the hearing to take place the next day. The time had finally come for Paul to be heard from again. Festus "convened the court" (καθίσας ἐπὶ τοῦ βήματος, *kathisas epi tou bēmatos*), a phrase which literally means that Festus "sat down on the *bēma*," or judgment seat.[3] From this position Festus would project the full authority of Roman law. Paul was brought in to stand before the judgment seat and hear his accusers present their case.

After Paul was in place, the accusations began to fly. Luke does not give details regarding the nature of these accusations, but characterizes them as "many serious charges" which the Jews "could not prove." The exact nature of the charges may be determined, however, by the response given by Paul.[4] His reply focused on three issues. First, he had "done nothing wrong against the law of the

---

[3]See the comments on 18:12 where Paul stood before Gallio, who sat on the judgment seat (βῆμα, *bēma*).

[4]For a discussion of the defense speeches of Paul in Acts see Veltman, "Defense Speeches," in *Perspectives on Luke-Acts*, pp. 243-256. For a discussion of the charges brought against Paul and their relationship to Paul's defense speeches in Acts see J.M. Gilchrist, "On What Charge Was St. Paul Brought to Rome?" *ExpT* 78 (1967): 264-266. See also note on 23:6.

Jews." This accusation had been made against Paul before. When he visited with James in Jerusalem, Paul had heard about the slander that he was teaching "Jews who live among the Gentiles to turn away from Moses, telling them not to circumcise their children" or live according to Jewish customs (21:21).[5] Such an accusation before Festus would have little effect by itself.

The second point on which Paul defends himself is that he had done nothing wrong against "the temple."[6] This charge stemmed from his visit to the temple for the purification. When the mob seized him, some of them shouted that he had brought a Gentile into the temple area (see 21:28-29; 24:6). Though this accusation was more serious,[7] the Sanhedrin still had no credible witnesses to verify their charge.

Finally, Paul denied committing any crime "against Caesar." For Festus this would be the most serious of the charges. An attempt had been made by Tertullus to pin this charge on Paul earlier (see 24:5), but no specific crime by Paul could be cited. Once again the Jews could not prove their accusations, nor provide any specific information which would demonstrate Paul's guilt.

When Paul finished his defense, he must have felt heartsick. Though Festus did not seem convinced by the facts, it seemed as if he wanted to extend "a favor" (see v. 3) to the Jews. He asked Paul if he would be willing to go to Jerusalem in order to stand trial for these charges. This suggestion did not necessarily mean that Festus would relinquish control over the proceedings. Festus asked, "Are you willing to go up to Jerusalem and stand trial *before me*?" The procurator had no intention of making it a Jewish trial. He was merely suggesting a setting which would allow the Sanhedrin the convenience of providing local witnesses, or even the possibility of having Jewish advisors in his judicial council.[8]

---

[5]Paul's attitude toward the Jewish law was one characterized by respect and participation (see Rom 7:12; 8:3-4; 1 Cor 9:20). His contention, however, was that Gentiles (or even Jews) should not be required to obey the law as a matter of their salvation.

[6]O'Neill sees in this defense a statement applicable not only to Paul, but also to believers in general who would deny the charge that they "had tried to profane the Temple." See his *Theology*, p. 76.

[7]See the comments on 21:28-29.

[8]Marshall notes that in some cases procurators used local officials in advi-

Paul had already experienced the aberration of justice that came with the extending of favors to the Jews. Felix had kept him in prison for two years as a result of this desire (see 24:27). His patience with the Roman system of justice was wearing thin. He was not interested in any accommodation of the Jews. A trial in Jerusalem, even with Festus as the judge, could not be an advantage for Paul. He thus decided to use the one option he had. He would once again use his Roman citizenship.

Paul spoke pointedly to Festus. Reminding him that the court did not belong to the Jews, Paul stated, "I am now standing before Caesar's court, where I ought to be tried." Festus would not have missed the subtle barb. Festus ought to be capable of rendering a decision without help from the Sanhedrin in Jerusalem.

Beyond this, Paul declared that he was innocent and that Festus knew it. Arguing that escaping punishment was not his motive, Paul announced that he would accept the death penalty if his crime deserved it. But, as a Roman citizen, he knew his rights. No one had authority to hand him over to the Jews if no crime could be proved against him. His appeal was to Caesar. Festus would no longer have jurisdiction over Paul's case.

Many questions about the appeal to Caesar by a Roman citizen remain unanswered for modern scholars. Cadbury lists a number of these.[9] To whom was the right of appeal to Caesar made available in the Roman world? How did one validate his Roman citizenship? In what cases was such an appeal permitted? At what point in the case could one make the appeal to Caesar? Once the appeal was made, what obligations did the governor have, especially if further evidence was discovered? Would the rights of a procurator in such cases be the same as those of a legate?

Since answers to these questions are unavailable, the best that can be said here is that the right of appeal to Caesar was already an ancient right when Paul employed it in Caesarea. It can be traced back to the founding of the Republic (509 B.C.). In its original form, the defendant could appeal to the sovereign people of Rome, an action known as *provocatio*. Under the dictatorships the right was

---

sory ways when rendering decisions (p. 385).

[9]Cadbury, "Roman Law and the Trial of Paul," *Beginnings*, 5:312-319.

still used, but the appeal was to Caesar himself. Usually the right of appeal was valid in cases where no established legal precedent could be found (*extra ordinem*).[10]

Festus had little reason to object. As a matter of fact, he may have felt great relief. He had seen a load removed from his shoulders.

8. The Visit of Agrippa II and Bernice to Festus (25:13-22)

[13]A few days later King Agrippa and Bernice arrived at Caesarea to pay their respects to Festus. [14]Since they were spending many days there, Festus discussed Paul's case with the king. He said: "There is a man here whom Felix left as a prisoner. [15]When I went to Jerusalem, the chief priests and elders of the Jews brought charges against him and asked that he be condemned. [16]I told them that it is not the Roman custom to hand over any man before he has faced his accusers and has had an opportunity to defend himself against their charges. [17]When they came here with me, I did not delay the case, but convened the court the next day and ordered the man to be brought in. [18]When his accusers got up to speak, they did not charge him with any of the crimes I had expected. [19]Instead, they had some points of dispute with him about their own religion and about a dead man named Jesus who Paul claimed was alive. [20]I was at a loss how to investigate such matters; so I asked if he would be willing to go to Jerusalem and stand trial there on these charges. [21]When Paul made his appeal to be held over for the Emperor's decision, I ordered him held until I could send him to Caesar." [22]Then Agrippa said to Festus, "I would like to hear this man myself." He replied, "Tomorrow you will hear him."

Only a few days after Paul's appeal to Caesar, Festus received a surprise visitor. King Agrippa II and his sister Bernice came to pay

---

[10]For further information on the right of appeal to Caesar, see Colin Hemer, *Book of Acts*, pp. 130-131; Sherwin-White, *Roman Society and Roman Law*, pp. 57-70; Conzelmann, pp. 203-204.

their respects due to the arrival of the new procurator. Extending their congratulations to Festus would also give the young king the opportunity to gain another political ally.

Agrippa II was the son of Agrippa I (the Herod of Acts 12). Born in A.D. 27, Agrippa II was raised in Rome and became king of Chalcis in A.D. 48 when he inherited the throne of his uncle. In A.D. 53 Agrippa II had the chance to trade his throne for the territories of Philip and Lysanias, including Abilene, Batanea, Traconitis, and Gaulinitis (see Luke 3:1). Then in A.D. 56 his rule was extended over several more towns around the Sea of Galilee, among which was Caesarea Philippi. Though his territories were largely Gentile, he was given by the Romans the right to appoint the high priest. As such he was known as "king of the Jews."[11]

Bernice was the sister of Agrippa II and had created quite a scandal in Palestine. When she was thirteen years old, she married her uncle, Herod of Chalcis. In A.D. 48 her husband died and she moved in with the new ruler of Chalcis, which happened to be her brother, Agrippa II. Rumors of her incestuous relationship with her brother spread far and wide. Then in A.D. 63 she married King Polemon of Cilicia, but the marriage did not last, and soon she was back with Agrippa. Finally in the 70s she became the mistress of the Roman general Titus, a relationship which created a huge stir in Rome. Titus apparently considered marrying the beautiful Oriental queen, but when political fortunes made it possible for him to become emperor in A.D. 79, Titus sent Bernice out of Rome for good.[12]

Agrippa and Bernice were to spend "many days" at Caesarea and in that time the issue of what to do about Paul came up for discussion. Festus was still looking for information which would help him to formulate a report for Caesar. He explained to Agrippa and Bernice exactly what had happened in connection with Paul, with a few interesting adjustments.

---

[11]Bruce observes that between A.D. 6 and 37 the priests were appointed by the procurators. Herod Agrippa I was granted the privilege of appointing the priests beginning in A.D. 41, but at his death in A.D. 44 a delegation of Jews traveled to Rome to argue to Claudius that the new procurator should not be granted this authority. The privilege went to Herod of Chalcis instead (p. 456, n. 20).

[12]See Bruce for more details about Agrippa II and Bernice, pp. 456-457.

Festus portrayed himself very much as the savior of Paul in this discussion. The Jews, he said, were on the verge of a grave miscarriage of justice when Festus prevented them from their objective. He had insisted that the Roman system grants a fair trial to all subjects (v. 16) and he came back to Caesarea to quickly arrange for a hearing (v. 17). He conveniently left out any reference to his desire to grant the Jews a favor.

What was revealed in the summary of Festus, however, was how confused he was regarding the declaration of Paul about the resurrection of Jesus. As he told Agrippa and Bernice, the dispute between the Jews and Paul seemed to center on a "dead man named Jesus who Paul claimed was alive." He did not understand that Paul's claim was that Jesus had been raised from the dead. He could only comprehend the debate to be about whether a man thought to be dead had perhaps not died at all. To Festus the whole controversy was a mystery. The concept of the resurrection was inconceivable to him. He was befuddled as to what to say in his report to Caesar.

Festus could only hope that Agrippa's experience with the Jews might unlock the mystery of this debate. The challenge sounded interesting to Agrippa and he agreed to listen to Paul's presentation.

9. Paul's Appearance before Agrippa (25:23–26:32)

The Presentation of Paul to Agrippa by Festus (25:23-27)

[23]The next day Agrippa and Bernice came with great pomp and entered the audience room with the high ranking officers and the leading men of the city. At the command of Festus, Paul was brought in. [24]Festus said: "King Agrippa, and all who are present with us, you see this man! The whole Jewish community has petitioned me about him in Jerusalem and here in Caesarea, shouting that he ought not to live any longer. [25]I found he had done nothing deserving of death, but because he made his appeal to the Emperor I decided to send him to Rome. [26]But I have nothing definite to write to His Majesty about him. Therefore I have brought him before all of you, and especially before you, King

Agrippa, so that as a result of this investigation I may have something to write. [27]For I think it is unreasonable to send on a prisoner without specifying the charges against him."

When the day arrived for Paul's hearing before Agrippa and Bernice, the occasion provided an opportunity for a show of royalty. Thus "with great pomp" the king and his sister entered the palace reception hall. The extravagant show was the result of the elaborate, flowing robes, the expensive jewelry, and the large entourage. Not only would Agrippa and Bernice have entered, but also "the high ranking officers," such as the tribunes (perhaps five of them),[13] as well as leaders of the city of Caesarea.

Then Paul was brought in to stand before the procurator. Festus opened the hearing by reviewing the facts of the case briefly. The summary corresponds to the facts of Paul's case which have been repeated frequently in the latter chapters of Acts (22–26). Festus reiterated how the Jews were determined to find Paul guilty of a capital crime (see 23:29; 25:15) and how he had found no reason for this sentence.

Concluding his opening remarks, Festus stated his purpose for the present hearing. Because Paul had appealed to Caesar, Festus had the obligation to send a report to the emperor, who, at that time, was Nero (A.D. 54-68). To say that it would be "unreasonable to send a prisoner without specifying the charges against him" is an understatement. It would not only be foolish (ἄλογος, alogos), it could be fatal![14] This formal report was called a *litterae dimissoriae* or a *litterae apostoli* and was required. The procurator felt the obligation to "His Majesty" (κύριος, kyrios)[15] and was taking every precaution possible.

So Festus had arranged for this session in order to get specific information. He was not sitting on the judgment seat and this was

---

[13]Polhill, p. 495.

[14]I owe this expressive observation to Polhill, p. 496. See also Sherwin-White, *Roman Society and Roman Law*, pp. 64-65.

[15]The use of the title "lord" for the king was common in the East. Later the Romans applied the term to the emperor, beginning especially with Caligula. By the time of Nero the use of the title was very common; by the time of Domitian it was required.

not a formal trial, but an informal or investigative hearing. Nevertheless, Paul would get one more opportunity to tell the story of the persecutor who came face to face with the resurrected Christ.

ACTS 26

9. Paul's Appearance before Agrippa (25:23–26:32)

Paul's Address to Agrippa (26:1-23)

[1]Then Agrippa said to Paul, "You have permission to speak for yourself." So Paul motioned with his hand and began his defense: [2]"King Agrippa, I consider myself fortunate to stand before you today as I make my defense against all the accusations of the Jews, [3]and especially so because you are well acquainted with all the Jewish customs and controversies. Therefore, I beg you to listen to me patiently. [4]The Jews all know the way I have lived ever since I was a child, from the beginning of my life in my own country, and also in Jerusalem. [5]They have known me for a long time and can testify, if they are willing, that according to the strictest sect of our religion, I lived as a Pharisee. [6]And now it is because of my hope in what God has promised our fathers that I am on trial today. [7]This is the promise our twelve tribes are hoping to see fulfilled as they earnestly serve God day and night. O king, it is because of this hope that the Jews are accusing me. [8]Why should any of you consider it incredible that God raises the dead? [9]I too was convinced that I ought to do all that was possible to oppose the name of Jesus of Nazareth. [10]And that is just what I did in Jerusalem. On the authority of the chief priests I put many of the saints in prison, and when they were put to death, I cast my vote against them. [11]Many a time I went from one synagogue to another to have them punished, and I tried to force them to blaspheme. In my obsession against them, I even went to foreign cities to persecute them. [12]On one of these journeys I was going to Damascus with the authority and commission of the chief priests. [13]About noon, O king, as I was on the road, I saw a light from heaven,

brighter than the sun, blazing around me and my companions. [14]We all fell to the ground, and I heard a voice saying to me in Aramaic,[a] 'Saul, Saul, why do you persecute me? It is hard for you to kick against the goads.' [15]Then I asked, 'Who are you, Lord?' 'I am Jesus, whom you are persecuting,' the Lord replied. [16]'Now get up and stand on your feet. I have appeared to you to appoint you as a servant and as a witness of what you have seen of me and what I will show you. [17]I will rescue you from your own people and from the Gentiles. I am sending you to them [18]to open their eyes and turn them from darkness to light, and from the power of Satan to God, so that they may receive forgiveness of sins and a place among those who are sanctified by faith in me.' [19]So then, King Agrippa, I was not disobedient to the vision from heaven. [20]First to those in Damascus, then to those in Jerusalem and in all Judea, and to the Gentiles also, I preached that they should repent and turn to God and prove their repentance by their deeds. [21]That is why the Jews seized me in the temple courts and tried to kill me. [22]But I have had God's help to this very day, and so I stand here and testify to small and great alike. I am saying nothing beyond what the prophets and Moses said would happen—[23]that the Christ[b] would suffer and, as the first to rise from the dead, would proclaim light to his own people and to the Gentiles."

[a]*14* Or *Hebrew*   [b]*23* Or *Messiah*

Now Paul had one final opportunity at Caesarea to present his case before the rulers. This time the hearing was not a formal one. He was not standing trial. The purpose of the session was merely to give Festus the information and clarification he needed to send Paul along to Caesar.

Agrippa would serve as an advisor to Festus. The Jewish king had a background which would enable him to interpret Paul's situation to Festus.

Thus Paul defended his life's mission in a climactic way.[1] Bringing together many of the themes he had enunciated in the previous

---

[1]For an analysis of the terminology in the defense speeches in 22–26 see Trites, "Legal Scenes." See note on 22:1. Also see Veltman, "Defense Speeches," 243-256.

five chapters of Acts, Paul once again focused on the resurrection as the one reason he was receiving such opposition from the Jews. As Paul stood in this position, his life again showed parallels with that of Jesus. Christ also had stood on trial before both a Roman procurator and a Jewish king (see Luke 23:6-12), and just like Christ, Paul also was found by both to be innocent of any crime deserving of death (see vv. 31-32; Luke 23:14-15).

The Introduction (26:1-3). Because the hearing was not a formal one, Agrippa took full control, granting Paul permission to speak, as Festus listened.[2] Paul began with a motion which indicated his stance as an orator (even though he was in chains). His address shows evidence of an oratorical formality that surpasses any of his earlier speeches.[3] Now he was ready to begin his "defense" (ἀπολέγομαι, *apolegomai*) of his life's mission.

His initial words followed the conventional introduction which included a flattering compliment to the ruler listening to the address (see 24:2-4,10).[4] In this part of his address he reflected on the expertise of Agrippa in matters of Jewish law and the controversies between the Jewish sects, in particular the issues which separated the Sadducees from the Pharisees.

At this point Paul also alluded to the accusations against him. By now only one accusation remained of the three which had been hurled against him before. No convincing evidence had been presented to prove that Paul was guilty of crimes against the state (see 24:5) and the charge that he had desecrated the temple had died for lack of witnesses (see 24:6). The only item left for discussion was Paul's alleged disrespect toward the Jewish law.

---

[2]Had the session been a formal trial, Festus would have taken direct control as procurator. But in this hearing he granted Agrippa authority over the proceedings.

[3]The gesture in Greek is ἐκτείνω τὴν χεῖρα (*ekteinō tēn cheira*), a motion which is not the same one as a motion for quieting a crowd, which is κατασείω τῇ χειρί (*kataseiō tē cheiri*) (13:16; 21:40). The word order of v. 2, as well as the alliterative περὶ πάντων (*peri pantōn*) are signs of elegant speech for this formal occasion.

[4]This part of the speech was technically known as the *capitatio benevolentiae.*

Paul's Pharisaic Heritage (26:4-8). As Paul did in his speech before
the temple crowd (see 22:2-3; also 23:6), he once again pointed to
his upbringing within Judaism as the starting point for his relationship to the law. The Jews who opposed him were well aware of his
childhood. He had lived as a Jew from the beginning of his life in
his "own country" (ἔθνει μου, *ethnei mou*), a phrase that probably
refers to his connection with Judea rather than Cilicia where Tarsus
was located (see 22:3).[5]

Paul's point throughout this part of his address was to show his
alliance with orthodox Judaism. He grew up in the "strictest sect
(αἵρεσις, *hairesis*)" of Judaism—the Pharisees. He was well known
among the Jews for his consistent life within the beliefs and practices of this sect.

The Pharisees were the Jewish sect which believed strongly in the
resurrection, as opposed to the Sadducees. The hope of the resurrection, said Paul, was the substance of "what God has promised"
to the Old Testament patriarchs. The promise was so important
to Jews that for it "they earnestly serve God day and night," a
phrase that includes continuous prayers.[6] Paul's use of the phrase
"twelve tribes"[7] indicates that the Jews continued to see themselves as the original people called by God out of Egypt and led
into the promised land.

Paul's emphasis here is that the promise of the resurrection
formed the very framework of the identity of the Jewish nation.
Why, then, should the Jews be his accusers when his preaching had
so much in common with Pharisaic Judaism? Paul expressed astonishment that the Jews whose faith was energized so by the hope of
the resurrection should resist his message that proclaimed the fulfillment of that hope.

Perhaps turning his eyes toward the rest of the audience, Paul
raised the burning question, "Why should any of you consider it
incredible that God raised the dead?" His reference to "the dead" is

---

[5]See Polhill, p. 499, n. 152.

[6]Luke gives Anna as an example of a godly woman who prayed to the
Lord "day and night" (Luke 2:37-38), while Simeon waited for the "consola-
tion of Israel (2:25).

[7]The term δωδεκάφυλον (*dōdekaphylon*) ("twelve tribes") appears only
here in the New Testament.

plural ("dead people"), but it is evident that Paul had one particular resurrection in mind (see v. 23). As Paul saw it, the possibility of the general resurrection hinged on the resurrection of Christ. In 1 Corinthians 15 Paul argues in the same way that the general resurrection and the resurrection of Christ stand or fall together (see vv. 12-20), only there he reverses the logic. Instead of saying there cannot be a general resurrection if Christ was not raised, 1 Corinthians says Christ was not raised if there is no general resurrection.

Paul's Former Zeal against Christians (26:9-11). Paul's sense of zeal was so intense that he once persecuted "the name of Jesus of Nazareth" (see 4:12,17,30; 5:40,41). He thus began a serious effort to rid Jerusalem of any disciples by forcing them into prisons under the supervision of the Sanhedrin. His efforts took him to several synagogues where he tried to find believers (8:1; 9:1-2; 22:4-5). Eventually he even went to "foreign cities" (such as Damascus) to persecute them. His goal in all of these efforts was to "force them to blaspheme," that is, to curse Christ (see 1 Cor 12:3).

Imprisonment was not as far as Paul went. When the "saints" (ἅγιοι, *hagioi*) were executed for their faith, Paul says that he cast his "vote against them." This statement is revealing in two ways. First, nowhere else in the New Testament is found any information about Paul's participation in the martyrdom of believers with the exception of Stephen (see 7:58; 8:1). Does his statement before Agrippa mean that other believers were executed because of Paul's efforts? There is no reason to deny that this is possible. The only other alternative is to take his comment here as a generalized plural in which his reference to the martyrdom of "saints" speaks of one saint in particular—Stephen.

The second point concerns his reference to casting his vote. Does this comment mean that he had been a member of the Sanhedrin? The language could imply that he was a voting member of the Jewish council that ordered the execution of such disciples as Stephen. But the language does not have to be understood in this way. The word ψῆφον (*psēphon*) can also be understood in a figurative sense with the idea that he merely consented to the decision (see 8:1). If Paul had been a member of the Sanhedrin it is surprising he did not mention it in such passages as Philippians 3:4-6, where it could have strengthened his argument about his Jewish heritage.

Paul's Experience on the Road to Damascus (26:12-18). For the third time in Acts the conversion of Paul is recounted here (see also 9:1-19; 22:4-21). No other event receives so much attention from Luke.[8] His heavy emphasis on this dramatic moment in the life of Paul and the church shows how important it was to the progress of the gospel in the story of the expanding church.

Paul told Agrippa the story of his conversion, but did not include all of the details which had been mentioned before. As a matter of fact, Paul's description of what happened to him on the road to Damascus is briefer here than in the other passages. In discussing the event here, Paul underscored the role of God in extending the call for Paul to become a proclaimer of the gospel.

The brilliance of the light received attention this time, as Paul described the light "from heaven, brighter than the sun, blazing around" the Apostle and his companions. This time he also mentioned that "all" of the party fell to the ground (rather than just Paul; see 9:4; 22:7).

In addition, he explicitly noted this time that the Lord Jesus spoke to him in Aramaic, and that the words he heard included the statement: "It is hard for you to kick against the goads." This ancient agricultural proverb referred to the pointed sticks used by farmers to move animals along. Though this reference has been considered a reflection of Paul's troubled conscience when he was on the road to Damascus, Krister Stendahl's classic article demonstrates convincingly that such a disturbed conscience was not a part of Paul's service to God (see 23:1).[9] The goads had nothing to do with the pangs of Paul's conscience, but rather with the will of Christ who was calling him to proclaim the truth of the gospel. Paul was fighting against what the Lord was goading him to do with his life.

---

[8]For a comparison of the accounts see Munck, *Paul,* pp. 13-35.

[9]See his "Introspective Conscience," *HTR* 56 (1963): 199-215; also found in his *Paul among Jews and Gentiles,* pp. 78-96. He argued that our tendency to interpret Paul as afflicted with a guilty conscience is more a product of the western habit of internalizing guilt than of any pangs of conscience Paul actually felt himself.

One other significant difference in Paul's retelling of his conversion is that Ananias does not appear. Rather than describing how Ananias was commanded by God to go speak to Paul (9:15), on this occasion Paul quotes the words which Ananias had spoken as if they came directly from the Lord Jesus. This is no accident. Paul was merely "telescoping" the details of the event, not feeling the need to mention the person of Ananias, but determined to mention the words he spoke to Paul. Since they were words Ananias had received from the Lord himself, Paul could attribute them to Jesus without mentioning the human servant.[10]

Thus Paul contended before Agrippa that he had indeed been extended a divine call to service. Much like the Old Testament prophets Jeremiah (see Jer 1:7-8) and Ezekiel (Ezek 2:1,3), Paul also had been commissioned. He was to be a "servant" (ὑπηρέτης, hypēretēs) like "the Servant of the Lord" described in Isaiah 42:1-7. When called upon to explain his ministry, his answer was that the Lord had called him to preach the good news. He would do so as a "witness," because he had seen Jesus, just as the other apostles had seen him. His duty was to bring the light where people lived in darkness (see Rom 13:12; 2 Cor 4:6; Eph 5:8-14).

It was at this point he had been interrupted on the previous occasion when he told this story. He had mentioned his mission to the Gentiles and the mob became angry (see 22:21-22). This time he finished his explanation of how God commissioned him to proclaim the message of salvation in a world filled with darkness. The Lord promised to "rescue" (ἐξαιρέω, exaireō) Paul from Jews and Gentiles, so that he would continue courageously in fulfilling his ministry.

In doing so he would be delivering people from "the power of Satan" and granting them the opportunity of "a place among those who are sanctified by faith" in Christ. These last words are expressions which Paul uses frequently in his letters as he argues for salvation by faith rather than the law (see Eph 2:8-10). The idea of believers who are "sanctified" (ἁγιάζω, hagiazō), or "set apart" for Christ, is also prominent in Paul's teaching (see 1 Cor 1:2; 6:11).

---

[10]Paul also combines the message he had received in the vision at the temple with the message given by the Lord on the road to Damascus (see 22:17-21).

Paul's Obedience to God (26:19-20). If Paul was confronted by the Lord Jesus in a revelation from heaven, (which he calls "the vision," ὀπτασία, *optasia*), he had only one choice. His immediate response was to obey the command of the Lord. Acts fills in the details of how he carried out this mission.

Paul went first "to those in Damascus," a historical note which is covered in detail in 9:20-25. Then Paul traveled "to Jerusalem and in all Judea," described in 9:28-29, though his work in Judea at large is not discussed. Then he went to the Gentiles. Three missionary journeys found him faithfully discharging his service given him by the Lord (see 13:1–14:28; 15:36–18:22; 18:23–21:17).

In his ministry, said Paul, he insisted that people should "repent and turn to God," language which appears both in Acts (see 3:19) and in Paul's letters (see 1 Thess 1:9).[11] Beyond this Paul declared that his preaching of grace did not involve salvation without obedience. He preached that converts should "prove their repentance by their deeds," that is, demonstrate by their obedience that their repentance was sincere. This concept does not contradict Paul's doctrine of justification by faith through grace, since Paul's doctrine of faith always required a faith ready to obey the will of Christ (see Rom 1:5).

Paul's Arrest (26:21). Paul thus came to the explanation of his arrest in Jerusalem. Speaking to Agrippa, he argued that it was this mission given him by God which was the reason he had faced the mob in the temple. These Jews had actually tried to kill him (see 21:31).[12] Thus he remained a prisoner to that very moment.

Paul's Continuing Preaching of Christ (26:22-23). In spite of these difficulties, Paul had found encouragement from the Lord to continue his efforts (see 23:11; Phil 4:10-19; 2 Cor 1:3-11; 4:16-18). For this reason he continued "to testify to small and great alike," so

---

[11]Dupont notes that this terminology summarizes Paul's preaching to the Gentiles. See his *Salvation*, p. 65.

[12]The Greek term for "kill" is διαχειρίσασθαι (*diacheirisasthai*), the same term used in 5:30 to describe the killing of Jesus. Trites sees in this parallel a connection made between Paul's sufferings and those of the Messiah. See his *Witness*, p. 131.

that Paul's ministry did not show partiality, not only in reaching all ethnic groups, but also all people whatever their social standing.

Paul reasoned that his message was simply the culmination of what Moses prophesied. Old Testament passages could be cited which described a Messiah who would suffer (see Isa 42:6-7; 49:6-7; see also Luke 24:27,44), but would be "the first to rise from the dead." In his letters Paul refers to Christ as the "firstfruits" from the dead (see 1 Cor 15:20; Col 1:18). Paul's language described a Christ who would proclaim light both to the Jews and to the Gentiles, just as the Servant of the Lord was foreshadowed in the Old Testament (see Isa 42:6-7).

The Interchange between Festus, Paul, and Agrippa (26:24-29)

[24]At this point Festus interrupted Paul's defense. "You are out of your mind, Paul!" he shouted. "Your great learning is driving you insane." [25]"I am not insane, most excellent Festus," Paul replied. "What I am saying is true and reasonable. [26]The king is familiar with these things, and I can speak freely to him. I am convinced that none of this has escaped his notice, because it was not done in a corner. [27]King Agrippa, do you believe the prophets? I know you do." [28]Then Agrippa said to Paul, "Do you think that in such a short time you can persuade me to be a Christian?" [29]Paul replied, "Short time or long—I pray God that not only you but all who are listening to me today may become what I am, except for these chains."

Festus had heard enough. He had tolerated what for him was an incomprehensible discourse from what appeared to be an educated Jewish rabbi. He had been patient through the details of the Old Testament references to the fathers and the twelve tribes (vv. 6-7), Paul's conflict with a sect of Nazarenes (vv. 9-11), his claims that he had seen a man named Jesus who had once been dead (vv. 12-18), and the words of some prophets who had once lived in Palestine (vv. 22-23). None of this was making sense to him.

Obviously Paul's education had gotten the best of him, Festus thought. "You are out of your mind (μαίνῃ, *mainē*)," Festus shouted at Paul, "your great learning is driving you insane." His diagnosis of Paul's state was in a sense a compliment. He was acknowledging, at least, that Paul possessed a credible education. But when it came to the concept of the resurrection, Festus could not make sense of Paul's message. The reaction was the same one which Paul had received in Athens with the Greek philosophers (see 17:32).

Paul's reaction was to reply respectfully to the "most excellent Festus." He insisted that his position was just the opposite of madness. His message was "true and reasonable" (σωφροσύνη, sōphrosynē).

Then directing his attention to Agrippa again, Paul observed that this Jewish king was "familiar with these things." After all, the events which formed the basis for his ministry had occurred right there in Palestine. Jesus' famous ministry was performed in Judea and Galilee. His miracles happened right under the noses of the royal Herodian family from which Agrippa came. It was impossible that Agrippa could have missed them, since none of it was "done in a corner."[13]

At this point Paul turned to challenge Agrippa directly, asking if he believed the message of the prophets. With his Jewish background, the question was not unreasonable. If Agrippa's knowledge of the Jewish Scriptures had generated an interest in Paul's message, perhaps he was now open to the truth that the prophets had spoken of Jesus. Paul now pressed the point. Even standing before a Roman ruler and a Jewish king did not intimidate him. He forced the issue in the same way he had done it so often in his missionary work. Would he be able to convert a king?

With some nervousness Agrippa responded to Paul's challenge. He was not interested in giving a serious reply to a prisoner whom the Roman procurator had just labeled a crazy man. Now Agrippa spoke with sarcasm. "Do you think that in such a short time (ἐν ὀλίγῳ, en oligō) you can persuade me to be a Christian?" he asked.[14]

---

[13]The sense of this idiom seems to be that the story of the gospel was very public in its development. This theme is a major emphasis of Luke-Acts where the basic facts of the gospel are linked with major rulers and events of the wider Roman world (see Luke 1:5; 2:1-3; Acts 12:1; 18:2,12; 25:1).

[14]The present tense is used here as a conative present, focusing on "the notion of incompleteness and attempt." See Moulton, Howard, Turner, *Grammar*, 3:63.

Agrippa was not seriously considering conversion. His question was in reality an exclamation. Paul was overreaching if he truly thought that with just a brief interview he could turn Agrippa into a Christian.[15]

Without hesitation Paul grasped the king's words and used them to make his final point. Whether it took a short time or a long time was of no consequence. His prayer[16] was that he could make of all who were listening what he had come to be in Christ. Then, perhaps holding up his chained arms, he gave his one reservation— "except for these chains,"[17] a reference to his desire to freely continue his ministry for the Lord.

The Agreement Regarding Paul's Innocence (26:30-32)

[30]The king rose, and with him the governor and Bernice and those sitting with them. [31]They left the room, and while talking with one another, they said, "This man is not doing anything that deserves death or imprisonment." [32]Agrippa said to Festus, "This man could have been set free if he had not appealed to Caesar."

King Agrippa had listened long enough. When he rose to his feet the conversation was over. Festus and Bernice rose with him, along with the royal attendants,[18] and left the reception hall. As they

---

[15]Bruce understands the infinitive "to make" (ποιῆσαι, *poiēsai*) to mean that Agrippa was asking "in just a brief time you are trying to make me play the Christian," a phrase which implies playacting as a Christian (p. 471). Turner takes the question to mean, "You seek to convince me that you have made me in a moment a Christian." See Moulton, Howard, Turner, *Grammar*, 3:147,262.

[16]"I pray" (εὐξαίμην, *euxaimēn*) is an aorist middle optative which expresses a wish, or possibility based on the fulfillment of an unexpressed conditional clause (Rienecker, p. 337). See also Moulton, Howard, Turner, *Grammar*, 3:123; Robertson, *Grammar*, p. 1021.

[17]Though this statement probably accurately reflects Paul's actual condition, the reference to chains here does not necessarily mean that Paul was still chained. Paul's preferential treatment under military custody may mean that he stood in this hearing without chains on his hands and feet.

[18]These people may have included the advisory council for Agrippa (Polhill, p. 510).

left the room, the three of them engaged in a very revealing conversation. They agreed that Paul was not guilty of a crime which
deserved the death sentence or even imprisonment. Festus now had
enough information to write his report for Caesar.

It was the fifth time in Acts where Paul's innocence had been
affirmed. The Pharisees (23:9), the Roman commander Lysias
(23:29), Festus on two occasions (25:18-19,25), and now Agrippa
had all come to the same conclusion. Paul was no threat to the
Roman government. As far as Agrippa was concerned, Paul could
have gone free except for the fact that he had appealed to Caesar. It
was beyond the power of any ruler in Palestine to prevent Paul's
case from going all the way to the emperor.[19]

---

[19]Though questions remain about the process of appeal to the emperor,
this statement by Agrippa corresponds to what is known of the legal procedures in the Roman system. See Sherwin-White, *Roman Society and Roman
Law*, p. 65. Festus would have brought the wrath of the emperor on himself
had he started the process of appeal and then suddenly withdrawn the
appeal.

ACTS 27

G. PAUL'S VOYAGE TO ROME (27:1–28:31)

1. The Journey from Caesarea to Sidon (27:1-3)

[1]When it was decided that we would sail for Italy, Paul and some other prisoners were handed over to a centurion named Julius, who belonged to the Imperial Regiment. [2]We boarded a ship from Adramyttium about to sail for ports along the coast of the province of Asia, and we put out to sea. Aristarchus, a Macedonian from Thessalonica, was with us. [3]The next day we landed at Sidon; and Julius, in kindness to Paul, allowed him to go to his friends so they might provide for his needs.

The final two chapters of Acts deal with Paul's journey to and arrival in Rome. This section of Acts allows Luke to finish his account of how the witness for Christ went all the way to the Imperial City itself. He thus concludes the narrative by showing how Paul fulfilled his mission even in the face of severe hardships (see 19:21; 23:11). These chapters also allow Luke to show that the gospel was victorious, breaking out of the geographical confinements of Palestine and ultimately impacting the whole Roman world (see 1:8).

Paul's journey to Rome as a prisoner is a fascinating and detailed report of an ancient sea voyage. The account of the voyage is so true to ancient seagoing practices that James Smith, the Scottish yachtsman and classical scholar from the last century, spent years in the study of this narrative, including personal experience at the sites mentioned in the text. His conclusion was that this report was written by someone who had actually observed the techniques used in a

voyage on a Roman vessel during a real journey on the Mediterranean Sea.[1]

Polhill argues that the chapter intends to be more than just a
record of the journey of a traveler to Rome. The account fulfills an
important role in the development of Acts. It is "narrative theology"
— the use of written history to communicate theological truth.[2]

Paul's adventure on this final journey began when Festus decided
that Paul must be sent to Rome. At this point the "we" narrative
begins again (resumed from 21:18) and continues until the travelers
reach Rome in 28:16. Apparently Luke was included in the journey
to Rome, perhaps after spending the two years in Caesarea during
Paul's imprisonment.

Other prisoners were also being sent to Rome with Paul. All of
them were placed in the custody of a centurion named Julius, a
character otherwise unknown in the New Testament. He was a
member of the "Imperial Regiment," or the "Augustan Cohort."
Evidence from inscriptions attests to the presence in Syria of a
cohort bearing the name of Augustus at this time.[3] This cohort was
apparently an auxiliary cohort, in which case most of the troops
came from the local population.

The presence of Paul's companions is indicated by the statement
"we boarded," but does not mean that they had taken the status of
slaves or attendants of Paul.[4] Since the vessel was privately owned
(and on lease by the Roman government), anyone who had enough
money would be permitted to board. Thus Luke, Aristarchus, and
any other friends of Paul might accompany him. The mention of

---

[1]James Smith, *The Voyage and Shipwreck of St. Paul* (3rd; London:
Longmans, Green, and Co., 1866). Other scholars have since disagreed.
Martin Dibelius, for example, argued that the author of Acts used an
ancient sea voyage narrative and inserted his own material within it. See his
Studies in the Acts of the Apostles (London: SCM, 1956), pp. 204-206. See also
Conzelmann, p. 215. For a discussion of the nautical terminology used in
Acts 27 see Robertson, *Luke the Historian*, pp. 206-216. For a discussion on
the "we-passages" of Acts see the note on 16:10.

[2]Polhill, p. 514.

[3]See Bruce, p. 477, n. 14.

[4]Ramsay assumes that Paul's companions boarded the vessel under the
guise of his slaves so they would be permitted to accompany Paul on this
imperial voyage. See his *St. Paul the Traveller*, p. 316.

Aristarchus here follows his listing among Paul's travel companions in 20:4.[5] He will continue as one of Paul's closest companions during the remainder of the ministry of the Apostle (see Col 4:10,14; Phlm 24).

The ship they boarded was from Adramyttium, a seaport in Mysia on the western coast of Asia, southeast of Troas. This ship was most likely a coasting vessel, one of the smaller ships which customarily sailed along the coast, stopping at major ports along the way. Such vessels were used for commercial purposes all over the Roman world. The Romans were quite content to transport their prisoners in a commercial vessel because it was as quick and inexpensive as any other procedure.[6] This ship had probably traveled down the coast and, after completing its business, was now headed back to the home port, Adramyttium.

Shoving off from shore, they began their voyage. Arriving on the Phoenician coast at Sidon (some seventy nautical miles away) the next day, the centurion in kindness (φιλανθρώπως, philanthrōpōs) permitted Paul to visit with friends. This was a courtesy extended to Paul probably because of his status as a Roman citizen, as well as the graciousness of the centurion.

Paul's "friends" were probably believers in Sidon of whom we hear nothing else in the New Testament. The church was likely established here when the early evangelistic efforts occurred in this area after the persecution of the disciples in Jerusalem (see 11:19). Paul's time with them would not have delayed the voyage because the ship would have spent time unloading and loading commercial cargo. The visit was helpful to Paul in tangible ways, because they provided "for his needs," a phrase which means they gave him food and other provisions for the journey.

2. The Journey from Sidon to Myra (27:4-6)

4From there we put out to sea again and passed to the lee of

---

[5]Aristarchus is also mentioned in 19:29 where the riot at Ephesus is described.

[6]See Lionel Casson, *The Ancient Mariners* (New York: Macmillan, 1959), p. 236.

Cyprus because the winds were against us. ⁵When we had sailed across the open sea off the coast of Cilicia and Pamphylia, we landed at Myra in Lycia. ⁶There the centurion found an Alexandrian ship sailing for Italy and put us on board.

After the stop in Sidon the journey continued. The ship left Sidon and "passed to the lee of Cyprus," a nautical term which meant sailing next to the land so as to be protected from the wind. Because the wind was from the west, this would mean they sailed to the east of Cyprus, then journeying northward and westward along the coast of Cilicia and Pamphylia.

Their immediate destination was Myra in Lysia, a journey which would take about two weeks. Although the wind across the Mediterranean was generally from the west, ships could make progress along the coast (especially at night) due to the land breezes blowing out to sea from the mountains. The difference in temperature between the mountains and the sea produced these breezes, and coupled with the strong westward current (of perhaps two miles per hour) close to the coast, they could tack along the coastline whenever necessary.[7]

Their arrival at Myra was by design, since "there the centurion found an Alexandrian ship sailing for Italy." Commercial trading had made this city a major port of call for vessels sailing from Alexandria in Egypt to the city of Rome. Because Rome imported some 150,000 tons of grain every year (much of this from Egypt), dozens of ships made the round trip from Rome to Alexandria and back again.[8]

Toward the end of the sailing season winds were normally from the west. This circumstance made it necessary for ships to sail straight north from Alexandria to the city of Myra, and then on to Rome. The centurion knew he would find a ship, filled with grain, on its journey from Myra to Rome. This vessel, known as the "merchantman," had become one of the most convenient means of travel in the Roman

---

[7]See Lake and Cadbury, p. 326. There is now plenty of evidence that Roman vessels were outfitted for tacking maneuvers in which a sail could be rotated to catch the wind from a variety of directions. See Casson, *Ancient Mariners*, pp. 219-222.

[8]See Casson, *Ancient Mariners*, pp. 233-239.

world, used frequently even by imperial officials.[9]

3. The Journey from Myra around Crete (27:7)

[7]We made slow headway for many days and had difficulty arriving off Cnidus. When the wind did not allow us to hold our course, we sailed to the lee of Crete, opposite Salmone.

Now the sailing became difficult. The prevailing winds were from the west and northwest. After leaving Myra the ship was more directly exposed to the wind. This made sailing toward Rome very difficult.

Reaching the port of Cnidus, some 130 nautical miles from Myra on the southwest tip of Asia Minor, took "many days." This port was frequently used by the Roman merchantmen, and the harbor facilities were well developed. It may be at this point that the decision was made to sail straight west to the island of Cythera, a run which would depend on finding a favorable wind. Because the wind did not cooperate, the ship was forced to choose an alternate route, sailing south to the eastern tip of Crete and then heading around to the lee (south) of the island in order to be shielded from the northwest wind.

4. The Arrival at Fair Havens (27:8-15)

Paul's Warning about the Coming Danger (27:8-12)

[8]We moved along the coast with difficulty and came to a place called Fair Havens, near the town of Lasea. [9]Much time had been lost, and sailing had already become dangerous because by now it was after the Fast.[a] So Paul warned them, [10]"Men, I can see that

---

[9]The Emperor Caligula advised the Jewish prince Agrippa if he wanted to travel from Rome to Palestine, "don't bother with galleys and the coastal routes but take one of our direct Italy-Alexandria merchantmen." Even the Emperor Vespasian used this means of travel in A.D. 70, despite the fact that he had available to him any galley in the navy (Casson, *Ancient Mariners*, p. 236).

our voyage is going to be disastrous and bring great loss to ship and cargo, and to our own lives also." [11]But the centurion, instead of listening to what Paul said, followed the advice of the pilot and of the owner of the ship. [12]Since the harbor was unsuitable to winter in, the majority decided that we should sail on, hoping to reach Phoenix and winter there. This was a harbor in Crete, facing both southwest and northwest.

[a]9 That is, the Day of Atonement (Yom Kippur)

The going was still slow for the voyagers as they hugged the southern coastline of Crete. Finally they arrived at Fair Havens on the coast of Crete. By now the season for sailing was nearing an end. Sailing on the Mediterranean Sea became dangerous between the middle of September and the middle of November. After this point ships discontinued sailing altogether until at least early February. The "Fast" mentioned in v. 9 is the Day of Atonement (Yom Kippur). The best calculations indicate that the year in which this journey occurred was A.D. 59. In this year the Day of Atonement fell on October 5.[10]

At this point a council meeting of some kind was held to decide whether to spend the winter in Fair Havens. The concern was that keeping the ship in Fair Havens would leave it too much exposed to damaging winds. The centurion, "the pilot" (κυβερνήτης, kybernētēs; the officer responsible for the navigation of the ship), and "the owner of the ship" (ναυκλήρος, nauklēros; merchant shipowner or his representative who acted as the captain of the ship) discussed their plans, perhaps with the sailors included.[11] The majority of the participants in this council argued for sailing on to reach Phoenix, a safer place to winter since the harbor faced "both southwest and northwest"(v. 12).[12]

---

[10]Vegetius, *On Military Affairs*, 4.39. W.P. Workman, "A New Date Indication in Acts," *ExpT* 11 (1899-1900): 316-317. Polhill, p. 518.

[11]The presence of the owner on board may imply that the ship was privately owned and merely leased to the Roman government for the shipment of the grain to Rome.

[12]Such a bay has been located at a site that today is called Phineka Bay, about thirty-three miles east of the western edge of Crete. See Colin Hemer, "First Person Narrative in Acts 27-28," *TB* 36 (1985): 97-98.

The role which Paul played in this decision is not clear. Perhaps he voiced his concerns in a formal meeting or in informal discussions with both sailors and officers.[13] What is clear is that he made his opinion known. He warned those making the decision that moving the ship now would lead to disaster, including "great loss to ship and cargo," as well as to the lives of those on board. Paul knew of this risk from firsthand experience (see 2 Cor 11:25).

The Storm at Sea (27:13-15)

[13]**When a gentle south wind began to blow, they thought they had obtained what they wanted; so they weighed anchor and sailed along the shore of Crete. [14]Before very long, a wind of hurricane force, called the "northeaster," swept down from the island. [15]The ship was caught by the storm and could not head into the wind; so we gave way to it and were driven along.**

The position held by the majority of sailors and officers was strengthened when suddenly a gentle wind from the south began to blow. This was all the encouragement they needed. They made arrangements to move the ship. They immediately weighed anchor and began to sail along the southern coast of Crete. The distance would be forty miles, only a one-day run.

Progressing perhaps a little more than half of the distance, the ship rounded a cape known as Cape Matala. When it did so, the ship was more open to prevailing winds. But what happened caught everyone by surprise. A "wind of hurricane force" (τυφωνικός, *typhōnikos*; "typhonic") came sweeping "down from the island." The wind was well known to ancient sailors, and it had been appropriately named the "northeaster" (Εὐρακύλων, *Eurakylōn*).[14] The burst of wind was sudden, perhaps because it flew down from the 7,000

---

[13]Ramsay takes the position that Paul was invited to the council discussion because of his experience as a traveler. See *St. Paul the Traveller*, pp. 322-325.

[14]*Eurakylōn* combines a Greek word *Euros* meaning "east wind" and a Latin word *Aquilo* meaning "north wind."

foot peaks of the mountains of Crete.[15]

The "typhoon-like" wind slammed furiously into the ship with such a force that it was immediately blown off course. Unlike a typhoon, this wind did not let up. It soon became obvious to the sailors that reaching Phoenix would be impossible. The ship "could not head into the wind," meaning that they were not able to adjust the sails so as to maintain their course. Ancient ships did not have the capability of heading into such gale-like conditions. They "gave way to it," meaning that they shortened the sail. Now they were at the mercy of the storm, being blown farther off course with each passing hour.

5. The Difficult Journey around Cauda (27:16-17)

[16]As we passed to the lee of a small island called Cauda, we were hardly able to make the lifeboat secure. [17]When the men had hoisted it aboard, they passed ropes under the ship itself to hold it together. Fearing that they would run aground on the sandbars of Syrtis, they lowered the sea anchor and let the ship be driven along.

Being driven in the storm, the ship was forced "to the lee" (south) of a small island called Cauda. Some twenty-three miles since the storm had struck them, they had found very little opportunity to respond with any of the techniques appropriate in such weather. Now with the brief protection from the wind provided by the land mass of Cauda, the crew took three important steps.

First, they hoisted the lifeboat aboard. The Roman merchantmen usually kept their lifeboats in tow behind the ship.[16] In a storm like this one the sailors had to tow it in, filled with water as it was.

---

[15]Lake and Cadbury note that it is possible to sail along the southern coast of Crete in calm water on one side of a mountain and on the other side of the outcropping of land, find a violent wind rushing down a ravine toward the sea.

[16]The small boat was towed, often with a hand stationed on board, so that easier rescue could be made of anyone who fell overboard. See Casson, *Ancient Mariners*, p. 220.

The second step was to run "ropes under the ship itself to hold it together." This maneuver probably describes the passing of cables "under the ship or around it,"[17] and then the use of an instrument which tightened these lines to draw the planks of the ship together. The additional support would keep the ship from "breaking its back" against the powerful waves. The third step was to lower a "sea anchor" on a line from the stern, just long enough to serve as a kind of "braking system." The ship would slow to a crawl, but would be less likely to be blown as far off course.[18]

These steps were essential because now the sailors realized that they could eventually be pushed far enough off course so as to be lost "on the sandbars of Syrtis." This dangerous section of the North African coast was well known to ancient seafarers as a ship graveyard. Even though it was located some 400 miles to the southwest of Cauda, these sailors did not want to take any chances.

6. The Shipwreck (27:18-44)

The Attempts to Lighten the Ship (27:18-19)

[18]We took such a violent battering from the storm that the next day they began to throw the cargo overboard. [19]On the third day, they threw the ship's tackle overboard with their own hands.

The next step in slowing the progress of the ship was to begin jettisoning some of the cargo. This maneuver would also help to prevent taking on water due to leaks which had opened up in the ship. Not all of the grain, however, was thrown overboard at this point (see v. 38).

Now it was the third day of the storm and the crew took further steps to lighten the ship. They "threw the ship's tackle (σκευήν,

---

[17]For a full discussion of the possible methods involved in this procedure, see Polhill, p. 521, n. 23.

[18]The Greek term σκεῦος (*skeuos*) may not, however, be a reference to a sea anchor, but the main sail. If so, the maneuver described here was the brailing up of the yard. See Lake and Cadbury, p. 332.

skeuēn) overboard," including such items as spare sails, rigging, and other gear, requiring the manual effort of the entire crew (and maybe even the passengers).[19]

Paul's Words of Encouragement (27:20-26)

[20]**When neither sun nor stars appeared for many days and the storm continued raging, we finally gave up all hope of being saved.** [21]**After the men had gone a long time without food, Paul stood up before them and said: "Men, you should have taken my advice not to sail from Crete; then you would have spared yourselves this damage and loss.** [22]**But now I urge you to keep up your courage, because not one of you will be lost; only the ship will be destroyed.** [23]**Last night an angel of the God whose I am and whom I serve stood beside me** [24]**and said, 'Do not be afraid, Paul. You must stand trial before Caesar; and God has graciously given you the lives of all who sail with you.'** [25]**So keep up your courage, men, for I have faith in God that it will happen just as he told me.** [26]**Nevertheless, we must run aground on some island."**

After the crew had gone "a long time" without food, it was obvious that they had lost "all hope of being saved" (σώζω, *sōzō*), a term perhaps used by Luke to carry a double meaning of "saved from the danger of the sea," but also "saved from spiritual death," as well. The sense of hopelessness would be increased by the fact that for many days neither the "sun nor stars" had been visible. Since ancient seafarers had no compass or accurate charts for navigation, the inability to see these heavenly points of reference would be very distressing. In addition, eating would be the last thing on their minds when the ship was being rocked around in the waves and seasickness was setting in.

Paul "stood up before them" to offer his advice one more time. Though it is true, as Haenchen argues, that this scene could be

---

[19]At this point Acts 27 shows some similarities with the story of Jonah (see 1:5). See David Clark, "What Went Overboard First?" *BTr* 26 (1975): 144-146. He points to some differences with the account of Jonah's voyage.

viewed as Paul's presenting an address before an attentive audience in a driving gale (as if he could even be heard), such an interpretation is not required. As Marshall points out, Haenchen's portrait depends too much on seeing Paul as an orator in this situation.[20] Luke does not give details about how Paul communicated his message to the ship's crew other than saying that "Paul stood up before them."

Perhaps in a moment which revealed his humanity, Paul reminded the sailors he had warned them previously about this danger. Now he wanted them to know they had reason to maintain their courage. Paul could now report that he had received a vision from God. This time he was not speaking his own words of warning (see v. 10) as he had before when he cautioned that even loss of life would result from this venture. This time he was speaking words from God in which the assurance had been given there would be no loss of life. Instead, Paul was guaranteed that he would be transported safely to Rome where he would stand trial before Caesar (see 23:11; 27:44). What this meant to the crew and passengers was that the Lord would also deliver them because of Paul.[21]

Thus Paul encouraged the sailors to keep up their strength. The time would come when it would be needed. Paul now predicted that the outcome of the ship's plight would be its beaching on some island. When he spoke these words there was only one island on which this could happen — Malta. If they missed Malta, there was no stopping point for the ship for 200 miles.

The Sighting of Land (27:27-29)

[27]**On the fourteenth night we were still being driven across the Adriatic[a] Sea, when about midnight the sailors sensed they were approaching land.** [28]**They took soundings and found that the water was a hundred and twenty feet[b] deep. A short time later they took soundings again and found it was ninety feet[c] deep.** [29]**Fearing that**

---

[20]See Haenchen, p. 704; Marshall, p. 411. Polhill notes that such speeches were not unusual, since examples can be seen in Odysseus, Caesar, Hannibal, and Aeneas (p. 523, n. 29).

[21]Marshall calls attention to a similar idea in Genesis (Gen 18:23-33) where the Lord would save Sodom if only a few righteous were present among the wicked (p. 410).

**we would be dashed against the rocks, they dropped four anchors
from the stern and prayed for daylight.**

[a]27 In ancient times the name referred to an area extending well south of
Italy.   [b]28 Greek *twenty orguias* (about 37 meters)   [c]28 Greek *fifteen
orguias* (about 27 meters)

Fourteen days after the storm hit the ship at Cauda, the vessel
was "still being driven across the Adriatic." This name applied at
that time to much of the Mediterranean Sea extending south of the
area between Italy and Macedonia (including the Ionian Sea and the
north-central Mediterranean).

Then came the moment the sailors had both hoped for and
feared. They could hear the sound of breakers on a shore. This
meant that they might soon see land, but it also meant that they
could be dashed against the rocks. As things turned out, they were
hearing the breakers that were active at the point of Koura, only a
mile from the point they were passing near the shore.

Now the sailors took soundings to determine the depth of the
water. All Roman merchantmen were equipped with a lead line for
testing depths. The lead had a "cup for tallow" to bring up samples
from the bottom.[22] These "soundings" probably came at intervals of
about thirty minutes and showed the water depth becoming more
shallow as they drew nearer the land. The first sounding was 120
feet and then another was ninety feet.

The sailors, working in a darkness which prevented their seeing
the land, became worried about being "dashed against the rocks."
For this reason they quickly dropped four anchors to prevent the
ship from moving closer to the rocks. The presence of such anchors
on the Roman merchantmen has been well documented by modern
archaeologists.[23] In this case they were dropped from the stern so
that the ship would remain headed toward the shore. The only

---

[22]See Casson, *Ancient Mariners*, p. 220. Casson gives further information in
his *Ships and Seamanship in the Ancient World* (Princeton: Princeton University
Press, 1973), p. 246. Luke uses the word βολίζω (*bolizō*), a technical term for
the act of getting the soundings. Also see Hemer, *Book of Acts*, p. 147.

[23]For the variety of sizes and shapes in ancient anchors see Casson, *Ships*,
pp. 248-258; Douglas Haldane, "Anchors of Antiquity," *BA* 53 (1990): 19-24.
Also see Nicolle Hirschfield, "The Ship of St. Paul — Part I: Historical
Background," ibid., 25-30.

thing left was to pray to their gods that daylight would come quickly.

The Attempt of the Sailors to Escape (27:30-32)

[30]In an attempt to escape from the ship, the sailors let the lifeboat down into the sea, pretending they were going to lower some anchors from the bow. [31]Then Paul said to the centurion and the soldiers, "Unless these men stay with the ship, you cannot be saved." [32]So the soldiers cut the ropes that held the lifeboat and let it fall away.

At this point some of the sailors had seen enough of the stormy sea. Evidently they did not trust their gods. Claiming that they were going to lay anchors from the bow of the ship, they lowered the lifeboat back into the sea.[24] Paul became suspicious (perhaps because he had seen sailors behave this way before) and spoke to the centurion about this action, warning that the men must stay on board if they were to be saved. To prevent further attempts in which the sailors might abandon the passengers, the soldiers simply cut the lines and permitted the lifeboat to fall into the sea.[25]

Paul's Encouragement of the Crew to Eat (27:33-38)

[33]Just before dawn Paul urged them all to eat. "For the last fourteen days," he said, "you have been in constant suspense and have gone without food—you haven't eaten anything. [34]Now I urge

---

[24]Haenchen finds this action incredible since the sailors were safer on the ship than in the lifeboat (p. 706), but after fourteen days in a raging storm, it is impossible to say what irrational behavior might have developed, especially if these sailors were experiencing such danger for the first time in their lives.

[25]The wisdom of the action by the soldiers may be questioned, but examples can be cited where sailors took whatever actions needed to save themselves while the passengers were left to fend for themselves. See Hemer, *Book of Acts*, p. 148; Polhill, p. 526.

you to take some food. You need it to survive. Not one of you will lose a single hair from his head." ³⁵After he said this, he took some bread and gave thanks to God in front of them all. Then he broke it and began to eat. ³⁶They were all encouraged and ate some food themselves. ³⁷Altogether there were 276 of us on board. ³⁸When they had eaten as much as they wanted, they lightened the ship by throwing the grain into the sea.

Very little sleep was possible on this night in the ship. The storm had robbed the crew not only of their sleep, but also of their appetites. For this reason, Paul "urged (παρεκάλει, *parekalei*) them all to eat."[26] For fourteen days they had eaten very little, if anything.[27] The work of beaching the ship would demand their full strength. Paul could assure them that they would come through this experience in safety.

To set the example, Paul took food himself. The verbs in this verse are familiar. Paul "took some bread" (λαβὼν ἄρτον, *labōn arton*), "gave thanks" (εὐχαρίστησεν, *eucharistēsen*), and "broke it" (κλάσας, *klasas*). The same language is used of the Lord's Supper (see Luke 22:19; 1 Cor 11:23-24) and also in the Gospels to describe Jesus' eating with his disciples (see Mark 6:41; 8:6; Luke 24:30). Such language was common among Jews in respect to the eating of food, drawing attention to the feeling of gratitude to the God who provides for the needs of his children. It is very doubtful that the language here is intended to associate this incident with the Lord's Supper.[28] Paul did, however, in this one incident present his witness to the pagan sailors and other passengers who were given the opportunity once again to observe his trust in the living God.

Paul's encouragement inspired the others to eat also. At this point Luke counts himself among the passengers and gives the total number as 276. This large number is not surprising when the report of Josephus is taken into account. About four years later he was involved in a shipwreck involving some 600 passengers; only eighty

---

[26]The imperfect tense suggests that Paul urged them repeatedly to eat.

[27]Paul's words may be understood as hyperbole to mean that they had not taken a full meal since the storm hit them. See also v. 21.

[28]Polhill, p. 527.

people survived.[29] The reason for Luke's report of the number of passengers may be connected with the way the food was distributed. Another possibility is that the number of passengers serves to highlight the magnitude of the rescue which was accomplished by God.

After eating, the crew began to finish what was begun in v. 18. Earlier the crew had begun the process of lightening the ship, throwing out any heavy equipment, and perhaps some of the grain.[30] Now all the grain was emptied from the ship. The ship needed to be as light as possible so that she would run as far as possible upon the beach.

The Running Aground of the Ship (27:39-41)

[39]**When daylight came, they did not recognize the land, but they saw a bay with a sandy beach, where they decided to run the ship aground if they could. [40]Cutting loose the anchors, they left them in the sea and at the same time untied the ropes that held the rudders. Then they hoisted the foresail to the wind and made for the beach. [41]But the ship struck a sandbar and ran aground. The bow stuck fast and would not move, and the stern was broken to pieces by the pounding of the surf.**

When daylight came the sailors knew immediately they were in unfamiliar territory. No one recognized the beach. Without accurate charts and compasses, Roman vessels often depended on simple recognition of landmarks. In this case there were none.

Nevertheless, they did see a spot which seemed appropriate for beaching the ship. It was a sandy area on the shoreline. They cut the anchors loose and they "untied the ropes that held the rudders." Roman vessels were steered by large paddles lowered into the

---

[29]Josephus, *Life*, 15. Passengers stayed on the deck of Roman vessels since the hold was completely filled with cargo and conditions were more pleasant outside than inside.

[30]Polhill notes that the Greek phrase ἐκβολήν ἐποιοῦντο (*ekbolēn epoiounto*) in v. 18 is a more general reference than here where it is the σῖτον (*siton*) (grain) which is thrown out (p. 528, n. 48).

water. When sailing in a storm, these paddles were raised and tied up in order to keep them out of the water.[31] One more step taken by the sailors was to hoist "the foresail to the wind." This sail was a small one on the bow of the ship used for guiding the vessel.

Unfortunately the sailors were not aware that a sandbar lay under the surface of the sea.[32] The bow settled into the sand and held in place, while the stern was left unsupported to be lashed by the wind and waves. This pressure was too much for the ship and the wood gave way. The ship was broken in two. Pieces of the vessel were floating in the water.

The Escape to Dry Land (27:42-44)

[42]The soldiers planned to kill the prisoners to prevent any of them from swimming away and escaping. [43]But the centurion wanted to spare Paul's life and kept them from carrying out their plan. He ordered those who could swim to jump overboard first and get to land. [44]The rest were to get there on planks or on pieces on the ship. In this way everyone reached land in safety.

The adventure was not yet over, especially for the prisoners. Now that land was in sight, the sailors and soldiers were ready to take their chances diving into the water and swimming ashore. But the soldiers felt keenly the responsibility for their prisoners. Since Roman law held them accountable for the escape of the prisoners, the soldiers had decided that the safest approach for them was to kill the prisoners so that none could escape.

The centurion stopped this plan. He was not merely showing kindness to his prisoners now. He had become impressed with Paul.

---

[31]See J. Smith, *Voyage*, p. 133-134. For plates showing the position of these rudders, see Casson, *Ships*, plates 139-147; Michael Fitzgerald, "The Ship of Saint Paul: Comparative Archaeology," *BA* 53 (1990), 31-39.

[32]J. Smith located this bay on the island of Malta. It is known today as St. Paul's Bay. Smith also demonstrates how perfectly Luke's description fits the features of this bay, including a bottom composed of "mud graduating into tenacious clay" that would explain the grounding and breaking apart of the ship (pp. 137-140).

Whether because of Paul's council which had spared the lives of the others, or perhaps because he sensed something about the God of Paul's prayers which inspired reverence, the centurion wanted Paul's life spared. As Paul had predicted (v. 24), God was truly sparing those with Paul, who might have been lost.

Thus the orders were given by the centurion that the prisoners be permitted to jump overboard and swim to shore. Those who could not swim were allowed to float on pieces of the ship which were floating in the water.[33] All persons aboard the vessel "reached land in safety,"[34] a remarkable development in light of the grave danger that had been faced as a result of the storm. The only explanation was the providence of God.

---

[33]The phrase translated "on pieces of the ship" is ἐπί τινων τῶν ἀπὸ τοῦ πλοίου, (*epi tinōn tōn apo tou ploiou*), and might mean that the nonswimmers were allowed to float on "persons from the ship," or on the backs of members of the crew.

[34]Gary Miles and Garry Trompf point out that this phrase reflects the theology of divine providence. Not only did his deliverance from the shipwreck indicate that God was protecting Paul and the other passengers, it also amounted to a statement of his innocence regarding the charges against him. See their "Luke and Antiphon: The Theology of Acts 27–28 in the Light of Pagan Beliefs about Divine Retribution, Pollution, and Shipwreck," *HTR* 69 (1976): 259-267. In this presentation of the shipwreck they find parallels with the description by Antiphon, the Athenian orator (c. 480–411 B.C.). See also David Ladouceur, "Hellenistic Preconceptions of Shipwreck and Pollution as a Context for Acts 27–28," *HTR* 73 (1980): 435-449.

ACTS 28

7. The Winter at Malta (28:1-10)

The Welcome by the Barbarians (28:1-6)

¹Once safely on shore, we found out that the island was called
Malta. ²The islanders showed us unusual kindness. They built a
fire and welcomed us all because it was raining and cold. ³Paul
gathered a pile of brushwood and, as he put it on the fire, a viper,
driven out by the heat, fastened itself on his hand. ⁴When the
islanders saw the snake hanging from his hand, they said to each
other, "This man must be a murderer; for though he escaped
from the sea, Justice has not allowed him to live." ⁵But Paul shook
the snake off into the fire and suffered no ill effects. ⁶The people
expected him to swell up or suddenly fall dead, but after waiting a
long time and seeing nothing unusual happen to him, they
changed their minds and said he was a god.

Not until the crew and passengers reached shore did they find
out where they were. The island was called Malta, a small land mass
some twenty miles long from east to west, and twelve miles wide.[1]
Malta was a part of the province of Sicily and was located some fifty-
eight miles from this larger island.[2] It possessed several harbors that

---

[1]Reese, *New Testament History*, p. 920.

[2]The identification of Malta with the islands off the coast of Dalmatia
(modern Yugoslavia) is built on a misunderstanding of the reference to
the Adriatic Sea in 27:27. See Angus Acworth, "Where Was St. Paul
Shipwrecked? A Re-examination of the Evidence," *JTS* 24 (1973): 190-193.
See also Otto Meinardus, "St. Paul Shipwrecked in Dalmatia," *BA* 39 (1976):
145-147. Most scholars disagree with them. It would have been a miracle of
major proportions for the vessel to travel so far north in the teeth of "the
Northeaster" (see 27:14).

were commonly used by Roman merchantmen vessels.

Luke notes how friendly the residents of Malta were. He refers to them as "barbarians" (βάρβαροι, *barbaroi*; the NIV translates "islanders"), a designation often used by the Greeks to describe anyone who did not speak Greek.[3] The Maltese were of Phoenician heritage and spoke a dialect of Punic.

The "unusual kindness" (φιλανθρωπίαν, *philanthrōpian*) of the islanders showed itself in their willingness to build a huge fire around which the passengers could warm themselves in the cold November rain.[4] As Paul was assisting in the work of gathering firewood, he was bitten by a poisonous snake (ἔχιδνα, *echidna*) as he placed the wood on the fire. Evidently the snake lay among the pieces of wood, inactive from the cold, but revived when it felt the heat of the fire. It "fastened" (καθάπτω, *kathaptō*) itself on Paul's hand. The Maltese gathered there assumed immediately that Paul was receiving some punishment from the goddess "Justice" (δίκη, *dikē*). He had escaped the shipwreck only to be fatally bitten by a viper.[5]

Identifying the species of this snake has occupied the minds of many commentators.[6] No poisonous snakes inhabit Malta today, but this does not impugn the accuracy of Luke's account since centuries of human habitation on such a small island could easily alter the snake population.

When Paul shook the snake off and showed no signs of being

---

[3]The term is onomatopoetic (meaning that it sounds like its meaning) and is used in the same way in 1 Cor 14:11.

[4]The time of the year can be discerned by noting that they waited three months for shipping to begin again (28:11), a time which came in early February for the Romans. Haenchen notes that the low temperature would be about 50°F (p. 713).

[5]Bruce points out that the ancients were fascinated by the notion of a sinner escaping from one punishment only to be caught by another (p. 498, n. 13). See Wisdom 1:8; Greek *Palatine Anthology* 7.290.

[6]See Lake and Cadbury, p. 341; Haenchen, p. 713; Marshall, p. 416; Reese, p. 922; Bruce, pp. 497-498; Polhill, pp. 531-532. Ramsay originally argued that the snake was the species *Coronella leopardinus*, which resembles a poisonous snake, but is not actually poisonous. See his *Luke the Physician* (London: Hodder and Stoughton, 1908), pp. 63-65. Such an interpretation runs into problems since the islanders themselves thought it was a poisonous snake.

harmed, the islanders jumped to the opposite conclusion that "he was a god." Luke's term for "swelling up" (πίμπρημι, *pimprēmi*) was the usual medical term for inflammation.[7] Perhaps with some humor Luke records this sudden shift in attitude, which must have seemed similar to the reaction of the Lystrans who were ready to proclaim Paul and Barnabas as gods (see 14:11-15). Luke knew, of course, that Paul was no god. Rather, he was just a godly man. But he was a man through whom God was working powerful deeds.

Paul's Ministry of Healing (28:7-10)

[7]There was an estate nearby that belonged to Publius, the chief official of the island. He welcomed us to his home and for three days entertained us hospitably. [8]His father was sick in bed, suffering from fever and dysentery. Paul went in to see him and, after prayer, placed his hands on him and healed him. [9]When this had happened, the rest of the sick on the island came and were cured. [10]They honored us in many ways and when we were ready to sail, they furnished us with the supplies we needed.

Even as a prisoner Paul's ministry continued. The "chief official (πρῶτος, *prōtos*) of the island" had a father who was sick. This official was named Publius, a common name in the Roman world. The term used by Luke to identify his office is accurate, a point that is confirmed by inscriptions discovered in the area.[8] This official provided hospitality, at least for Paul and his companions,[9] providing the travelers with a place to stay for three days. The father of Publius was

---

[7]Rienecker, p. 343.

[8]Bruce notes that one of the inscriptions is in Greek and uses the term πρῶτος of one L. Castricius, "first of the Maltese." The other inscription uses the Latin equivalent of the Greek term (p. 499). Compare Luke's accuracy on other official titles, such as "proconsul" (ἀνθύπατος, *anthypatos* in 13:7), "magistrates" (στρατηγοί, *stratēgoi* in 16:20), "city officials" (πολιτάρχαι, *politarchai* in 17:6), and "officials of the province" ('Ασιάρχαι, *Asiarchai* in 19:31).

[9]The "us" does not necessarily include all 276 aboard the ship that wrecked on the island.

suffering from "fever and dysentery," a gastric condition which has been identified by modern scholars as caused by a "microbe in goat's milk."[10]

Paul entered the room to pray for him and also to lay his hands on him. After doing so, the man was healed.[11] The result was that the population in general took note of Paul's healing power and brought those who needed healing. The fact that different terms are used for these healings (ἰάομαι, *iaomai* in v. 8 and θεραπεύω, *therapeuō* in v. 9) does not imply that Luke's skill as a physician was involved when the crowds of sick people came. The fact that "they honored" the Christian workers does not necessarily imply that a physician's fee was involved, but that the islanders felt grateful for the efforts of Paul and his companions and did what they could to supply for the necessities of the travelers.

8. The Journey to Syracuse (28:11-12)

[11]**After three months we put out to sea in a ship that had wintered in the island. It was an Alexandrian ship with the figurehead of the twin gods Castor and Pollux. [12]We put in at Syracuse and stayed there three days.**

Paul and his companions did not put out to sea again until "after three months." This period of time corresponds to the beginning of the sailing season, which began no earlier than at the beginning of February.[12]

The ship that was boarded by the 276 passengers and crew had also wintered on Malta, perhaps in a harbor at Valleta. This ship was

---

[10]This affliction is known as "Malta fever" (Bruce, p. 499, n. 17).

[11]This example is the only one in Acts where healing results from the laying on of hands with prayer, though James 5:14 speaks of this same method of physical healing. See Polhill, p. 534.

[12]Two ancient references may be cited regarding the opening of the sailing season. The elder Pliny (*Natural History* 2.122) refers to February 8 as the time when the west winds begin to blow again and shipping can begin. Vegetius (*On Military Affairs* 4.39) states that the sea lanes were closed until March 10. No doubt the shorter voyages could begin earlier than the trans-Mediterranean voyages.

also sailing from Alexandria to Rome, probably loaded with grain. Frequently these vessels were given an identity which linked them with a favorite deity. In the case of this ship, the figurehead on the vessel told the story. The "twin gods Castor and Pollux" were known as the sons of Zeus, or in Greek the term was *Dioscouroi* (Διόσκουροι). These deities were the favorites of sailors since they were considered the guardians of seafarers and the punishers of evildoers.

Sailing north they reached Syracuse, some ninety miles from Malta. Syracuse was the capital city of Sicily and possessed two important harbors. The city had been under Roman control since 212 B.C., having been established as a Corinthian colony in 734 B.C. Here the ship remained for three days, probably waiting for favorable winds.

9. The Journey to Rhegium and Puteoli (28:13-14)

[13]**From there we set sail and arrived at Rhegium. The next day the south wind came up, and on the following day we reached Puteoli.** [14]**There we found some brothers who invited us to spend a week with them. And so we came to Rome.**

The next segment of the journey took the ship as far as Rhegium, seventy-five miles away. The passengers and crew had finally reached Italy. Rhegium was located at the southwestern tip of Italy just south of the point where the Straits of Messina are narrowest.

The next day the journey continued. The "south wind" was so favorable that the ship was pushed along at a rapid pace, running some 210 miles to Puteoli (the modern Pozzuoli) in only one day's time. The crew apparently had no trouble navigating the Straits of Messina in the beginning of the run. Reaching this principal port of southern Italy brought the ship to a point frequently used by the grain ships of the Roman world. Located some 130 miles south of Rome, the city served as Rome's major port city. This remained true until the efforts of Claudius to construct a harbor facility at Ostia in the mouth of the Tiber River outside of Rome were brought to completion.

Believers could be found in Puteoli. For reasons that are not stated, the journey paused for a week. Bruce suggests that perhaps the centurion had official business of some kind.[13] At any rate, Paul's easy custody continued and he was permitted freedom to spend time with these disciples (see 27:3).

Now Luke seems to summarize what follows immediately. As he puts it, "so (οὕτως, *houtōs*; or "in this way") we came to Rome."[14] Details of the final leg of the journey are then given.

10. The Welcome at Three Taverns (28:15)

[15]The brothers there had heard that we were coming, and they traveled as far as the Forum of Appius and the Three Taverns to meet us. At the sight of these men Paul thanked God and was encouraged.

Believers in Rome traveled south to meet Paul on the last bit of his journey to Rome. Traveling along the Appian Way, the oldest road in Roman Italy, they were walking on a heavily-traveled and well constructed highway.[15] The Appian Way would take them straight to Rome. The presence of these believers from Rome would provide moral support, as well as help with material needs along the five-day walk. Showing their dedication and interest in the mission work of the Apostle Paul, some of these believers came as far as the Forum of Appius, some forty-five miles south of Rome. They walked along with Paul for about ten miles until the company reached Three Taverns, where they met a second group of Christians from Rome.[16] Without a doubt the occasion was an emotional one for

---

[13]Bruce, p. 502.

[14]Marshall, p. 419. Polhill suggests that the redundancy between vv. 14 and 16 might be explained by seeing in Luke's first reference to Rome the larger metropolis which may have included Puteoli (p. 536).

[15]This road was constructed by Appius Claudius in 312 B.C. and became the most famous of Roman roads. Some 800 years later when Procopius of Caesarea (in Palestine) was traveling on it he wrote that the joints in the pavement were so tight that they were barely perceptible. See Hamey, *Roman Engineers*, p. 19.

[16]Haenchen's suggestion that Luke struggles to make Paul the first missionary to preach in Rome is incomprehensible in light of the attention Luke gives to these believers (see p. 720).

Paul. What a thoughtful and generous act of support! When he saw them Paul "thanked God and was encouraged."

11. The Imprisonment at Rome (28:16-29)

The Arrival at Rome (28:16)

[16]When we got to Rome, Paul was allowed to live by himself, with a soldier to guard him.

Finally the company of travelers came to the Imperial City. Luke's long travel narrative which began with Paul's journey to Jerusalem (see 19:21) comes to a conclusion with this verse.

Paul's living arrangements are described by Luke in terms of his independence. He remained a prisoner, but was granted a degree of freedom. Rather than being held with the other prisoners in the barracks, Paul was permitted to "live by himself" (καθ᾽ ἑαυτόν, *kath' heauton*; see also v. 30). As was customary for Roman prisoners, however, a Roman soldier was always present, chained to Paul's arm (see v. 20). Every four hours or so the guard would be changed. Such an arrangement would allow Paul to receive friends, maintain correspondence,[17] and perhaps even continue his trade to some extent.

Paul's Preaching to the Jews (28:17-29)

[17]Three days later he called together the leaders of the Jews. When they had assembled, Paul said to them: "My brothers, although I have done nothing against our people or against the customs of our ancestors, I was arrested in Jerusalem and handed over to the Romans. [18]They examined me and wanted to release me, because I was not guilty of any crime deserving death. [19]But when the Jews objected, I was compelled to appeal to Caesar—not that I had any charge to bring against my own people. [20]For this

---

[17]If the Roman imprisonment was the setting for the writing of any or all of the "Prison Epistles" (Ephesians, Philippians, Colossians, and Philemon), Paul would have been able to compose them under these circumstances. In these letters Paul often refers to his chains (see Eph 6:20; Phil 1:13-14,17; Col 4:3,18; Phlm 10,13).

reason I have asked to see you and talk with you. It is because of the hope of Israel that I am bound with this chain." [21]They replied, "We have not received any letters from Judea concerning you, and none of the brothers who have come from there has reported or said anything bad about you. [22]But we want to hear what your views are, for we know that people everywhere are talking against this sect." [23]They arranged to meet Paul on a certain day, and came in even larger numbers to the place where he was staying. From morning till evening he explained and declared to them the kingdom of God and tried to convince them about Jesus from the Law of Moses and from the Prophets. [24]Some were convinced by what he said, but others would not believe. [25]They disagreed among themselves and began to leave after Paul had made this final statement: "The Holy Spirit spoke the truth to your forefathers when he said through Isaiah the prophet: [26]'Go to this people and say, "You will be ever hearing but never understanding; you will be ever seeing but never perceiving." [27]For this people's heart has become calloused; they hardly hear with their ears, and they have closed their eyes. Otherwise they might see with their eyes, hear with their ears, understand with their hearts and turn, and I would heal them.'[a] [28]Therefore I want you to know that God's salvation has been sent to the Gentiles, and they will listen!"[b]

[a]27 Isaiah 6:9,10　　[b]28 Some manuscripts *listen!" [29]After he said this, the Jews left, arguing vigorously among themselves.*

One final opportunity for the Jews to hear the gospel is presented by Luke as a conclusion to his masterful work. Strangely, many of the details the modern reader might wish to know are not included in this description of Paul's custody in Rome. Details concerning Paul's appearance before Caesar and the results of his trial are passed over in silence. Instead Luke focuses on Paul's preaching to the Jews of Rome who come to hear his message.

Paul's Defense (28:17-20). Three days after arriving in Rome the "leaders of the Jews"[18] were invited by Paul to come to his place of

---

[18]The term for "leaders" (πρῶτοι, *prōtoi*) has been discovered in inscriptions found at Rome (Polhill, p. 539, n. 78).

residence. Paul stressed the fact that his imprisonment was the result of false charges brought against him. He had committed no sin against the Jewish people nor had he transgressed "the customs" of the Jews, the very charges which had come from the Asian Jews (see 21:28). Paul argued that he had lived as a Jew who obeyed the law (see 22:3; 24:14; 26:4-5). In Jerusalem he was "handed over (παραδίδωμι, *paradidōmi*) to the Romans," a phrase that shows similarities with the end of Jesus' journey to Jerusalem when he was "handed over to the Gentiles" (see Luke 9:44; 18:32; 24:7). Just as Jesus was considered innocent by Pilate (see Luke 23:22), so Paul was thought to be innocent by Agrippa II (see 26:32), and he might have been free by now except for the appeal to Caesar.

Paul argued that his continued imprisonment was due to the fact that he was forced to make this appeal because of the Jewish attempts to have him tried in Jerusalem (25:9). But in making this point, Paul also insisted that he held nothing against his "own people." Though they had obviously set themselves against him, he did not share the sentiment toward them.

As far as Paul was concerned, his reasons for being held in custody came down to one point—"the hope of Israel." This conclusion had been proclaimed before by Paul (see 23:6; 24:15; 26:8,23). Because he believed that the resurrection of Christ was the fulfillment of the promises made by God to Israel, the Jews opposed him. This was the root cause of the differences between Paul and his Jewish accusers. If not for his conviction about Christ's resurrection, he could be free of his chain (see v. 16).

The Request for Further Information by the Jews (28:21-22). Now a familiar pattern developed. As Paul had experienced in his previous experiences with the Jews, they first showed interest in his message, only to reject it later. In Pisidian Antioch it had happened (see 13:42-48), as well as in Corinth (see 18:5-7) and in Ephesus (see 19:8-10).

In this case the Jewish leaders insisted they had received no word from Jerusalem concerning Paul. Letters could have been sent from the Sanhedrin, as had happened with the situation between Jerusalem and Damascus (see 9:2). But it had not happened. The Jews had no direct information from the authorities in

Jerusalem.[19] All they knew was that "people everywhere" were "talking against this sect." Thus they had no reason not to listen to Paul's presentation.[20]

The Interview with the Jews (28:23). Paul found himself again in the position of explaining "the kingdom of God" and its connection with Jesus. These twin themes have been prominent throughout Acts. Arguing from "the Law of Moses and from the Prophets," Paul tried to prove what sermon after sermon in Acts emphasizes— that Jesus was the promised servant of God who had to be crucified, but was raised from the dead (see 2:16-21, 25-28, 34-35; 3:22-23; 4:25-26; 8:32-33; 13:33-35).

Thus in this final example of Paul's preaching, the issues were raised which began the Book of Acts. In 1:6 the question of the disciples was whether the kingdom would be restored to Israel. Now the Apostle Paul contended for the fulfillment of this promise in terms of the gospel.

The Mixed Response (28:24-29). Paul's message produced a divided audience. Some "were convinced" (ἐπείθοντο, *epeithonto*),[21] while others would not believe. Once again in Acts, the "believing minority" from the Jewish synagogue responded to Paul's word.[22] But the majority did not accept the gospel, making Paul's use of the quotation from Isaiah 6:9-10 appropriate. Just as in Jesus' ministry these words were applied to the obstinacy of the Jews (see Matt 13:14-15; Mark 4:12; Luke 8:10), so now Paul applied them to the Jews from Rome. In this last recorded opportunity for them to hear the word from Paul, they showed themselves to be people whose

---

[19]The words of the Jewish leaders have been used to argue that the Jews in Rome looked to Jerusalem for direction. See Raymond Brown, *Antioch and Rome* (London: Paulist Press 1983), p. 97.

[20]Their words cannot mean that they had no direct experience with Christianity since the evidence indicates the presence of Christians in Rome at least as early as A.D. 49 (see comments on 18:2). Evidently Rome had seen some friction between Jews and Christians during the reign of Claudius.

[21]The imperfect tense could be understood as repeated action or as an inceptive imperfect—"some began to be persuaded." See Rienecker, p. 345.

[22]See 13:43; 14:1; 17:4,12; 18:8; 19:9.

physical senses were functional, but not their spiritual senses.

Paul's final sentence was a repetition of earlier pronouncements. "God's salvation" (σωτήριον, *sōtērion*) had been sent to the Gentiles (see 13:46). Whether Paul was giving up on salvation for the Jews as a nation has been seriously debated.[23] Paul's words in Romans 9-11, however, seem to indicate that he looked for (or at least, hoped for) a day when the nation of Israel would come by faith to Christ (see especially Rom 11:26). Nevertheless, the more significant successes would come from the Gentiles, Paul maintained.[24]

12. Paul's Two Years in Rome (28:30-31)

[30]**For two whole years Paul stayed there in his own rented house and welcomed all who came to see him.** [31]**Boldly and without hindrance he preached the kingdom of God and taught about the Lord Jesus Christ.**

Luke's final words in Acts portray the Apostle Paul still in chains, but the gospel unchained. Paul remained in "his own rented house" (ἐν ἰδίῳ μισθώματι, *en idiō misthōmati*). Though it may have been a humble dwelling,[25] it gave Paul the opportunity to receive friends and continue his contact with those who might be open to the gospel.

The phrase "two whole years" remains a puzzle to commentators. Earlier scholars took the mention of this time period to indicate that Paul's case was dismissed. Much of this conclusion was built on a misunderstanding of an edict from a later period. It was assumed that a case would lapse in two years if the accusers did not arrive to press their charges.[26] This interpretation of the "two whole years" lacks definitive evidence.

---

[23]See Polhill, pp. 544-545.

[24]Because of a lack of solid manuscript evidence, the NIV text omits v. 29.

[25]Bruce suggests that the dwelling may have been a "hired apartment," maybe even three floors up in a tenement building (p. 509). Sherwin-White notes that Paul's custody was probably supervised by the pretorian guard, though not personally handled by Afranius Burrus who was sole prefect from A.D. 51-62. See his *Roman Society and Roman Law*, pp. 108-109.

[26]See Bruce, p. 510.

That cases could be dropped after this period of time, however, was always a distinct possibility. The motive might be the overload of cases and the legal procedure involved would be clemency. Whether this development occurred in the case of Paul is uncertain. It is possible that the "two whole years" defined the lengthy period during which Paul waited before the trial finally took place. If so, the mention of the two years may be intended to emphasize how long Paul went on preaching freely right in the heart of Rome. His gospel, so furiously opposed by the Jews, was tolerated by the Roman government for such a long time that it should be obvious that Paul's preaching was not a threat to the state.

At any rate, the Book of Acts closes with the fulfillment of the words of Jesus (1:8). The gospel had reached to the ends of the earth, extending to the far regions of the western Roman empire, to the preeminent city of the civilized world. Though the servants of the gospel were subjected to opposition and persecution; though one of the greatest missionaries was placed in chains by the powerful Roman government, the gospel continued to be preached "boldly and without hindrance."[27]

Explaining what happened to Paul after this period of time is very difficult. If Luke recorded Paul's story to the point where the story was current, the date of Acts must be placed in the early 60s. This would force a very early dating of Luke's Gospel, perhaps making it the earliest of all the four Gospels. Most scholars reject this possibility.

If Paul was judged guilty, he may have been executed at that time. Then Luke may have been aware of Paul's martyrdom, but Luke did not want this part of the story to detract from his major theme of the triumphant gospel. A similar explanation would be offered to explain why Luke would omit any reference to the outcome of the trial if Paul was found innocent. The events recorded in the Pastoral Epistles do suggest that Paul was released from this imprisonment and that he carried on a later ministry.[28]

Perhaps Luke wanted to maintain his emphasis on the unchained

---

[27]The term translated "without hindrance" is ἀκωλύτως (akōlytōs) and may be a "quasi-legal term" that describes the manner in which the Romans "put no obstacle in the way" of Paul's testimony (Polhill, p. 546).

[28]See comments in the Introduction, pp. 15-16.

gospel. To describe what happened to Paul would have drawn attention to the human instrument in God's plans for the gospel's worldwide conquest. So Luke's final words ring through the corridors of time. The message of Christ can never be locked up. Even when the preachers of God's salvation are made prisoners of a world which does not know God, the truth of Christ will always run free.